CENTRAL ASIA AND IRAN: GREEKS, PARTHIANS, KUSHANS AND SASANIANS

UNIWERSYTET JAGIELLOŃSKI
INSTYTUT HISTORII

ELECTRUM

Journal of Ancient History

Editor-in-Chief: Edward Dąbrowa

Assistant Editor: Sławomir Sprawski

Scientific Committee:

Michael Alram (Universität Wien)
Getzel M. Cohen (University of Cincinnati)
Michał Gawlikowski (University of Warsaw)
Antonio Invernizzi (Università di Torino)
Peter F. Mittag (Universität zu Köln)
Federicomaria Muccioli (Università di Bologna)
Robert Rollinger (Universität Innsbruck)
Giusto Traina (Université Paris IV – Sorbonne)

VOL. 22 (2015)

CENTRAL ASIA AND IRAN: GREEKS, PARTHIANS, KUSHANS AND SASANIANS

JAGIELLONIAN UNIVERSITY PRESS

Electrum, vol. 22 (2015)

COVER DESIGN
Barbara Widłak

The publication of this volume was financed by the Jagiellonian University in Krakow – Faculty of History.

ISBN 978-83-233-3967-0
ISSN 1897-3426
e-ISSN 2084-3909

The digital version of the "Electrum" (ISSN 2084-3909) – which counts as the original – is published in the journals section of the Jagiellonian University Press website (www.ejournals.eu/electrum/).

Number of copies: 250

www.wuj.pl

Jagiellonian University Press
Editorial Offices: Michałowskiego St. 9/2, 31-126 Krakow
Phone: +48 12 663 23 80, +48 12 663 23 82, Fax: +48 12 663 23 83
Distribution: Phone: +48 12 631 01 97, Fax: +48 12 631 01 98
Cell Phone: + 48 506006 674, e-mail: sprzedaz@wuj.pl
Bank: PEKAO SA, IBAN PL80 1240 4722 1111 0000 4856 3325

CONTENTS

ABBREVIATIONS

The journals *sigla* utilized are similar to the rules used in *L'Année Philologique*.

ELECTRUM * Vol. 22 (2015): 9–15
doi: 10.4467/20800909EL.15.001.3491
www.ejournals.eu/electrum

ALEXANDER THE GREAT AT BACTRA: A BURNING QUESTION

Frank L. Holt

University of Houston

Abstract: Scholars have generally claimed that Alexander the Great's extraordinary order that his army burn all of its non-essential personal possessions occurred in Hyrcania, on the eve of the Bactrian invasion. The evidence, however, shows that the event more likely happened at Bactra several years later, at the end of the Bactrian campaign.

Key words: Alexander the Great, Hyrcania, Bactria, India, logistics.

Alexander the Great spent more of his reign in Bactria and Sogdiana than in any other part of his vast empire, including Macedonia and Greece. Yet, many aspects of the king's long sojourn in Central Asia remain obscure due to the poor quality of the surviving narrative sources. All five of these accounts are late and derivative; one of them (Arrian) chooses at just this point to switch from a chronological to a thematic approach, and another (Diodorus) suffers a frustrating lacuna (Holt 2012, 165–172). In some cases, archaeological and documentary evidence can be marshaled to good effect (Naveh/Shaked 2012; Rtveladze 2002), but nagging problems still remain. One of these is the question of when, why, and where Alexander issued the extraordinary order for his entire army to burn its personal baggage. This was certainly a demoralizing loss of valuable loot that had been gathered along the triumphant march through Persia, some of it already carried for many miles only to be abandoned by royal decree. Departing from the opinion of most scholars, this paper argues that the event occurred at Bactra at the end of spring 327 BC in circumstances that signal a new experiment in Alexander's logistical thinking.

Historical sources give two versions of when and where the Macedonian army first destroyed its spoils of war.[1] According to Curtius, the order was issued in Hyrcania soon after the death of Darius in 330 BC. Curtius situates the burning at the end of an

---

infamous series of stories: Alexander rescues his beloved horse Bucephalus from the
Mardi (6.5.11–21); Alexander receives as a gift the beloved eunuch Bagoas (6.5.22–23);
Alexander meets and mates with the queen of the Amazons (6.5.24–32); Alexander begins to succumb to his passions under the corrupting influence of Persian luxury, which
alienates his veteran soldiers (6.6.1–10); Alexander avoids mutiny with gifts and bo-
nuses, then circumvents the men's dangerous idleness through an opportune war against
the rebel Bessus (6.6.11–13). At this point the unexpected order comes from Alexander
(6.6.14–17):

> And because the marching of the army was impeded by burdensome spoils and instruments of
> luxury, he commanded that all of the non-essential baggage beginning with his own be centrally
> collected. There was a large level area into which the loaded wagons were driven. While everyone
> wondered what their leader was going to do, he ordered the draught animals led away and that first
> his and then the rest of the belongings be burned. They set ablaze all that had been snatched intact
> from the burning cities of their enemies, daring not to weep over their spoils since the king's was
> being destroyed as well. Soon reason assuaged their grief, and suited for military service and ready
> for everything, they were glad to have shed their packs and not their discipline. Therefore, they set
> out for the region of Bactria.

Diodorus runs through a similar list of events in Hyrcania: the recovery of Bucephalus from the Mardi (17.63.3–8); the dalliance with the Amazon queen (17.77.1–3); Alexander's adoption of Persian luxury and habits (17.77.4–7); and the silencing of dissent
among the Macedonians with gifts (17.78.1). Diodorus then introduces the rebellion of
Bessus, but mentions nothing at all about circumventing idleness or the burning of baggage to speed the army's march to Bactria. Justin's epitome of the lost work of Pompeius
Trogus offers a similar mélange of tales, including the Amazons and the army's resent-
ment toward Alexander's changing personality, but no order to lighten the army (12.3.4–
12.5.8). Arrian describes the Mardi campaign, but without reference to the Bucephalus
story (3.24); he likewise omits all of the other sensationalized elements found in Curtius,
Diodorus, and Justin. Arrian reports nothing about destroying the army's baggage.

Besides Curtius, the only other sources that do describe such an incident place it three
years later at Bactra in 327 BC. According to Plutarch (*Alexander* 57.1–2, and repeated
in *Aemilius Paulus* 12.6):

> Intending to cross the mountains into India, and seeing that the army was already laden with spoils,
> making it weighed down and hard to move, at dawn when the wagons were marshaled he first set
> fire to his own and the Companions' baggage, then ordered the same for the Macedonians. The
> planning of this expedient turned out to be more troublesome than its execution, for it upset only
> a few. Most of the men shouted loudly with enthusiasm, shared their necessities with those in need,
> and then utterly burned and destroyed whatever was unessential, filling Alexander with eagerness.
> Besides, he was already regarded with fear and considered a merciless punisher of those displeas-
> ing him.

Polyaenus includes the event among his *Strategems of War* (4.3.10):

> Alexander turned back toward India. Because the soldiers had in train wagons weighed down with
> the heavy Persian spoils they had amassed, which were not essential to the Indian campaign, he set
> fire first to the royal wagons and next the others. The Macedonians, having lost their plunder, were
> keener to obtain more in the coming war.

The details of these three versions are sufficiently alike to rule out the possibility that this event actually happened twice, as separate actions in Hyrcania (Curtius) and then again in Bactria (Plutarch, Polyaenus). In each source, the baggage had already been loaded into wagons as part of a secret plan (its calculation emphasized by Plutarch) to catch the unsuspecting soldiers off guard.[2] Alexander obviously anticipated opposition to the order and that, if his men suspected anything beforehand, many items might be surreptitiously held back from the train. All versions point out that Alexander's possessions were torched first to set an example and that in the end most men obeyed with a measure of enthusiasm. Curtius and Plutarch note that all who were disturbed by the order held their tongues out of disciplined respect, or growing fear.

Since the accounts are so similar, and because tricking and dispossessing the army twice in this way would hardly keep up morale for new campaigns, we are surely dealing with a single occurrence that must be situated either in Hyrcania or in Bactria. In current Alexander scholarship, the former is by far the dominant position. In his pioneering study of Alexander's logistics, Donald Engels (1978, 86–87) opted for Hyrcania. Scholars such as A.B. Bosworth (1988), Jona Lendering (2004), Ian Worthington (2004), and Krzysztof Nawotka (2010) have agreed. The few choosing Bactra include N.G.L. Hammond (1997, 161) and J.R. Hamilton (1969, 157).[3] Yet, the question has never been thoroughly argued on either side. Proper methodology requires us to explain how and why this conflict in the sources might have arisen, and ultimately which version makes better sense of the evidence.

In Alexander *Quellenforschung*, it is often possible to use Diodorus as a useful check on Curtius since both tend to follow the same so-called Vulgate source tradition. It has been shown above, for example, that Curtius and Diodorus present the same package of stories for Hyrcania, except notably the burning of baggage. Thus, either Curtius has inserted this story or Diodorus has omitted it. The testimony of Plutarch and Polyaenus would suggest the former explanation, but this would be much more certain if Diodorus, too, situated the burning in Bactria. Unfortunately, Diodorus' account of Alexander's departure for India is missing.[4] It is worth noting, however, a possible trace in Curtius' history of the story's transference from Bactria to Hyrcania. When introducing Alexander's decision to invade India in the aftermath of recent sedition, Curtius remarks (8.9.1): "But in order not to promote idleness (*otium*), which naturally sows rumors, he set out for India." These words echo Curtius' earlier description of Alexander's decision to invade Bactria as a response to Macedonian opposition in Hyrcania (6.6.12): "Therefore, lest the situation turn seditious, it was necessary to replace their idleness (*otium*) with war." The former marker probably locates the burning story's original context, before it was moved by Curtius (along with its trigger about Macedonian unrest fostered by idleness) to serve as the tailpiece to his series of Hyrcanian anecdotes. For Curtius, the discipline

---

 [2] *Contra* Hammond (1983, 29), the notion that there are two distinct source traditions because the wagons were burned in one version, but only the unloaded baggage in the other, is not supported by the texts. The animals (of course) were led away, but not necessarily the wagons. Except for a transposition of time and place, there is a single source tradition for this incident.

 [3] Although he confuses Egypt for India, Atkinson (1994, 205–206) seems also to favor Bactra over Hyrcania.

 [4] The lacuna stretches from the capture of Bessus in 329 to the Swat campaign of 327.

of the soldiers when ordered to burn their possessions balances his account at the key moment when one phase of the war has ended and another begins, when Alexander wavers between Macedonian and Persian kingship, and when his army first teeters on the fulcrum of discipline/disorder.

Trying to identify and explain a transposition in the other direction, from Hyrcania to Bactria, is less fruitful. Plutarch covers some of the same Hyrcanian stories as Curtius and Diodorus (rescue of Bucephalus, growing Persian influence, the Amazon queen), but squarely locates the baggage incident at Bactra. Why he, or Polyaenus for that matter, should bother to shuffle the event out of Hyrcania is unclear: Neither author is attempting to spotlight major themes or draw special attention to India. Plutarch puts the burning rather artlessly between the magnificent burial of old Demaratus and a recitation of portents, while Polyaenus just lists the incident randomly between Alexander's later battle with Porus and his much earlier campaign in Thrace.[5] If artifice rather than error accounts for the transference of the burning from one time and place to another, then Curtius seems the likely person to have done so.

We must next consider which circumstances, those in Hyrcania or those in Bactria, better explain the king's order to destroy the personal baggage of his troops. In Curtius there exists a troubling incongruity. In the face of growing opposition to his policies, Alexander allegedly dispensed gifts to his troops to win back their favor and then straightaway had these possessions destroyed. Diodorus also mentions the largesse, but of course not the immediate purging of it. Indeed, it makes no sense to antagonize the troops in this bizarre fashion. In addition, it is unlikely that Alexander would be pressed to take such drastic measures at this point in his march. The more urgent pursuit of Darius had not occasioned such an order, and the terrain between Hyrcania and Bactria posed no sudden new challenge to Alexander's logistics.[6] In Hyrcania the king was already managing the situation by sending most of the baggage wagons along flatter roads (Curtius 6.4.3; Arrian 3.23.2) where needed.

On the other hand, the circumstances in Bactria fit the incident perfectly, and furthermore help make sense of other pieces of evidence. Whereas Curtius has the men gladly destroying possessions they had just been given to keep them quiet, the accounts of Plutarch and Polyaenus are internally consistent. Curtius offers no real explanation for why the troops became enthusiastic about the order, but Plutarch and Polyaenus do. Plutarch writes that the army dared not complain about the order because of recent actions by the king, and then gives appropriate examples from the campaigns in Bactria and Sogdiana to make his case (*Alexander* 57.3). These examples obviously could not follow the migration of this story from Bactria to Hyrcania. Polyaenus stresses the Macedonians' zeal to acquire more plunder in India, which (as will be shown below) they certainly did. Both explanations correspond to the situation in Bactria, and are inappropriate for Hyrcania.

More importantly, the pending march of Alexander's army at Bactra did warrant a new and somewhat drastic change in logistics. Unlike Hyrcania, from Bactra the men

---

[5]   Polyaenus is, however, writing in general at this point about marches, wagons, and transport barges. There would be no reason to change Hyrcania to Bactria.

[6]   Engels (1978, 86) describes an initial march "through an uncultivated and sparsely settled region" which he notes gave way to a fairly easy invasion route via Merv to Bactra (89). This does not explain a sudden need to abandon baggage that had already been hauled across the mountains and deserts of Persia.

were about to cross mountains that had once already wrecked their baggage train. When struggling over the treacherous Hindu Kush Mountains in spring 329 BC, the Macedonian army was forced to kill and eat its baggage animals (Arrian 3.28.8–9; Diodorus 17.83.1; Curtius 7.4.22–25; Strabo 15.2.10). It was this challenge that Alexander faced again in spring 327. To avoid another disaster, the king chose a different route over these mountains that took his forces ten days to accomplish rather than the previous 15–16 (Arrian 4.22.4; Strabo 15.1.26). Not only a shorter path, but also a lighter army would contribute to the efficiency of the second trek. The peremptory burning of all non-essential possessions accords well with these circumstances. Another recent experience surely influenced the king's novel solution to this logistical challenge. For two years leading up to the departure of the army for India, the soldiers had not been burdened in their operations by the transport of personal baggage. Beginning with his first arrival at Bactra in 329 BC, Alexander had lightened his army by ordering that the soldiers' packs and other impedimenta be stored there (Curtius 7.5.1). This is the same Curtius who had reported these very packs burned back in Hyrcania. It should not be imagined that Curtius means here new packs weighted with fresh plunder gathered since the alleged burning in Hyrcania, because in those intervening months no plundering is recorded by our sources and, in fact, Alexander had taken measures to prevent his men from looting along the way (Arrian 3.25.2).

Throughout the long campaign in Bactria and Sogdiana, the city of Bactra remained the base camp and major supply hub for the army.[7] As Macedonian forces fanned out across the region in annual missions, they left behind anything that might encumber them (their sick and injured, non-combatants, personal belongings) at the guarded depot in Bactra. This was the only period in Alexander's conquest of the East during which the baggage train was not a ubiquitous adjunct of the field army, and the advantages were not lost on Alexander as he planned to move back across the Hindu Kush in 327 BC. If ever there was a time to rid the army of personal baggage, this was it: the troops had not been attached to it for two years, the increased efficiency of the unburdened army had been demonstrated, and ahead lay the challenge of recrossing the mountainous spine of what is today Afghanistan.

Curtius, Plutarch, and Polyaenus all note the readiness of Alexander's troops to move forward after the firing of their belongings, although Curtius never explains their motivation. According to Polyaenus, the Macedonians were eager to make good their losses by acquiring more plunder in India. Yet, it is Curtius' history (8.5.3) that emphasizes in other contexts the prospects for plunder in India, "a land filled not only with gold but also gems and pearls." Curtius adds that after the Battle of the Hydaspes, Alexander addressed his assembled army on this very theme (9.1.2–3):

> He promised them rich spoils ahead in regions celebrated for their wealth. Therefore, he said, the loot taken from the Persians should be seen as cheap and ordinary (*vilia et obsoleta*). Now the men would fill not only their homes, but all of Macedonia and Greece, with gems, pearls, ivory, and gold. The soldiers, eager for money and glory, trusted the king because he had not lied to them, and promised to serve him.

---

[7] For this very reason, the Sogdian leader Spitamenes raided Bactra: see the discussions in Holt (1994; 2012, 71–73).

This is the sort of speech that complements a recent loss of plunder at Bactra rather than Hyrcania. The Persian goods being replaced in India would be a distant memory if they had been abandoned four years earlier in Hyrcania, but not if lost at Bactra. The recent blow would be softened by Alexander's alleged description of the lost spoils from Persia as "cheap and ordinary" compared to those in India. The implication is that Alexander had not misled them about fresh spoils in India, a promise appropriate to the situation at Bactra on the eve of the Indian invasion, thus renewing their enthusiasm for the campaign. From other sources (Diodorus 17.94.4; Arrian 6.16.2), we learn that the king did indeed give his troops free rein to plunder everything of value in India. One prominent member of Alexander's court managed to amass more than 28 tons of gold and silver while in that region (Plutarch, *Eumenes* 2). Circumstances clearly suggest that the Macedonian army burned its baggage at Bactra and then recouped its losses on the other side of the Hindu Kush Mountains.

One final point is that in the same context as Alexander's speech about the wealth of India and his encouragement of the troops to seize what they wished, the king also introduced new measures to care for the dependents traveling with the army. Diodorus (17.94.4) reports:

> While the soldiers were out plundering, Alexander held a meeting with their wives and children. He instituted a monthly ration for the women and another for the children calculated on the basis of the father's rank.

This innovation, like the looting, was meant to regain the good will of his armed forces. The royal provisioning of the camp-followers may have been necessary because the men, still replenishing their spoils, were hard-pressed to provide for their dependants. At Bactra they had clearly jettisoned their spoils, but not the ongoing expense of these familiars.

The burning question of where, when, and why Alexander took the extraordinary measure of destroying the personal possessions of his entire army has now been considered at some length. Among the extant sources for this event, Curtius is at odds with Plutarch and Polyaenus because one or the others has transferred this incident to the wrong time and place. As a whole, the evidence supports the conclusion that the baggage was burned at Bactra in 327 BC and not in Hyrcania some three years earlier.

BIBLIOGRAPHY

Atkinson, J.E. (1994), *A Commentary on Q. Curtius Rufus' Historiae Alexandri Magni, Books 5 to 7.2*, Amsterdam.

Bosworth, A.B. (1988), *Conquest and Empire: The Reign of Alexander the Great*, Cambridge.

Engels, D. (1978), *Alexander the Great and the Logistics of the Macedonian Army*, Berkeley.

Hamilton, J.R. (1969), *Plutarch, Alexander: A Commentary*, Oxford.

Hammond, N.G.L. (1983), Army Transport in the Fifth and Fourth Centuries, *GRBS* 24: 27–31.

Hammond, N.G.L. (1997), *The Genius of Alexander the Great*, Chapel Hill, North Carolina.

Holt, F. (1994), Spitamenes against Alexander, *Historikogeographika* 4 (1): 51–58.
Holt, F. (2012), *Into the Land of Bones: Alexander the Great in Afghanistan*, updated ed., Berkeley.
Lendering, J. (2004), *Alexander de Grote: De ondergang van het Perzische rijk*, Amsterdam.
Naveh, J., Shaked, S. (eds.) (2012), *Aramaic Documents from Ancient Bactria (Fourth Century BCE) from Khalili Collections*, London.
Nawotka, K. (2010), *Alexander the Great*, Newcastle upon Tyne.
Rtveladze, E. (2002), *Makedoniyalik Aleksandr Baqtria va So'g'diyonada*, Tashkent.
Worthington, I. (2004), *Alexander the Great: Man and God*, London.

ELECTRUM * Vol. 22 (2015): 17–46
doi: 10.4467/20800909EL.15.002.3218
www.ejournals.eu/electrum

Ai Khanoum and Greek Domination in Central Asia[1]

Laurianne Martinez-Sève

Lille 3 Université

Abstract: Ai Khanoum is probably the most important and the best-known of the Greek settlements founded in Bactria by the Seleucid kings. The site was excavated between 1964 and 1978, but its chronology remains unclear. The purpose of this article is to give a more accurate view of its history, taking into account the results of recent research. As yet, we are still unable to date with precision the time of its foundation, which was not a single event but a process, going on for several decades between the time Alexander the Great entered eastern Bactria in spring 328 and the time a true city was planned there under Antiochos I. Nevertheless, the development of Ai Khanoum occurred only from the beginning of the second century BC, when the city had become, along with Bactra, the major city of the Graeco-Bactrian kingdom. Under the Seleucids as well as the Graeco-Bactrian kings, Ai Khanoum was thus a royal city and its history was subordinate to those of the Greek kings.

Key words: Hellenistic Bactria, Ai Khanoum, Alexander the Great, Seleucid kings, Graeco-Bactrian kings, Greek colonization.

Central Asia was one of the territories conquered by Alexander the Great, leading subsequently to Greek immigration (Fig. 1). After his death, the region was initially incorporated into the Seleucid kingdom, then saw the emergence of independent dynasties that laid claim to Greek culture and exercised characteristically Hellenistic royal power.[2] Literary sources and numismatics long constituted the only sources of information about its history,[3] but they are not sufficiently numerous or comprehensive to allow it to be re-

---

[1] In this paper, my intention is not to give a veridical historical account – something that is difficult to achieve in general, and even more so with respect to the history of Central Asia – but to present the current state of our knowledge of Ai Khanoum and to formulate a number of hypotheses derivable from this knowledge. Any new discoveries are likely to call them into question. I thank Paul Bernard, Frantz Grenet, Georges Rougemont and Claude Rapin for their always enlightening comments and for their help. But I alone am responsible for the opinions expressed in the paper.

[2] Coloru 2009 and Widemann 2009, recently published, provide a historical study of Greek ruling dynasties in Bactria.

[3] See in particular Coloru 2009, 25–102; Martinez-Sève 2012a, 367–370.

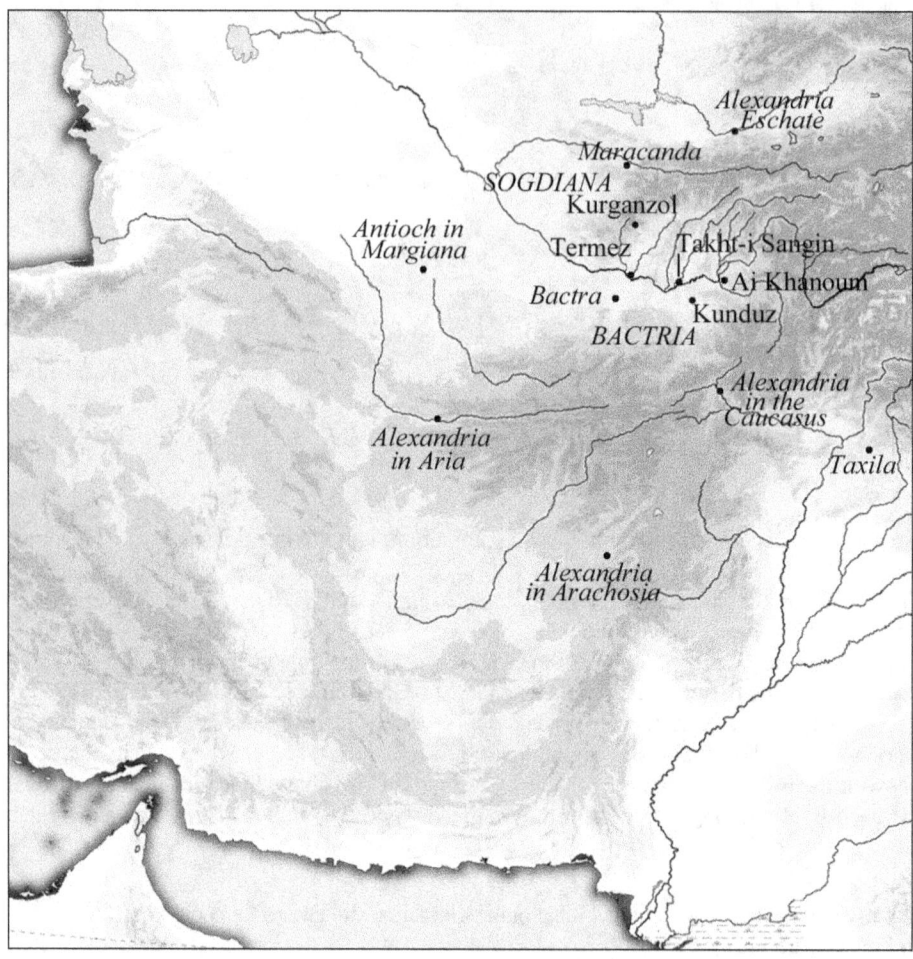

Fig. 1. Map of Hellenistic central Asia (Ancient cities are shown in italics, modern
cities are shown in roman, drawing by L. Martinez-Sève)

constructed in detail. Archaeological documentation provides welcome additions, and for
the Hellenistic period reveals many settlements inhabited by people who were Greek or
were in contact with the Greek world.[4] One of the most important is Ai Khanoum, located
on the current border between Afghanistan and Tajikistan on the left bank of the Darya-i
Pandj, at the confluence with the River Kokcha. The site was excavated between 1964
and 1978 by the French Archaeological Delegation in Afghanistan, under the direction of
Paul Bernard, and was home to the only truly known city of the Hellenistic era in Central
Asia (Fig. 2). Founded in the early third century BC in ancient Bactria, it was occupied by
settlers from more western regions. For nearly a hundred and fifty years their descendants

---

[4]   Leriche 2007, 130–134, for an account of the Greek occupation of Bactria, see also Ball 1982;
Košelenko 1985, 204–350; Cohen 2013.

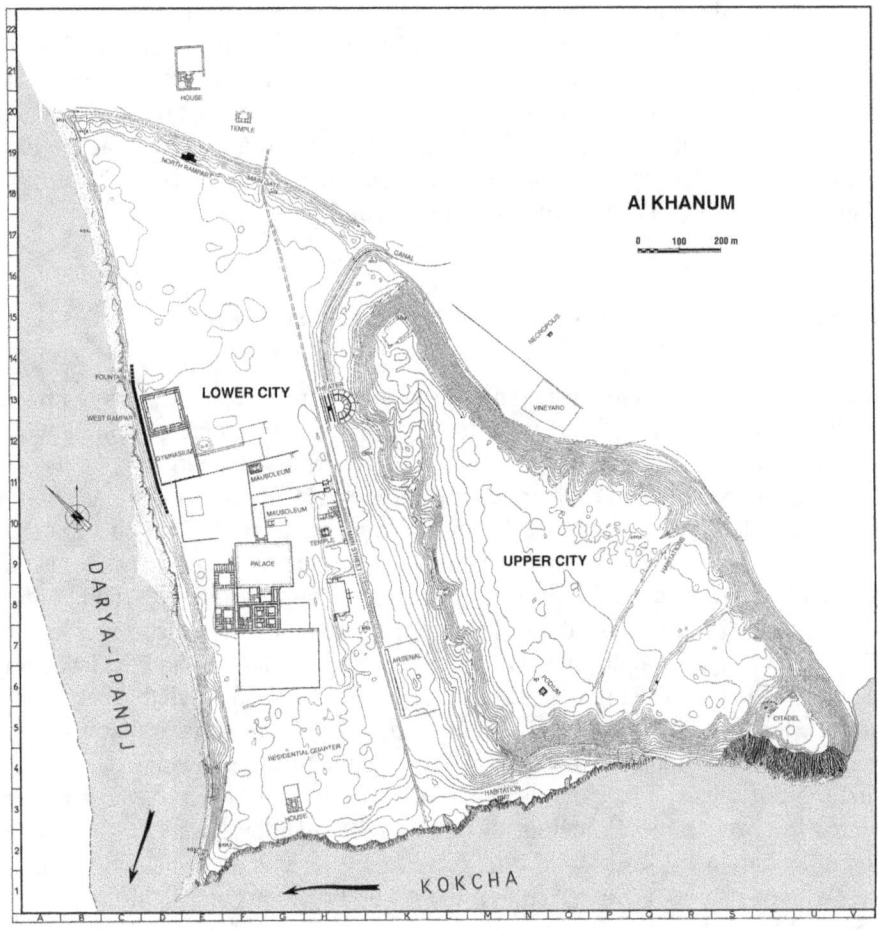

Fig. 2. Plan of Ai Khanoum (drawing by J. Liger and G. Lecuyot)

perpetuated traditions strongly influenced by Greek culture, before being forced to leave the city around 145 BC under the combined pressure of nomads and local people, and withdrawing to areas south of the Hindu Kush. Ai Khanoum was also a royal residence. Its history is therefore particularly revealing with regard to Greek administration in the region, and sheds light on the development of Greek domination, which had three main stages in Central Asia. The first was Alexander the Great's expedition, which proceeded through Bactria and Sogdiana from spring 329 to spring 327, subsequently reaching as far as the Indus Valley. It was during this period that Central Asia fully entered the Greek world. Then, after Alexander's death in June 323, everything had to be rebuilt, a task that was implemented by the Seleucid kings, Alexander's successors, from 305. Thus began the second stage, covering the first half and the beginning of the second half of the third century. Their power, however, was increasingly challenged by Diodotus, the governor who represented them in Bactria and who created the Graeco-Bactrian kingdom between 250 and 235 BC. The third stage was characterised by the domination of the Graeco-Bactrian kings. They survived until about 145 BC in the areas north of the Hindu Kush, even though they were sometimes involved in the dynastic rivalries that resulted in the break-up of their kingdom into a number of principalities. After 145, they fell back to the south of this mountain range, to Arachosia and the region of Kabul, as well as the territories of the Punjab they had conquered from the early second century BC.

1. The plain of Ai Khanoum at the time of Alexander

The discovery of Ai Khanoum in 1961 during a hunting expedition by the king of Afghanistan, and the results of the excavations started in 1964, were so remarkable that it is sometimes forgotten that the city was built on a territory that already had its own history, extending over several millennia.[5] The choice of location was not made at random. It is often pointed out, rightly, that this city occupied a commanding position that controlled several strategic routes. It was situated at the southwest corner of a fertile plain of roughly triangular shape, covering an area of 300 square kilometres, and bordered by the Darya-i Pandj to the west, the Kokcha to the south, and to the east by a line of hills leading to the Darya-i Pandj. The plain was the richest in the area and the last before the highlands of the eastern Hindu Kush and the Pamirs.[6] It commanded access to the valleys of the Kokcha and of the Kizil Su, a tributary on the right bank that flows into the Darya-i Pandj ten kilometres upstream of Ai Khanoum. The Kokcha valley led to the Badakhshan heights and its garnet and especially lapis lazuli mines,[7] whose riches were exploited from the third millennium BC. The Kizil Su valley gave access to the present region of Kuliab in Tajikistan, and from there to the various routes leading to the ranges of the Western Pamirs, an area rich in minerals and precious and semi-precious stones, and beyond to what eventually became Chinese Turkestan.[8] The city was at a crossroads of regional and inter-regional communications, used by merchants as well as by nomadic and mountain populations, who were at once partners and potential adversaries needing to be watched.[9] The Kizil Su valley thus formed the first potential invasion corridor once the mountains were crossed via the upper Wakhsh Valley. The plain was under cultivation from the third millennium, an era during which the first parts of a major irrigation network were dug, and continued to be extended thereafter. The evolution of its occupation is known to us through the work of a team of researchers, archaeologists, ceramologists and geographers, under the leadership of Jean-Claude Gardin, who prospected the area from 1974 to 1976 before exploring the neighbouring regions in 1977 and 1978.[10]

---

[5] On what follows, see also Mairs 2014.

[6] Gardin/Gentelle 1976, 63–65; Gentelle 1978.

[7] Bernard 1978a.

[8] However, there is no evidence that contact existed at that time between the regions on either side of the Pamirs.

[9] Bernard 1978b, 14–15.

[10] Gardin/Gentelle 1976; Gentelle 1989; Lyonnet 1997; Gardin 1998.

The foundation of Ai Khanoum was certainly an important event in the history of this region, even though it occurred relatively late. The first major settlement on the plain, excavated under the direction of Henri-Paul Francfort, was Shortugai, located about 20 kilometres north of Ai Khanoum.[11] As well as farming, its inhabitants engaged in artisanal activities and trade in metals (such as gold, copper and lead) and semi-precious stones including lapis lazuli. Shortugai maintained close links with settlements in the Indus Valley, either because it was something of a colony founded by settlers from there, or because it was part of a broad cultural area defined by shared characteristics of the Indus civilisation. The site existed for several centuries in the second half of the third millennium and in the early part of the second millennium BC, when it underwent a phase of autonomous, and more specifically Bactrian, development. The irrigation system was further developed during the second half of the second and the first half of the first millennium, so that when the Greeks arrived, most of the fertile lands were already supplied with water. Two large main canals were fed from the upstream Kokcha and then flowed northward, against the prevailing slope of the land, an achievement that reflects the expertise of the Bactrian engineers. The Greeks then exploited this mastery of hydraulic techniques and completed the cultivation of the plain: a third canal was dug at the foot of the eastern hills, extending to the land furthest away from the course of the rivers. Between the middle of the third millennium and the last centuries BC, the plain of Ai Khanoum thus continued to grow in population and to develop, and the Greeks simply contributed to this process of expansion that had existed before their arrival.

Establishing a major town at Ai Khanoum, which could benefit from the various resources of the plain and its surroundings, was therefore particularly tempting for a political power. The site also enjoyed considerable defensive strengths. It was naturally protected by the Kokcha and Darya-i Pandj rivers and by a 60-metre tabular acropolis that dominated the plain. These three features defined a large triangular area, in which a substantial population could be housed. But the date of the founding of the city is not easy to determine with any certainty.[12] Although the plain had been cultivated since the third millennium, it seems not to have had any real cities prior to Ai Khanoum, since Shortugai cannot be accorded such a status. Ai Khanoum appears to have been founded in the Hellenistic period, on a site that had not been occupied on a large scale before the arrival of the Greeks, even under the Achaemenids, who were the first to develop an extensive and relatively organised state infrastructure in Bactria and Sogdiana, as the recently published archives of the satrap of Bactra (modern Balkh) reveal.[13] This infrastructure rested on a number of important settlements, including Cheshme Shafa,[14] situated 30 kilometres south of Bactra, and Kok Tepe,[15] 30 kilometres north of Samarkand, both of them recently discovered. There is no doubt now that the Achaemenid kings firmly held these regions, and it seems unlikely in these circumstances that the plain of Ai Khanoum and its resources escaped their control, or at least their knowledge. Moreover, some finds from Ai Khanoum lie within the Achaemenid artistic tradition, such as

---

[11] Francfort 1989.
[12] Cohen 2013, 231–232.
[13] Naveh/Shaked 2012, 22–33.
[14] Besenval/Marquis 2008, 982–987; Besenval/Engel/Marquis 2011, 181–184.
[15] Rapin 2007.

a number of torus column bases, a bell-shaped base found in the palace, and stoneware, seals and intaglios.[16] Some of the ceramic artefacts of the third century are no different from those of previous centuries.[17] The layout of certain public buildings also seemed inspired by Achaemenid models, particularly the palace.[18] The hypothesis that the site was occupied from the Achaemenid period has therefore been considered.[19] But no archaeological layers from that time have ever been found, and the deeper levels already contained material attributed to the Greeks. The oldest structures are both buildings, one buried under the eastern wall of the citadel and the other at the outside base of the north wall of the lower town. Both were constructed from large mud-bricks, the calibre of which seems to be typical of the Achaemenid period.[20] But it is possible that they were built at the beginning of the Hellenistic period, in accordance with traditional standards and at a time when the characteristic architectural traditions of the Greeks had not yet developed. We now know that these Achaemenid influences are accounted for mainly by the persistence of older artistic and technical traditions during the Hellenistic period.[21] If Ai Khanoum was occupied during the Achaemenid period, it was thus more likely by a garrison, stationed on the citadel. Indeed, use was probably made of the defensive strengths of the site and its acropolis use before the arrival of the Greeks. Moreover, its indigenous name was perhaps *Oskobara, a toponym which can be understood as signifying "the high fortress."[22] The largest site was at the time situated 1.5 kilometres upstream at Kohna Qala, from where the Achaemenid authority probably exercised its control over the plain. Covering an area of about 25 hectares, semi-circular in layout and protected by two lines of ramparts, it was located near the main crossing point of the Darya-i Pandj, thus allowing the river to be kept under surveillance. The site has not been excavated, but from the surface material it seems to have been occupied from the Achaemenid period up until the eighth century AD.[23]

It is thus still currently believed that the city of Ai Khanoum was founded by the Graeco-Macedonians. This event had considerable impact on the history of the plain and its occupants. The function of the site changed, from a simple military post to a major city. The transformation was the result of a political decision, motivated by considerations pertaining not solely to the local plain, which formed the territory of the new city, but to the whole of Bactria. Yet the question of who made the decision remains unresolved. Alexander the Great, who is considered one of the great city founders of antiquity, seems to be the ideal candidate. But another is Seleucus I, who also founded numerous colonies and was very active in Central Asia. Both possibilities have been considered, without any definite conclusions being reached.[24] Upon arrival in Bactria

---

[16] Bernard 1970, 333–334; Bernard *et al.* 1973, 28, 119–120; Francfort 2005, 336, 338, 340; Francfort 2013a, 24–37, 41–50, 59–64, 97–101.

[17] Lyonnet 2001, 142; Lyonnet 2012, 147–155.

[18] Bernard 1976a, 252–257; Rapin 1992, 272–278. See also Lecuyot 2013, 201–207 for the great aristocratic residences.

[19] For example Francfort 2005, 338.

[20] Leriche 1986, 21, 44, 71–72.

[21] Francfort 2013a.

[22] Rapin 2005, 146–147.

[23] Bernard 1978b, 15; Gardin 1998, 42, 45–46.

[24] Particularly Bernard 1978b, 12–15.

in 329, Alexander met with unanimous opposition from the local population. He had to contend with guerrilla operations, led in Bactria and Sogdiana by aristocrats who possessed castles and private armies and had no intention of giving up their privileges. To defeat them, Alexander responded blow for blow to the attacks, not hesitating to use violence to terrorise the population and get them to submit. He overcame the remaining pockets of resistance by dividing his army into a number of contingents, under the command of those who were close to him, whose task it was to go up the valleys, carry out reconnaissance and crush any opposition. He also established a network of foundations designed to secure his control of the region, in which he installed mercenaries and demobilised veterans and wounded soldiers unable to campaign. These foundations were of two kinds. Some were destined to become towns, bearing the name of Alexandria. These would be the key points of the network and would serve as a home to the regional administration. Bactra, the main Achaemenid capital, nonetheless retained its name. The rest were simple forts and guard posts, where large military forces were stationed. Alexander left the region without having managed to pacify and take complete control of it, but his strategy was probably continued.[25]

It is unlikely that Ai Khanoum remained on the side-lines of operations. Both the site and the already cultivated plain were probably visited by the Greek armies. Alexander took control of the Achaemenid administration and benefited from the knowledge that it had accumulated. He found out about the location of the richest valleys and oases in the region, and of the access routes he needed to keep under observation and defend. Even if we can rely solely on the argument of plausibility, everything that is known about Alexander's personality and political and military capabilities suggests that he or one of his generals took possession of the plain of Ai Khanoum and left men there.[26] He was thus able to build one of his many Alexandrias, the list of which tradition has preserved for us. It is also sometimes suggested that Ai Khanoum was in fact Alexandria Oxiana, mentioned by Ptolemy (6.12.6).[27]

The date when Alexander's army entered eastern Bactria can be specified thanks to the Historians of Alexander, who provide a relatively detailed account of the operations in Bactria and Sogdiana between 329 and 327, particularly Quintus Curtius (6.2.12–8.8.23) and Arrian (*Anab.* 3.23–4.22.2), among others. But their accounts leave a considerable amount of uncertainty and raise many questions when one tries to pinpoint the localities and features of the landscape they refer to. Efforts have nonetheless been made to identify them and to trace the routes taken, and several studies based on field work have recently been published.[28] Given the timing of the campaigns of Alexander and his army, it is most likely that they operated in eastern Bactria in the spring of 328. What follows is the reconstruction proposed by Claude Rapin (Fig. 3).[29] After leaving Bactra (Balkh), Al-

---

[25] For Alexander's strategy: Holt 1989, 52–69; Bosworth 1993, 104–119; Briant 2002, 50–55; Martinez-Sève 2012a, 371–375.

[26] Bernard 1982, 135–136.

[27] Bernard 1978b, 3–15. Lastly Cohen 2013, 269–271 with all previous references, including Fraser 1996, 153–156.

[28] The most comprehensive analysis is now Rapin 2013. Cf. also Grenet/Rapin 2001; Rapin *et al.* 2005, and Sverchkov 2008.

[29] Rapin 2013, 46–54.

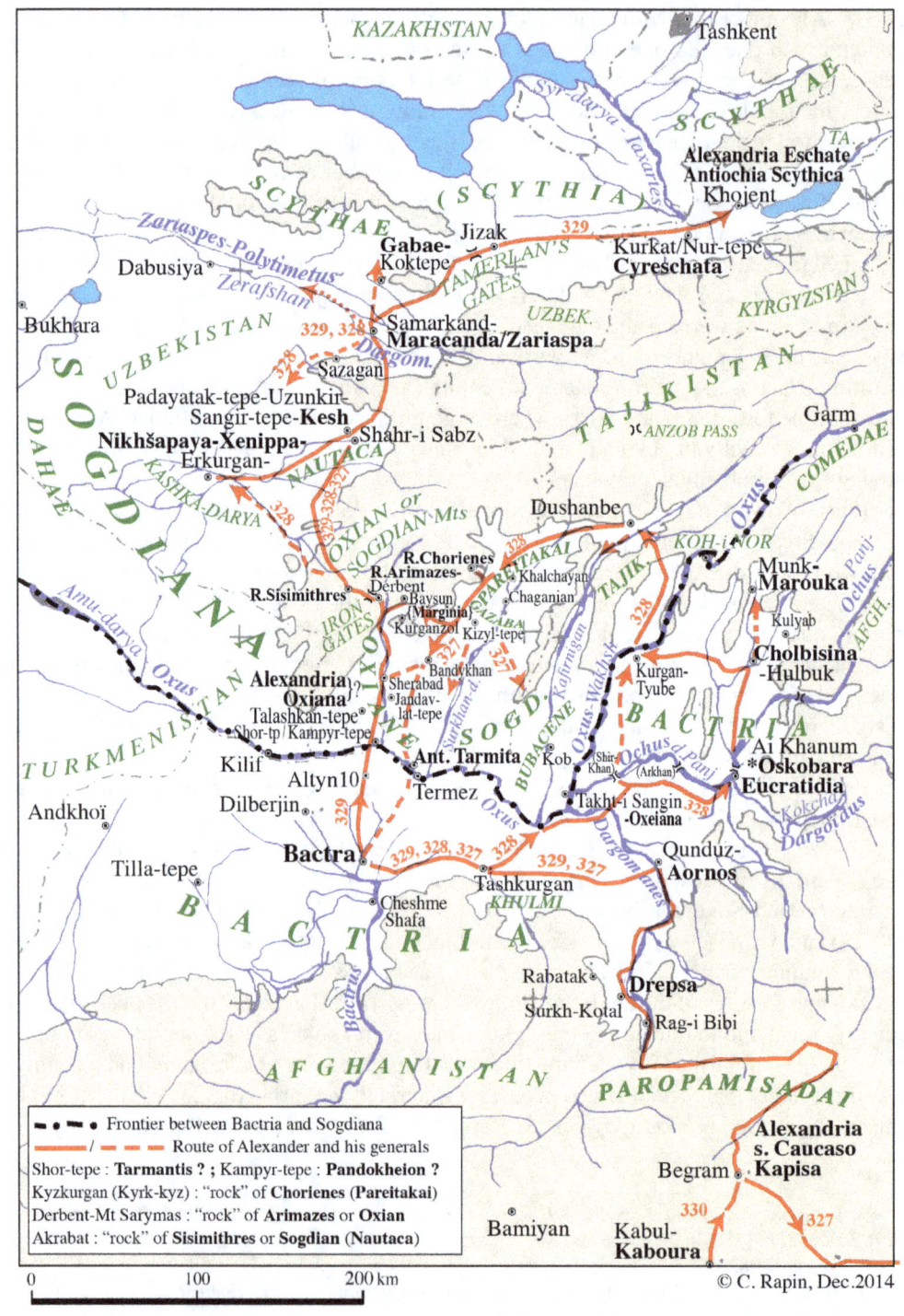

Fig. 3. Map of Hellenistic Central Asia with the route taken by Alexander the Great in 329–327 BC according to Rapin 2013 (drawing by Cl. Rapin)

exander first went in the opposite direction along the route he had taken into Bactria the previous year, then reached the banks of the Oxus. After that, he first crossed the River Ochus, then the Oxus itself,[30] and continued by marching into Sogdiana. Gradually, as he progressed, he divided his army into different contingents that he dispatched to operate in adjoining areas. Polyperchon, Attalus, Gorgias and Meleager were the commanders detached to intervene in the oases of eastern Bactria, and probably in the plain of Ai Khanoum as well. Alexander himself may have gone there if he used the Kohna Qala ford to cross the Darya-i Pandj, as this was the River Ochus. It is often assumed that this was the Oxus, as it forms the headwaters of the Amu Darya, which was unquestionably the Oxus of the ancient Greeks. In actual fact, the headwaters of the Oxus coincide with the present-day Wakhsh, a river in Tajikistan that flows into the Amu Darya at the point where the great sanctuary of Takht-i Sangin stood, consecrated to the god Oxus, a hundred kilometres downstream of Ai Khanoum. The name Oxus is, moreover, retained in the name Wakhsh, derived directly from the old Iranian *Waxšu-*, which designated the Oxus and was transcribed by the Greek Ὦξος.[31] On the other hand, the Greek Ὦχος corresponds to the Iranian *Wahu-* and the modern name of Wakh, which was sometimes used to designate the Darya-i Pandj, including by the Arab geographer Ibn Rustah, active in the early tenth century.[32] Thus Alexander crossed first the Daria-i Pandj/Ochus and then the Wakhsh/Oxus. If an Alexandria was founded on the site of Ai Khanoum, therefore, there is little chance that it was the Alexandria Oxiana of the literary tradition. The qualifier indicates that this Alexandria was situated on the banks of the Oxus, which was not the case for Ai Khanoum. Of the other Alexandrias in Central Asia whose names have been preserved, none are located in the region, with the exception of an Alexandria near Bactra (κατὰ Βάκτρα) cited by Stephenus of Byzantium (under the word *Alexandreia* 11). Its existence remains doubtful, and in any case its location hardly seems suitable for Ai Khanoum, which is located about 300 kilometres to the east of Bactra.[33]

Therefore, the available information suggests that Alexander took the plain of Ai Khanoum, but rather than founding a city there, he left troops stationed in Kohna Qala and the acropolis of Ai Khanoum. If this hypothesis is correct, it may be concluded that he simply took over the system of domination established by the Achaemenids. None of the ruins at Ai Khanoum known at present indicate that Alexander undertook the building of a proper city, or even that he planned to do so. Elsewhere in Bactria and Sogdiana, it has been possible to demonstrate the presence of ceramic assemblages characteristic of the period running from the reign of Alexander to the beginning of the reign of Antiochus I, the period of transition between the Achaemenid and Hellenistic eras. They may be seen at Maracanda and Kok Tepe,[34] as well as Kurganzol, a fort built by the Macedo-

---

[30] Quintus Curtius 7.10.13–15; the Metz Epitome, 14.

[31] Grenet/Rapin 2001, 80.

[32] Ed. M.J. de Goeje, *Bibliotheca Geographorum Araborum*, vol. 7 (Leiden 1892), 93. Cf. Grenet/Rapin 2001, 80, for a translation of the text and additional references. This proposal is also based on the new interpretation of the Ptolemy map suggested by Rapin (2001).

[33] Cohen 2013, 262. One of the contributions of P.M. Fraser's book (Fraser 1996, 153–154 for this Alexandria) was, moreover, to show that a large number of unwarranted foundations had been attributed to Alexander by virtue of his reputation as a founder. Cf. also Rapin 2005, 147–148 for the identification of Alexander's foundations.

[34] Lyonnet 2012, 167–169; Lyonnet 2013a, 364–365.

nian king near the present city of Baysun to monitor a crossing point of the mountains of Hissar, which separated the Surkhan Darya and Kashka Darya valleys, on one of the roads leading from Bactra to Maracanda.[35] But these ceramic assemblages have not been found at Ai Khanoum. This absence does not imply that the site was then unoccupied; if Graeco-Macedonians did live there, though, they were not sufficiently numerous to leave substantial traces. They were probably stationed on the citadel, where the deeper layers were reached only over very limited areas.

2. The city of Ai Khanoum, a largely unknown Seleucid foundation

Following the death of Alexander, Central Asia was not one of the main theatres in the conflict that erupted among his Friends, eager to assume his mantle, and it remained a peripheral region. Around 315, the political and military infrastructure he had set up still existed, particularly because the Diadochi – and especially Antigonus Monophthalmus – had not succeeded in eliminating Alexander's former satraps.[36] The Greek presence had then been weakened by the departure or death of many soldiers and settlers. After 323, many of them revolted and departed from this region, viewed by the Greeks as a distant and hostile land, where Achaemenid kings deported their opponents. They were slain by an army sent to suppress them.[37] In addition, the hostility of the local population had not abated. It is not certain whether the contingent possibly left at Ai Khanoum could have managed to maintain its presence there. But around 306–305, a new expedition was successfully led into Central Asia by Seleucus, who had already established control over Iran and Babylonia. Shortly afterwards, in 305, he adopted the royal title and founded the Seleucid kingdom. Although we have no definite knowledge of the campaigns he conducted, it is likely that he fought against the local population, as well as against adventurers and former satraps who had subjected to their control the remnants of Alexander's army and settlers. A certain Sophytos minted coins in his own name in a Bactrian workshop with his portrait, which was particularly innovative.[38] Oxyartes, the father of Roxanne, whom his son-in-law Alexander had made responsible for controlling the Paropamisadae, may also have issued coins in his name, along with other satraps such as Stasanor.[39] It is not surprising that these men invested with military commands operated in this manner, since the authorities they were supposed to be subordinate to were distant and in disarray. Seleucus managed to re-establish Graeco-Macedonian rule in Bactria,[40] and took energetic measures to strengthen his power. From 294, his oldest

---

[35]   On Kurganzol in general, cf. Sverchkov 2008.

[36]   Olbrycht 2013, 161–168.

[37]   Diodorus 17.99.5–6; Quintus Curtius 9.7.1–11 (first revolt of 325) and Diodorus 18.7 (revolt of 323). Cf. Bernard 1985a, 127–128; Holt 1989, 82–86; Coloru 2009, 130–134; Martinez-Sève 2012a, 374–375.

[38]   Bopearachchi 2006.

[39]   Košelenko 2006 and Atakhodjaev 2013, 220–222. The name stamped on coins attributed to Oxyartes is Vakhshuvar. It refers to Wakhsku, the Oxus of the Greeks, as we have seen previously. The name Oxyartes thus corresponds to its Greek form.

[40]   According to Capdetrey (2007, 42–43), he mostly succeeded in obtaining the allegiance of the local satraps and dynasts, who held the real power.

son Antiochus was appointed co-regent and made responsible for governing the eastern part of the kingdom. He remained in Central Asia, where he rebuilt an administrative and military structure inspired by what Alexander the Great had put in place.[41] Antiochus benefited from support in Bactria, where he also had interests and kin, as he was Bactrian through his mother Apama, the daughter of Spitamenes, who had been one of Alexander main adversaries. Seleucus had married her in Susa in 324, at the same time as Alexander and his other generals had also married Iranian princesses. Apama was not repudiated by Seleucus, and occupied an important position at the Seleucid court. Antiochus conducted reconnaissance operations in Caspian through Patroclus, one of his top generals,[42] and beyond the Syr Darya through Demodamas, a general of Milesian origin.[43] It is also believed that he recovered some of Alexander's colonies that had collapsed or been attacked. Pliny (*HN* 6.46–48) refers to Antioch in Margiana, which would have succeeded an Alexandria in Margiana – whose existence nonetheless seems very doubtful[44] – as well as to the refounding of one of Alexander's former colonies, known as Heracleia or Achais.[45] W.W. Tarn also speculated that Alexandria Eschata met the same fate: Demodamas would have refounded it during his operations in an Antioch of Scythia, attested to in Stephanus of Byzantium (s.v. *Antiocheia* 10).[46] We do not have any evidence to support these claims, and it is therefore important to be cautious.[47] But the fact remains that the Seleucids' involvement was extensive. This policy was expensive, obliging the kings to mint large amounts of coinage.[48] This development was significant for the region, which had never before encountered locally produced coinage, even at the time of Alexander, who had never set up a mint there.[49] The Seleucids recreated a network of establishments, many of them small forts and places to station garrisons,[50] among which the one at Kurganzol, for example, remained functioning. They also founded more sizable centres, including Antioch in Margiana, which was probably located on the site of the present-day Gyaur Kala in the oasis of Merv, about 30 kilometres east of the modern town of Mary.[51] Contrary to what has sometimes been believed, they also endeavoured to securely hold Sogdiana and Maracanda (Samarkand), where bronze and silver coins issued by Seleucus I and Antiochus I were in circulation.[52] Thus, we have to examine

---

[41]   Bernard 1985, 38–39; Holt 1999, 21–29; Capdetrey 2007, 79–81; Martinez-Sève 2012a, 375–376.

[42]   Strabo 11.7.3, 11.11.5 (Patroclus had left an account of this expedition, and it is in this context that he is mentioned by Strabo); Pliny, *HN* 6.58.

[43]   Pliny, *HN* 6.49.

[44]   Fraser 1996, 31, 117–118; Cohen 2013, 244–247.

[45]   Cohen 2013, 274–276.

[46]   Tarn 1985, 83, note 3. An Alexandreschata of Scythia is also designated by Appian (*Syr.* 57) as one of the foundations of Seleucus I. Cf. Cohen 2013, 252–255.

[47]   Fraser 1996, 34–40.

[48]   Holt 1999, 29–37; Houghton/Lorber 2002, 99–103, no. 257–303 for Bactria alone, but see pp. 88–304 for the whole of Central Asia.

[49]   Bopearachchi 2004.

[50]   Martinez-Sève 2012a, 376.

[51]   Cohen 2013, 245–250. Its impressive upper storey ramparts are especially known for the Hellenistic period: Zavyalov 2007.

[52]   Atakhodjaev 2013. A workshop there may have minted small-denomination coins under a king Antiochus, probably Antiochus I (cf. note 65 in Atakhodjaev 2013).

the situation of Ai Khanoum under the first Seleucids, taking into account this particular historical and political context.

None of the monuments excavated in the city date back to the reign of Seleucus I, and, as we have seen, the oldest ceramic assemblages date from the reign of Antiochus I at the earliest. The same goes for the buildings.[53] It is certain that the shrine near the main street, which later housed the temple with indented recesses, was built under Antiochus I.[54] The Heroon of Kineas and the first ramparts are likely to have been constructed at roughly the same time.[55] Based on what we know at present, it thus seems that the Greeks moved there in stages and that the development of the city proper occurred no earlier than the personal reign of Antiochus I (281–261 BC). This installation process must have been accompanied by a royal deed of foundation, but it is not possible to say when, and these events remain very imprecise. Only epigraphic documents could allow the modalities and stages of the foundation of Ai Khanoum to be determined, and these are lacking. All we can be sure about is the time when enough Greeks were living in Ai Khanoum to leave substantial traces. There was apparently a change of scale under Antiochus I, an occurrence that gives rise to various questions, because Seleucid power was established in Central Asia as early as the reign of Seleucus I. It possibly took some time to do what was needed for the Seleucids to secure their presence in Ai Khanoum. Perhaps they also devoted their early efforts to other parts of central Asia, while retaining for the plain of Ai Khanoum a system based on what had been introduced by Alexander and simply installing troops there.

A notable shift nevertheless seems to have occurred at the time of the co-regency, with substantial changes to the status of Ai Khanoum. According to Brian Kritt, a mint was opened there in the last years of co-regency, after 285, and produced bronze and silver coinage.[56] He argues that the coinage which E.T. Newell[57] previously attributed to the Bactra mint was in fact produced in Ai Khanoum, basing his argument on a very thorough technical study and the fact that these coins bore as a monogram a sign also found stamped on baked bricks used in the masonry of the oldest tomb of the Heroon of Kineas.[58] Another of these bricks was discovered within the floor of a building in the east wing of the Seleucid sanctuary. Paul Bernard had already emphasised this fact, and he too considered – before rejecting – the hypothesis that coins with this monogram should be reattributed to Ai Khanoum. If accepted, this would have resulted in removing from Bactra most of the Bactrian coinage struck under not only Seleucus I, but also Antiochus I. The coinage of Antiochus I cannot in fact be separated from his father's, with which it forms a homogeneous whole. Bernard therefore preferred to retain the

---

[53]   Martinez-Sève 2013a, 214–215; Martinez-Sève 2014, 270.

[54]   The temple with indented recesses was built in the time of Diodotus I or Diodotus II during the foundation of the Graeco-Bactrian kingdom, or soon after. He had a predecessor in the Seleucid era, which was then levelled (Martinez-Sève 2010).

[55]   See below.

[56]   Kritt 1996. These currencies are referenced in Houghton/Lorber 2002, 103–107, no. 276–290. Both authors initially accepted Kritt's proposals, but then rather reconsidered their position and became more cautious (Houghton/Lorber/Hoover 2008, 643).

[57]   Newell 1978. Note that the first edition of this study was published in 1938; the author therefore did not know of the existence of Ai Khanoum.

[58]   Bernard et al. 1973, 9, 88.

attribution to Bactra, maintaining that the main Bactrian workshop could not be any-where else than in the region's capital city.[59] For a long time, the idea prevailed that each Seleucid satrapy possessed a mint that issued coins for the needs of the area. Recent work has shown the situation to have been more complex. The Seleucids minted coins on an irregular basis to meet specific needs, but not to supply monetary circulation on the scale of a given region. The latter requirement was mainly met by coinage of very varied origins, which circulated throughout the kingdom. The Seleucids also struck coins when they were short of currency, most of which typically consisted of money obtained through various levies. If workshops of regional scope did exist, it was not the general rule, and other mints were opened when the need arose.[60] Furthermore, our conception of the organisation of the Seleucid kingdom has also been refined, and the very idea of a capital is open to question. The Seleucid kingdom was not a modern state governed from a single capital city, any more than the various satrapies were truly administrative districts governed solely from satrapy capitals. The kingdom was more an area where royal power was deployed through a network of establishments in which armed forces and administrators were stationed. This network was hierarchical, variously comprising the ancient indigenous royal cities, new foundations, secondary urban settlements and simple guard posts. It is unlikely that the region of Bactria was a uniform space for the Seleucids, administered from Bactra alone, although it was the largest city in the region and the seat of the satrap who represented them.[61] The impossibility of placing Bactria's main Seleucid mint in Ai Khanoum nonetheless constitutes the main argument mounted in opposition to Kritt.[62] As long as his technical arguments are not invalidated, his hy-pothesis remains sound. Let us look at it in more detail.

In Kritt's opinion, the Seleucids began by setting up a mint in Bactra that was in operation for six to eight years during the co-regency of Antiochus I. Its first coins were struck between 290 and 286 BC.[63] After 285, probably in the latter years of the co-regency, a second mint was opened in Ai Khanoum under the supervision of a monetary magistrate transferred from Bactra, with some coins from Ai Khanoum bearing his con-trol mark. The Bactra mint ceased operations at the beginning of the reign of Antiochus I, whereas the one at Ai Khanoum issued coinage for the duration of the Seleucid presence in Bactria. Kritt explains this transfer through the fact that the mines were closer to Ai Khanoum and that sourcing the metal was easier. In particular he maintains that it was at this time that the city of Ai Khanoum was founded, under the authority of Antiochus.[64] Even though the oldest known remains date back to the reign of Antiochus I, it can be

---

[59]   Bernard 1985b, 39.

[60]   These points clearly emerge from Houghton/Lorber 2002 and Houghton/Lorber/Hoover 2008. See also Aperghis 2004, 213–246 and Martinez-Sève 2012b for further references.

[61]   Capdetrey 2007, 69–72, 359–383 and Capdetrey 2012. Cf. also Martinez-Sève 2003, 232–234; Mar-tinez-Sève 2004, 22–32; Martinez-Sève 2012b, 217–219 (for the example of Bactria).

[62]   Notably by Osmund Bopearachchi: 1999 and 2004. See Kritt's response in Kritt 2001, 167–183.

[63]   In Kritt 1997, 65, 106–108, the suggested date is 288/287, i.e. when, in Kritt's view, Antiochus I would have arrived in Bactria after first staying at Seleucia and then Susa. Kritt attributes a set of silver and bronze coins to the Bactra mint, which were originally, but wrongly, thought to have been issued in Susa (Houghton/Lorber 2002, 99–102, no. 257–271).

[64]   Kritt 1996, 31–34. According to Kritt, Ai Khanoum did not replace Bactra as the capital of Bactria because it was too far away from the centre (on the idea of capital city, see above).

agreed that the first operations related to the founding of the city began from the time of the co-regency, when the first settlers arrived. The transfer of the mint in any case reflects a shift in the Seleucids' focus of interest to eastern Bactria, which took on a new importance. It is probable from this time onwards that the Seleucids decided to organise the control of Bactria through two main urban centres, Bactra in western Bactria and Ai Khanoum in eastern Bactria.[65] From this point, their area of control was to extend northward to the Kuliab region in Tajikistan and to the Kizil Su Valley, and perhaps westward to Kunduz, the former Aornos. This situation is more evident in the Graeco-Bactrian era,[66] but it was probably inherited from the co-regency of Antiochus, which shaped the contours of Greek power in Central Asia.[67] Their larger investment in eastern Bactria forced the Seleucids to make a financial effort that was all the greater because this region had no monetary tradition and must have had very little money in circulation. They were thus obliged to mint large amounts of coinage to finance the founding of the colony and to pay the military, which were probably stationed in greater numbers than hitherto. The name of the new city is not known, but it was probably a Seleucid dynastic name, as with all other Seleucid foundations comparable in size to Ai Khanoum. Tradition has retained the names of the two Antiochs in Central Asia mentioned above: Antioch in Margiana and Antioch in Scythia. But no texts mention an Antioch, a Seleucia or an Apamea in Bactria or on the Ochos. This absence is not altogether surprising, and no hasty conclusions should be drawn from it. Several Seleucid foundations are known only through epigraphic documents and were not mentioned by the authors of antiquity, for example Seleucia on the Eulaios, on the site of the former Susa, or Antioch in Persis and Seleucia on the Erythrean Sea, both located near the Persian Gulf.[68] Few epigraphic documents have been found in Central Asia, and most of those that have been found are private in nature and make no mention of a city. Further discoveries will be needed to make progress in this respect.

Of the various monuments in Ai Khanoum, the Heroon of Kineas is the only one associated with the first settlers. It was built in the centre of the lower town to house the remains of this individual, whose name is well attested to in Thessaly. The identification of this building is not in doubt, thanks to an inscription made by one Clearchus, which states that the monument was a place of worship dedicated to Kineas: Clearchus refers to the *temenos* of Kineas. He had erected a stele there bearing a set of maxims, some of which, owing to a lack of space, were engraved on the base itself.[69] It is considered

---

[65] On this point, cf. Leriche 2007, 130–134.

[66] See below.

[67] Rapin also stresses the advantageous position of Ai Khanoum in an area that in his view extended from the Wakhsh valley to the Kunduz region, but had already formed in the Achaemenid period (Rapin 2013, 48–49).

[68] Seleucia on the Eulaios is mentioned in several inscriptions found in Susa (Rougemont 2012, no. 13, 14, 17?, 19, 20?, 23?, 33?) as well as in the acceptance decree of the *Leukophryena* of Magnesia on the Maeander by Antioch of Persis (Rougemont 2012, no. 53). Antioch of Persis is known through this document, as is Seleucia on the Erythrean Sea.

[69] Rougemont 2012, 200–209, no. 97 (first edition of the text: Robert 1968). The base bore Clearchus's dedication in verse: Ἀνδρῶν τοι σοφὰ ταῦτα παλαιοτέρων ἀνάκει[τ]αι / ῥήματα ἀριγνώτων Πυθοῖ ἐν ἠγαθέαι / ἔνθεν ταῦτ[α] Κλέαρχος ἐπιφραδέως ἀναγράψας / εἵσατο τηλαυγῆ Κινέου ἐν τεμένει (*The wise words of men of old, words of celebrated men / are set up in most holy Pytho / From there Clearchus copied them meticu-*

that Kineas was the Seleucid officer responsible for founding the colony, though Antiochus would have been able to go there himself had he been in Bactria. Kineas probably
belonged to the first generation of settlers living in the city, where he was to die. His
body was placed in a sarcophagus inside the tomb;[70] it was thus not simply a cenotaph.
Kineas was nevertheless considered to be the founder of the city, the only assumption
that accounts for the fact that he was worshipped and interred in his own mausoleum.[71]
Therefore it was he who specifically organised the settling of the city and was the main
representative of Seleucid power. These first settlers lived in temporary buildings, of
which nothing remains, except possibly an initial defensive wall located at the site of the
future north rampart.[72]

The momentum generated by Antiochus while co-regent did not stop when he became king in 281. It was in fact at this point that Ai Khanoum really began to exist as
a city. Conceived as a royal city, it embodied the power of the sovereigns who ruled over
it. On the death of Seleucus I, Antiochus was either in Babylonia or, more probably, in
Central Asia. He was obliged to make his way quickly to Asia Minor and contend with
various problems there, and subsequently spent long periods in the western parts of the
kingdom.[73] It is not even certain that he ever returned to Central Asia, though that did
not prevent his administration continuing to consolidate Seleucid domination there. This
policy came at a cost, and large amounts of coinage were minted. Nearly a third of the
bronze coins found at Ai Khanoum were issued in this period,[74] testifying not only to
continuing royal investment but very much to its amplification. It was at this time that the
city took its initial form. The oldest constructions are, as we have seen, the sanctuary, the
Heroon of Kineas, and probably the ramparts, which all had a utilitarian and a symbolic
function. The ramparts functioned as a defence, but also defined and enclosed the urban
space, the future expansion of which was foreseen, while concretely expressing the power of newcomers. The total area was very large (about 150 hectares), and even though it
was customary to keep non-built-up spaces so as to allow people in the surrounding area
to fall back in the event of danger and to have arable land in the event prolonged siege,
it is evident that the construction of a major city was planned from the outset. There was
also a concern to install the settlers' gods as guarantors of their safety and their future,
and to pay tribute to the founder, who had died in the meantime. The main street was
laid out at the same time as the sanctuary, at least in its surroundings, suggesting that
the general plan of the city was conceived during this period. Considerable work was
undertaken, an indication of royal involvement. The sanctuary was built on an intermedi-

---

lously / and had them drawn up, brilliant from afar, in the temenos of Kineas, trad. Lerner 2003/2004). The
last five lines of maxims remained on the base, and two other very fragmentary lines were found on the fragment of the lower left corner of the stele, the only one preserved: Παῖς ὢν κόσμιος γίνου / ἡβῶν ἐγκρατής /
μέσος δίκαιος / πρεσβύτης εὔβουλος / τελευτῶν ἄλυπος and on the fragment ε[ὐλόγει πάντας] / φιλόσοφ[ος
γίνου] (*In childhood, be well behaved / in youth, have self-control / in middle age, behave justly / in old age,
be of wise counsel / in death, be without sorrow*, trad. Lerner 2003/2004).

[70] Bernard *et al.* 1973, 87–88.
[71] This hypothesis is, for example, accepted by Fröhlich 2013, 245–247.
[72] Leriche 1986, 52, 72.
[73] For the chronology of the reign of Antiochus I, cf. Will 1979, 135–152.
[74] Bernard 1985, 7 (the coins found in hoards are excluded from this count). Some of these coins were
still in circulation during the second century BC.

ate terrace between the upper town and the palace area stretching out below. Its layout was remodelled before the construction of the religious complex: in some places, some of the natural land was removed, while in others the surface was raised by a thick layer of fluvial pebbles. The slopes forming the edge of the terrace were also equalised. These operations were dated from a coin of Antiochus I,[75] buried under pebbles a metre thick, which constitutes a chronological milestone of major importance. Through it we can date the foundation of the sanctuary to his reign.[76] The date of the Heroon can also be established. As well as pottery, comparable to that of the first period of the sanctuary,[77] a very important source is the inscription by Clearchus, whose characteristic writing can hardly be dated to a period after the reign of Antiochus I.[78] This inscription shows that Kineas was by then dead, but we must take account of the fact that he also lived in Ai Khanoum for some time before his death, the length of which we unfortunately cannot estimate. The oldest pottery collected during the excavation of the rampart is also of the Seleucid era,[79] which remains imprecise. But it is likely that once the decision was taken to construct the first buildings, the Seleucid authorities did not wait long before protecting them against external attack. The rampart is therefore probably contemporaneous with them. A further influx of settlers was perhaps also necessary, but there is no trace of it, and we still know nothing about the houses of the first inhabitants.

This was also the time when Clearchus erected the stele with the Delphic maxims in the Heroon. The inscription is a valuable source of information on the mentality of the early settlers. Clearchus was probably not acting in a private capacity.[80] Erecting a monument in the precinct of a public building required that prior approval be obtained from the city authorities.[81] The symbolic importance of the Heroon even suggests that these

---

[75] Bernard 1985, no. 68.

[76] Martinez-Sève 2010, 201; Martinez-Sève 2014, 274–275. Although the date provides only a *terminus ante quem*, the other coin finds and the architectural sequence of the sanctuary do not allow it to be lowered much.

[77] Lyonnet 2012, 147–155; Lyonnet 2013a, 361–362. This pottery was found in the embankment that supported the second version of the building. It is certainly from the Seleucid period, but it is difficult to come up with more precise dating given the present state of our knowledge.

[78] Rougemont 2012, 202, 204–208 (the inscription dates from a period spanning the reigns of Alexander to Antiochus I). Rougemont thus confirms the date originally proposed by Louis Robert (1968), which has been challenged by several authors, including recently by J.D. Lerner (2003/2004, 392–395, with the oldest bibliography).

[79] Leriche 1986, 53–54, 69, 105–106. This pottery dates from period I–II, which roughly corresponds to the Seleucid era (Lyonnet 2012, 147, who combines periods I, II and III).

[80] Following Robert (1968, 441–454), many commentators believe that Clearchus was Clearchus of Soli, known to have been a direct disciple of Aristotle: see most recently Rougemont 2012, 203–206, which focuses on the issue and examines conflicting opinions, including that of Lerner 2003/2004, 392–394. I for one am very doubtful. This implies that Clearchus met Aristotle toward the end of Aristotle's life and came to Ai Khanoum early in the reign of Antiochus I. Although not intrinsically impossible, the current evidence suggests that the city was little developed in the third century and that it was mainly occupied by the military. The environment was therefore not very likely to attract the philosopher, unless the road he took went to Ai Khanoum and his journey had a different purpose. According to Frantz Grenet, Clearchus may have been the source of Diodorus (1.94.2), comparing Zoroaster with Moses. Diodorus seems to have known and transmitted an Iranian tradition, obtained straight from Iranian intermediates (Grenet 2005, 49, note 24). He could have travelled in Badakhshan to meet them, because he is known to have been interested in Oriental wisdom.

[81] I thank Pierre Fröhlich for this suggestion.

authorities did not simply give their permission, but were directly involved. This monument embodies the birth of the settler community, the first moment of its collective history. The stele originally bore a set of about 150 maxims, six of which have been more or less preserved: "speak well of everyone," "practice wisdom," "Be a well-behaved child / a self-controlled young man / a just mature man, an old man of good council / die without affliction."[82] The others are easy to reconstruct, because these precepts are known through epigraphic and literary documents found elsewhere in the Greek world, including Miletopolis in Mysia (*Syll.*,[3] no. 1268), where they were exhibited in the gymnasium, as well as in Stobaeus, who attributed them to a certain Sosiades.[83] The significance of these maxims should not be exaggerated, since they were not unusual.[84] They consisted of short phrases providing a series of rules of life and behaviour characteristic of Greek identity that were learned by heart and recited in schools and were also a means of teaching children how to read.[85] The settlers of Ai Khanoum thus proclaimed their community, founded in a remote and barbarous land and composed of individuals from diverse backgrounds. They were bound together through the sharing of these core values, which were constitutive of their identity and more generally that of Greek culture, and which distinguished them from other populations. Respecting these values was thus the basis for the success of the foundation.

We know little about Ai Khanoum for the decades following the death of Antiochus I, an indication perhaps that Seleucid involvement was less extensive than previously. The city nevertheless kept its mint and struck gold, silver and bronze coins in the name of Antiochus II.[86] Its fortifications were maintained, and even improved, as was evident at the north rampart, which was excavated over several metres about 200 metres west of the end point of the main street. It contained a tower, the outside of which was reinforced first with a brick lining (ceramics period I–II[87]) and then by a buttress probably intended to counter the use of siege engines (ceramics period III), an operation that was contemporary with the adding of a brick facing to the inner side of the curtain wall.[88] A similar veneer may be seen on the walls bordering the Darya-i Pandj, where a stone fountain was later erected. The inner side of the curtain wall was covered with a facing (ceramics period I–II). A little later, the wall collapsed as a result of the infiltration of water, and was rebuilt. It was then that the fountain was placed at the bottom of the outer face (ceramics period III).[89]

However, under Antiochus II, who succeeded his father in 261 and ruled until 246, Seleucid control of Bactria seems to have been more remote. It was contested by Diodotus, the governor who administered the region on behalf of the king and then seceded and created the Graeco-Bactrian kingdom. It is believed that he took power gradually, as

---

[82] Cf. note 65.

[83] Robert 1968, 427–429 (for Stobaeus, ed. Meineke, vol. 1: 90–92).

[84] For the links with Delphi, cf. Mairs 2014.

[85] Oikonomides 1987; Huys 1996 (papyrus edition from the first century AD that included these maxims following a list of heroes, and perhaps was an educational papyrus).

[86] Kritt 1996, 26; Houghton/Lorber 2002, 215–218, no. 616–627.

[87] Eight chronological stages have been distinguished. Only period IV, which covers the first decades of the second century BC, can be more or less dated with absolute chronology.

[88] Leriche 1986, 44–45, 49, 51, 53–54.

[89] Leriche 1986, 35–36. For the fountain: Leriche/Thoraval 1979.

indicated by the coinage. Diodotus began by replacing the type of coins and the portrait of Antiochus with his own, but left the name of Antiochus unchanged in the legend. The name of Diodotus, accompanied by the royal title (*basileus*), then replaced that of the Seleucid. The Seleucid kings ruled over an empire whose functioning was complex, largely based on the links in terms of individuals and influence that the king forged with his subordinates at various levels of the administrative hierarchy. In many areas, local or regional governors enjoyed considerable power, sometimes equivalent to that of a king, but continued to act within an imperial sphere that they themselves acknowledged as Seleucid. The strongest and most enterprising of them were eventually able to break away, though gradually, so as to obtain the support of all those who were previously tied to Seleucid power. For instance, this is what happened in Asia Minor with the foundation of the Attalid kingdom of Pergamum.[90] A similar process appears to have occurred in Bactria. An important step towards independence came when Diodotus adopted the royal title of *basileus* on his coinage. It is difficult to specify exactly when this occurred, though various suggestions have been made. It was thought that this step was taken not by Diodotus himself, but by his son, also called Diodotus (II), who would have taken the title when he succeeded his father around 235 BC.[91] However, Jens Jakobsson has nevertheless recently put forward an alternative hypothesis that alters our understanding of Diodotus's secession. He proposes that the coins in the style of Diodotus minted in the name of Antiochus were not issued by Diodotus I, as previously thought, but by a Graeco-Bactrian king named Antiochus who succeeded Diodotus II, probably his brother, and continued to strike coins characteristic of the new dynasty.[92] This proposal implies that the revolt by Diodotus I was sudden, since in that case he would have adopted the royal title from the beginning, while he was changing the coin style and the portrait.[93] Jakobsson considers that he reigned only briefly, around 255–250 BC, followed by Diodotus II from around 250 to 240, and then by Antiochus between 240 and 225. Although revolutionary, this assumption seems to be supported by some die-links among gold staters struck by this Antiochus and others struck by Euthydemus I, who would therefore have succeeded him.[94] These different proposals do not make much difference for the chronology of Ai Khanoum.[95] But they create uncertainties that prevent more exact placing, under the Seleucids or under the Diodotids, of various maintenance and construction

---

[90] Chrubasik 2013.

[91] Holt 1999, 87–125; Kritt 2001, 7–47. Cf. also Kovalenko 1995/1996. A new analysis of their currency suggests that Diodotus I himself took the decision and, if so, probably in the second part of his life: cf. Bordeaux, forthcoming (I thank Olivier Bordeaux for letting me read this paper prior to publication).

[92] Jakobsson 2010. The fact that a son of Diodotus I could bear the name of Antiochus presents no problem insofar as Diodotus was for part of his life a member of the royal Seleucid entourage; it is therefore understandable that he could have chosen this name for one of his sons. Diodotus may also have maintained links of kinship with the Seleucids, as proposed by Jakobsson (2010, 21). This implies, however, that once he became king, this Antiochus did not change his name to a regnal name.

[93] He would therefore have behaved like Molon in 222 and like Timarchus around 162 (Jakobsson 2010, 23–24).

[94] Zeng 2013. These Bactrian staters came to light recently from a large hoard discovered in 2001. The staters of Euthydemus I had been struck from an obverse die previously used by Antiochos.

[95] They do, however, affect the identification of the mints where coins were struck, including possibly that of Ai Khanoum. According to Jens Jakobsson, Diodotus I struck all his silver coins in the mint identified by Frank Holt as the Bactra mint (workshop B: Holt 1999, 114, 124–125).

operations that have been observed there.[96] Jakobsson's proposal also implies that the Seleucids retained possession of Ai Khanoum for a very short time after the reign of Antiochus I.

These political events probably had an impact on the development of Ai Khanoum. It does not appear that the initiatives taken under Antiochus I were fully implemented. Nothing in the known documentation shows that the city grew and increased in population. The pottery used by the people who lived there was largely undecorated, and the vases were simple in form and varied little, suggesting that the population was small in size and that their activities were all much the same. From this evidence, Bertille Lyonnet has concluded that residents were mostly soldiers and that the city essentially housed a garrison.[97] The oldest excavated houses are, in addition, solely from the early second century.[98] Diodotus and his son (or sons) did not completely lose interest in the city, however. They were the architects of the complete reconstruction of the temple and its sanctuary, after one or the other officially assumed the royal title.[99] This operation is dated by four bronze coins minted in the name of King Diodotus, found within the floor of the new temple and in a layer of fill supporting the floor of a portico in the courtyard.[100] The reconstruction of the temple complex was also perhaps motivated by taking the royal title, because it was important for the new king to obtain divine favours and place himself under the protection of the gods, the guardians of royal legitimacy.[101]

3. Ai Khanoum, the royal residence of the Graeco-Bactrian kings

The Graeco-Bactrian kings were truly responsible for the development of Ai Khanoum that occurred from the beginning of the second century, when, in a related process, the Graeco-Bactrian kingdom itself entered into a growth phase. The first architects of this change were Euthydemus I (about 235–190) and his son Demetrius I (about 190–180).[102]

---

[96] Pierre Leriche found traces of a fire that destroyed the river rampart at the end of ceramics period II (Leriche 1986, 38). It is tempting to account for then by an attack made against the city in the context of Diodotus's secession. But it is better to remain cautious. An attack made in a strictly local context, or even simply an accident, may also have caused it. It is nonetheless likely that ceramics period III corresponds to the time of Diodotides, whether or not it is possible to finely delineate the chronological limits. Examination of the pottery found at the sanctuary may provide additional items, because a period of occupation in the Diodotid era has been clearly identified there.

[97] Lyonnet 2012, 158–159. In her opinion, this comment applies to the city at the time of Antiochus I. But as she considers the ceramics of periods I, II and III to form the same set and that the real change occurred in period IV (Lyonnet 2012, 147), the comment should also be applicable to the following decades.

[98] Cf. the recent publication on private housing in Ai Khanoum (Lecuyot 2013) and, for the chronology, Lyonnet 2013b, and Martinez-Sève 2013a.

[99] Martinez-Sève 2010, 202–203. Drawing on the findings of Holt and Kritt, in this publication I have assumed that coins minted in the name of Diodotus were produced by Diodotus II.

[100] Bernard 1985, no. 85, 91, 97, 101. These coins are part of coinage attributed to Diodotus II by Holt and Kritt. This places the rebuilding of the temple between 235 and 225 BC (or between 250 and 240 BC if we accept Jakobsson's hypothesis).

[101] Kritt 2001, 101 believes, moreover, that Ai Khanoum was the first capital of Diodotus I; Martinez-Sève 2010, 202–203.

[102] Coloru 2009, 175–193.

Euthydemus seized power by overthrowing Diodotus II (or Antiochus).[103] He then firmly established himself on the throne and even resisted an attempt to reconquer Bactria by the Seleucid king Antiochus III. After besieging Bactra from 208 to 206 but failing to remove Euthydemus, Antiochus III finally acknowledged his royal title.[104] Antiochus III did not spend all this time besieging Bactra, and probably led operations elsewhere in Bactria. He possibly went to Ai Khanoum, where he would have minted currency. Brian Kritt attributes two bronze coins in the name of Antiochus to the Ai Khanoum mint, made with the same technique as those of Euthydemus and possibly struck on coin blanks prepared for him, but which had not yet been used. Antiochus would also have stamped an anchor countermark on bronze coins issued by Antiochus I and Antiochus II that had been in circulation for a long time. Kritt thus postulates that, on his arrival in Ai Khanoum, Antiochus III was obliged to pay for his expenditure using countermarked coins, before arranging for coins bearing his name to be minted locally.[105] Kritt also attributes to Antiochus III the destruction of parts of the rampart, which would have retained evidence of his assault.[106] Indeed, a section of the north rampart collapsed as a result of being undermined, while traces of a large fire were found on the river wall, where the external face of the rampart near the fountain also collapsed.[107] This destruction was followed by the restoration of the rampart, which was repaired or partially rebuilt, a phenomenon also observed in the citadel.[108] But these events have been dated to period IV in the history of the city, and if the dating is correct, it must be assumed that they occurred after the arrival of Antiochus III, since period IV covers the first decades of the second century.[109]

Euthydemus managed to prevail over the Seleucid king, and his successes helped consolidate his power. The kingdom was organised on the model of the Seleucid kingdom, the political and administrative structures of which were emulated.[110] The last years of Euthydemus's reign and the reign of Demetrius were taken up by military campaigns that enabled them to extend their dominance, particularly to the south. Demetrius was the first to cross the Hindu Kush and establish himself in Paropamisadae and Arachosia, the regions of Kabul and Kandahar.[111] Ai Khanoum benefited from this new situation. The city acquired a new impetus, reflected in an increase in its population, which also affected its territory, where the Greeks appear previously not to have been very numerous.[112] It also seems to have been more affected than before by influences from the Mediterranean

---

[103] Polybius 11.34.

[104] Polybius 10.48–49, 11.34; Holt 1999, 126–133.

[105] Kritt 2001, 152–157; Houghton/Lorber 2002, 466–467, no. 1283–1284.

[106] Cf. also Lerner 2003/2004, 396–398.

[107] Leriche 1986, 37, 38, 45, 54, 82 (the attack has been attributed to Euthydemus, but the chronology adopted needs to be corrected).

[108] Leriche 1986, 23, 25.

[109] Cf. note 114 for the dating of period IV.

[110] Coloru 2009, 265–269.

[111] Bernard in Bernard/Pinault/Rougemont 2004, 269–276; Coloru 2009, 187–193.

[112] Lyonnet 1997, 148–149. A number of farms have been excavated on the Ai Khanoum plain, whose date is not always easy to specify. The one for which historical data is available dates from this period (Francfort 2013b, 161–165).

world. Very marked changes were observed in the area of ceramics.[113] The shapes of vases were enriched with new models, many of them directly adapted from the production of potteries in the eastern Mediterranean, such as the so-called "Megarian" bowls, which copied dishes made of precious metal. Manufacturing and cooking techniques also underwent development.[114] The growth of the city resulted in the construction of private houses, including the house in the southwest quarter and smaller installations in the vicinity of the sanctuary,[115] and a house under the remains of the gymnasium.[116] Several public buildings also date from this period, including the monumental Propylaea, through which one passed to reach the buildings located under the remains of the palace and the gymnasium.[117] The sanctuary underwent a complete renovation: the temple with indented recesses remained operational, but all the buildings in the courtyard were rebuilt to a completely revised plan. The Heroon of Kineas, which had deteriorated, was also completely rebuilt. The new building, larger in size, was constructed on a terrace covering the remains of the previous Heroon.

The creation and then the strengthening of the Graeco-Bactrian kingdom had a decisive impact on the development and role of the city. Even though the Seleucid kings had made it one of the major centres of Bactria, it was hitherto but one element in an extensive network of colonies extending as far as the Mediterranean. Now, along with Bactra, it was a cornerstone of a smaller kingdom, but unlike Bactra, it was a new city that it was possible to organise more freely. The Graeco-Bactrian kings could concentrate their efforts on it and display their power through monumental and prestigious buildings, while using its location to maintain their control of the surrounding area. An inscription found recently near Kuliab thus suggests that a member of the royal entourage called Heliodotus was in the vicinity, and assumed command or completed a mission shortly after the victory over Antiochus III. He dedicated an altar to the goddess Hestia and erected it in a sacred grove of Zeus in honour of King Euthydemus and his son Demetrius.[118] It may be deduced that there was a settlement there occupied by a Greek community, in all likelihood a small fort where a military detachment was stationed, along with some civilians. These men depended on a military and civilian command based in a larger settlement located in eastern Bactria: it is reasonable to suppose that this was Ai Khanoum. But

---

[113] Lyonnet 2001, 151–152 (the chronology adopted here is too high); Lyonnet 2012, 155; Lyonnet 2013b, 187–188.

[114] This pottery is typical of period IV, originally dated from the third century. But with the publication of the ceramics of the agora of Athens it has emerged that these Megarian bowls could not be from a date earlier than the beginning of the second century. The dating of period IV has been brought forward and placed in the first decades of the second century, consistently with the proposal that J.D. Lerner has formulated in various papers (Lerner 2003/2004; Lerner 2005; Lerner 2010; Lyonnet 2013b), which has contributed significantly to changing our perception of the history of Ai Khanoum.

[115] Lecuyot 2013, 13–74 for the house, and 59–61 for its former states (Lyonnet 2013b, 183–189 for the chronology); Martinez-Sève 2013b, 137–138 for houses in the neighbourhood of the sanctuary. Barracks were also built on the Acropolis; they probably served to house soldiers (Leriche 1986, 62–63; Lecuyot 2013, 198–199).

[116] Veuve 1987, 107–109. This building is located at the site of the future round exedra in the south-west corner of the courtyard.

[117] For the Propylaea: Guillaume 1983, 5–10, 29. For the remains beneath the gymnasium, consisting of a large bath-house collection: Veuve 1987, 52–58.

[118] Bernard/Pinault/Rougemont 2004, 333–356; Rougemont 2012, 255–258, no. 151.

does this new momentum alone explain the regeneration of Mediterranean influences? If Antiochus III did come to Ai Khanoum between 208 and 206, he may have decided to leave behind soldiers and even a new group of settlers, and to set about rebuilding the city. The policy he implemented during his reign was guided by the desire to remodel the Seleucid kingdom and rebuild the political structures put in place by his ancestors. Restoring the Seleucid colony of Ai Khanoum might have been one of his objectives. But he did not remain in Bactria long enough to leave a lasting imprint there. Euthydemus thus played an important role that was all the more decisive since Antiochus had recognised his legitimacy and confirmed him in his royal function. If new settlers were installed at Ai Khanoum, they remained there with his consent and under his control. We can also assume that some of the soldiers who came with Antiochus preferred to stay put and enter the service of Euthydemus rather than undertake the long journey home. The strengthening of the kingdom must also have helped the resumption of trade with the Mediterranean and perhaps attracted new immigrants.[119] Euthydemus's victory thus created the conditions for renewal and, for Ai Khanoum, a new situation that succeeded the initial impetus provided by the Seleucid kings.

The city further developed during the first half of the second century, especially in the reign of Eucratides I, the most well-known of the Graeco-Bactrian kings (circa 171–148).[120] He seems to have spent part of his time restoring the unity of the kingdom, which had broken up into a number of principalities under the impact of competing kings.[121] One such principality was probably centred around the city of Ai Khanoum.[122] Eucratides also expanded his realm, particularly towards India, where he pushed the Indo-Greek King Menander back beyond the Punjab. Eucratides acquired large amounts of booty in India, some of which remained in the treasury of the Ai Khanoum palace: Indian silver coins and precious objects, including agate and rock crystal vases, a wooden throne decorated with inlays, and the lid of a casket (or the back of a mirror) made of shell and decorated with scenes from Indian mythology by means of coloured glass inlays.[123] Ai Khanoum benefited from the consequences of this exceptional reign. An extensive architectural programme was undertaken and the city was completely renovated and rebuilt. It was endowed with prestigious monuments, the enormous size of which rules out

---

[119] Lerner 2003/2004, 399.

[120] Here I take the dates proposed by Wilson/Assar 2007. The authors rely on the fact that according to Justin the death of Eucratides coincided with the conquest by Mithridates I of the Medes (41.6.5.). This conquest is dated by G.F. Assar as late 148/early 147 BC. An inscription in the Ai Khanoum treasury suggests that Eucratides reigned for at least 24 years, which would place his accession in 171 (Bernard et al. 1980, 23–27; Rougemont 2012, 226–227, no. 117). This is a minimum. Rapin believes that the treasury operated for another four years before suffering an attack, possibly related to the death of Eucratides (Rapin 1992, 114). He would therefore have ascended the throne four years earlier, around 175 BC. Note that this date has been proposed for the beginning of the "Yavana" Greek era, commemorating an important event in the history of the Graeco-Bactrian kings (Falk and Bennett 2009). For another proposal see Rapin 2010. The chronology of Graeco-Bactrian history is virtually unknown and is based on various very tentative hypotheses that may be called into question by any new documents.

[121] Coloru 2009, 195–230; Rapin 2010.

[122] Rapin 2010, 242–246 stresses that Euthydemus II, Agathocles I and then Demetrius II were based in eastern Bactria during the decade 180–170 BC.

[123] Rapin 1992, 281–287.

their having been funded solely by the inhabitants of the city.[124] It therefore seems very likely that Ai Khanoum was the main residence of Eucratides, his "capital." But other large-scale schemes had been implemented by some of the kings who had reigned before him, though these remain unidentified.[125] For example, the gymnasium from the time of Eucratides was preceded by one or more monuments of impressive dimensions.[126] To the north, there was a large courtyard, bordered by buildings on two of its sides, altogether covering an area of 17,200 square metres. To the south, there was a rotunda building as well as an impressive bath complex. The reconstruction of the sanctuary, which I have suggested to have dated from the reign of Euthydemus I, or more likely of Demetrius I, may in fact have occurred a little later, being contemporary with these monuments. Indeed, a fragment of a Megarian bowl was found in a preparatory layer under the floor of the buildings.[127] We now believe that these vases began to spread throughout the Greek world from around 175 BC,[128] i.e. a little after the death of Demetrius I, which is usually put around 180 BC.[129]

Eucratides endowed himself with a capital rivalling the main centres of the Hellenistic world.[130] The regal character of the city was now amplified by the substantial mass of the palace, extending over seven hectares in the centre of the lower town. The public buildings alone occupied about a third of this lower town. The king's power was also expressed through imposing buildings such as the theatre[131] and the gymnasium,[132] which placed Eucratides on a par with other Hellenistic kings and showed that he, like them, was also a protector of Greek arts and culture. It is also noteworthy that literary papyri and parchments were kept in a room in the treasury.[133] Eucratides probably supported artists from the Mediterranean world at his court, as we know the Parthian kings did at the same period in their capital city of Nisa[134] and as Macedonian and Hellenistic kings had always done. Moreover, Bernard pointed out the many similarities between some of the capitals in the bouleuterion of Miletus, dating from the reign of Antiochus IV, and

---

[124] The palace occupied an area of over seven hectares. The gymnasium covered a square of about one hectare and the adjacent courtyard extended over a fairly wide area; the theatre was 85 metres in diameter and could accommodate nearly 5,000 spectators.

[125] To these should be added the construction work on the ramparts that we mentioned above, which dates from the transition between periods IV and V.

[126] Veuve 1987, 43–52, 106–107.

[127] In Gardin/Lyonnet 1976, 48, it is stated that these fragments were lying on the floor of a chapel built on the south side of the courtyard. They were attributed to levels 4 or 5 of the sanctuary, then dated at 270–250. The fragments were collected in 1972, in the sector of the chapel, but from the relevant preparatory layer, not from the floor.

[128] Rotroff 1982; Rotroff 1997; Lerner 2003/2004, 381; Rotroff 2006.

[129] Wilson 2003 has nevertheless proposed bringing forward the reign of Demetrius I by a few years, and considers that it ended around 170–167 BC.

[130] I will say less about this period in the history of Ai Khanoum, which is rather better known than the previous ones. See, most recently, Francfort *et al.* 2014, and Martinez-Sève 2014 with the older bibliography.

[131] Bernard 1976b, 314–322; Bernard 1978c, 429–441.

[132] Veuve 1987, 23–41, 103–106.

[133] Rapin 1987; Rapin 1992, 115–130; Rougemont 2012, 236–242, no. 131–132.

[134] Invernizzi 2007, 174–176. For examples of achievements that can be attributed to some of these artists, see Invernizzi 2009 and Invernizzi 2010.

those of the hypostyle hall of the palace.[135] The members of the royal entourage thus lived luxuriously, in rich houses calling for numerous servants.[136] Eucratides was also responsible for the rehabilitation of the city's defences, which were renovated or rebuilt.[137] His presence and investment left his mark on Ai Khanoum to such an extent that it has seemed reasonable to view this city as the Eucratidea mentioned by Strabo (11.11.2, 15.1.3) and Ptolemy (6.2.8).[138]

The king and the elite also liked to present themselves as people of Greek culture, educating their children in the traditional manner within the confines of the gymnasium. The many bathrooms excavated in the palace, beneath the gymnasium and in aristocratic houses, reveal the importance they attached to bodily care, a characteristic Greek practice unknown among Iranian populations.[139] The Greek character of the city and its architectural decoration is, moreover, what made its discovery so important. But we know very little about the appearance of the other eastern Greek colonies and of other royal towns. We know that there was a theatre in Babylon and Seleucia on the Tigris,[140] and probably a gymnasium at Susa,[141] where a wealthy aristocratic house was also excavated.[142] These large cities must have common features, and Ai Khanoum was no exception in this respect. If we accept, therefore, that it was the main residence of Eucratides, his "capital," it is not impossible that like the other great Hellenistic royal residences it had the attributes of a true Greek city and was endowed with traditional civic institutions. One sometimes gets the idea that Greek cities, because they were subject to royal power, were opposed to it. But it was the kings who were the main promoters of civic life. They were the only people authorised to found cities or to grant civic institutions to a community. They were also often the protectors of these institutions. For a king like Eucratides, promoting Greek culture meant erecting prestigious buildings such as the theatre and gymnasium, as well as perhaps encouraging civic life, since this was a characteristic part of Greek culture, as the Greeks were fully aware. The status of Ai Khanoum may be comparable to that of Alexandria, Seleucia on the Tigris, Antioch or Pergamum,[143] especially since the Graeco-Bactrian kingdom functioned much like other Hellenistic kingdoms.[144] Thus Ai Khanoum may well have possessed traditional institutions, assemblies and magistrates, but in close association with the king and his administration, which

---

[135] Bernard 1968, 120–129. According to Henri-Paul Francfort, these capitals were made by artists of Milesian origin, sent to Ai Khanoum from Ecbatana at the time when Timarchus, himself a Milesian, usurped the power (Francfort 1984, 121–122).

[136] Lecuyot 2013, 13–74, 103–136, 193–197.

[137] Leriche 1986, 13, 25, 39, 41, 68–69.

[138] Bernard et al. 1980, 38. This identification is now generally accepted. Note, however, that in this paper it was proposed tentatively.

[139] Bernard 1971, 389–402; Veuve 1987, 107–108; Lecuyot 2013, 6, 30–34, 40–41, 47–48, 59, 76–77, 85–87, 108, 125–128, 194–196.

[140] Babylon: Wetzel/Schmidt/Mallwitz 1957; Mohammed Ali 1979; Bergamini 2011; Seleucia: Messina 2010.

[141] The building itself is not known, but an inscription, probably a decree, mentions a gymnasiarch called Nikolaos (Rougemont 2012, 46–47, no. 10).

[142] Martinez-Sève 2002, 39–44. For Susa in the Hellenistic period, see also Martinez-Sève 2011.

[143] Only Pergamum's status is relatively well known, thanks to the epigraphic documentation found there. See in particular Allen 1983, 159–174.

[144] Coloru 2009, 265–269.

oversaw their activities.[145] We know nothing of these because the citizens of the city appear not to have been in the habit of engraving the administration's decisions in stone.[146]

Ai Khanoum is a special case in Central Asia. A city of prime importance and the only one known for the Greek period, it is often cited as an example on account of the dynamism of the Greek traditions manifested there. But it alone does not provide evidence as to the forms taken by the Greek presence in the region. It was primarily a royal city, founded by the Seleucid kings as their seat of power in eastern Bactria. It later became one of the principal residences of the Graeco-Bactrian kings, who designed it based on the model of the great capitals of the Hellenistic world. Its history was thus often determined by the dynasties that controlled it, and the city experienced the same fate as these dynasties, their periods of glory as well as their setbacks, the latter exemplified by the events that impacted it around 145 BC and led to its ruin. The city was under attack at about the time when Eucratides was assassinated by one of his sons (Justin 41.6.5). It was assaulted by nomadic groups and probably also by Bactrian populations opposed to the emblems of Graeco-Bactrian power, particularly the palace, which was devastated,[147] and the large statue of the temple with indented recesses, so antithetical to the aniconic practices of Iranian peoples.[148] These events led to the flight of the Graeco-Bactrian administration, along with all the inhabitants associated with royal power and more generally the various elites, leaving the city occupied by the local component of the population, which had no interest in Hellenism and its manifestations.[149] Shortly afterwards, Graeco-Bactrian power abandoned eastern Bactria, and then the whole region. There is no better example to show that the city's destiny was bound up with that of its kings.

BIBLIOGRAPHY

Allen, E.R. (1983), *The Attalid Kingdom: A Constitutionnal History*, Oxford.

Aperghis, G.G. (2004), *The Seleukid Royal Economy*, Cambridge.

Atakhodjaev, A. (2013), Données numismatiques pour l'histoire politique de la Sogdiane (IVe–IIe siècles avant notre ère), *Revue de Numismatique*: 213–246.

Ball, W. (1982) avec la collaboration de J.-C. Gardin, *Catalogue des sites archéologiques d'Afghanistan*, Paris.

---

[145] For the links between Ai Khanoum and the various kings who held it, see Martinez-Sève 2012b.

[146] We must also take into account the fact that the city was subject to very considerable damage at the end of its existence and its stone resources and metal objects were systematically looted. Some steles could also have been destroyed at this time.

[147] It was severely damaged by a huge fire started in several places at once (Bernard *et al.* 1973, 2–3), and its buildings were then systematically demolished.

[148] Martinez-Sève 2010, 204–205.

[149] Martinez-Sève 2013a, 218–220. The many dead, whose remains were exhumed in the orchestra of the theatre, appear to have been killed in this attack (Grenet, in Francfort *et al.* 2014, 66).

Bergamini, G. (2011), Babylon in the Achaemenid and Hellenistic Period: The Changing Landscape of a Myth, *Mesopotamia* 46: 23–34.

Bernard, P. (1968), Chapiteaux corinthiens hellénistiques d'Asie centrale découverts à Aï Khanoum, *Syria* 45: 111–151.

Bernard, P. (1970), Quatrième campagne de fouille à Aï Khanoum (Bactriane), *CRAI*: 313–355.

Bernard, P. (1971), La campagne de fouille de 1970 à Aï Khanoum, *CRAI*: 385–452.

Bernard, P. (1976a), Les traditions orientales dans l'architecture gréco-bactrienne, *Journal Asiatique* 264: 245–275.

Bernard, P. (1976b), Campagne de fouilles 1975 à Aï Khanoum (Afghanistan), *CRAI*: 287–322.

Bernard, P. (1978a), Les mines de lapis lazuli du Badakhshan, in: P. Bernard, H.-P. Francfort (eds.), *Études de géographie historique sur la plaine d'Aï Khanoum (Afghanistan)*, Paris: 49–51.

Bernard, P. (1978b), Le nom de la ville grecque du Tepe Aï Khanoum, in: P. Bernard, H.-P. Francfort (eds.), *Études de géographie historique sur la plaine d'Aï Khanoum (Afghanistan)*, Paris: 3–16.

Bernard, P. (1978c), Campagne de fouilles 1976–1977 à Aï Khanoum (Afghanistan), *CRAI:* 421–463.

Bernard, P. (1982), Alexandre et Aï Khanoum, *Journal des Savants*: 125–138.

Bernard, P. (1985), *Fouilles d'Aï Khanoum*, IV : *Les monnaies hors trésor. Questions d'histoire gréco-bactrienne*, Paris.

Bernard, P. *et al.* (1973), *Fouilles d'Aï Khanoum*, I, *(Campagnes 1965, 1966, 1967, 1968)*, Paris.

Bernard, P. *et al.* (1980), Campagne de fouille 1978 à Aï Khanoum (Afghanistan), *Bulletin de l'École Française d'Extrême-Orient* 68: 1–103.

Bernard, P., Pinault, G.-J., Rougemont, G. (2004), Deux nouvelles inscriptions grecques de l'Asie Centrale, *Journal des Savants*: 227–356.

Besenval, R., Marquis P. (2008), Les travaux de la Délégation Archéologique Française en Afghanistan (DAFA) : résultats des campagnes de l'automne 2007–printemps 2008 en Bactriane et à Kaboul, *CRAI*: 973–995.

Besenval, R., Engel, N., Marquis, P. (2011), Les travaux de la Délégation Archéologique Française en Afghanistan, *Bulletin de la SFAC*, *Revue Archéologique*, fasc. 1: 172–188.

Bopearachchi, O. (1999), Les monnaies Séleucides de l'Asie Centrale et l'atelier de Bactres, in: M. Amandry, S. Hurter (eds.), *Travaux de numismatique grecque offerts à Georges Le Rider*, Paris: 77–93.

Bopearachchi, O. (2004), La politique monétaire de la Bactriane sous les Séleucides, in: V. Chankowski, F. Duyrat (eds.), *Le roi et l'économie*, *Topoi*, Suppl. 6: 349–369.

Bopearachchi, O. (2006), Sophytes, the Enigmatic Ruler of Central Asia, Νομισματικά χρονικά 15: 15–32.

Bordeaux, O. (forthcoming), *Le monnayage de Diodote I et II, nouvelles données et étude des coins*.

Bosworth, A.B. (1993), *Conquest and Empire*, Cambridge.

Briant, P. (2002), *Alexandre le Grand*, Paris.

Capdetrey, L. (2007), *Le pouvoir séleucide. Territoire, administration, finances d'un royaume hellénistique*, Rennes.

Capdetrey, L. (2012), Fondations, diasporas et territoires dans l'Asie hellénistique au IIIe siècle, in: L. Martinez-Sève, *Les diasporas grecques du VIIIe à la fin du IIIe siècle av. J.-C.*, *Pallas* 89: 319–344.

Chrubasik, B. (2013), The Attalids and the Seleukid Kings, 281–175 BC, in: P. Thonemann (ed.), *Attalid Asia Minor. Money, International Relations, and the State*, Oxford: 83–119.

Cohen, G.M. (2013): *The Hellenistic Settlements in the East from Armenia and Mesopotamia to Bactria and India*, Berkeley–Los Angeles.

Coloru, O. (2009), *Da Alessandro a Menandre. Il regno greco di Battriana*, Pisa–Roma.

Falk, B., Bennett, Ch. (2009), Macedonian Intercalary Months and the Era of Azes, *Acta Orientalia* 70: 197–216.

Francfort, H.-P. (1984), *Fouilles d'Aï Khanoum*, III : *Le sanctuaire du temple à niches indentées, 2 : Les trouvailles*, Paris.

Francfort, H.-P. (1989), avec des contributions de Ch. Boisset, L. Buchet, J. Desse, J.-C. Echallier, A. Kermorvant, G. Willcox, *Fouilles de Shortugaï. Recherches sur l'Asie Centrale Protohistorique*, Paris.

Francfort, H.-P. (2005), Asie Centrale, in: P. Briant, R. Boucharlat (eds.), *L'archéologie de l'empire achéménide : nouvelles recherches*, Paris : 313–352.

Francfort, H.-P. (2013a), *L'art oublié des lapidaires de la Bactriane aux époques achéménide et hellénistique*, Persika 17, Paris.

Francfort, H.-P. (2013b), Habitat rural achéménide, hellénistique et kouchan dans la plaine d'Aï Khanoum-Shortugaï, in: G. Lecuyot, *Fouilles d'Aï Khanoum*, IX : *L'habitat*, Paris: 157–178.

Francfort, H.-P., Grenet, F., Lecuyot, G., Lyonnet, B., Martinez-Sève, L., Rapin, Cl. (2014), *Il y a 50 ans... la découverte d'Aï Khanoum*, Paris.

Fraser, P.M. (1996), *Cities of Alexander the Great*, Oxford.

Fröhlich, P. (2013), Funérailles publiques et tombeaux monumentaux *intra-muros* dans les cités grecques à l'époque hellénistique, in: M.-C. Ferriès, M.P. Castiglioni, F. Létoublon (eds.), *Forgerons, élites et voyageurs d'Homère à nos jours*, Grenoble: 227–309.

Gardin, J.-C. (1998), *Prospections archéologiques en Bactriane orientale (1974–1978)*, vol. 3 : *Description des sites et notes de synthèse*, Paris.

Gardin, J.-C., Gentelle, P. (1976), III. Irrigation et peuplement dans la plaine d'Aï Khanoum, de l'époque achéménide à l'époque musulmane, *Bulletin de l'École Française d'Extrême-Orient* 63: 59–110.

Gardin, J.-C., Lyonnet, B. (1976), La céramique, in: P. Bernard *et al.*, Fouilles d'Aï Khanoum. Campagne de 1974, *Bulletin de l'École Française d'Extrême-Orient* 63: 45–51.

Gentelle, P. (1978), Étude géographique de la plaine d'Aï Khanoum et de son irrigation depuis les temps antiques, Paris.

Gentelle, P. (1989), *Prospections archéologiques en Bactriane orientale (1974–1978)*, vol. 1 : *Données paléographiques et fondements de l'irrigation*, Paris.

Grenet, F. (2005), An archaeologist's approach to Avestan geography, in: V.S. Curtis, S. Stewart (eds.), *Birth of the Persian empire*, London: 29–51.

Grenet, F., Rapin, Cl. (2001), Alexander, Aï Khanum, Termez: Remarks on the Spring Campaign of 328, in: O. Bopearachchi, C.A. Bromberg, F. Grenet (eds.), *Alexander's Legacy in the East, Studies in Honor of P. Bernard, Bulletin of the Asia Institute* 12 [1998]: 79–89.

Guillaume, O. (1983), *Fouilles d'Aï Khanoum*, II : *Les propylées de la rue principale*, Paris.

Holt, F.L. (1989), *Alexander the Great and Bactria*, 2nd ed., Leiden.

Holt, F.L. (1999), *Thundering Zeus. The Making of Hellenistic Bactria*, Berkeley–Los Angeles–London.

Houghton, A., Lorber, C. (2002), *Seleucid Coins: A Comprehensive Catalogue*, Part I: *Seleucus I through Antiochos III*, NewYork–Lancaster–London.

Houghton, A., Lorber, C., Hoover, O. (2008), *Seleucid Coins: A Comprehensive Catalogue*, Part II: *Seleucus IV through Antiochus XIII*, New York–Lancaster–London.

Huys, M. (1996), P. Oxy. 61.4099: A Combination of Mythographic Lists with Sentences of the Seven Wise Men, *Zeitschrift für Papyrologie und Epigraphik* 113: 205–212.

Invernizzi, A. (2007), The Culture of Parthian Nisa between Steppe and Empire, in: J. Cribb, G. Herrmann (eds.), *After Alexander. Central Asia before Islam*, Oxford: 163–177.

Invernizzi, A. (2009), *Nisa Partica. Le sculture ellenistiche*, Firenze.

Invernizzi, A. (2010), *Nisa Partica. I rhyta ellenistici*, Firenze.

Jakobsson, J. (2010), Antiochus Nicator, the Third King Of Bactria?, *Numismatic Chronicle*: 17–33.

Košelenko, G.A. (1985), Srednjaja Azija v antičnuju epoxu, in: G.A. Košelenko (ed.), *Drevnejše gosudarstva Kavkaza i Sredniej Azii*, Moskva: 204–350.

Košelenko, G.A. (2006), Stanovlenie denežnogo obraščenija na ellinističeskom vostoke, *Rossijskaja Arxeologija* 3: 95–105.

Kovalenko, S. (1995/1996), The Coinage of Diodotus I and Diodotus II, Greek Kings of Bactria, *Silk Road Art and Archaeology* 4: 17–74.

Kritt, B. (1996), *Seleucid Coins of Bactria*, Lancaster.

Kritt, B. (1997), *The Early Seleucid Mint of Susa*, Lancaster.

Kritt, B. (2001), *Dynastic Transitions in the Coinage of Bactria*, Lancaster.

Lecuyot, G. (2013) avec des contributions de P. Bernard, H.-P. Francfort, B. Lyonnet et L. Martinez-Sève, *Fouilles d'Aï Khanoum*, IX : *L'habitat*, Paris.

Leriche, P. (1986), *Fouilles d'Aï Khanoum*, V : *Les remparts et les monuments associés*, Paris.

Leriche, P. (2007), Bactria. Land of Thousand Cities, in: J. Cribb, G. Herrmann (eds.), *After Alexander. Central Asia before Islam*, Oxford: 121–153.

Leriche, P., Thoraval, J. (1979), La fontaine du rempart de l'Oxus à Aï Khanoum, *Syria* 56: 171–205.

Lerner, J.D. (2003/2004), Correcting the Early History of Āy Kānoum, *Archäologische Mitteilungen aus Iran und Turan* 35–36: 373–410.

Lerner, J.D. (2005), Greek Ceramic Period IV of Aï Khanoum, in: E.A. Antonova, T.K. Mkrtychev (eds.), *Central'naja Azija: istočniki, istorija, kul'tura*, Moscow: 464–476.

Lerner, J.D. (2010), Revising the Chronologies of the Hellenistic Colonies of Samarkand-Marakanda (Afrasiab II–III) and Aï Khanoum (Northeastern Afghanistan), *Anabasis* 1: 58–79.

Lyonnet, B. (1997), *Prospections archéologiques en Bactriane orientale (1974–1978)*, vol. 2 : *Céramique et peuplement du Chalcolithique à la conquête arabe*, Paris.

Lyonnet, B. (2001), Les Grecs, les Nomades et l'indépendance de la Sogdiane, d'après l'occupation comparée d'Aï Khanoum et de Marakanda au cours des derniers siècles avant notre ère, in: O. Bopearachchi, C.A. Bromberg, F. Grenet (eds.), *Alexander's Legacy in the East. Studies in Honor of P. Bernard, Bulletin of the Asia Institute* 12 [1998]: 141–159.

Lyonnet, B. (2012), Questions on the Date of the Hellenistic Pottery from Central Asia (Ai Khanoum, Marakanda and Koktepe), *Ancient Civilizations from Scythia to Siberia* 18: 143–173.

Lyonnet, B. (2013a), La céramique hellénistique en Asie centrale, in: N. Fenn, C. Römer-Strehl (eds.), *Networks in the Hellenistic World according to the pottery in the Eastern Mediterranean and beyond*, Oxford: 351–368.

Lyonnet, B. (2013b), La céramique de la maison du quartier sud-ouest d'Aï Khanoum, in: G. Lecuyot, *Fouilles d'Aï Khanoum*, IX : *L'habitat*, Paris: 179–191.

Mairs, R. (2014), The Founder's Shrine and the Foundation of Ai Khanoum, in: N. Mac Sweeney (ed.), *Foundation Myths in Ancient Societies. Dialogue and Discourses*, Philadelphia, Pennsylvania: 103–128.

Martinez-Sève, L. (2002), La ville de Suse à l'époque hellénistique, *Revue Archéologique*: 31–54.

Martinez-Sève, L. (2003), Quoi de neuf sur le royaume séleucide ?, in: F. Prost (ed.), *L'Orient méditerranéen de la mort d'Alexandre aux campagnes de Pompée. Cités et royaumes à l'époque hellénistique*, Rennes: 221–242.

Martinez-Sève, L. (2004), Peuple d'Antioche et dynastie séleucide, in: B. Cabouret, P.-L. Gatier, C. Saliou (eds.), *Antioche de Syrie. Histoire, images et traces de la ville antique*, *Topoi*, Suppl. 5: 21–41.

Martinez-Sève, L. (2010), À propos du temple aux niches indentées d'Aï Khanoum : quelques observations, in: P. Carlier, Ch. Lerouge (eds.), *Paysage et religion en Grèce antique. Mélanges en l'honneur de Madeleine Jost*, Paris: 195–207.

Martinez-Sève, L. (2011), Suse et les Séleucides au IIIᵉ siècle avant J.-C., in: E. Dąbrowa (ed.), *New Studies on the Seleucids*, *Electrum* 18: 41–66.

Martinez-Sève, L. (2012a), Les Grecs d'extrême Orient : communautés grecques d'Asie Centrale et d'Iran, in: L. Martinez-Sève, *Les diasporas grecques du VIIIᵉ à la fin du IIIᵉ siècle av. J.-C.*, *Pallas* 89: 367–391.

Martinez-Sève, L. (2012b), Roi et cités en Asie Centrale : un roi indispensable ?, in: C. Feyel *et al.* (eds.), *Communautés locales et pouvoir central dans l'Orient hellénistique*, Nancy: 211–233.

Martinez-Sève, L. (2013a), Données historiques, in: G. Lecuyot, *Fouilles d'Aï Khanoum*, IX : *L'habitat*, Paris: 213–220.

Martinez-Sève, L. (2013b), Le quartier du temple principal, in: G. Lecuyot, *Fouilles d'Aï Khanoum*, IX : *L'habitat*, Paris: 137–143.

Martinez-Sève, L. (2014), The Spatial Organization of Ai Khanoum, a Greek City in Afghanistan, *American Journal of Archaeology* 118: 267–283.

Messina, V. (2010), *Seleucia al Tigri. Il monumento di Tell 'Umar. Lo scavo e le fasi architettoniche*, Firenze.

Mohammed Ali, S.M. (1979), The Greek Theatre, *Sumer* 35: 94–111.

Naveh, J., Shaked, S. (2012), *Aramaic Documents from Ancient Bactria from the Khalili Collections*, London.

Newell, E.T. (1978), *The Coinage of the Eastern Seleucid Mints from Seleucus I to Antiochus III*, 2nd ed., New York.

Oikonomides, Al.N. (1987), Records of "The Commandements of the Seven Wise Men" in the 3rd c. B.C. The Revered "Greek Reading-book" of the Hellenistic World, *Classical Bulletin* 63: 67–76.

Olbrycht, M.J. (2013), Iranians in the Diadochi Period, in: V.A. Troncoso, E.M. Anson (eds.), *After Alexander, the Time of the Diadochi (323–281 BC)*, Oxford: 159–182.

Rapin, Cl. (1987), Les textes littéraires grecs de la trésorerie d'Aï Khanoum, *BCH* 111: 225–266.

Rapin, Cl. (1992), *Fouilles d'Aï Khanoum, VIII : La trésorerie du palais hellénistique d'Aï Khanoum*, Paris.

Rapin, Cl. (2001), L'incompréhensible Asie centrale de la carte de Ptolémée. Proposition pour un décodage, in: O. Bopearachchi, C.A. Bromberg, F. Grenet (eds.), *Alexander's Legacy in the East. Studies in Honor of P. Bernard, Bulletin of the Asia Institute* 12 [1998]: 201–225.

Rapin, Cl. (2005), L'Afghanistan et l'Asie centrale dans la géographie mythique des historiens d'Alexandre et dans la toponymie des géographes gréco-romains. Notes sur la route d'Hérat à Bégram, in: O. Bopearachchi, M.-F. Boussac (eds.), *Afghanistan. Ancien carrefour entre l'est et l'ouest*, Turnhout: 143–172.

Rapin, Cl. (2007), Nomads and the Shaping of Central Asia: From the Early Iron Age to the Kushan Period, in: J. Cribb, G. Herrmann (eds.), *After Alexander. Central Asia before Islam*, Oxford: 29–72.

Rapin, Cl. (2010), L'ère Yavana d'après les parchemins gréco-bactriens d'Asangorna et d'Amphipolis, in: K. Abdullaev (ed.), *Tradicii vostoka i zapada v antičnoj kul'ture srednej Azii*, Tashkent: 234–252.

Rapin, Cl. (2013), On the way to Roxane. The route of Alexander the Great in Bactria and Sogdiana (328–327 BC), in: G. Lindström *et al.* (eds.), *Zwischen Ost und West. Neue Forschungen zum antiken Zentralasien*, Darmstadt: 43–82.

Rapin *et al.* (2005), Recherches sur la région des Portes de Fer de Sogdiane : bref état des questions, *Istorija Material'noj Kul'tury Uzbekistana* 35: 102–112.

Robert, L. (1968), De Delphes à l'Oxus, inscriptions grecques nouvelles de la Bactriane, *CRAI*: 416–457.

Rotroff, S. (1982), *Hellenistic Pottery. Athenian and imported Moldmade Bowls* (The Athenian Agora, vol. 29.1), Princeton, New Jersey.

Rotroff, S. (1997), *Hellenistic Pottery. Athenian and imported Wheelmade Table Ware and Related Material* (The Athenian Agora, vol. 29.2), Princeton, New Jersey.

Rotroff, S. (2006), The Introduction of the Moldmade Bowl Revisited: Tracking a Hellenistic Innovation, *Hesperia* 75: 357–378.

Rougemont, G. (2012), *Inscriptions grecques d'Iran et d'Asie Centrale* (Corpus Inscriptionum Iranicarum), London.

Sverchkov, L.M. (2008), The Kurganzol Fortress (on the History of Central Asia in the Hellenistic Era), *Ancient Civilizations from Scythia to Siberia* 14: 123–191.

Tarn, W.W. (1985), *The Greeks in Bactria and India*, 3rd ed., Chicago, Illinois (1st ed. 1938).

Veuve, S. (1987), *Fouilles d'Aï Khanoum, VI : Le gymnase*, Paris.

Wetzel, F., Schmidt, E., Mallwitz, A. (1957), *Das Babylon der Spätzeit*, Berlin.

Widemann, F. (2009), *Les successeurs d'Alexandre en Asie Centrale et leur héritage culturel*, Paris.

Will, E. (1979), *Histoire politique du monde hellénistique (323–30 av. J.-C.)*, Nancy.

Wilson, L.M. (2003), King Demetrios of India and Eukratides of Bactria, *Journal of the Oriental Numismatic Society* 174: 17–23.

Wilson, L.M., Assar, G.R.F. (2007), Re-dating Eukratides I relative to Mithradates I, *Journal of the Oriental Numismatic Society* 191: 24–25.

Zavyalov, A.V. (2007), The Fortifications of the City of Gyaur Kala, Merv, in: J. Cribb, G. Herrmann (eds.), *After Alexander. Central Asia before Islam*, Oxford: 313–327.

Zeng, C.D. (2013), Some Notable Die-links among Bactrian Gold Staters, *Numismatic Chronicle*: 73–78.

ELECTRUM * Vol. 22 (2015): 47–85
doi: 10.4467/20800909EL.15.003.3941
www.ejournals.eu/electrum

LA DÉCOUVERTE DE L'ANCIENNE TERMEZ, MÉTROPOLE DE LA BACTRIANE DU NORD*

Pierre Leriche

CNRS, Paris

Abstract: The main aim of the paper is a presentation of results of the Franco-Uzbek Archaeological Expedition in Northern Bactria in ancient Termez and its region. Archeological excavations that have been conducted from 1993 up to the present day shed new light on the past both of the city and the area of the Northern Bactria. Chronologically, discoveries cover periods from Hellenistic to Islamic.

Key words: ancient Termez, Northern Bactria, Franco-Uzbek Archaeological Expedition of Northern Bactria.

Introduction

La Bactriane, aux confins orientaux du monde antique, est longtemps restée un sujet d'interrogations historico-littéraires. C'est en Bactriane, après avoir franchi l'Hindou Kouch, qu'Alexandre aurait mis fin à la dynastie des Achéménides. C'est là qu'il a éprouvé ses plus graves revers, mais aussi rencontré Roxane qu'il a épousée à Bactres. C'est là qu'est né un puissant royaume gréco-macédonien, conquérant de l'Inde et c'est là, enfin, que, deux siècles plus tard, s'est formé le Tokharestan, cœur du mystérieux empire kouchan, entre la Chine, l'empire parthe et Rome.

Il n'a jamais fait de doute que, sur le plan géographique, le nom de « Bactriane » désigne la grande plaine qui s'étend entre Amou Daria et Hindou Kouch et où s'étendent les ruines impressionnantes de Balkh, Surkh Kotal et Aï Khanoum. En revanche, de nombreux débats s'étaient développés concernant la frontière entre Bactriane et Sogdiane que d'aucuns plaçaient sur le cours de l'Amou Darya.[1] Mais ces dernières années,

---

* Je tiens à remercier ici le Dr Ségolène de Pontbriand pour son aide dans l'élaboration et la formalisation de cet article.

[1] Comme le Rhin entre la France et l'Allemagne, selon le principe des frontières naturelles, une théorie qui date de Ph. Labbe (+1667). D'aucuns considèrent ce concept comme naturel, ignorant que, dans

s'est imposée l'évidence que la Bactriane historique s'étendait également aux vallées des affluents de rive droite du fleuve (Fig. 1).[2] En fait, ce serait la chaîne du Hissar et ses ramifications occidentales (Bayssoun Tau et Kugitang Tau) qui aurait été la véritable frontière septentrionale de la Bactriane (Fig. 2).

Cette vision nouvelle repose essentiellement sur les résultats des recherches archéologiques actives de plusieurs missions soviétiques puis ouzbèques, tadjiques et étrangères. Parmi celles-ci, la Mission Archéologique Franco-Ouzbèque de Bactriane Septentrionale (MAFOuzB) a joué un certain rôle dans la province ouzbèque du Surkhan Daria, en particulier à l'Ancienne Termez[3], grande et opulente cité médiévale qui a disparu quand sa population a été intégralement mise à mort en 1220 par Gengis Khan.

Depuis cette tragédie, l'Ancienne Termez n'a, en effet, jamais été réoccupée et ses ruines demeurent techniquement accessibles à l'exploration archéologique.[4] Après d'autres missions archéologiques soviétiques et ouzbèques, la MAFOuzB a contribué à y mettre en évidence les vestiges antiques d'une ville puissamment fortifiée qui était, sans doute, la capitale de la Bactriane du Nord. C'est cette Ancienne Termez dont je voudrais présenter ici les traits principaux en rappelant rapidement ceux qui ont déjà fait l'objet de publications pour présenter plutôt les *nouveaux développements* et quelques conclusions qu'on peut en tirer.

1. La Bactriane du Nord, une découverte progressive

La Bactriane du Nord s'étend dans les anciennes Républiques soviétiques d'Asie Centrale et c'est dans ce cadre que s'est déroulée sa découverte progressive. A la fin de 1866, la prise d'Oura-Tiube et de Djizzak (au Nord du Zeravchan) par l'armée du Tsar conduit à l'annexion de Samarcande et à l'établissement du protectorat de Boukhara puis de Khiva. L'émir de Boukhara Mozaffar concède alors aux Russes le droit d'établir des postes le long de l'Amou-Daria et de naviguer sur ce fleuve qui traverse ses états.[5] Dix ans plus tard, en 1897, l'édification de la forteresse russe de Termez à Pata Khissar, à l'embouchure du Surkhan Daria, consacre la présence des armées du Tsar dans la région et l'intégration de la rive droite de l'Amou Daria à l'Empire russe.[6]

---

l'antiquité et au Moyen-Age, les vallées sont traditionnellement des foyers de vie et de circulation et rarement des frontières.

[2] Kyzyl Su, Vakhch, Kafirnigan, Surkhan Daria et Cherabad Darya, ce qui correspond aux provinces (*oblast*) du Surkhan Daria, en Ouzbékistan, et du Khatlon au Tadjikistan.

[3] Je ne reviens pas ici sur les assauts d'érudition et les discours plus polyglottes que scientifiques auxquels a donné lieu le nom de Termez. Un débat aujourd'hui obsolète. Voir, sur ces généralités : Leriche / Pidaev 2007 : 181.

[4] A l'époque timouride, Termez a, en effet, été reconstruite plus à l'Est puis s'est éteinte au XVIIe s. L'actuelle Tarmiz, capitale de l'*oblast* du Surkhan Daria, a été fondée en 1897 à une dizaine de kilomètres plus au Sud que l'Ancienne Termez, près de l'embouchure du Surkhan Daria.

[5] C'est ainsi que le 5 décembre 1886, sont mis à l'eau deux vapeurs russes « Piotr » et « Alexandre » destinés au service du chemin de fer transcaspien qui devait relier Krasnovodsk à Tachkent et le 10 septembre 1887, est lancé le premier vapeur militaire, le « Tsar » en présence du *beck* de Tchardjoui.

[6] Avec, en particulier, le développement de la culture du coton pour vêtir l'armée russe.

Au lendemain de la première Guerre Mondiale, la victoire de Frunze et Kuibychev sur les troupes des émirs de Khiva et de Boukhara provoque, en septembre 1920, l'émigration en Afghanistan de Saïd Alim Khan, dernier émir de Boukhara, et la proclamation de la république soviétique populaire du Boukhara. Les terres des riches sont confisquées et distribuées aux paysans pauvres, eux-mêmes invités à se regrouper en communes agraires. C'est alors que se pose la question du sort des ruines de l'Ancienne Termez.

A. L'archéologie en Bactriane au lendemain de la première Guerre Mondiale

Les premières fouilles archéologiques en Asie Centrale débutent dans les années 1880, à Anau et à Samarcande, mais ce n'est qu'après la fin de la première Guerre Mondiale que la Bactriane accueille ses premiers archéologues, à Bactres, puis à l'Ancienne Termez.

Située à quelques kilomètres au Nord de l'entrée de la ville moderne de Tarmiz (capitale de la province ouzbèque du Surkhan Daria), l'Ancienne Termez s'étend sur cinq cents hectares dans une courbe de la rive droite de l'Amou Daria. Ses ruines, comme celles de Bactres, sont parfaitement identifiées,[7] mais sont nettement moins spectaculaires, avec quelques pans de fortifications qui émergent de la végétation ou des cultures et une citadelle confinée au bord de l'Amou Daria dans la zone frontière interdite (Fig. 3).

Au milieu de ces ruines se dresse, au sein d'un parc fleuri, le mausolée médiéval du savant érudit Abou Abdallah Mohamad bin Ali, dit « Hakim al-Termezi ».[8] Autour de ce mausolée, on reconnaît les trois éléments traditionnels des cités médiévales d'Asie Centrale :

- au Sud, la **citadelle** puissamment fortifiée (*kokendoz*) longe l'Amou Daria sur 600 m de long. Son sommet domine le fleuve d'une vingtaine de mètres de hauteur et forme une plateforme large de 300 m. Visible de loin, cette citadelle manifeste la grandeur passée de la ville ;
- à l'Est, l'enceinte basse de la **ville** (*chahristan*) forme approximativement un rectangle allongé Nord-Sud de 900 m sur 450 m qui communique au Sud directement avec le fleuve à l'Est de la citadelle ;
- au Nord et à l'Est et de la ville, court la muraille basse en grande partie noyée dans les vignes et les champs de coton d'un double **faubourg** (*rabad*) dans lequel s'élèvent les ruines d'un château médiéval appelé « kourgane ».

Une deuxième zone d'environ un kilomètre de côté, en grande partie occupée par des installations contemporaines, s'étend à l'Ouest de ce premier ensemble, jusqu'à la rive du fleuve qui marque ici la frontière naturelle militarisée du pays. Cette zone est limitée au Nord par une longue et étroite dépression est-ouest qui correspond au tracé d'un ancien canal. Aux approches du fleuve, on voit se développer, au Nord de cette dépression,

---

[7] Voir, par exemple, G. Bonvalot (1889 : 237–238 avec gravure), qui conduit des fouilles sur la citadelle du 9 au 19 novembre.

[8] Le Hakim al-Termezi (820–930) est connu pour être l'auteur de plusieurs hadiths (commentaires sur la traduction du Coran) : Gobillot 2006. Son mausolée, d'époque timouride, est depuis quelques années l'objet d'un pèlerinage hebdomadaire actif. Il a été récemment fortement restauré et un musée et des installations diverses liées à l'afflux des pèlerins ont été construits autour.

une ample colline appelée Tchingiz Tepe, longtemps pratiquement inexplorée, qui se prolonge au Sud par un petit plateau rectangulaire nommé Tchingiz 2. Ces deux Tchingiz Tepe portent d'importants vestiges archéologiques antiques qui ont été l'objet d'une attention soutenue de la part de la MAFOuzB.

Enfin, à une certaine distance hors des remparts de l'Ancienne Termez se trouvent trois sites importants de monastères bouddhiques. Au Sud-Est, vestige impressionnant d'un monastère aujourd'hui disparu, un stoupa en forme de tour cylindrique haut de douze mètres appelé Zourmala émerge des champs de coton. Au Nord du site, d'importants vestiges de deux grands monastères bouddhiques, Kara Tepe et Fayaz Tepe, ont été dégagés.[9]

Tous ces vestiges anciens ont rapidement attiré l'attention des nouvelles autorités soviétiques et, en 1925, le premier inventaire des vestiges de l'Ancienne Termez est réalisé. Peu après, une mission d'histoire de l'art dirigée par le P_2 B.P. Denike, procède, en 1926 et 1928[10] à l'étude des principaux vestiges architecturaux alors conservés : le mausolée de Hakim al-Termezi, le vaste palais des Termez Chahs[11] (Fig. 5) et, nettement plus à l'Est, le château de Qyrq Qyz (« Les quarante jeunes femmes »).

C'est alors que sont découverts les premiers monuments bouddhiques de l'Asie Centrale soviétique. A. Strelkov reconnaît dans la « Tour de Zourmala » un stoupa bouddhique, trouve à l'Ancienne Termez les fragments d'une sculpture bouddhique en pierre et reconnaît à Kara-tepe les vestiges de grottes cultuelles qu'il rapproche de celles trouvées en Inde, en Afghanistan et au Sin Kiang (Xin-Qiang). C'est alors aussi que l'archéologue G. Parfenov fonde le Musée d'Étude de la Région de Termez, pour recevoir le matériel archéologique provenant de l'Ancienne Termez et des autres sites de la région. L'Ancienne Termez devient alors célèbre jusqu'à l'étranger : ainsi, en 1929, P. Pelliot publie un article sur Termez dans les « Comptes rendus de l'Académie des sciences de l'URSS ».[12]

En 1934, une drague remonte du fond de l'Amou Daria, en amont de Tarmiz, de grands fragments d'une frise de calcaire en haut relief représentant des musiciens entre des feuilles d'acanthes provenant sans doute d'un monastère bouddhique. La présentation de cette « frise d'Ayrtam » au IIIe Congrès International d'Iranologie à l'Ermitage impose l'idée que des recherches archéologiques doivent être entreprises à grande échelle dans l'ancienne Bactriane-Tokharestan, en particulier à l'Ancienne Termez.

C'est pourquoi, M.E. Masson de l'Université de Taškent crée en 1936, la TAKE[13] qui reprend les travaux à l'Ancienne Termez et l'étude des monuments d'époque médiévale

---

[9]   Huit kilomètres séparent Fayaz Tepe de la Tour de Zourmala et cinq kilomètres et demi la muraille orientale des faubourgs (*rabad*) de la rive du fleuve.

[10]   L'inventaire a été réalisé par le Comité centre-asiatique pour la Conservation des Monuments antiques, des Œuvres d'Art et de la Nature de l'URSS. L'expédition archéologique était lancée par le Musée des Cultures d'Orient de Moscou.

[11]   Ce palais était en cours d'embellissement à l'arrivée de Gengis Khan. De la salle de réception, l'expédition rapporte un choix de panneaux de stuc incisé de motifs décoratifs géométriques ou de type coufique, d'autres ornés de médaillons de verre sculpté de motifs animaliers, dont l'un comporte une inscription arabe en l'honneur du Sultan Bahramshah.

[12]   Pelliot 1929. Article complété par Y. Rerik en 1963 et 1964.

[13]   Termezskaja Arkheologičeskaja Kompleksnaja Ekspeditsija [Mission Archéologique Pluridisciplinaire de Termez], créée par le Comité Scientifique de la République d'Ouzbékistan, devenu plus tard filiale de l'Académie des Sciences de l'URSS, puis de l'Académie des Sciences de l'Ouzbékistan.

alors encore debout : un quartier d'artisans, la mosquée de Tchor Soutoun, le palais des Termez Chahs et, en partie, le château appelé « kourgane ». Un plan schématique mais exact de la partie médiévale du site est alors dressé.

Parallèlement, des vestiges antiques, accompagnés de monnaies d'Euthydème et d'Hélioclès ont été explorés sur la citadelle et sur le Tchingiz Tepe, cependant que des grottes bouddhiques étaient fouillées à Kara-tepe.[14] Ainsi pouvait-on déjà en conclure que, sous la citadelle et la ville médiévale, se trouvaient les vestiges d'une ville remontant à l'époque hellénistique.

B. Après la deuxième Guerre Mondiale

La multiplication des fouilles soviétiques (Fig. 6)

Après la deuxième Guerre Mondiale, l'importance de la province du Surkhan Daria, avec ses deux vallées, le Surkhan Daria et le Cherabad Daria, apparaît de plus en plus clairement pour l'histoire de l'Asie Centrale antique, à l'égal du Khorezm et de la Turkménie méridionale.[15] Le Musée Historique de Tachkent crée alors une Mission dirigée par L. Al'baum qui, à partir de 1948, lance un grand programme de recherches archéologiques dans la vallée méridionale du Cherabad Daria (région d'Angor, au Nord-Ouest de l'Ancienne Termez). L. Al'baum ouvre plusieurs chantiers d'époque hellénistique et/ou kouchane : Zang Tepe dès 1950 puis deux sites kouchans de la même région ; Zar Tepe et Khayrabad Tepe, puis un site kouchano-sassanide et ephtalite : Balalyk Tepe, jusqu'en 1960. Dans la même région, A. Askarov explore à partir de 1973 plusieurs sites de l'Âge du Bronze : Sapalli Tepe, Mollali Tepe et, surtout, le site monumental de Djarkutan.

Dix ans plus tard, G. Pugatchenkova qui dirige l'Institut des Beaux-Arts Hamza à Tachkent crée l'UzIskE[16] qui, à partir de 1959, fouille de nombreux sites de la vallée du Surkhan Daria et multiplie les découvertes. Elle met au jour le palais prékouchan de Khaltchayan avec ses étonnantes frises de combats en haut relief d'argile stuquée et peinte (1959–1963), la ville fortifiée gréco-kouchane de Dal'verzine Tepe (1960–1963, reprise en 1967), les deux villes fortifiées d'époque achéménide de Kyzyl Tepe et Bandykhan (1970–1986) et plusieurs sites antiques, dont Khaytabad qui s'avère également d'origine achéménide.

Non loin du cours du Surkhan Daria, en 1974, une fouille préventive sur l'emplacement de l'aéroport de Tarmiz, à Mirzakul Tepe, provoque la découverte d'une petite agglomération d'époque kouchane avec des bases de colonnes du type de celles d'Aï Khanoum et une céramique typiquement d'époque kouchane.[17] Sur la rive de l'Amou

---

[14] Ces travaux ont été conduits par E.G. Ptchelina avec V.D. Joukov sur la citadelle et le Tchingiz Tepe et, avec G. Parfenov et A. Strelkov (de l'Ermitage) sur les grottes de Kara-tepe dont les relevés ont été exécutés par G.A. Pugatchenkova.

[15] Le Khorezm activement exploré par Tolstov et la Turkménie méridionale avec la première fouille d'Asie Centrale à Anau et la grande cité de Merv, capitale de la Margiane, vers laquelle s'est tourné M.E. Masson et son équipe dès 1946.

[16] Expédition Archéologique permanente pour l'Histoire de l'Art en Ouzbékistan.

[17] Pidaev 1976.

Daria, outre le monastère d'Ayrtam, à nouveau exploré (1964–66 et 1979), un chantier régulier est ouvert à partir de 1983 sur le site de la ville hellénistique et kouchane de Kampyr Tepe, en aval de Termez.

En 1973, E.V. Rtveladze et Z.A. Khakimov publient un impressionnant inventaire de plus de cinquante sites pour la vallée du Surkhan Daria puis une liste complémentaire d'une vingtaine de sites pour la région d'Angor, sur le delta intérieur du Cherabad Daria. Quelques années plus tard, en 1981, l'inventaire des sites présentant un niveau médiéval, mais qui sont pour la plupart nettement plus anciens, atteint deux cent vingt ![18] Enfin, une première synthèse est publiée en 1990, désignant la région du Surkhan Daria sous le nom de « Bactriane – Tokharestan ».[19]

L'Ancienne Termez

Dans la périphérie de l'Ancienne Termez, deux opérations importantes sont lancées. De 1964 à 1994, B.Ja. Staviskij, à la tête d'une expédition conjointe des Musées et des Académies de Moscou et de Léningrad met au jour, avec l'aide de T. Zejmal, plusieurs monastères rupestres à Kara Tepe. De son côté, Al'baum découvre et fouille, de 1968 à 1978, un troisième grand monastère bouddhique, celui de Fayaz Tepe, au Nord de Kara Tepe.[20]

A l'Ancienne Termez même, Al'baum dégage le « kourgane » et un vaste édifice interprété comme une église arménienne (?) du XIe s. Il complète alors le plan de l'Ancienne Termez publié par la TAKE. Enfin, le long de l'Amou Daria, il fouille une nécropole kouchane tardive sur le Tchingiz 1 et, sur le Tchingiz 2, il dégage partielle ment un édifice qu'il interprète comme un fortin douanier d'époque hellénistique.

D'autre part, en 1980, est créée une Mission Archéologique de Termez chargée d'établir la topographie historique et l'histoire de l'Ancienne Termez sous la direction de Ch.R. Pidaev. Ce dernier cherche à atteindre les niveaux les plus anciens puisqu'il n'existait ni source écrite, ni matériel archéologique concernant les origines et la date de fondation de la ville. Sur la citadelle, des fouilles facilitées par l'emploi de la pelle mécanique sont ouvertes sur trois secteurs proches du fleuve (Fig. 4). Au point culminant de la citadelle, une tranchée perpendiculaire à la face interne de la puissante fortification méridionale, révèle, à 14 m de profondeur, la présence de céramique gréco-bactrienne sur le sol vierge. Le décapage de la paroi orientale d'une large dépression (*maydan*) qui conduit au fleuve, non loin de l'angle sud-Est de la citadelle, confirme la présence de puissantes fortifications kouchanes.

D'autres opérations de même type font également apparaître quelques constructions d'époque kouchane, au centre et aux angles sud-Ouest et nord-Ouest de la citadelle, mais aussi sous le rempart de la ville islamique, au Nord de la citadelle. Pour la plupart les résultats de ces opérations sont restés inédits. Par la suite, les recherches sur la Termez

---

[18]   Rtveladze / Khakimov 1973 ; Rtveladze 1974.

[19]   Pugačenkova / Rtveladze 1990. Cet ouvrage avait été précédé d'un recueil sur les recherches de l'Institut Hamza en Ouzbékistan méridional : Pugačenkova 1989.

[20]   Rappelons pour mémoire, en 1965, l'étude de la « Tour de Zourmala » par G. Pugačenkova et Z. Khakimov.

islamique se sont poursuivies: deux petites mosquées des XI–XIVᵉ s., un quartier de potiers et une importante nécropole médiévale ont alors été fouillés.

Développement et internationalisation de l'archéologie ouzbèque

Une troisième étape est franchie lorsqu'est créé l'Institut d'Archéologie d'Ouzbékistan
dirigé par le Pr A. Askarov, non pas à Tachkent, mais à Samarcande. La recherche archéologique en Bactriane ouzbèque connaît alors une impulsion nouvelle. Puis, à partir
de 1989, l'Institut d'Archéologie s'ouvre à des collaborations étrangères, précédant de
peu l'indépendance du pays.

Dans la province du Surkhan Daria, cette évolution se manifeste d'abord par la création, en 1992, de la MAFOuzB qui, sous la direction de T. Annaev et P. Leriche,[21] explore la vallée du Surkhan Daria et l'Ancienne Termez. Au sein de l'Institut Hamza, la
Mission de Dal'verzine Tepe, dirigée depuis 1989 par B. Turgunov devient une mission
ouzbéko-japonaise avec K. Kato comme co-directeur. Par la suite, la fouille de Kara
Tepe est relancée en 1999 par Ch. Pidaev associé à K. Kato qui, lui-même, est remplacé
à Dal'verzine Tepe par K. Tanabe.

Quelques années plus tard, dans l'oasis d'Angor, c'est une mission ouzbéko-ger-
manique qui en 2001 reprend la fouille de DjarKutan (Sh.B. Shaydullaev – D. Huff),
puis, en 2003, une mission tchéco-ouzbèque poursuit l'exploration de Djandavlat Tepe
(L. Stanco / K. Abdullaev).

En 2002–2006 un programme d'étude, de restauration et de conservation du monastère bouddhique de Fayaz Tepe est lancé par l'UNESCO, sous la direction de Ch. Pidaev
puis de T. Annaev auquel s'associe l'équipe du P_2 G. Fussman du Collège de France.[22]

Plus récemment, une équipe du fond Humboldt dirigée par N. Borofka fouille plusieurs petits sites du Surkhan Daria et découvre dans les monts du Hissar un fort du début
de l'époque hellénistique à Kurganzol. Le long de l'Amou Daria, un groupe moscovite
dirigé par N. Dvurechenskaja s'associe en 2007 à la mission d'E.D. Rtveladze dans
l'exploration du site de Kampyr Tepe puis, à partir de 2010, il reprend les recherches de
Rtveladze sur la forteresse d'Uzun Dara dans le Bayssoun Tau.

Toutes ces recherches débouchent sur une masse de données nouvelles qui s'ajoutent
à celles obtenues par de très nombreuses autres missions archéologiques ouzbèques. Le
tableau de la civilisation de la Bactriane septentrionale s'en trouve profondément enrichi
et modifié, à l'image des résultats obtenus par la MAFOuzB. Désormais, cette partie de
la Bactriane antique et médiévale est devenue l'une des régions historiques d'Asie Centrale les mieux connues par l'archéologie.

---

[21] MAFOuzB est un fruit de la convention entre la France et l'Ouzbékistan (Académie des Sciences et
Institut d'Archéologie dirigé par R. Kh. Souleïmanov) sous la direction de T. Annaev et P. Leriche. En 1997,
Ch.R. Pidaev remplace T. Annaev qui, lui-même remplace en 2009 Ch.R. Pidaev.

[22] Pidaev / Annaev / Fussman 2011.

C. Les recherches de la MAFOuzB à l'Ancienne Termez

De 1993 à 2003, les travaux de la MAFOuzB ont plus particulièrement concerné trois sites répartis sur l'ensemble de la province du Surkhan Daria : deux sites fortifiés de petites dimensions (Khaytabad et Payon Kourgane) et l'Ancienne Termez, afin de mieux saisir les caractères propres de cette partie de la Bactriane antique.[23] Mais, à partir de 2003, l'ampleur des découvertes a conduit la MAFOuzB à faire de l'Ancienne Termez son objectif unique, facilité par l'établissement d'une carte topographique détaillée de l'ensemble du site sur plus de cinq cents hectares, une carte qui sert désormais de référence à toutes les données topographiques sur le site de l'Ancienne Termez.

Les efforts de la MAFOuzB se sont d'abord concentrés sur l'étude des premières étapes de l'existence de l'Ancienne Termez, c'est-à-dire sur la citadelle à laquelle elle avait accès grâce à l'appui particulier de l'Académie des Sciences de l'Ouzbékistan. Puis, à partir de 1997, l'enquête s'est élargie à l'ensemble de la ville, en particulier à la zone des deux Tchingiz Tepe et à la ville islamique.[24]

2. Géographie historique de l'Ancienne Termez

A. La citadelle

Premier lieu à porter une installation humaine, dernière partie du site à avoir été occupée, la citadelle de l'Ancienne Termez porte les traces de toutes les périodes de l'existence de la ville. Trois chantiers ouverts par la MAFOuzB ont clairement montré que c'est sur la citadelle qu'a été fondée une forteresse gréco-bactrienne (*phrourion*) sur une butte naturelle, à une douzaine de mètres au-dessus de l'eau. Cette implantation militaire qui ne couvrait qu'environ la moitié de la surface de la citadelle actuelle était destinée à contrôler le passage du fleuve facilité par la présence de l'île d'Aral Pay Gambar.

Après l'effondrement de la Bactriane macédonienne, à l'époque Yue Tche (vers 140 av. n. è.–1ʳᵉ moitié du Iᵉʳ s. de n. è.), cette modeste implantation a été agrandie. Mais c'est sous les premiers Kouchans (début de notre ère) qu'a été fixé, dans sa configuration définitive, le tracé de ses puissantes fortifications, contre lesquelles s'adossait, au point le plus élevé de la rive sud, un édifice important, palais ou temple, orné de colonnes à bases attiques monumentales.

---

[23] On a ainsi pu établir que la petite ville fortifiée de Khaytabad, dans la basse vallée du Surkhan Daria, avait été dévastée à la fin de l'époque achéménide puis réoccupée et refortifiée à l'époque hellénistique tardive. D'un autre côté, dans les montagnes du Hissar (Bayssoun), Payon Kourgane se révèle être un fortin de frontière hellénistique qui a donné naissance à une petite cité kouchane prospère et (?) non fortifiée.

[24] Précisons que la ligne de barbelés qui délimite la zone frontière de l'Ouzbékistan avec l'Afghanistan interdit aujourd'hui l'accès, au fleuve, mais aussi à la partie méridionale de la citadelle. En outre, le secteur du Tchingiz Tepe et de Kara Tepe sont englobés dans l'emprise d'une caserne de gardes-frontière. Le site est donc protégé de toute tentative de pillage, mais le travail des archéologues y est soumis à l'autorisation particulière du commandement de la frontière. Celle-ci est généralement accordée pour les Tchingiz Tepe et pour Kara Tepe (sauf en cas d'exercice militaire), mais a été supprimée pour la citadelle.

Lors de la crise du VI–VIIᵉ siècle qui voit les villes décliner et les châteaux se multi-plier, la citadelle semble avoir été abandonnée. Mais avec la conquête arabe (667), elle retrouve sa fonction militaire. Les Ghaznévides (XIᵉ s.) en font une véritable place forte, ce que confirme la découverte d'une longue muraille en briques cuites pourvue de petites tours rectangulaires massives bordant le fleuve et protégeant la citadelle, le port et la ville basse. Au début du XIIIᵉ siècle, les Khorezmchahs renforcent encore les défenses de la citadelle et édifient de puissants bastions à l'angle sud-est de celle-ci. C'est à l'abri de ces puissantes fortifications que, en 1220, Termez a imprudemment cru pouvoir résister à Gengis Khan, ce qui lui a valu l'épitaphe, glorieuse mais vaine, de « Madinat al Rej-jal » (« La Ville des Vrais Hommes »).

Après 1220, seule la citadelle retrouve une fonction défensive au XVIIᵉ siècle, lorsque les Chaybanides, édifient à son point culminant un fort carré pourvu de tours circulaires aux angles. Ce fort est abandonné au bout d'un siècle, jusqu'à l'époque soviétique où des défenses enterrées sont établies sur le pourtour de la citadelle.

Malheureusement, depuis peu, on l'a vu, les impératifs de la sécurité des frontières du pays nous ont interdit l'accès à la zone de la citadelle proche du fleuve (Fig. 3). Nos travaux ont donc été arrêtés avant qu'aient pu être mis au jour les vestiges de la mu-raille hellénistique originelle. Et l'on doit se résoudre à ce que cette première enceinte, masquée par une puissante maçonnerie kouchane, ne nous soit connue que par sa seule céramique typiquement hellénistique.

B. La zone de Tchingiz Tepe 1

La colline de Tchingiz Tepe 1 est plus haute que la citadelle, à huit cents mètres au Nord-Ouest de laquelle elle se trouve. Son sommet a la forme d'une longue crête gréseuse perpendiculaire à la rive abrupte de l'Amou Daria. Sur cette colline, à peine explorée par les premières missions, la présence d'indices archéologiques antiques a conduit la MAFOuzB à ouvrir plusieurs chantiers. Par la suite, l'exploration s'est étendue au ravin qui sépare au Sud cette colline du petit plateau du Tchingiz Tepe 2 (Fig. 7).

Le ravin

La fouille de la longue dépression qui limite au Sud la colline de Tchingiz Tepe a révélé que celle-ci est le fruit d'importants travaux d'aménagement datant de la période immé-diatement postérieure au départ de Grecs (vers 140 av. n. è.). Cette dépression, en effet, correspond à un canal de 12 m de large alimenté par les eaux du Surkhan Daria. Ce canal irriguait cette zone sableuse, permettait à la population de la ville de vivre et servait *in fine* d'exutoire majeur aux eaux usées. Il a donc véritablement permis le développement très rapide de la ville aux époques kouchane et islamique. Bien entendu, le système défensif de la ville nouvelle du Tchingiz Tepe 1 avait intégré ce canal, puisque le grand fossé qui borde la fortification orientale de la colline débouchait sur ce dernier.

La colline du Tchingiz Tepe 1

Les fortifications du Tchingiz Tepe 1

A partir de 1997, sur la colline du Tchingiz 1, la présence d'une épaisse fortification de briques crues de direction Nord-Sud, descendant jusqu'au ravin, a été mise en évidence (Fig. 7). Accolées à cet ouvrage rectiligne long de 300 m, neuf tours sont conservées. Dans son dernier état, la fortification était précédée par un avant-mur et par un impressionnant fossé large de 12 m et profond de 4 m. Au Nord, couronnant la crête sinueuse est-ouest de la colline, subsistent les vestiges très dégradés de cette fortification avec cinq tours sur une longueur de plus de 350 m.[25]

L'ouvrage possédait deux niveaux de tir, avec un corridor intérieur percé d'archères nombreuses. Sa façade était ornée d'un décor d'archères sagittales et de *garudas* stylisés de type kouchan.

Edifiée au début de l'époque kouchane (Ier s. de n. è.), cette muraille est le résultat d'une grande phase de reconstruction qui suit un abandon prolongé. Un grand fossé a été creusé à l'avant de la muraille orientale, puis le système de fortification tout entier a été abandonné. De l'habitat, puis des tombes constituent le dernier état d'occupation des tours et des courtines.

A l'Est, à l'arrière de cette puissante ligne fortifiée, une rue et quelques maisons, d'époque kouchano-sassanide ou plus récente, ont été fouillées sans livrer de matériel autre que céramique.

La plateforme du sommet du Tchingiz Tepe 1

Au sommet de la colline qui est le point culminant du site, un bâtiment carré de 15 m de côté avait été construit au début du Ier siècle de n. è. Temple bouddhique ou dynastique dont la façade à décor mouluré était peinte en rouge, il abritait au moins une statue de culte de taille humaine, modelée et stuquée, dont quelques fragments du visage doré à la feuille ont été retrouvés en fouille. Ce petit temple qui s'élevait dans un espace (sacré ?) limité par un mur de péribole à 90 m au Sud du sommet de la colline, a été volontairement détruit et nivelé lors de la construction de la fortification de la colline qui enjambe le péribole.

Lorsqu'après plusieurs siècles la fortification est abandonnée et s'écroule en partie, ses briques servent à la reconstruction d'une plateforme bouddhique portant un stoupa et un décor sculpté en pierre de type gréco-indien. Au VIe s. au plus tard, cette nouvelle plateforme cultuelle est abandonnée.

Le temple central

Au centre même de la colline, un deuxième édifice cultuel a été identifié et partiellement fouillé. Il s'agit d'un grand sanctuaire de plus de 80 m de côté, qui comporte des corridors périphériques, dont certains ornés de peintures murales présentant des traces de

---

[25] A l'Ouest et au Sud, cette fortification a totalement disparu, sans doute victime du recul de la rive du fleuve et de l'érosion pluviale.

feuilles d'or, entourant des cours. Au centre un édifice probablement cultuel à deux *cellae* adossées, possédant, l'une une entrée vers le Nord, l'autre une entrée vers le Sud. La fonction de cet édifice n'a pas encore été déterminée. D'après les rares objets recueillis, on sait que le culte bouddhique était pratiqué dans ce bâtiment incontestablement religieux, mais il n'est pas exclu qu'un autre culte (*synnaos*) y ait également eu sa place.

Conclusion

Ces vestiges monumentaux en partie explorés sur la colline de Tchingiz Tepe 1 sont incontestablement ceux d'une ville volontanement établie dans une aire dépourvue de toute installation antérieure. Ils révèlent la volonté d'un dynaste de créer ici une ville nouvelle symbole extérieur bien visible de son pouvoir, peut-être la première capitale de l'époque Yue-Tche (fin IIe–Ier s. av. n. è.). Entretenue à l'époque kouchane, l'enceinte est entièrement restaurée et notablement renforcée à l'époque kouchano-sassanide. Enfin, à la fin du IVe–milieu du Ve s., la fonction militaire de la colline est abandonnée. Les monuments sont investis par des occupants tardifs, apparemment bouddhistes, puis la muraille nord est transformée en nécropole-ossuaire collectif.

C. Le plateau du Tchingiz Tepe 2

Sur le petit plateau qui s'étend sur une centaine de mètres au Sud du ravin, deux importants bâtiments, ont été découverts : à l'Est, l'édifice A, partiellement fouillé par L. Albaum, et, au Nord, l'édifice B, allongé d'Est en Ouest et dont seule la partie orientale nous était accessible, le reste du bâtiment s'étendant largement vers l'Ouest, probablement jusqu'à la rive du fleuve, très au-delà de la ligne de barbelés (Fig. 13). Ces deux bâtiments ont été en grande partie détruits (Fig. 8), mais ce qui en reste nous apporte une lumière nouvelle sur l'histoire de l'Ancienne Termez, en particulier dans des périodes mal connues.

Le bâtiment B

Sur la bordure nord du plateau, le bâtiment (B), dont la fouille est maintenant achevée, avait servi de carrière à briques et ne subsiste plus que sous la forme de la base de ses murs (Fig. 9). Nous avons tout de même pu déterminer que, dans sa partie orientale, la seule qui nous était accessible, ce bâtiment a connu trois états de construction depuis l'époque hellénistique avant d'être abandonné et pillé, sans doute après la conquête sassanide.

Le premier état de ce bâtiment (au moins 23 m est-ouest x 14 m nord-sud) a été édifié en grandes briques de 46 cm de côté marquées d'un *phi*, typiques de l'époque hellénistique (deux monnaies d'Euthydème et d'Hélioclès y ont d'ailleurs été trouvées).

Dans un deuxième état, l'édifice a été élargi vers le Nord, grâce à la construction d'un grand *analemma* fondé sur la rive sud du canal et soutenant une terrasse.

Dans le troisième et dernier état, moins large que les deux précédents, plusieurs fragments de frise bouddhique ont été trouvés, ce qui nous incite à y voir un temple bouddhiste.

A travers ce dernier état, un canal voûté d'évacuation d'eau a été installé. Ce canal est orienté vers le Nord jusqu'à l'arrière de l'*analemma* où, visiblement il déversait son eau. On ignore encore le sens de ce dispositif. Enfin, précisons que, dans les parois de ce canal, cinq tambours de colonnes en calcaire, de plus d'un mètre de long chacun, ont été remployés. Ceci indique sans doute qu'à proximité de l'édifice B ou en façade de celui-ci, à une période que l'on ignore, devait s'élever un portique.

Le bâtiment A

Ce grand bâtiment allongé du Nord au Sud a également subi de nombreuses destructions, mais cette fois sur sa périphérie et surtout à une époque récente. Il ne mesure plus que près de 80 m de long et une trentaine de mètres de large (Fig. 7 et 12). Ses façades ont presque totalement disparu (Fig. 13), mais sa partie centrale a été heureusement préservée.

L'action des engins mécaniques a créée une coupe sur la partie méridionale de l'édifice (Fig. 11a et 11b). On y constate que ce bâtiment a été construit à l'époque kouchane et qu'il a été agrandi peu de temps après. Ce deuxième état a ensuite été abandonné, s'est dégradé et a été recouvert d'une forte accumulation de sable éolien. Plus tard, sur le monticule ainsi formé une puissante plateforme de terre battue (*pahsa*) a été construite pour constituer une vaste plateforme sur laquelle un troisième bâtiment a été édifié. Au centre de l'édifice, cette plateforme n'existe pas et c'est l'état antérieur qui continue à fonctionner dans le troisième état architectural du bâtiment A.

L'entrée officielle du bâtiment A comportait un hall large de près de 4 m, dans lequel un four à céramique du haut Moyen-Age a été installé, détruisant en grande partie les parois de l'entrée (Fig. 14). A l'arrière de ce hall, un couloir long de près de 14 m traverse tout le bâtiment d'Est en Ouest, conduisant, à l'Est, à une grande salle à banquettes qui a toutes les apparences d'une Salle de Conseil. Sous les décombres d'écroulement recouvrant le sol de l'état dernier de ce corridor, se trouvaient plusieurs fragments de sculptures de type bouddhique : bas-relief cultuel, chapiteau de *harmika* (porte-parasol sur un *stoupa*), bases de colonnes moulurées, etc., ce qui indique qu'à la fin de son dernier état, le bâtiment avait une fonction religieuse bouddhique. Ce sol bien régulier de terre battue masquait des dalles très usées d'un état antérieur. Une fouille de la moitié occidentale de ce sol, a révélé que ce tout dernier état du sol était fait d'une succession de quatre sols superposés, soigneusement disposés qui masquaient le véritable sol du troisième état du bâtiment.

L'étude attentive de ce corridor au début de son dernier état a révélé que, du portail occidental à la « salle du conseil » il fallait franchir pas moins de cinq portails – dont quatre sur une longueur de 8 m. Ces portails étaient pourvus de seuils monumentaux de bois ou de pierre qui ont disparu, comme leurs montants verticaux. Mais les traces de ces montants demeurent sous la forme de trous verticaux juxtaposés, de part et d'autre des seuils et le long des murs du grand hall d'entrée ouest du bâtiment (Fig. 15).

Ces trous cylindriques du diamètre d'une poutre apparaissent dans l'épaisseur d'une sorte de banquette formée de couches superposées d'enduits muraux très fins blancs qui couvrent la base des murs. A certains endroits, l'épaisseur de ces couches d'enduits accumulées atteint plus d'un demi-mètre, ce qui implique une durée très longue de fonctionnement du corridor.

Le sol correspondant à cet état était un pavement de pierres calcaires disposées sur toute la largeur du corridor entre les quatre premiers seuils et le portail donnant accès à la « salle du conseil » (Fig. 16). Nombre de ces blocs étaient ornés de motifs dérivés de l'architecture grecque (bases attiques de pilastres ou de colonnes, linteaux finement moulurés, montants de pilastres, etc.) ou bouddhique (frises, motifs de barrières à claire-voie, bouddhas sous arcature, etc.). L'état d'usure de la surface supérieure des pierres dont certaines ont perdu jusqu'à 8 cm d'épaisseur, montre qu'on a circulé sur ces pierres durant une longue période.

Dans cet ensemble dont le nombre dépasse largement la centaine, se trouvaient deux blocs sculptés d'un très grand intérêt (Fig. 17). Le premier provient d'une frise en haut-relief et représente un couple vêtu à l'indienne, très finement sculpté et conservant des restes de dorure à la feuille d'or. Le second faisait visiblement partie d'un bas-relief plus fruste représentant un personnage debout, de face, en costume kouchan,[26] à côté d'un pilastre à dépression à lunule. De toute évidence, le haut relief provient de la démolition d'un temple bouddhique orné d'une ou plusieurs frises sculptées à décor figuré caractéristique, alors que le bas-relief pourrait être un fragment de relief votif ou avoir orné une partie du palais lui-même. De toute évidence, cet ensemble de pierres sculptées peuvent être datées de la haute époque kouchane.

Ce dallage, qui comportait parfois deux épaisseurs de blocs, a été soigneusement retiré pour l'étude et la préservation des blocs. Sous la couche de blocs de pierre, est apparu un sol bien régulier de briques correspondant visiblement au deuxième état du corridor du palais. Sur cette surface régulière les pierres avaient clairement été disposées sans grand soin apparent, avec parfois de grands espaces entre elles. Du sable pur, volontairement versé entre elles, contenait quelques monnaies kouchanes et d'autres plus tardives qui pourraient être kouchano-sassanides ou plus tardives, ce qui indique que cette sort de dallage est largement postérieur à la conquête sassanide.

En ce qui concerne l'entrée ouest du palais et l'accès à ce corridor, la couche de blocs de pierre s'interrompt selon une ligne nette correspondant clairement à un seuil disparu (seuil 5). Contre la face occidentale de ce seuil, se trouvait un massif de maçonnerie, épais et large de trois rangées de briques crues, visiblement destiné à rattraper le niveau du sol tardif recouvrant les blocs (Fig. 18). Le démontage des deux assises supérieures de ce massif au cours de la campagne de 2014 a fait apparaître un seuil de belle pierre calcaire large de 40 cm et long de 2 m, constitué de deux dalles d'environ un mètre de long chacune, très bien jointoyées.[27] Il s'agit de toute évidence du seuil de la porte d'entrée du corridor, au sommet d'un escalier dont les marches inférieures n'ont pas encore été dégagées sous le reste de la maçonnerie de briques crues – à moins qu'elles n'aient été détruites en même temps que le portail 1, lors de la construction du four tardif (Fig. 19).

---

[26] Dont on ne voit qu'une jambe du pantalon et le bas de la tunique.

[27] A chaque extrémité de cette marche, se trouve un agencement complexe de pierre maçonné au mortier qui comporte des saignées en angle droit et un trou vertical circulaire visiblement destinés à recevoir un placage et l'axe de rotation de la porte du corridor. La longueur totale de ce dispositif est d'environ 3,5 m, avec une largeur du passage de 2 m.

On pénétrait donc dans le palais par l'Ouest, dans un hall s'ouvrant dans la façade et au fond duquel un portail (1) donnait accès à un escalier monumental de trois marches probablement en pierre. Au sommet de cet escalier s'ouvrait un deuxième portail (5), puis il fallait franchir deux autres portails (4 et 3), en passant entre une salle de garde et une salle d'attente à foyer central, pour atteindre enfin le dernier portail (2) qui permettait d'entrer dans la grande Salle du Conseil à banquettes.

Malheureusement on ignore si, comme on peut le supposer, un trône ou un lit d'apparat (selon Song Yun) se trouvait dans cette salle de prestige. Le fond de cette grande salle a, en effet, disparu, peut-être à la suite d'un séisme, et, dans la phase bouddhique du bâtiment, un nouveau mur de façade orientale du palais a été construit plus à l'Ouest, rétrécissant cette salle. On peut également noter que, dans ce dernier état, la banquette méridionale de la salle du conseil a été recouverte d'un massif de maçonnerie au sommet duquel on distingue encore l'encastrement d'un socle carré sur lequel s'élevait sans doute une statue de Bouddha.

Le reste du palais, reconstruit sur la plateforme de *pahsa* qui recouvre le deuxième état de l'édifice, est aujourd'hui très fortement détruit. Au Sud, on y trouve une série de pièces allongées dans le sens nord-sud, avec, à l'Ouest, une grande salle à pilastres dont ne subsiste pratiquement plus que le mur oriental (Fig. 12). Certaines pièces ont été recoupées et la fonction de nombreux locaux n'a pas encore pu être précisée. Au Nord, sur la plateforme de *pahsa*, apparaissent plusieurs maçonneries aujourd'hui pratiquement arasées.

Il est clair que ce bâtiment était un lieu de prestige, un palais qui a connu trois grands états architecturaux en conservant curieusement le même plan. A chaque fois, ce plan a été agrandi au Sud comme au Nord. Le troisième grand état, consécutif à une longue phase d'abandon, a fonctionné longtemps comme l'indiquent clairement l'usure du seuil et du dallage de blocs de pierre, ainsi que l'impressionnante épaisseur des enduits du corridor. Puis, le pouvoir lié à cet état disparaît et le palais subit quelques destructions. Il est ensuite transformé en lieu de culte bouddhique, dernier avatar avant son abandon définitif qui le livre au pillage, aux injures du temps et aux impératifs du fonctionnement de la frontière actuelle.

Synthèse historique du Tchingiz Tepe 2

L'histoire de cette partie du site peut donc se résumer ainsi :

1. Les premières constructions, dont le premier état du temple (bâtiment B), paraissent remonter à l'époque hellénistique.

2. A l'époque kouchane, construction du deuxième état du temple et du premier état du palais (bâtiment A) à l'Est du temple.

3. Dernière reconstruction du temple (état 3) et deuxième grand état du palais. En façade de l'un ou l'autre de ces bâtiments de prestige, ou dans l'aire ouverte qui s'étendait entre eux, on pourrait peut-être restituer une colonnade dont les tambours (les seuls découverts à ce jour au Nord de l'Amou Daria) ont ensuite été remployés dans la canalisation du temple.

4. Abandon du temple et du palais. Ce dernier s'écroule en partie et disparaît sous une épaisse couche de sable éolien.

5. Puis, à une époque ultérieure (tardo kouchano-sassanide ou ephtalite), construction du troisième grand état du palais en pillant l'ornementation de pierre du temple et de l'état antérieur du palais pour la remployer dans le dallage du corridor du palais. Longue durée de cette phase.

Peut-être est-ce de cette période que date la canalisation creusée dans le temple en y intégrant des tambours de colonnes.

6. Disparition du pouvoir en question et transformation du palais en édifice de culte bouddhique.

7. Abandon du palais en façade duquel s'installe un atelier de potier dont le four est construit dans la dépression que forme la grande entrée. Plus tard, quelques maisons de l'époque islamique s'installent dans ce secteur.

D. Le secteur de la ville islamique et de ses environs

La partie du site à l'Est du mausolée du Hakim al Termezi se trouve hors de la zone militaire, dans le domaine accessible à tous. Nous sommes ici dans le secteur de la ville prémongole et de sa périphérie, où des prospections et sondages ponctuels ont révélé la présence de maisons, de plusieurs forges métallurgiques et de nombreux ateliers et fours de potiers.

Trois chantiers proches les uns des autres y ont été ouverts. Le premier à l'intérieur des murailles de la ville, un deuxième sur l'enceinte urbaine elle-même et un troisième dit « du bâtiment kouchan » entre cette muraille et le mur du parc aménagé autour du mausolée du Hakim al Termezi (Fig. 3).[28]

Le chantier de la ville islamique

En 2000, un chantier a été ouvert dans la ville islamique sur une légère éminence à environ une cinquantaine de mètres de la muraille occidentale de cette ville. Ce secteur, d'une surface de 50 m de côté, a pris l'aspect d'une fouille urbaine médiévale avec des séries de murs de briques crues ou cuites, superposés ou se chevauchant et datant du Xe au XIIe s. Malheureusement, ces murs et les sols associés ont été fortement dégradés par des inhumations tardives et offrent un tableau relativement confus. Du verre, de la céramique glaçurée ou incisée et un grand nombre de « grenades » ou « poires à mercure » (*simop kuzachas*), de céramique grise fortement grésée typiques des XI–XIIIe s. y ont été récoltés.

Cet état médiéval repose sur une couche d'abandon bien nette scellant des niveaux antiques. Bien qu'eux aussi très perturbés par de multiples *badrabs* (fosses d'aisance) et creusements divers, ces derniers datent des IIIe–Ve s. et témoignent, de l'importance de la pratique du culte bouddhique. On y a, en effet, mis au jour une base de stoupa do-

---

[28] Citons pour mémoire la fouille sans surprise d'une petite nécropole islamique sur la butte de Dunya Tepe, au Sud du troisième chantier.

mestique (?) d'environ un mètres de côté, associée à deux cellules souterraines d'ermites bouddhistes (telles qu'on en a découvert une vingtaine autour du Mausolée). C'est dans ce secteur qu'a été trouvé un beau chapiteau en calcaire de type gréco-bouddhique orné sur chaque face d'un buste du Bouddha.

Dans ce secteur, la fouille a donc permis de mettre en évidence deux grandes phases d'occupation. La plus ancienne, d'époque kouchane, correspond à un édifice religieux à colonnade et chapiteaux à buste. Suit une période d'abandon datant du VIIe s. au Xe s. Puis, jusqu'à l'irruption de Gengis Khan (1220), se développe un habitat urbain associé à des installations artisanales qui confirme la prospérité économique de Termez prémongole vantée par les sources arabes. Malheureusement, les constructions de cette période ont été très endommagées par de très nombreuses fosses et tombes plus récentes, ce qui limite l'intérêt de leur étude.

Le chantier de la fortification islamique

L'enceinte de la ville islamique est encore bien visible sur le terrain. Elle se compose de deux murailles basses parallèles renforcées à intervalles réguliers de tours pleines semi circulaires. Il s'agit plus d'une clôture contre le brigandage que d'un dispositif militaire. Une fouille a été lancée sur cette muraille, non loin du chantier de la ville, à l' endroit où une brèche ancienne avait été ouverte dans la courtine pour faire passer une route de terre. Cette route est aujourd'hui abandonnée et, dans les années quatre-vingts et une petite tranchée perpendiculaire à la ligne de la muraille avait été creusée à l'aide d'une pelle mécanique.

La MAFOuzB a procédé au nettoyage des deux faces de la muraille, de part et d'autre de la brèche, incluant une tour de chaque côté et a allongé et approfondi la tranchée jusqu'au sol vierge (Fig. 20). Il ressort de ces travaux que l'enceinte a été édifiée en *pahsa* avec des courtines d'une épaisseur de 3 m portée à 5 m par un doublage ultérieur. Sa hauteur n'excédait pas 6 m au chemin de ronde et des locaux (casernements ?) étaient accolés à sa face interne. La muraille a été pourvue de tours pleines semi-circulaires d'un diamètre de 5 m ensuite épaissies par un placage extérieur qui porte leur diamètre à 8 m (Fig. 21). La distance entre ces tours est irrégulière.

En outre, on a eu la surprise de découvrir que cette partie du rempart médiéval repose sur les vestiges très arasés d'une muraille antérieure de direction légèrement divergente. Le matériel associé est entièrement d'époque kouchane et kouchano-sassanide. A cette muraille, édifiée, elle aussi en *pahsa*, est accolé sur sa face orientale un départ de tour quadrangulaire en brique crue (Fig. 22). Nous avons donc probablement ici la muraille qui protégeait à l'Ouest la ville kouchane et kouchano-sassanide. Au-delà, vers l'Est se développaient déjà des faubourgs, puisque dans toute la zone des faubourgs d'époque islamique, on trouve en abondance de la céramique kouchane et kouchano-sassanide.

Le chantier du « Bâtiment kouchan »

Ce chantier a été ouvert en 2010 à la suite de la découverte d'un médaillon de plâtre en tous points comparable aux médaillons de Begram au sein d'une architecture de brique crue mise en évidence lors de travaux d'aménagement de la zone du mausolée. A la fin de la campagne de 2014, le chantier mesurait 25 mètres dans le sens Nord-Sud comme dans le sens Est-Ouest (Fig. 23).

Les maçonneries en brique crue, dont certaines atteignent deux mètres d'épaisseur, sont celles d'un bâtiment qui avait incontestablement un caractère de prestige. Malheureusement de nombreuses fosses à argile ont été creusées à cet endroit, probablement lors de l'édification du rempart de la ville islamique situé à faible distance, rendant l'établissement du plan de l'édifice très problématique. Au Nord, et au Sud, les limites réelles du bâtiment semblent avoir été atteintes. Mais à l'Ouest, une série de maçonneries s'enfoncent sous la route moderne et, à l'Est, certains locaux se développent vers le rempart de la ville kouchane. Enfin, dans la paroi de l'angle sud-est du chantier, s'amorce un couloir d'accès à une nouvelle grotte bouddhique.

Dans la partie méridionale du chantier, à l'extérieur d'un mur de 1,2 m d'épaisseur qui semble bien être le vestige de la façade sud du bâtiment kouchan (Fig. 24), se trouve un four à arcades orienté Est-Ouest. On a donc ici le témoignage incontestable d'une activité artisanale de céramique et de coroplastie qui explique sans doute le grand nombre de figurines de terre cuite de style kouchan découvertes dans ce secteur.

Les murs qui occupent le centre du chantier révèlent l'existence d'au moins deux périodes de construction séparées par une couche de sable éolien d'abandon. Le bâtiment aurait donc connu deux états principaux nettement distincts séparés par une phase d'abandon et de remblaiement naturel. Parmi le matériel permettant de dater les divers états de cet ensemble de maçonneries, dont la signification et la fonction n'apparaissent pas toujours très clairement, les éléments les plus anciens sont des monnaies gréco-bactriennes dont une petite en argent et de la céramique grise, dite « Yue-Tche ».

Cet édifice aurait donc été construit dans la période qui suit immédiatement le départ des Macédoniens. Après une période d'abandon, il aurait à nouveau fonctionné jusqu'à à la fin de la période kouchane. Plus tard, en limite sud-ouest du chantier, une grotte destinée à un ermite bouddhiste a été creusée.

3. L'apport de l'archéologie à l'histoire de l'Ancienne Termez

A. Un site longtemps ignoré

Jusqu'à la publication des travaux de la TAKE en 1942 et 1945, l'histoire de la Bactriane du Nord pré arabe n'était documentée que par un texte tibétain du VIIe s. mal compris et par les légendes recueillies par les premiers historiens arabes qui faisaient de Termez une création de Dhul' Karnain (Alexandre le Bicornu). S'y sont ensuite ajoutés les résultats de l'archéologie bouddhique issus des fouilles des monastères de Kara Tepe et Fayaz Tepe. Mais on ne savait presque rien de la ville elle-même ce qui ouvrait la porte aux hypothèses les plus diverses et parfois les plus aventurées.[29]

Puis, fait majeur pour les chercheurs non russophones, en 1970 est paru le premier ouvrage en anglais consacré à l'Archéologie en Asie Centrale soviétique.[30] Toutefois,

---

[29] Leriche 2002 : 411–415.
[30] Frumkin 1970.

sur les dix pages qu'occupa la présentation des travaux dans la province du Surkhan Darya, l'auteur n'a consacré qu'un seul paragraphe à l'Ancienne Termez elle-même. N'y sont mentionnés que les vestiges d'époque islamique et le « kourgane » ainsi que le pèlerin chinois Hsuan Tsang qui (vers 630) voyait à Termez un très grand nombre de moines bouddhistes. Sont, cependant décrits en deux pages les monastères bouddhiques d'Ayrtam et de Kara Tepe.

Sept ans plus tard, B.Ja. Staviskij[31] publiait en russe un ouvrage majeur *Kušanskaja Baktrja* mis à jour en 1986 à l'occasion de la traduction en français de ce livre sous le titre *La Bactriane sous les Kushans*. On trouve dans cette édition, remise à jour par l'auteur, page 62, une excellente carte de quarante quatre sites archéologiques kouchans de la province du Surkhan Daria. L'auteur ne consacre à Termez qu'un paragraphe, mais, dans une annexe d'un peu plus d'une page, il fait la liste des travaux au « Vieux Termez », situe le centre de la ville kouchane sur la citadelle, décrit brièvement les trois monastères de Kara Tepe, Fayaz Tepe et Zourmala et cite une dizaine de notices archéologiques et de brefs articles, tous en russe.

En 1993, lorsque la MAFOuzB a été créée, on savait donc peu de choses sur l'histoire de l'Ancienne Termez. Les circonstances de sa naissance et l'origine de son nom n'avaient pas été élucidées faute de document écrit antérieur au VIIe s. de n. è. Néanmoins, certains historiens soutenaient sans preuve sérieuse que la ville avait été fondée par Alexandre et toutes sortes d'hypothèses avaient fleuri pour expliquer le nom de la ville. L'archéologie avait révélé qu'à l'époque kouchane (Ier s. av. n. è.–IIIe s. de n. è.) des monastères bouddhiques s'étaient implantés dans sa périphérie et les textes montraient qu'au Moyen-Âge, Termez jouait un rôle militaire et économique majeur en Asie centrale.

Aujourd'hui, les résultats des recherches de la MAFOuzB, conduites avec l'appui des autorités archéologiques et la confiance des autorités militaires, ont dépassé nos espérances. Et l'on peut dès lors, tenter de tracer avec une marge d'erreur acceptable les grandes lignes de l'histoire de l'Ancienne Termez.[32]

B. Contributions à l'histoire de l'Ancienne Termez

Origines de la cité

A l'époque hellénistique, l'Ancienne Termez n'était qu'un petit établissement grec composé du *phrourion* installé sur la citadelle et du sanctuaire de bord de fleuve du Tchingiz 2 qu'accompagnait probablement une agglomération qui lui était liée. Mais on ignore encore la taille et le nom de ce noyau originel de la ville.

L'époque Yue-Tche

Peu avant 130 av. n. è., les Macédoniens abandonnent la Bactriane pour s'installer en Inde. Ils sont remplacés, selon Tchang Kien, par des Yue-Tche, eux-mêmes chassés par

---

[31]   Staviskij 1986.

[32]   Pour un exposé plus détaillé des premiers résultats : Leriche / Pidaev 2008.

les Hiong Nou du Sin-kiang (Xinjiang) oriental où ils vivaient de manière sédentaire. Loin d'être un « âge obscur », comme l'ont écrit un grand nombre d'historiens, la période qui suit est apparemment une ère de prospérité.

C'est alors, en effet, qu'est creusé le grand canal qui amène l'eau du Surkhan Daria à l'Ancienne Termez, condition indispensable au développement agricole de la région et d'une ville. Du coup, la zone du Tchingiz Tepe 1 et 2 que traverse ce canal connaît un développement architectural rapide comme l'indique le matériel céramique de cette époque et surtout d'époque kouchane recueilli sur tous les chantiers de ce secteur. Au sommet de la colline de Tchingiz Tepe 1, un temple bouddhiste entouré d'un péribole est édifié.

L'époque kouchane

L'époque kouchane voit le doublement de la surface de la citadelle de l'Ancienne Termez jusqu'à ses limites actuelles et le renforcement de celle-ci. Un grand édifice, probablement palatial à colonnes monumentales à bases attiques y est construit contre le rempart sud.

Sur la colline du Tchingiz Tepe 1, une ville nouvelle est créée avec une puissante muraille doublée de tours nombreuses, ce qui entraîne la destruction du temple du sommet de la colline. Par compensation (?), au centre de l'espace circonscrit, un grand temple nouveau est créé avec une double *cella* au centre d'une série de cours, elles-mêmes entourées de longs corridors. L'ensemble couvre au total un espace de près de cent 100 m de côté.

Sur le petit plateau du Tchingiz 2, le temple est reconstruit en surplomb du canal et embelli. Un grand édifice probablement palatial, mesurant une soixantaine de mètres du Nord au Sud, est édifié à l'Est de celui-ci. Ces deux édifices connaissent ensuite une nouvelle phase de reconstruction : le temple est somptueusement orné d'une frise sculptée en haut relief et dorée.

Le palais à l'Est du temple est lui-même intégralement reconstruit plus grand mais avec un même plan. Une colonnade ornait peut-être l'espace qui se développait devant ces deux monuments de prestige.

Enfin, très largement à l'Est de la zone des deux Tchingiz, un habitat domestique et artisanal s'est développé à l'abri d'une muraille qui, partant du pied de la citadelle, se développait au Nord jusqu'au grand canal dont elle devait suivre ensuite le tracé pour rejoindre la fortification du Tchingiz Tepe 1. Au milieu des maisons, des ateliers et des résidences de cette nouvelle agglomération, des cellules souterraines bouddhiques sont creusées et des stoupas domestiques sont élevés. Puis des faubourgs se créent à l'Est de cette enceinte et, à l'apogée de l'époque kouchane, la zone habitée de l'Ancienne Termez couvrait, avec le secteur des Tchingiz Tepe 1 et 2 et la citadelle, une surface de trois cent cinquante hectares. Enfin, c'est semble-t-il à cette époque que de grands monastères bouddhistes s'implantent à la périphérie de la ville, à Kara Tepe, Fayaz Tepe et Zourmala.

L'époque kouchano-sassanide

Cette rapide et extraordinaire période de croissance de l'Ancienne Termez connaît un brusque coup d'arrêt avec la conquête sassanide qui met à bas la dynastie kouchane. Ceci est nettement visible au Tchingiz Tepe 2 où le temple et le palais sont abandonnés, tandis qu'à Kara Tepe des graffitis en *pehlevi* sont incisés sur les murs.

Suit une période suffisamment longue pour que le palais du Tchingiz 2 se ruine et soit enfoui sous le sable éolien au point de disparaître presque complètement.

La renaissance ephtalite

C'est alors qu'on assiste à un étonnant regain d'importance de l'Ancienne Termez.

Au Tchingiz Tepe 1, les fortifications sont reconstruites, nettement renforcées et protégées à l'Est par un énorme fossé.

Le palais du Tchingiz Tepe 2 est véritablement reconstruit à une échelle nettement supérieure. Débarrassé de son décor de pierre antérieur, le corridor axial du palais comporte désormais un décor armé de poutres verticales plaquées conte les murs et régulièrement enduit au lait de chaux. Ce corridor comporte cinq portails dont certains devaient être fermés par de simples tentures, et devient le lieu de cérémonies spectaculaires durant une longue période qu'on peut évaluer à près d'un siècle.

Dans le temple B à proximité du palais, un court et large canal couvert est construit avec un émissaire vers le Nord. Y sont remployées cinq fûts de colonnes, provenant sans doute d'un portique proche du temple.

Dans la ville basse, cette période est celle d'une grande activité de forge et de production céramique.

Abandon et deuxième période bouddhique

Cette période de relative grandeur de l'Ancienne Termez s'interrompt brusquement. Les fortifications du Tchingiz Tepe 1 sont totalement abandonnées et, au sommet de la colline, le temple bouddhiste est reconstruit. Le palais du Tchingiz Tepe 2 est, à nouveau, abandonné, puis, après une période de dégradation des maçonneries, la salle du Conseil est transformée en lieu de culte bouddhiste.

A cette période de rétractation qui est peut-être celle de la visite de Hsuan Tsiang, succède une phase d'abandon relativement durable qui voit, au Tchingiz Tepe 1, les couloirs des fortifications transformées en nécropoles et les tours en lieux d'habitation et, au Tchingiz Tepe 2, un potier installe son atelier et son four dans la dépression du terrain que forme l'entrée du palais.

L'époque islamique

Suit alors une longue période de marasme qui dure jusqu'au Xᵉ siècle où, d'un seul coup, l'Ancienne Termez connaît une période de renouveau, sans doute sous les Ghaznévides qui, on le sait, renforcent de manière notable les fortifications de la citadelle. Une nouvelle ville se crée, nettement plus petite, à l'Est et au Nord de la citadelle avec une enceinte au tracé grossièrement rectangulaire. L'artisanat et les échanges y semblent prospères.

Termez passe ensuite sous la domination des Khorezmshahs qui en font un point d'appui de leur puissance. Mais à l'automne 1220, Gengis Khan met tragiquement fin à l'existence de l'Ancienne Termez.

C. Bilan provisoire

Les acquis des recherches archéologiques à l'Ancienne Termez sont donc très nombreux et essentiels pour notre connaissance de l'histoire de la Bactriane du Nord.

Ils nous révèlent l'importance de la période Yue-Tche, période de développement et non un âge obscur comme semblent l'entendre ceux qui en parlent comme d'un « danger nomade ». Le matériel archéologique indique que ce sont les Yue-Tche qui seraient à l'origine du creusement du grand canal grâce auquel le pouvoir kouchan a pu entreprendre l'aménagement urbain de la colline de Tchingiz Tepe 1. Les maîtres de la Bactriane ont sans doute cherché à se doter d'une capitale, au moins régionale, en Bactriane du Nord et ont choisi pour cela à l'Ancienne Termez.[33] En creusant le canal qui sépare la colline du grand Tchingiz Tepe 1 et le plateau du Tchingiz 2, les Yue-Tche et les Kouchans ont créé les conditions de l'extraordinaire développement urbain du site. Et il n'est pas interdit de penser que des mesures énergiques ont été prises pour peupler cette ville nouvelle. C'est ce qui pourrait expliquer le brusque arrêt, à l'époque de Kanichka, de l'existence de la ville kouchane de Kampyr Tepe – proche de Termez et née elle aussi d'un *phrourion* grec – par transfert de sa population à Termez.

Cette volonté délibérée de développement de l'irrigation et de multiplication des agglomérations est également perceptible dans toute la Bactriane du Nord, mais aussi au Sud de l'Amou Daria. D'où le surnom de « Bactriane aux mille villes » que, selon Strabon, on attribuait à cette région dans l'Antiquité.

Les époques Yue-Tche et kouchane sont celles d'une incontestable prospérité pour l'Ancienne Termez, une prospérité que l'on retrouve dans toute la province du Surkhan Daria où les villes connaissent une incontestable expansion en nombre et en surface grâce au développement de l'irrigation ou grâce au commerce qui se développe entre l'Inde et Rome.

Au milieu du III\ :sup:`e` siècle, on le sait, l'Empire kouchan est brusquement abattu par la conquête sassanide et la période qui suit, celle des Kouchano-sassanides et des Ephtalites est très mal connue en Asie Centrale. A l'Ancienne Termez, en revanche, il apparaît qu'à l'époque ephtalite la ville est devenue un lieu d'affirmation rituelle du pouvoir.

On peut donc dire qu'après la fin du royaume macédonien de Bactriane, l'Ancienne Termez est devenue l'objet d'une véritable politique de développement avec ses impressionnantes fortifications de la citadelle ou celles du Tchingiz Tepe 1 précédées d'un fossé large de 12 m et profond de 4 m ou avec son architecture palatiale si particulière.

Mais l'Ancienne Termez apparaît aussi comme un lieu de civilisation à travers les vestiges architecturaux du palais, ses colonnes de pierre, son chapiteau d'inspiration achéménide tétracéphale, ses bases de colonnes ou de pilastres attiques ou un nouveau bas relief de type kouchan a été récemment découvert. De même, le médaillon de plâtre

---

[33] Et non, comme le soutenait G. Pugatchenkova, Dal'verzine Tepe dont la surface n'excédait pas 30 ha.

découvert dans le bâtiment d'artisanat kouchan atteste l'existence à l'Ancienne Termez d'au moins un atelier de toreutique de même niveau qu'à Aï Khanoum ou Begram.

Enfin, la ville était aussi un important centre religieux où le bouddhisme s'est implanté dès le Ier s. de n. è. C'est ce que montrent ses chapiteaux gréco-bouddhiques et ses décors de stoupas (*harmikas*, *chattras* et *chatravalis*) mais aussi les fragments de statues couverts de feuille d'or du temple du Tchingiz Tepe ou le haut-relief découvert en novembre 2012 en remploi dans le palais et provenant visiblement du temple bouddhiste du Tchingiz 2.

L'Ancienne Termez est donc, au Nord de l'Oxus, le témoin de la brillante civilisation de la Bactriane kouchane qui combine l'important héritage hellénistique, la tradition des steppes portée par des peuples venus des confins de la Chine, le rayonnement du bouddhisme indien et l'influence croissante de l'Empire romain à travers le commerce actif entre l'Inde et la Bactriane. Une civilisation qui touche toutes les agglomérations de la région qui se dotent de monuments nouveaux, comme en témoigne la profusion de bases de colonnes de type attique qu'on retrouve jusque dans les moindres sites de cette période.

C'est aussi ce que signifie la présence des trois monastères bouddhistes qui entouraient l'Ancienne Termez de la même façon que, à 60 km au Sud, plusieurs monastères entouraient Bactres-Balkh, capitale de la Bactriane-Tokharistan. Ces trois monastères logeaient la communauté bouddhique de l'Ancienne Termez et, sans doute, les moines et les missionnaires de la Bactriane-Tokharistan et de l'Inde. Ils contribuaient par là à propager le bouddhisme dans les régions au Nord de l'Oxus.

Conclusion

L'histoire antique de la Bactriane du Nord et de l'Ancienne Termez dont nous venons de tracer les grands traits était totalement inconnue il y a quelques décennies. Des matériaux solides ont été apportés, faisant apparaître en pleine lumière le rôle, jusque-là méconnu, des régions de rive droite du Moyen Oxus dans l'Antiquité et au Moyen-Âge. Nombre d'hypothèses dont certaines très aventurées peuvent ainsi être éliminées. C'est là un résultat exceptionnel dû aux remarquables initiatives de l'Académie des Sciences de l'Ouzbékistan et de l'Institut Hamza et à l'action de nombreuses missions ouzbèques ou ouzbéko-étrangères. Une entreprise collective remarquable qui a fait de la Bactriane du Nord l'une des régions historiques les mieux connues d'Asie Centrale.

Les recherches de la MAFOuzB sur l'Ancienne Termez sont donc venues heureusement enrichir l'histoire antique, trop longtemps ignorée de la plus grande cité de la Bactriane du Nord. Mais nombre de faits demandent encore à être précisés et plusieurs questions majeures attendent une réponse. Il importe donc, tant que les conditions favorables actuelles sont réunies, que ces recherches de la MAFOuzB soient soutenues pour conduire à leur terme les recherches très prometteuses à Termez même et dans toute la province du Surkhan Daria.

Quant aux publications et aux synthèses, elles sont en chantier et devraient, si les moyens nous sont donnés, voir le jour prochainement.

BIBLIOGRAPHIE

Aršavskaja Z.A., Rtveladze E.V., Xakimov Z.A., *Szedneve Kovye pamyatniki Surxandazy*, Taykent 1981.

Bonvalot, G. (1889), *Du Caucase aux Indes à travers le Pamir*, Paris.

Frumkin, Gr. (1970), *Archaeology in Soviet Central Asia*, Leyde.

Gobillot, G. (2006), Al-Hakim al-Tirmidhi, *Le livre des Nuances ou De l'impossibilité de la synonymie*, tr. par G. Gobillot, Paris.

Leriche, P. (2002), Termez fondation d'Alexandre?, *Journal Asiatique* 290 : 411–415.

Leriche, P. (2011), *Le chapiteau tétracéphale de l'Ancienne Termez*, Mesopotamie XIV, 2011, p. 321–334.

Leriche, P. (2013), *Héráclès, l'anguipède et le géant. Le médaillon (emblêma) de Termez : un nouvel épisode de gigantomachie*, dans: A. Peruzzetto, F.D. Metzger, L. Dirven (ed.), *Animals, Gods and Men from East to West : Papers on archaeology and history in honour of Roberta Venco Ricciardi*, Oxford 2013 (BAR S2516).

Leriche, P. (2013), *L'apport de la Mission archéologique franco-ouzbeque (MAFOu²) de Bactriane du Nord à l'histoire de l'Asie Centrale.*

Leriche, P., Pidaev, Ch. (2007), Termez in Antiquity, dans : J. Cribb, G. Herrmann (éd.), *After Alexander. Central Asia before Islam* (*Proceedings of the British Academy* 133), Oxford: 179–211.

Leriche, P., Pidaev, Ch. (2008), *Termez sur Oxus. Cité-capitale d'Asie Centrale*, Paris.

Pelliot, P. (1929), Termez dans les textes chinois et tibétains, dans : *Doklady Akademii Nauk SSSR*, ser. A, Leningrad : 297–298.

Pidaev, Ch.R. (1976), Mirzakul-tepe – pamjatnik rannekushanskogo vremeni v Severnoj Baktrii [Mirzakul Tepe – monument de la haute époque Kouchane en Bactriane du Nord], dans : *Baktrijskie Drevnosti. Predvaritel'nye soobščenia ob arkheologičeskikh rabotah na juge Uzbekistana*, Leningrad.

Pidaev, Ch., Annaev, T., Fussman, G. (2011), *Monuments Bouddhiques de Termez / Termez Buddhist Monuments* ; tome I : *Catalogue des inscriptions sur poteries* ; I.1 : *Introductions, catalogues, commentaires* ; I. 2 : *Planches, index et concordances*, Paris.

Pontbriand, S. de, Leriche, P. (2012), *Un bâtiment d'artisanat Kouchan à l'Ancienne Termez*, PIFK (Problemy Istorii, Filologii i Kul'turi), p. 14–23.

Pugačenkova, G.A. (éd.) (1989), *Antičnyje i rannesrednevkovyje drevnosti Južnogo Uzbekistana*, Taškent.

Pugačenkova, G.A., Rtveladze, E.V. (1990), *Severnaya Baktriya – Tokharistan. Očerki istorii i kul'tury. Drevnost'i srednevkove*, Taškent.

Rtveladze, E.V. (1974), Razvedočnoe izučenie baktrijskikh pamjatnikov na juge Uzbekistana [Recherches préliminaires sur les monuments bactriens d'Ouzbékistan méridional], dans : V.M. Masson (éd.), *Drevnjaja Baktrija. Predvaritel'nye soobščenia ob arkheologičeskikh rabotah na juge Uzbekistana*, Leningrad.

Rtveladze, E.V., Khakimov, Z.A. (1973), Maršrutnye issledovanija pamjatnikov Severnoj Baktrii [Prospections des monuments de la Bactriane du Nord], dans : *Iz istorii antičnoj kul'tury Uzbekistana*, Taškent.

Staviskij, B.Ja. (1986), *La Bactriane sous les Kushans. Problèmes d'histoire et de culture*, tr. par P. Bernard, M. Burda, F. Grenet, P. Leriche, Paris (= Staviskij, B.Ja., *Kušanskaja Baktrija*, Moscou 1977).

Fig. 1. Un paysage typique de Bactriane du Nord ; la vallée du Cherabad Darya; © MAFOuz de Bactriane

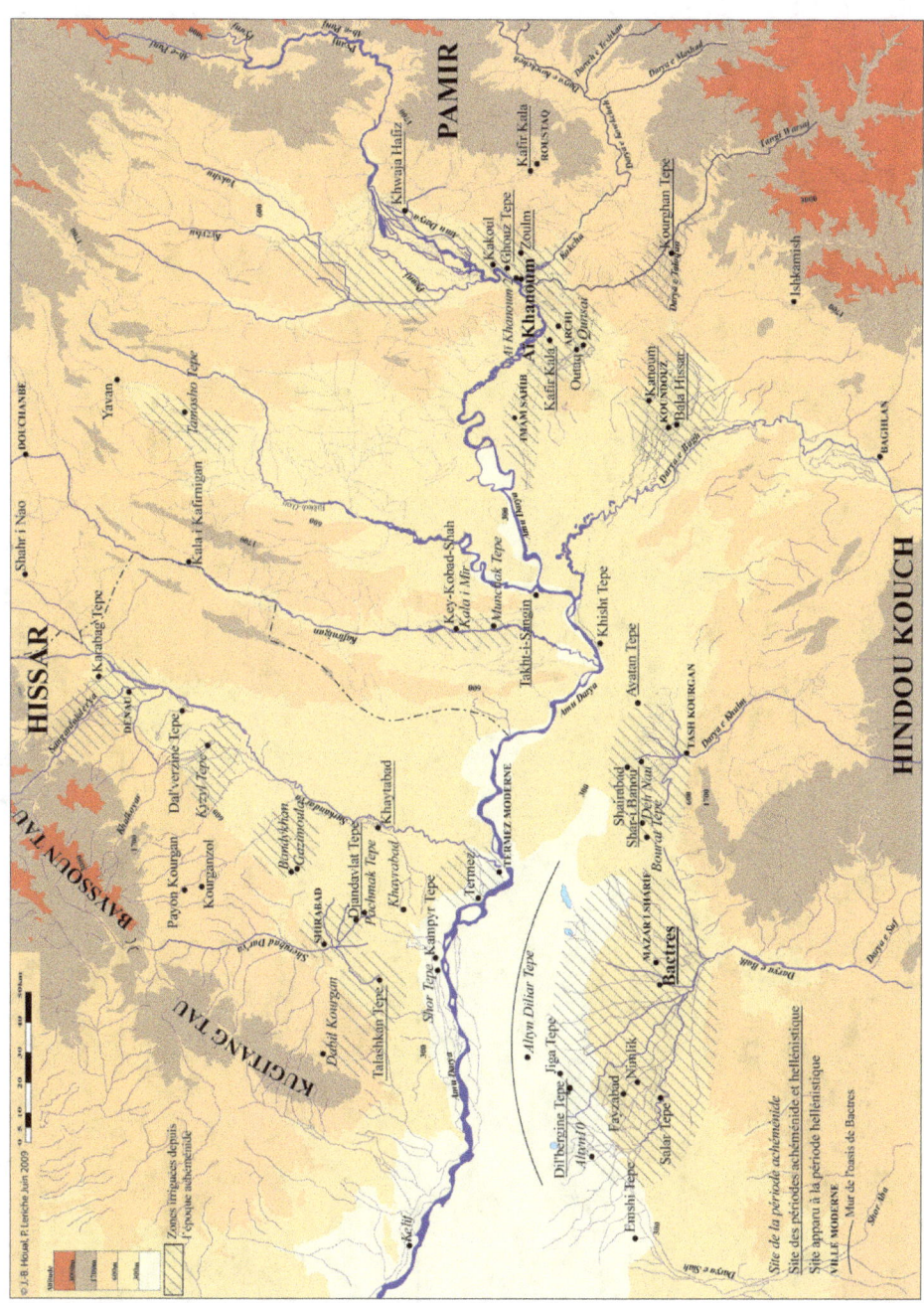

Fig. 2. Carte de la Bactriane antique ; © MAFOuz de Bactriane

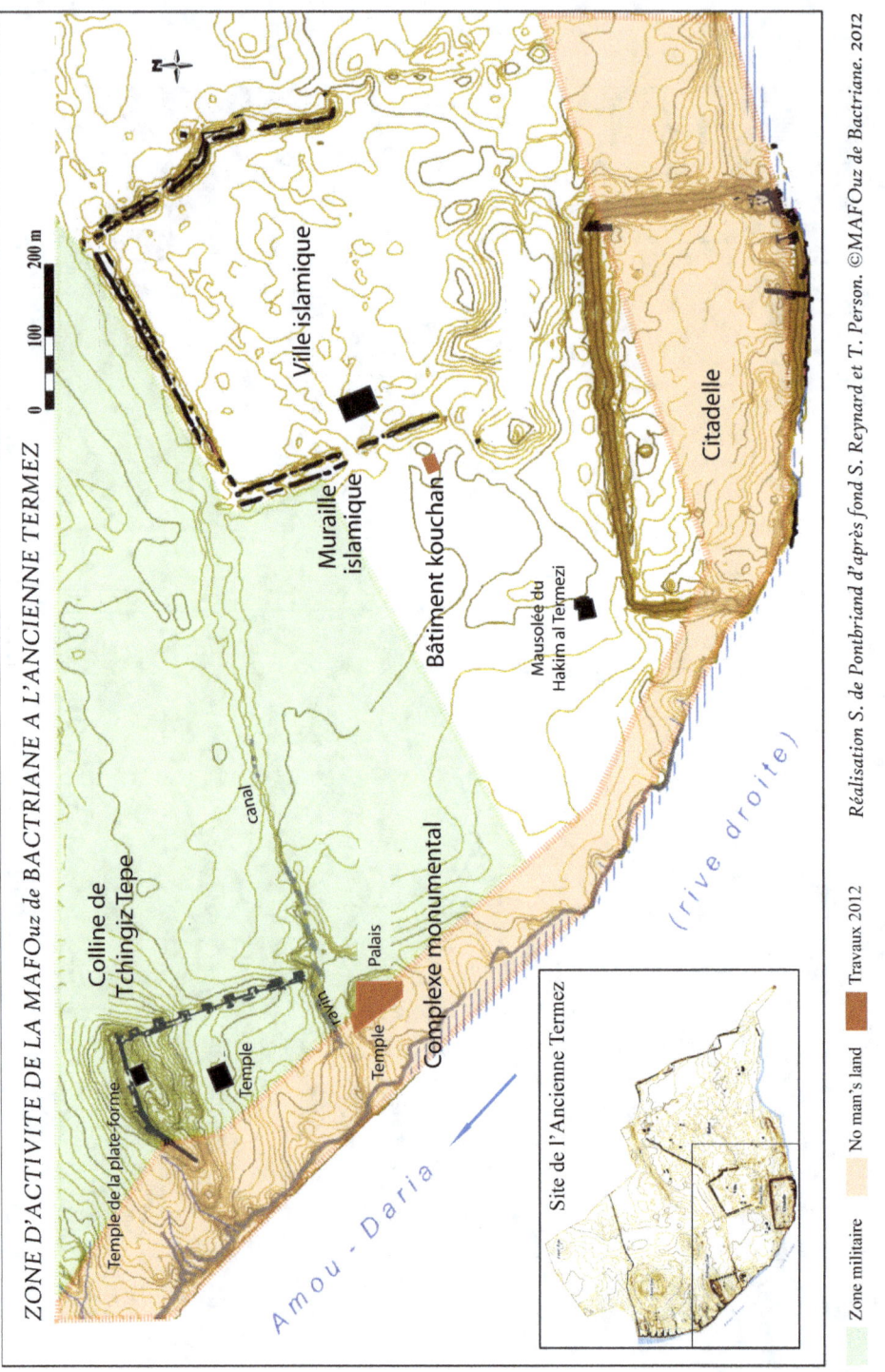

ZONE D'ACTIVITÉ DE LA MAFOuz de BACTRIANE A L'ANCIENNE TERMEZ

0   100   200 m

Colline de Tchingiz Tepe

Temple de la plate-forme

Temple

Temple

ravin

canal

Palais

Temple

Complexe monumental

Amou - Daria

Muraille islamique

Ville islamique

Bâtiment kouchan

Mausolée du Hakim al Termezi

Citadelle

(rive droite)

Site de l'Ancienne Termez

Zone militaire   No man's land   Travaux 2012

Réalisation S. de Pontbriand d'après fond S. Reynard et T. Person. ©MAFOuz de Bactriane. 2012

Fig. 3. Zone d'activité de la MAFOuz B à l'Ancienne Termez. En encart, plan topographique de l'Ancienne Termez MAFOuz B, 2003. Réalisation S. de Pontbriand ; © MAFOuz de Bactriane

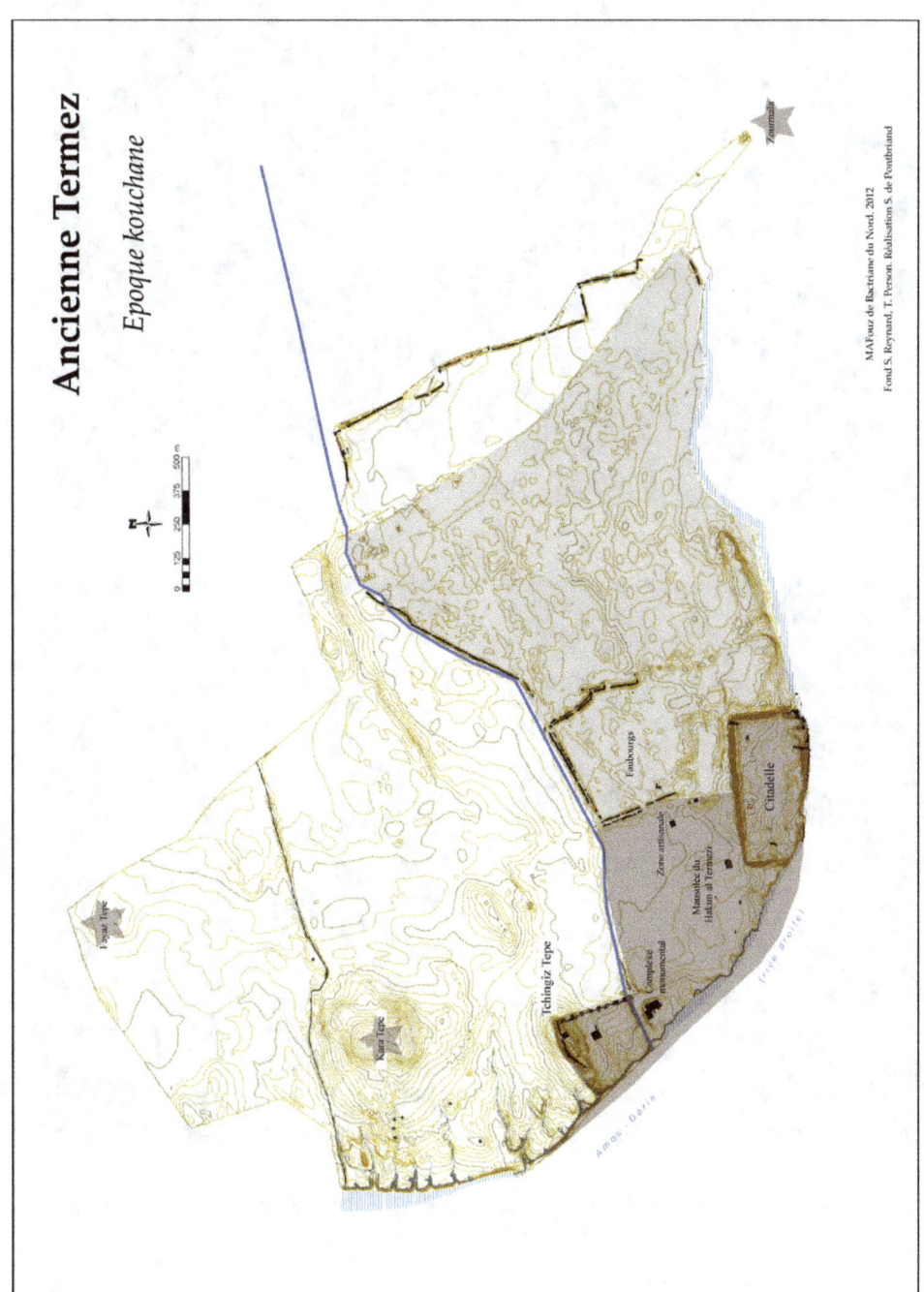

Fig. 4. Plan du site de l'Ancienne Termez à l'époque kouchane ; © MAFOuz de Bactriane

Fig. 5. Décor de stuc sculpté du palais des Termez Chahs (XIᵉ–début XIIIᵉ s.) aujourd'hui disparu ;
d'après Aršavskaja *et alii* (1981), p. 63.

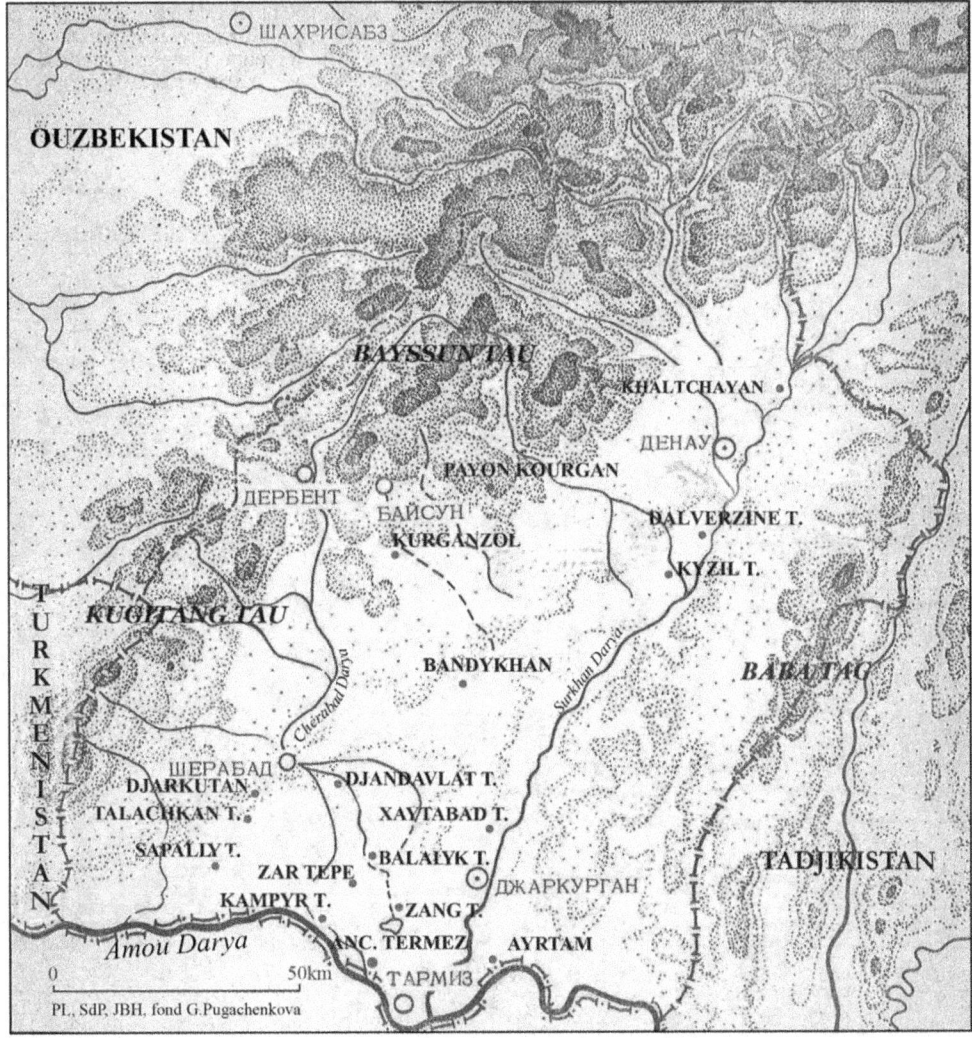

Fig. 6. Carte des principales missions archéologiques de la province ouzbèque du Surkhan Darya.
Fond G. Pugatchenkova, 1989. Réalisation P. Leriche, S. de Pontbriand et J.-B. Houal ; © MAFOuz
de Bactriane

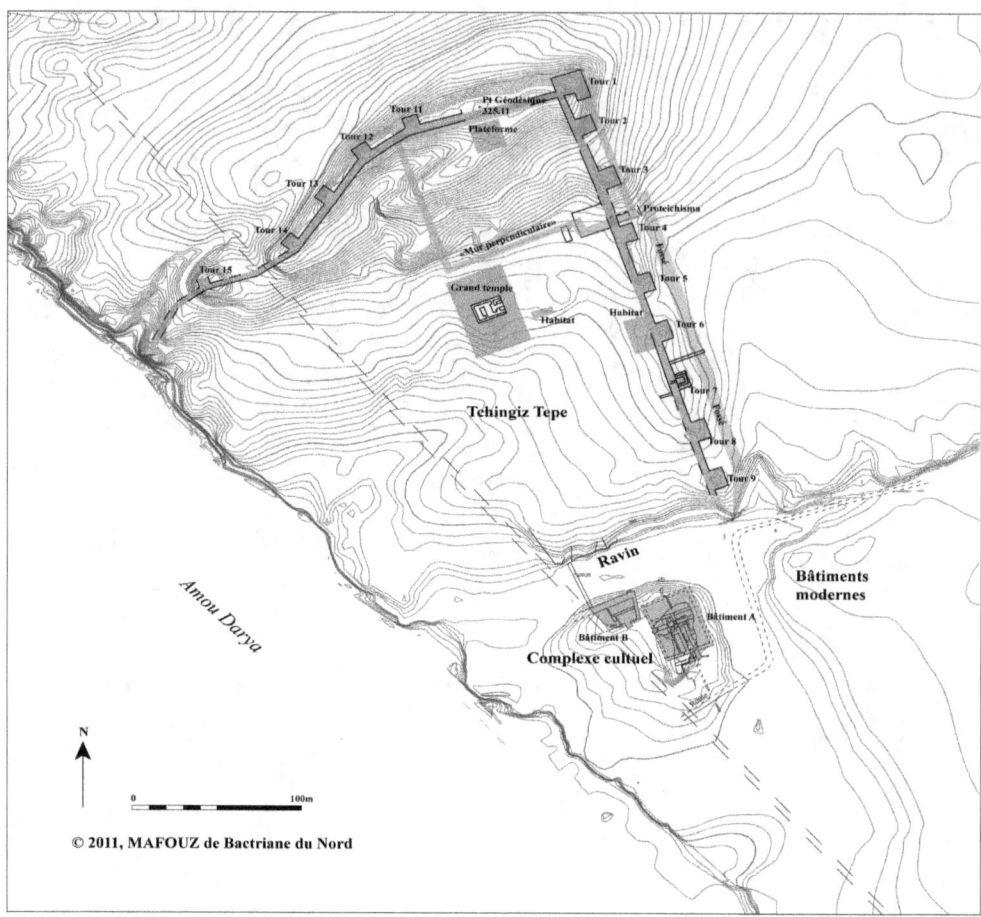

Fig. 7. Plan-masse des monuments antiques mis au jour sur les deux Tchingiz Tepe ; © MAFOuz de Bactriane

Fig. 8. Le plateau de Tchingiz Tepe 2 avant la fouille de la MAFOuz de Bactriane en 1995.
Vue vers le Sud ; © MAFOuz de Bactriane

Fig. 9. Le plateau de Tchingiz Tepe 2 en 2011. Vue vers le Sud. Au premier plan, le temple
(bâtiment B) qui surplombe le ravin ; à gauche, le palais (bâtiment A) ; © MAFOuz de Bactriane

Fig. 10. Tchingiz 2. Bâtiment B. Le canal d'évacuation d'eau creusé dans la maçonnerie du temple et remployant des fûts de colonnes en calcaire. Vue vers le Sud ; © MAFOuz de Bactriane

Fig. 11a. Tchingiz 2. Bâtiment A : a. Vue des destructions récentes de la partie sud du Palais. Vue vers le Nord-Ouest; © MAFOuz de Bactriane

Fig. 11b. Coupe sur la partie sud détruite du palais après retaillage. Noter la plateforme de pisé du troisième état reposant sur l'épaisse accumulation de sable éolien ennoyant les deux premiers états du bâtiment. Vue vers le Nord ; © MAFOuz de Bactriane

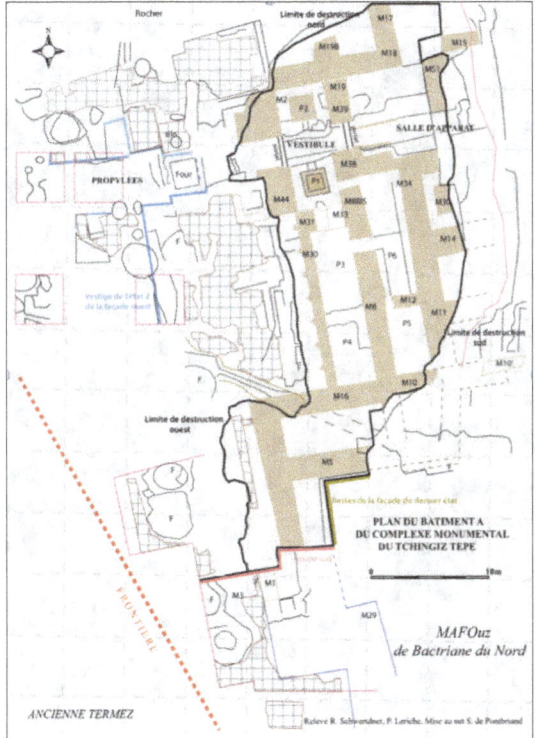

Fig. 12. Tchingiz 2. Bâtiment A. Plan masse des parties préservées du palais ; © MAFOuz de Bactriane

Fig. 13. Tchingiz 2. Bâtiment A. En haut : Vue générale de la face orientale, fortement dégradée, du palais ; en bas : entrée sur la face occidentale du palais et corridor axial ; © MAFOuz de Bactriane

Fig. 14. Tchingiz 2. Bâtiment A. Four de potier installé ultérieurement dans l'entrée du palais et corridor dans son dernier état. Vue vers l'Est ; © MAFOuz de Bactriane

Fig. 15. Tchingiz 2. Bâtiment A. Le corridor du palais dans son troisième état partiellement dégagé avec son dallage de blocs architecturaux en remploi. Noter les logements des poutres verticales et l'épaisseur des enduits de chaque côté du corridor. Vue vers l'Ouest ; © MAFOuz de Bactriane

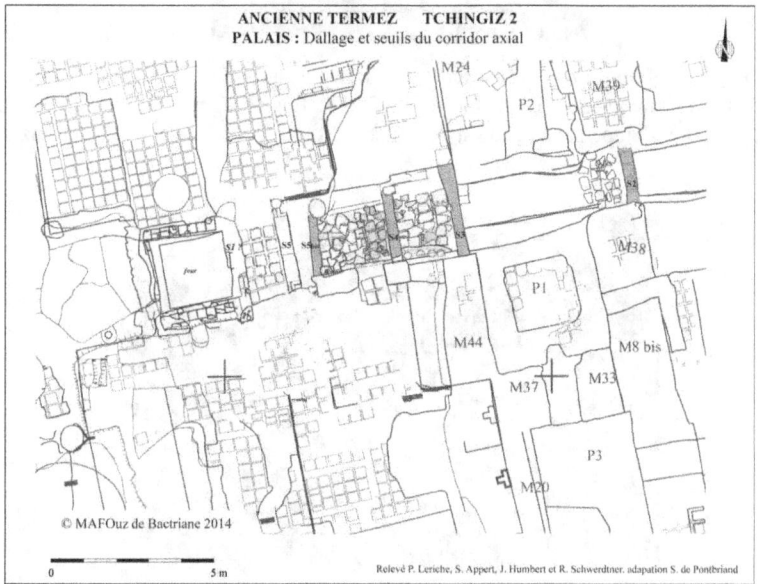

Fig. 16. Tchingiz 2. Bâtiment A. Plan de la partie occidentale du corridor avec les blocs architecturaux qui forment le dallage ; © MAFOuz de Bactriane

Fig. 17. Tchingiz 2. Bâtiment A. Haut : Elément de frise en haut-relief représentant deux personnages de style indien. Calcaire avec traces de dorure à la feuille. Bas : Fragment de bas-relief en calcaire représentant une partie d'un personnage de style kouchan et un pilier à lunule ; © MAFOuz de Bactriane

Fig. 18. Tchingiz 2. Bâtiment A. Extrémité occidentale du corridor du palais : Agencement des blocs architecturaux entre deux seuils disparus et avant le dégagement du massif de briques crues masquant le seuil n°5. Vue vers le Nord ; © MAFOuz de Bactriane

Fig. 19. Tchingiz 2. Bâtiment A. Extrémité occidentale du corridor du palais. Le seuil n°5 après son dégagement. Noter, au premier plan, le dispositif d'encastrement du montant nord et, au deuxième plan, les fragments architecturaux pris dans l'épaisseur des couches d'enduit recouvrant le mur du corridor. Vue générale vers le Sud ; © MAFOuz de Bactriane

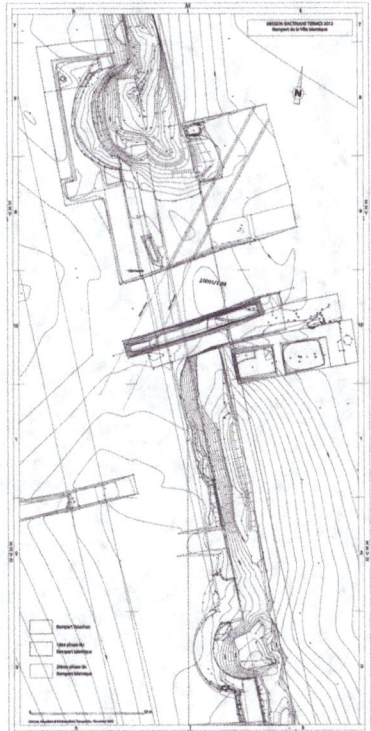

Fig. 20. Rempart de la ville islamique. Plan de la fouille en fin de campagne 2012. Relevé R. Schwerdtner ; © MAFOuz de Bactriane

Fig. 21. Rempart de la ville islamique. Tour massive semi-circulaire et brèche de la route moderne.
Vue vers l'Est ; © MAFOuz de Bactriane

Fig. 22. Rempart de la ville islamique. Tranchée dans la brèche. Au fond de la tranchée, le rempart
kouchan, avec, à l'extrémité, le départ d'une tour. Vue vers l'Est ; © MAFOuz de Bactriane

Fig. 23. Chantier du Bâtiment Kouchan en fin de campagne 2014. Vue Générale vers le Sud-Est. Au fond, la citadelle ; à gauche, la levée du rempart islamique ; © MAFOuz de Bactriane

Fig. 24. *Emblêma* de plâtre provenant du Bâtiment Kouchan, représentant une scène de gigantomachie de type hellénistique ; © MAFOuz de Bactriane

ELECTRUM * Vol. 22 (2015): 87–106
doi: 10.4467/20800909EL.15.004.3942
www.ejournals.eu/electrum

Ὁμόγλωττοι παρὰ μικρόν?

Antonio Panaino

Università di Bologna, Ravenna

Abstract: This article analyses the historical and linguistic implications that emerge from a very famous passage preserved by Strabo (XV, 2, 8 [C 724]), but probably belonging to Eratosthenes' *Geographika*, which states that Persians, Medes, Bactrians and Sogdians would "speak approximately the same language, with but slight variations" (εἰσὶ γάρ πως καὶ ὁμόγλωττοι παρὰ μικρόν). This assumption is untenable, because even before Eratosthenes' time the Iranian languages were well distinguished. The suggested *homoglossia* should be explained in political terms, as the result of a practical diffusion of a variety of Old Persian in the army and in the satrapal administration. In the framework of a socio-linguistic and ethno-linguistic analysis of the historical situation attested in the Persian Empire, this study also tackles the problem of the meaning to be attributed to the word *arya*- in a linguistic context, as that of § 70 of Bisutun inscription. This terminology is discussed not only in connection with the one attested in the recently discovered Rabatak Inscription, but also with the documentation preserved in the Khotanese *Book of Zambasta* 23, 4–5, and – outside of the strictly Iranian milieu – in the *Aitareya Āraṇyaka* III, 2, 5.

With regard to the frequently claimed *homoglossia*, this study concludes that any description of the linguistic semi-unity of the Iranian *ethne*, or only of the North-Eastern Iranian ones, is a dream, and, as far as we know about the linguistic history of these peoples, not only a conclusion insufficiently grounded, but a highly improbable linguistic mirage. A "permafrosted" Irano-Aryan still spoken by all the Iranians as a sort of "Esperanto" *ante litteram* has no historical basis, nor does the idea that *arya*- was the name of a still preserved "common language," if this expression should be interpreted as a surviving unifying archaic jargon of all the Iranians (and not a practical Western Iranian *koiné*, imposed by the Old Persian authorities as a comfortable medium). The "Aryan" linguistic identity thus assumed other, fully historical, implications, although it was based on a tradition, partly original and derived by an ancestral cultural heritage, partly invented, especially in its socio-linguistic and sociopolitical implications, as normally happens when power and its legitimacy are strongly involved.

Key words: Multilingualism and communication, Iranian languages, Achaemenian Empire, Sogdian and Bactrian, "Aryan" languages, glottonyms.

In this contribution[1] I would like to challenge the real contents of a very well-known quotation[2] preserved by Strabo (XV, 2, 8 [C 724]), but certainly derived by Eratosthenes;[3] there we find, in the framework of a geographic description of the "Ariana," a remarkable statement concerning the mutual linguistic comprehension apparently shared by some Iranian *ethne*, a subject that deserves to be properly discussed and understood. The passage is as follows:

[...] ἐπεκτείνεται δὲ τοὔνομα τῆς Ἀριανῆς μέχρι μέρους τινὸς καὶ Περσῶν καὶ Μήδων καὶ ἔτι τῶν πρὸς ἄρκτον Βακτρίων καὶ Σογδιανῶν· εἰσὶ γάρ πως καὶ ὁμόγλωττοι παρὰ μικρόν.[4]

[...] and the name of Ariana (Ἀριανή) is further extended to a part of Persia and Media, as also to the Bactrians and Sogdians on the north; for these speak approximately the same language, with but slight variations.[5]

In the past, these lines have been mostly studied and commented upon for their patent importance with regard to the territory of the Ἀριανή, and consequently related closely to the problem of the ancestral "Aryan" identity of the various *ethne* belonging to the earliest Iranian stock. In particular, this document has also been considered as testimony to the Eastern origin of the Western Iranian *ethne*.[6] In the present study, I would like to focus on the fact that, contrary to any expectation, this particular passage has never been properly discussed in a more "historicised" way, with a crude evaluation of the strictly linguistic and dialectological implications involved by the statements apparently deducible from (the interpretation of) its contents. We can, in fact, explain the sentence in question in at least two ways:

1) as a reference to a state of "restricted" *homoglossia* referring only to the last two mentioned *ethne*, i.e. the Bactrians and the Sogdians, so excluding Persians and Medians.

2) as a generic (and then inclusive) reference to all the four *ethne* previously quoted (all of them in genitive). In this second case, we will have to do with a short linguistic statement covering the whole *airiiō.šaiiana-* – "the Aryan space" (*Yt.* 10, 13) of the *Avesta*, as Gnoli supposed.[7]

Unfortunately, as previously noted before, in spite of the necessary prudence, the amphibolic implications of such an extraordinary *notitia* have not been clarified. Tradition-

[1] I wish to thank for their kind remarks and suggestions Dr Gian Pietro Basello (University of Naples, L'Orientale), Prof. Serena Bianchetti (University of Florence), Prof. Mauro Maggi (University of Rome, La Sapienza), Prof. Rüdiger Schmitt (Laboe), Prof. Adriano Valerio Rossi (University of Naples, L'Orientale), Prof. Velizar Sadovski (Institut für Iranistik, Österreichische Akademie der Wissenschaften, Vienna), and Prof. Nicholas Sims-Williams (SOAS, University of London).
[2] See apud Strabo, XV, 2, 8, ed. Jones 1930, 140, 141; Radt 2005, 236; Biffi 2005, *ad locum*.
[3] See in particular Berger 1880, 238–239 (Fragm. III B, 20). Bernhardy (1822, 97–98), who considered just the quoted passage as not belonging to Eratosthenes. Roller (2010, 84–85) also does not include it in his translation, but without giving any explanation for that choice. Contrariwise, the quotation is inserted in the *Eratosthenica* by Aujac 2001, 192. Cf. also Marcotte 2005, 149–155, in particular note 9; see also Geus 2007, 111–122. Specifically consulted on the opportunity to consider this passage as part of the original material belonging to Eratosthenes or not, Prof. Serena Bianchetti expressed her positive opinion, confirming the assumption already proposed by Berger.
[4] See Strabo, XV, 2, 8, ed. Jones 1930, 142.
[5] Translation according to Jones 1930, 142. German translation by Radt 2005, 237.
[6] See in particular Gnoli 1966b; 1967, 85; 1980, 140–142.
[7] See Gnoli 1966a; 1966b; 1983, 20, 68; 1987, 519; 1989, 77–78.

ally, the ambiguous meaning of the alleged *homoglossia* has been regarded with a strong enthusiasm, but without particular caution in terms of whether the mutual intelligibility of the Eastern Iranian languages (or, alternatively, of all the early Iranian languages) could still be uncritically considered as very high around the beginning of the Vulgar era. We connect this datum with the age of the final report given by Strabo, and certainly before it, as an external witness of a substantial conservatism preserved by all the Old Iranian dialects around the period of the fall of the Achaemenid Empire, if – as we should – we prudently antedate the origin of such a σφραγίς to the times of Eratosthenes and, probably, of his earlier informants.[8]

It is for this reason that I would like to insist that a serious evaluation of this passage from the historical and linguistic points of view can and must be attempted only after the determination of a relative chronology of the textual material embedded by Strabo's tradition. Actually, the contents of this particular section have already been attributed by Berger[9] to a lost geographical work of Eratosthenes (born in the mid-280s BC/died around the end of the third century or, more probably, the beginning of the second [probably 194 BC] at the age of 82 years),[10] who, in his turn, should have taken and/or re-worked part of his Iranian ethno-cultural material from the reports of some historians of Alexander.[11]

We may then suppose that the description of the linguistic proximity between the Sogdian and the Bactrian languages or, alternatively, among all the languages of the four mentioned Iranian *ethne* (Persians, Medes, Bactrians and Sogdians), could theoretically be connected with a *direct* observation (if correct or not, or in what sense, is another matter we will try to discover) made around the end of the fourth century BC, and later acquired (orally or through a written intermediation) by Eratosthenes, when the multi-ethnic and multilingual complexity of the Persian Empire had directly appeared in its whole intriguing complexity also to Western observers.

After this basic appraisal of the chronological implications of Strabo's final statement, we can try to discuss its two possible interpretations, starting from the one supposing a strong state of *homoglossia* only between Sogdian and Bactrian. As previously remarked, the textual stratification compels us to refuse any simplistic judgment about the Eastern Iranian linguistic situation for the period of Strabo himself. This external caveat is confirmed by the observation that it appears highly improbable, if not impossible, that the Bactrians and Sogdians might really still have been *homoglottoi* in the period between the first century BC and first century AD, in spite of the slight dialectological variations (παρὰ μικρόν) prudently admitted in the Greek source itself. So, although Bailey[12] assumed that Strabo himself, writing two centuries later (his *Geography* was probably finished in the earliest years of the first c. AD) than Eratosthenes, and one century after the Tocharian invasion of Bactria, might have more or less consciously again

---

[8] In his *Geographika*, Eratosthenes divided the world into portions, named σφραγίδες "gem or seal stones;" "Ariana" was described in the third book, second "seal-stone." See Briant 1996, 197 and note 7; Geus 2002, 276–277; Roller 2010, 25–27, 84–87.

[9] Berger 1880, 239.

[10] See Geus 2002, 7–15; cf. Roller 2010, 7–15.

[11] See Auberger 2001. Cf. Berger 1880; Eggermont 1975; Radt 2002; Roller 2010, 17–20, *passim*.

[12] Bailey 1937, 893; cf. Tarn 1938, 288, note 1.

adopted this statement, but as a fitting reference to the Kushan and Tocharian presence in Eastern Iran, such a conclusion seems to be very speculative and highly hazardous. Its implausibility is due to the evidence that Strabo had no direct knowledge of or any fitting competence on the Kushan dialects and, again, no direct access to them, so it appears simply groundless to make any *deliberate* adaptation of an older statement concerning two earlier Iranian *ethne* like the Bactrians and the Sogdians to the new historical situation occurring in Iran (if this was really what Bailey presumed). In other terms, it is much more prudent to consider this statement as simply referring to the period described by Alexander's historians rather than to that of Strabo's contemporaries.

However, if we admit – as seems reasonable – that Eratosthenes took this piece of news by an earlier Greek (written or oral) source obtained on the basis of a direct or indirect witness (although in any case deduced by means of a certain practical, empirical experience), what did it properly mean in ethno-linguistic terms? In other words, if a Greek officer or traveller in the footsteps of Alexander's army had the opportunity to hear Sogdians and Bactrians talking together, was he actually technically in the position to discriminate between the mutual comprehensibility of their two different languages? How might he be so conversant in Iranian dialectology to discriminate between the current everyday use of Bactrian and Sogdian to properly understand that two Iranians were not speaking, for instance, in (Old) Persian (perhaps with a peculiar or local accent) – as nowadays (educated) German and French tourists might easily speak together in English – if they had the chance to meet at the bazaar of Samarkand? This does not imply that Europeans are ὁμόγλωττοι παρὰ μικρόν, or that all the peoples of the former Soviet Union shared such a quality, when most of them were certainly able to speak each other in Russian, but not necessarily thanks to the common ancestral origin of their own different languages; in fact, this would have been true only for Slavonic peoples, but not for all the other ones.

A real state of *homoglossia*, like the one presumed by Eratosthenes and/or his earlier original informant(s), would probably confirm the existence of a widespread imperial tradition, in which Achaemenian officers and functionaries were (or should have been) able to communicate among themselves with a reasonable freedom! This result could be obtained, for instance, by means of the Persian language (or a certain variety of it), and it is reasonable to imagine that a few of these individuals were trained, at least in the scribal frameworks, in order to currently write and read Aramaic documents, which might probably also be offered to a public audience (or the local satrapal authorities) accordingly in Persian or in any other relevant (local) language of the kingdom, including Sogdian and Bactrian. In this sense, we must presume that at least some Sogdians and Bactrians had the appropriate education and training to read and speak Old Persian, but also to read aloud Aramaic basic texts which in an oral performance transformed their contents in Sogdian or in Bactrian as well. If not only and strictly *homoglottoi*, some of them surely could be also *homographoi*, and, by means of (written) Aramaic and (spoken) Old Persian, these people were able in practical terms to communicate in a more or less direct way in spite of their own different ethno-linguistic origins.

On the other hand, we must seriously doubt that even in the fifth century BC Sogdian and Bactrian languages were still so close to their archetypal model, i.e. to a northeastern form of Proto-Iranian, that in an oral practical performance two native speakers, one Bactrian and the other Sogdian, still might easily feel themselves practically *homoglottoi*. It seems to me very difficult to believe in an uncritical way that a scenario like this could be real, because more or less in the same period Iranian priests speaking Later Avestan were probably no more able to properly understand all the nuances of the whole Old Avestan liturgies, and in fact some of their adaptations show that the linguistic material belonging to the most archaic, but probably also dialectologically different, Avestan tradition[13] produced improper reinterpretations of the original composition.

Furthermore, we must insist on the striking evidence – which has never been done before – contained in some Babylonian inscriptions of Darius I and Xerxes, which counter any conclusion based on a simplistic evaluation of the data preserved by Strabo: in fact, an important sequence of the Achaemenian standard titles was translated (although with minimal varieties) in Akkadian as follows:

šar mātāte ša napḫar li-ša-na-a-ta *gabbi*[14]
the king of the countries of all languages
O.P. *xšayaθiya dahyūnām vispazanānām*
the king of the countries of all the (kinds of) peoples.

See also DPg[15] 1, 7; 2, 16, where we find the following statement:

Parsu Madaja u mātāte šanītima li-ša-nu šanitu[16]
Persia, Media, and other lands (with) other languages [...][17]

So, while the Elamite version just introduced a loanword for O.P., *vispazana-* "of all the peoples," i.e. *viššatanaš*, the Akkadian one had *lišanu* or *lišanu gabbi*, where the reference was to "all (*gabbi*) the languages (*lišanu*)." The same phenomenon also occurs with O.P. *paruzana-* – "of many (kinds of) peoples/men," which was systematically translated in Akkadian as *lišanu* or *lišanu gabbi* (and minor variants), while Elamite still has a loanword (pár-ru-za-na-na-um, etc.).[18] There is no reason (as on the contrary we read in the *CAD, sub voce*)[19] to hide this difference by translating "of all the nationalities." In fact, *lišanu* strictly concerns languages,[20] and in particular *foreign languages* as a sign of distinction; it is therefore clear that the Babylonian scribes adopted this mark, as Dr Basello has also independently assumed,[21] in order to distinguish the different *ethne*.[22] I would like to argue that the variant attested in the Akkadian scribal tradition might reflect not exactly O.P. *vispazana-* or *paruzana-* (or again "Echt-Per-

---

13   On the Avestan dialectology see Panaino 2007.
14   Weissbach 1911, 103, § 2: 12; 87, § 2: 5; 119, § 2: 12.
15   Lecoq 1997, 229–230. Cf. Schmitt 2009, 13, with additional bibliography.
16   Weissbach 1911, 85, § 1: 7; § 2: 16.
17   Lecoq 1997, 229–230.
18   In this case, however, there is a number of variants and sometimes few Elamite genuine forms.
19   CAD 9, 1973, 209–215; see in particular the entry 4c, at p. 214.
20   See Zadok 1981, 665; 2003.
21   I must again thank Gian Pietro Basello for his kind generosity in placing at my disposal his notes on the pertinent (parallel) passages in Old Persian, Akkadian and Elamite.
22   Briant (1996, 193) translates the passage of DPg "[...] la Perse, la Médie et les autres pays aux autres langues," insisting that Persia and Media are more strictly linked for ethno-cultural reasons, which is correct, but does not support the idea that all the other countries had mutually understandable languages, as we could deduce from Strabo/Eratosthenes.

sisch" stems as *visadana-/parudana-* or hybrids like **vispa-dana-*),[23] but unattested compounds like **vispahizan(a)-* "of all the (different) languages" or **paruhizan(a)-* "of many (different) languages," with O.P. *hizan-* "tongue"[24] as the second element. In the genitive plural, two forms like *vispazanānām/paruzanānām* might easily cover **vispahizanānām/*paruhizanānam*. In any case, the Akkadian tradition confirms that the idea of a linguistic multiplicity was current, and that the *homoglossia* was never existent a priori. In addition, we must postulate the existence of an Old Persian correspondent form from which it should have been possible to literally translate an Akkadian sentence referring to "people of other languages," and contrariwise.

If we now again examine our main problem, we must consider that Eratosthenes' statement gives us only few actually usable pieces of information; the Sogdians and Bactrians were certainly in a position to communicate among themselves with a certain efficacy, but we have no statement about the fact that this happened, when they pro-miscuously used their own native languages just with slight variations (παρὰ μικρόν) and without proper training. In addition, the Greek text does not clarify at which level this mutual understanding was possible, so it has been presumed that the Greek pas-sage just meant that Sogdian and Bactrian were substantially similar, an assumption that must be considered false. We know that certain dialectological features of Bactrian were also shared by some varieties of Sogdian,[25] or that in "word-formation and syn-tax Bactrian shows some particular affinities to Sogdian,"[26] but we cannot forget, as al-ready remarked by Henning,[27] that Bactrian "occupies an intermediary position between Pashto and Yidgha-Munji on the one hand, Sogdian, Choresmian, and Parthian on the other: it is thus in its natural and rightful place in Bactria." This simple description of the facts supports the prudent working hypothesis that around the epoch of the fall of the Achaemenian Empire Bactrians and Sogdians already spoke two well-differentiated languages, in which, in spite of its Eastern position, Bactrian shared some isoglosses with more Western languages, although its dialectological proximity with Sogdian was higher. But "higher" does not signify "complete," as if the two languages were just two minor branches of a common linguistic "Sogdico-Bactrian league."

Thus, a different approach to the whole passage is necessary. In fact, if we consider the *homoglossia* as referring to all the peoples of the "Ariana"[28] – so including Persians and Medes as well – the same statement could be no more compellingly interpreted as referring to the mutual intelligibility of all these languages among the various speakers and indifferently from their own native tongues. Rather, it would be interpreted as the description of a factual and pragmatic possibility to speak, at least in certain occasions

---

[23] See Schmitt 2014, 229, 280.

[24] Schmitt 2014, 194.

[25] Sims-Williams 1981, 353.

[26] Sims-Williams 1996a; 1996b, 649.

[27] Henning 1960, 47.

[28] On the fact that "Ariana" was not a "general term to designate the whole of Iran from east to west," see Gnoli 1980, 140–141, with an important discussion of Strabo's passage. See also Gnoli's critical discussion of some political interpretations concerning this area, which should be considered, in the light of Schmitt (1964, 66–67, note 4, 76–80), "a purely geographical conception to Eratosthenes" (Gnoli 1980, 142). Cf. also Geus 2002, 277, note 84. Also very important are two recent articles by Bianchetti (2010 and 2012), both concerning Eratosthenes' chronology and the description of the "Ariana."

and at certain socio-linguistic levels, approximately by means of a "common" language[29] used as a *medium*. Presumably, such a *medium* should have been a variety of Old Persian as a sort of *lingua franca* of the Empire, in particular for the Irano-Aryans who had been "unified" under the Achaemenian power.

If the reference to *ariya-* has to be connected (in which way is a problem that should be further discussed here) with (the name of ?) the language by which, according to § 70 of the Bisutun inscription (*θāti Dārayava.uš xšāyaθiya vašnā A.uramazdāha ima dipiçiçam, taya adam akunavam patišam ariyā* [...]),[30] King Darius denominated the Persian *dipiçiçam* ("form of writing/version of the inscription"),[31] the adoption of this "ethnolinguistic" denomination could perhaps imply that from the point of view of the Persian administration a specific variety of Old Persian was marked as the "official language" of all the Aryans and of the Aryan lands. Through that standard *medium* (also in its graphic manifestation),[32] it would follow that the imperial officers were expected to be able to communicate among themselves, because that was the very language (and script) of the king. This statement does not suggest that such an Iranian variety (*ariyā* [instr. sg. of the adjective ²*ariya-*], Elamite *har-ri-ia-ma*), was a language spoken on an everyday basis by all of the Aryans or commonly understood everywhere by all of them. On the other hand, we cannot exclude that such a denomination seems to satisfy a political[33] and ritual need more than a simply informative notion. For this reason, *ariya-* could be taken as a technical reference to a "formal" linguistic dimension with pretences, in an official

---

[29] This expression was already suggested by Lecoq (1974a, 62), but with other arguments and implications; cf. also Diakonoff (1970, 122, 65), and for earlier suggestions Junge (1944, 63). In my view, by means of the designation *ariyā* the text was presented as if it was expressed in a superior form, which should have been heard and appreciated by all the Aryans of the Empire, but also respected and recognised as fully authoritative by the other peoples, in particular by their local leaders. This pretension presupposes ideological aims to play a certain role in the transmission of the orders, and necessarily a compelling action in the determination of some linguistic media. See Kellens 2005 about *arya-*.

[30] Schmitt 2009, 87; 1991, 73 (DB IV, lines 4–5); 1990, 58–60. See now Schmitt 2014, 136–137. Cf. Hinz 1936; 1942; 1952; Lecoq 1974a, 62; 1974b, 77–84; Lazard 1976; Gnoli 1989, 13–14; Rossi 1981, 186–187, note 209; 1984, 62; 1985, 203; 1985, 204–208; Harmatta 1966; Herrenschmidt 1989; Huyse 1999; Bahari 2001; Tuplin 2005, 224. For the Elamite version see in particular Rossi 1985, 55–56, *passim*; Grillot-Susini/Herrenschmidt/Malbran-Labat 1993, 38, 58–59; Vallat 2011, 264–268, 280–281, who assumes that the royal action was a translation of the text in "Aryan." We must also recall that Rossi (2000, 2090–2010) has tried to explain O.P. *ariyā* and El. *hariyama* as meaning "on the rock" ("sulla roccia"). In a forthcoming article, the same scholar has revised his own view on the subject. In any case, for the complexity of the semantic field covered by El. *tuppi* "document, message," but also "inscription," see again Rossi 1985, 206–208; 2000, 2097–2098.

[31] Schmitt 2014, 169–170. Cf. Lecoq 1997, 212–213; Bahari 2001; Chul-Hyun 2003.

[32] For the inevitable implications connected with the assumption that *ariyā* might also refer to the introduction of a new Old Persian script, see Gershevitch 1979, 143, note 1; 1982, 103–107; cf. Rossi 1984, 58–62, and in particular notes 44 and 45. In my view, this interpretation is not exclusive, in the sense that the use of the term "Aryan" maintained an ideological and religious value, which was larger and, then, also inclusive of the glottonymical and graphemic levels evoked by the language and form of the inscription.

[33] My adoption of the term "political" does not counters Gnoli's considerations (1989) of the fact that *ariya-* did not play a main "political" force in the taxonomy of the Achaemenid Empire, but that it maintained a substantial religious role, in particular with contrastive reference to what happened in Sasanian times. I simply observe that the invocation of a "religious" concept in an official document as Bisutun, which, in itself, had an extraordinary political dimension, necessarily implies, willy-nilly, "political" involvements for the semantics of this stem.

(i.e. politically symbolic and liturgical) framework, to be the only one, strictly connected with an inner tradition, fitting to record all the events performed by the Irano-Aryans under the "divinely chosen" leadership of the Persian Emperor.

More precisely, I suspect that *ariya-*, in spite of a very simple and traditional inference, was not *sic et simpliciter* the standard name of the Old Persian language, because we can suppose that Persians and Medes, as well as the other Iranian peoples, knew very well that they were speaking different languages (although cognates) belonging to different Iranian *ethne*, and that more easily each one of these distinguished languages would have been designated according to the name of the corresponding *ethnos* usually speaking them.[34] Otherwise, we should be compelled to suppose that every Iranian *ethnos* presumed to speak *ariyā*, or denominated its language as "Aryan," a solution that suggest an objective state of terminological confusion (in which different people with different languages and proper ethnic denominations used the same unique term to refer to their distinct languages!), which then at least needs to be justified.

Actually, it is important to consider the theoretical doubt that all the Iranian *ethne* used to self-denominate their own mother tongues as "Aryan," because the same phenomenon seems to happen in Bactrian (see below), while we cannot forget that another important linguistic tradition like the Avestan one did not preserve any special name for itself, so we are compelled to designate it "Avestan" after the traditional name of its written textual collection. Furthermore, in the *Aitareya* (or *Kauṣītaki*), *Āraṇyaka* III, 2, 5, *āriyā- vāk-* (in the plural: *āriyā vācaḥ*)[35] indicates a plurality of "Aryan tongues," as a reference to the speeches of the Brāhmins and probably in opposition to non-Aryan languages.[36] Although this expression reasonably covers an area where Vedic was spoken, as observed by Witzel,[37] it would be risky to conclude that such a syntagm strictly concerned a special dialect or a particular "separate" variety of Vedic, while, on the contrary, it represented a "cultural" term, fitting for what was presumed to be (by its performers, of course) a superior way of speaking.[38] In fact, in this *Āraṇyaka*, it seems to make reference to the best human oral expression, and again we have confirmation of the supposition that by means of *āriyā- vāk-* a kind of ideological supremacy was meant, based on an ethnocentric perspective. In addition, we can doubt that all the Indo-Iranian *ethne* had such a low self-consideration and self-distinction that they called any of their languages "Aryan," a possibility which seems to me very improbable,[39] if not openly countered by internal competitions such as, for instance in the Iranian context, those between Medes and Persians. On the contrary, we may assume that O.P. *ariya-* and Later Ved. *ārya-* represented a general idea of ancestral prestige, shared by many (if not all the)

---

[34]   See already Lecoq 1974a, 62 on this particular problem.

[35]   See Keith 1909, 138; 255, note 3. Cf. Schmitt 2014, 137.

[36]   Cf. Keith 1909, 196, note 19.

[37]   Witzel 2001, 2.

[38]   See Kuiper 1955; 1991. Cf. Witzel 2001, 3.

[39]   Although Rossi 1985, 52–55 emphasises all the difficulties to be prudently seen in the ancient references on auto-glottonyms, their diffusion, in spite of the attested contradictions and mistakes, authorises us to deduce that, according to the ancient Greeks, Persian people spoke περσιστί "in Persian" even at the times of Herodotus. The fact that in some cases Greek authors were not able to properly distinguish between Persian and Median does not allow us to suspect that these two languages had no clear differences, nor to assume that only Persian was "Aryan" or that all the Iranians were *homoglottoi*.

Indo-Aryan and Arya-Iranian *ethne*, but taken as a unifying title, not as a mean of separation. Thus, apart from other probable ethnic self-denominations,[40] I suggest that the explicit adoption of the term *ariya-* or *ārya-* for the language itself (and, when necessary, the script) of any text involved other implications, in particular as a sort of conservative declaration of belonging to a common (and presumably higher) ethno-religious heritage. The evocation of a linguistic "Aryanity" probably gave the text (and its form) a superior authoritative force, as an archaising flavour putting it closer to a divine performance or to a superior anthropological condition. When a text was offered "in Aryan" or "Aryanly," this statement could probably mean that it was expressed not only in the main current language of that particular country, but in a superb form, which was the closest one to the mythical heritage of a whole *oikoumene*. For this reason it would be a *diminutio* to consider this definition as just a reference to the jargon of one more or less strong *ethnos*. We therefore have to postulate a deliberate archaising mark, as a re-foundation of a tradition, for ideological, contrastive reasons of prestige with respect to the others (peoples and/ or languages) and for a sort of self-satisfaction. In this respect, I think that Henkelman's discussion[41] of the term "Aryan" in the framework of the Achaemenid traditions results in a very fitting way, although improvable in all its implications:

> As far as our perception goes, it would seem that 'Aryan' is very different from 'Persian.' Though it potentially describes more people, namely all the Iranian-speaking nations of the empire, it is used in a restrictive and less neutral sense – the antonym non-Aryan seems to be in the air every time 'Aryan' is used. Also, judging from Greek and other secondary sources, 'Aryan' did not become a label for Achaemenid Persians or for Iranian-speaking nations in the empire in general; it was, apparently, not a name used by Persians or Iranophones when they introduced themselves to others. [...] The perception of an 'Aryan' heritage and past, provided, with its epic associations, a backbone for the imperial claim.

Although the reality should have been much more complicated, the idea of Iran[42] as well as its abstraction, i.e. that of "Aryanity," should have played a certain role in the Iranian and in the Indo-Iranian frames, as the later, truly "political" uprising of the *Ērān*-ity would confirm in Sasanian times. The problem is that we do not directly know the different layers of the Achaemenid ideology, nor those of the priestly leading centres, whose actions can be only guessed, but which remain another *incognitum*. Thus, I think that by means of *ariya-* the language (and the form) of that (Persian) inscription (or text, message, document, etc.) was attributed a sort of "universal" force, endowed with a liturgical investiture, raising it to the level of a court international language, although it was not so from an historical and linguistic point of view (which, of course, was not at all in the perspective of the royal ambiance). If this interpretation should only in part be sound, we might also presume that as the "court language" and when presented as *ariyā*, Old Persian (language and script) temporarily became something of a ritual sermon, so that *ariyā* could also indicate the solemn modality of any official expression of the king's words. With regard to this point, I have found myself to be in "resonant" agreement with

---

[40] See again Lecoq 1974a, 62.
[41] Henkelman 2011, 12.
[42] See again Gnoli 1989.

Rossi,[43] who has written on the subject "that OP *aryā* / AE har-ri-ya-ma indicates, if not a location, a modality ('in an *arya-* way') of the royal dedication," a solution which does not imply that the language was not meant, but that strongly emphasises the authority of the "speaker."

In the light of this ideological background, we can suppose that the Old Persian language performed the function of a prestigious *passpartout*, probably full of Median and other dialectological variants, open to loanwords, in particular from other important linguistic traditions (also non-Iranian and/or non-Indo-Europaean), and that, necessarily, it should have been known for practical reasons throughout the whole empire, in particular in the higher strata of the Irano-Aryan *ethne* and in the local administrations of the different satrapies. It should therefore come as no surprise that for any historian of Alexander (as for Eratosthenes and, later, for Strabo as well), the Persians, the Medes, the Bactrians and the Sogdians would "have spoken approximately the same language, with but slight variations." The problem, in fact, concerned who were the speakers involved and in which conditions. If they were officers and functionaries of the high administration, they were, as we noted before, certainly *homoglottoi*, and a few of them *homographoi* too!

Owing to the same tradition, some centuries later, in the Rabatak Bactrian inscription, King Kaniška declared (line 3f) that the language of the engraved text was in "Aryan" (αριαο).[44] This can be simply considered as a plain denomination of Bactrian, but was it really so? Or only so? We must not rule out the idea that by means of this special ethno-religious term the authority emitting the text was raising the status of the document, probably also including an idea of leadership over Iranian and Indo-Aryan *ethne* as well and, furthermore, deliberately distinguishing an "Aryan" meta-linguistic identity with respect to a Greek text (ιωναγγο), in which Kaniška had previously issued the same edict. It is clear that Kaniška insisted on the impact of this edict both on Indian and Iranian areas, so that the use of Bactrian αριαο inevitably possessed larger ideological implications as well. If we consider that in the Later Vedic tradition *āryā- vāk-* was already attributed to "Aryan tongues," we must suspect that Kaniška's choice to self-denominate his own language as αριαο should appear not so distinctive, and perhaps, I suppose, this was not at all his main target. The linguistic "Aryanity" involved a different perspective, not simply that of a formal categorisation of one (single and distinct) language among the others. Upon hearing (or reading) the word αριαο, a Hindu or a Buddhist educated servant of Kaniška would presumably never have restricted this determination to Bactrian, but would reasonably have appreciated the fact that the king was using a very "fair" and "high" language (or that, at least, he pretended to do this), as he too was a true "gentleman." In other terms, we must suspect that from a strictly pragmatic point of view, αριαο worked as a synonym of Skt. *samskṛta- "confectus*," which not only quali-

---

[43] Rossi, in print. In this new article, Rossi revises some of his interpretations proposed in Rossi 2000. Cf. Baghbidi 2009, 54–55, just to point out structural similarities between Dba/AE + DB/AE L and Middle Elamite dedicatory inscriptions. I thank Dr Gian Pietro Basello, who kindly reminded me of this unpublished article of Prof. Adriano Rossi, and Prof. Rossi himself for his kind support in making it fully available to me before its final publication.

[44] Sims-Williams/Cribb 1995/1996, 78; in this article Sims-Williams (p. 83) insisted on the direct comparison with Darius' Bisutun inscription. Cf. Sims-Williams 1998, 81. For a new edition of this inscription, see Sims-William 2008; in particular p. 56. I thank Prof. Sims-Williams again for his kind additional remarks on the text of the Rabatak Inscription.

fied the ethnicity of a linguistic tradition, but its "perfection." We must also remark that in line 10 of the same inscription we find another ethno-cultural reference; with regard to the god Srošard (σροþαρδο),[45] corresponding to Av. Sraoša, it is specified, by means of an short addition in smaller characters,[46] "who in Indian is called Mahāsena and is called Viśāka" [(κ)ιδι ργδοοαο μαασηνο ριζδι οδο βιζαγο ριζδι). Sims-Williams underlines that the "formation of ργδοοαο 'in (the) Indian (language)' (= Khot. *himduvau*)[47] is the same as that of αριαο 'in the Aryan (language)' in line 3."[48] However, in spite of the fact that this occurrence would apparently counter my previous considerations establishing a proportion like

ιωναγγο "in the Greek (language)"
αριαο "in the Aryan (language)"
ργδοοαο "in (the) Indian (language)."

I must observe that here the main distinction concerns the Indian denomination of an Iranian divinity, Sraoša[49] (who corresponded to a divine "diad" in India), and then it was more pertinent to the religious codex than wholly and solely to the linguistic one. The reference to Mahāsena and Viśāka does not strictly answer a linguistic need (how can this god be referred to in this or that speech?), but a religious pattern (to whom would these or those divine functions correspond?). It would in fact be embarrassing to try to circumscribe the dialectological limits covered by a designation such as "Indian." Which language or languages were meant? In the two divine names mentioned, the first one, μαασηνο, can reflect both a Sanskrit as well as a Middle Indian spelling, while βιζαγο seems to present two intervocalic sonorisations (ζ e γ) of Middle Indian derivation. "Indian" could therefore be taken as a generic "nickname" for religious names of Hindu origin, certainly being Mahāsena and Viśāka,[50] well attested Hindu divinities known both in Sanskrit literature and in languages spoken in the areas where the political influence of the Kušānas was relevant,[51] while, consequently, "Aryan" would mean "Bactrian." The witness of the Khotanese tradition seems to confirm that "Indian" probably became a sort of technical reference to "Sanskrit."[52] However, reversing the frame, we can assume that by means of this wide geographic determination the Bactrian text actually emphasised a socio-religious dimension, not simply linguistic evidence! Also in this case, therefore, the apparently simple "glottonymic" terminology contains some ambiguities, in which different levels are present and mutually play a number of subtle interferences.

---

[45] Sims-William 2008, 56.

[46] See Sims-Williams 2008, 64.

[47] For the Khotanese suffix, see Degener 1989, 172–173.

[48] *Ibidem.*

[49] We must remind that Sraoša, as the divinity of the 17th day of the month, was identified with Guha (Son of Śiva) and Baga (a different aspect of Śiva) in the calendrical lists of the Maga Brāhmaṇas, see Panaino 1996.

[50] Samad 2010, 35, 94, 98, *passim.*

[51] See Mann 2011.

[52] "Indian" is probably another reference to "Sanskrit" also in an Arabic alchemical text attributed to Ostanes and reasonably belonging to the Hermetic tradition; see Berthelot 1893, 13–17 (French translation), 116–123 (in particular p. 121); (Arabic Text) 79–88; van Bladel 2009, 54.

To add to the evidence a different situation with very pertinent results for our discussion, I would like to enter a very famous passage contained in the *Book of Zambasta* 23, 4–5:[53]

Z 23.4 *tterä hāḍe karma ne ysvā're hvatana kari hvatanau dātu*
Z 23.4 *hiṃduvau dīru buvāre hvatanau ni dātä nä saittä*
Z 23.5 *ciṅgānu ciṅgau dātä kaspärau tterä khaṣṣa-phaṣṣä*
Z 23.5 *kaspärai hāḍe tta sājīndi kvī rru arthu buvāre*

23.4 "But such are their deeds: the Khotanese do not value the Law at all in Khotanese. They understand it badly in Indian. In Khotanese it does not seem to them to be the Law."

23.5 "For the Chinese the Law is in Chinese. In Kashmirian it is very agreeable, but they so learn it in Kashmirian that they also understand the meaning of it."

Here, we actually find in order:

hvatanau "in Khotanese,"[54]
hiṃduvau "in Indian,"[55]
ciṅgānu "in Chinese,"[56]
kaspärau "in Kashmirian."[57]

It is evident that the context concerns a more complex and sophisticated dimension,[58] in which the choice of the language to be adopted for learning the "Law," as well as that of its translations, is fundamental. In other terms, the main matters are authority and comprehension with respect to a revealed *Vorlage*. But also in this case, we must observe that two (from our modern point of view) Indian languages are mentioned; one is called "Kashmirian" (in Skt. *Kaśmīrās* or *Kaśmīra* is the name of the corresponding land), which today denominates a speech belonging to the Dardic group, but we cannot presume the pertinence of its present meaning in this Khotanese framework. The latter should surely be Sanskrit, as the formal and highest written expression of the Buddhist Law, the main language from which Khotanese translators usually prepared their editions. Although a full discussion of the glottonymical distinctions attested in this passage has not been properly developed (with the exception of a long discussion offered by Konow; see below), I can note that Emmerick,[59] later followed by Nattier,[60] was inclined to think that by *hiṃduvau* it was in fact "Sanskrit" that was meant. On the other hand,

---

[53]   See Emmerick 1968, 342–343. Cf. Leumann 1933/1936, 290–291. In the discussion of the Khotanese linguistic material I have benefited enormously from the competence of Prof. M. Maggi, whom I would again like to thank.

[54]   See Bailey 1967, 431–432 (with many pertinent examples of contexts in which the language and the scripture are mentioned).

[55]   See Bailey 1967, 414.

[56]   See Bailey 1967.

[57]   See Bailey 1967, 44–45.

[58]   It is useful to recall that Leumann (1933/1936, 290, 291) interpreted *kha ṣṣa Phaṣṣä*, albeit with a question mark, "wie auch in Persisch." Cf. Konow 1939, 29. This interpretation has been already ruled out by Bailey; it has been quoted here only in order to give a complete information about the history of the interpretations of this passage, but it has no more relevance for the present discussion.

[59]   Emmerick 1983, 964.

[60]   Nattier 1990, 173 and note 66.

we cannot be sure that the Khotanese author did not make reference to other similar linguistic varieties and scripts, so that the same language could be referred to by means of different names according to the different writing and scribal traditions. The prudent caveat advanced by Degener, who simply preferred to speak of scripts "in der indischen Originalsprache" (i.e. *hiṃduvau*), and then also evoked a limited "Kenntnis des Sanskrit oder anderer indischer Sprachen," shows the complexity of the subject, which, for instance, has not been endorsed at all by Scherrer-Schaub.[61] This scholar, in fact, did not try to explain *kaspärau*, and simply maintained a generic reference to "Indian." Only Nattier,[62] and more largely Konow,[63] have tried to offer a more profound treatment of the whole problem, and both have concluded that *hiṃduvau* and *kaspärau* should be interpreted as both referring to "Sanskrit." Konow,[64] in particular, has supported his conclusions by means of a very accurate argument in which he pointed out all the complex and fitting cultural relations occurring between Gilgit (Kashmir) and Khotan, with particular regard for the pertinent fact that a number of Sanskrit texts from Gilgit are also attested in Khotanese translations. Furthermore, Konow stressed the remarkable importance that the Kashmirian area played in the earlier introduction of Buddhism to Khotan, so that (Sanskrit) texts from there would have been reasonably considered as particularly sacred. In turn, Nattier[65] has also adduced a very technical reason focusing on the evidence that the adoption of these two different ways of referring to "Sanskrit" would possibly answer a poetic reason; in fact, not only did the chosen differentiation between "Indian" and "Kashmirian" offer a synonymous alternative, but the introduction of *kaspärau* would also have produced a fitting alliteration with *khaṣṣa-phaṣṣä*, which occurs in the same stanza. Although we cannot exclude the possibility that *kaspärau* might refer to Gāndhārī, the local Prakrit, at the moment this solution does not seem to be sufficiently supported to reverse the one advanced by Konow.

I am not in a position to judge aesthetic criteria in Khotanese, but the choice remains to me worthy of attention, and I would like to note that a rhetoric solution also needs a cultural background in which it could immediately be understood by the audience. Furthermore, I would insist on the fact that Konow[66] himself did not completely rule out the possibility that "Kashmirian" could refer to an old North Western Prakrit. For these reasons, the relations between the two terms must be further investigated; in fact, also in the case that both terms were equally addressed to Sanskrit, the different denomination might involve a further distinction, perhaps connected with the style, shape, orthography and script of these texts.

Coming back to the inscriptional context, it is not by chance that in Bisutun and in Rabatak, the "Aryan" character was introduced to mark a distinction with the different ones of other ethno-linguistic traditions; in Bisutun with respect to the previously engraved Elamite and Babylonian versions, and in Rabatak to the Greek edict. Again, we have foreign languages previously adopted by royal authorities, which are now re-emit-

---

[61] Scherrer-Schaub 2009, 160.
[62] Nattier 1990, 210–211.
[63] Konow 1939, 28–31.
[64] *Ibidem*, 30–31.
[65] Nattier 1990, 219, note 41.
[66] Konow 1939, 30.

ted in the very language of the king, through a *medium* whose "Aryanity" is underlined. The choice of this term does not answer just the need of a profane technical designation, but enters and emphasises the innermost essence of this speech, its obvious pretension to obtain a superior status. Furthermore, if the reconstruction *dipi[ciçam]* is the correct one for Bisutun § 70, we cannot avoid observing that *ciça-*, although in a different context, occurs again with *ariya-*. In spite of the fact that we can postulate two distinguished stems, a ^1ciça- and a ^2ciça-, a solution in which I do not believe,[67] the use of *ariyā* is in any case ideological, and not just technical or even formal. When the king declared (DNa 13–15; DSe 12–14; Dse 12–14; XPh 12–13) to be "Aryan, of Aryan stock, Persian and Achaemenid" (*Haxāmanišiya pārsa pārsahyā puça ariya ariya ciça*), his reference to an *ariyā* document (emitted by himself) would necessarily imply[68] that the main (i.e. "his own") language of his edicts was doubtless also "Achaemenid, Persian, (performed by an authority) of Persian stock, Aryan and of Aryan stock." Furthermore, I cannot avoid another observation: in the Elamite text of DB IV, chapters 62 and 63,[69] A^{h}uramazdā is presented as "the God of the Aryans." This suggests that from the external, i.e. Elamite, point of view the highest god of the Persians was an "Aryan" divinity, one for all the peoples belonging to the same stock, and not that specifically of only one *ethnos*, the Persian one!

The formal similarity between Darius' and Kaniška's inscriptions also concerns other aspects,[70] such as the insistence on the fact that all the events narrated in the texts were realised in the space of a single year. This evidence can support the theory, advanced by Skjærvø[71] and Huyse,[72] that we have to do with the enduring presence of an ancestral oral tradition. Therefore, in the adoption of these ethnic terms (O.P. *ariya-*, Bact. αριαο) in a linguistic framework, I prefer to see a ritual/ceremonial "qualification" (of course, "politically" determined)[73] of the text and of its language transcending our strictly linguistic considerations. In fact, this denomination tried to further promote a certain textual written document on a higher sort of liturgical, performative and authoritative dimension. It is also to be considered that these expressions are used (in Iran) for texts *specifically* composed in order to be written, and not for documents composed orally (but later committed to writing or suitable to be preserved by means of written recordings), as whether the modality required an additional qualification, probably because this was an innovation with respect to a basically quasi-exclusively oral tradition.

I would again insist that an "Aryan" text was therefore not just a profane document in Old Persian or in Bactrian, but represented a consecrated (written) edict, a higher speech, a legal and official word, in spite of the fact that it was transmitted in an uncommon way,

---

[67] See Panaino 2009.

[68] Cf. Baghbidi 2009.

[69] Weissbach 1911, 65–66; Lecoq 1997, 210.

[70] See again Sims-Williams/Cribb 1995/1996, 83.

[71] Skjærvø 1985.

[72] Huyse 1990, 183, note 31.

[73] It is difficult to establish whether the O.P. inscription of Bisutun played an indirect influence on the Bactrian one by means of the intermediation of an Aramaic version or of oral echoes. See Sims-Williams/ Cribb 1995/96, 83 with bibliography. But if the prestige of the O.P. tradition was still so strong, we should consider the possibility that the adoption of the same terminology had an ideological meaning, and not simply a neutral description of the name of the language.

valid for the whole ethno-religious and ethno-linguistic community of the Aryans, which every leading *ethnos* aimed to represent at the highest level. For this reason, it is fitting to consider again that the Indian-speakers (i.e. Sanskrit-praying, but probably every day speaking other Prakrit- and Middle-Indian languages) were "Aryan" too, and that they probably could still use *āryā-* in order to qualify their own *vāk-* together with "Indian."

In conclusion, coming back to the small notice preserved by Strabo, it remains a very useful witness of a very intricate situation, which cannot be uncritically analysed just as the negation of the linguistic richness of Ancient Iranian *ethne* in the last years of the Achaemenian Empire. Strabo's ultimate statement probably refers to various forms of *homoglossia* and *homographia* adopted among the various communicative strategies of the Persian Empire and that enabled a number of higher officers belonging to a few of different Aryan *ethne* to be sufficiently conversant with an Aryan *koiné*, based on the court language in Old Persian (plus Median elements and other socio-linguistic varieties). For this reason, serious consideration is due to the possibility that the alleged *homoglossia* was adopted to describe the actual possibility of intercommunicating with a sort of *lingua franca*, favoured also by the authority of the "Aryan" self-promoting (and partly re-invented) tradition, adopted in order to write the royal text of the Bisutun inscription, in the light of the fact that mutual understanding could be obtained only by means of a basic instruction and a reasonable training (at least derived by practice and not necessarily by school). A new Empire needed a linguistic solidarity, although in conditions of multilingualism and multi-ethnicity, a situation confirmed, as previously noted, by the Akkadian Achaemenid inscriptions. The king did not insist on the "Persian" statute of his documents, but seems to declare that his script and language were in conformity with the Aryan (alleged) prestige, in a sort of performative *superbia* that had to implicitly promote (Old) Persian in the name of all the Iranian submitted *ethne* and without offending their traditions. It is not by chance that in the same chapter of Bisutun Darius also declared that after the sealed and authorised transcription of his edict, the document was placed on clay tablets and parchment and then was sent everywhere into the various countries. The active role of the *kāra-*, which in fact *hamātaxšatā*, i.e. "strove"[74] to follow the edict and its contents, also means that linguistic cooperation was expected.

This evidence, perhaps, can open a new path for further investigations. In fact, we must consider that in the case of Bisutun § 70, it has been normally assumed[75] that *arya-* should be strictly explained in the ethno-cultural borders of the Old Persian text, and that the Elamite version was just a translation. This is an evident solution, probably obvious enough to result in misleading, if uncritically considered as the unique key of interpretation. On the contrary, if we assume that with the term *arya-* a multilingual chancellery wished, on the one hand, to promote the ideological tradition of the Aryan heritage, but also, on the other hand, to produce a different synthesis, in which this kind of "Aryanity" was thought in order to fit in both versions, we could find a different scenario: thus, *arya-* did not simply represent a restricted reference to the mother tongue of the Achaemenians – a minimalist and minimising solution – but the superb perfection of the royal

---

[74] See Rossi 2003, 346–349; Rossi in print; Schmitt 2014, 253–254.
[75] With few exceptions, see Rossi 2000.

message, indifferently from the adopted language. In this sense, the word of the king, in Old Persian, Elamite, and Akkadian and Aramaic as well, could become, according to need, "Aryan," because the asseveration's power went by the king himself and its legitimacy. Thus, the reference to the "Aryan" dimension would have been transformed into a pervasive ideological message, connected with the prestige of the leading authority, and not simply and intrinsically with the linguistic *medium*. In other terms, the Elamite text could also have deserved to be defined as an "Aryan" edict, because what had now assumed an essential importance was the meaning, its authority and compelling force.[76] This is just a working hypothesis concerning a potential consequence of the political impact produced by the para- and meta-linguistic use of *ariya-*, but I hope that it could stimulate positive reactions.

With regard to the supposed *homoglossia*, we must conclude that the image of linguistic semi-unity of the Iranian *ethne*, or only of the North-Eastern Iranian ones, seems to be just a dream, and, as far as we know of the linguistic history of these peoples, not only a conclusion insufficiently grounded, but a highly improbable linguistic mirage. A "permafrosted" Irano-Aryan still spoken by all the Iranians as a sort of "Esperanto" *ante litteram* has no historical basis, as the idea that *arya-* was the name of a still preserved "common language," if this expression should be interpreted as a surviving unifying archaic jargon of all the Iranians (and not a practical Western Iranian *koiné*, imposed by the Old Persian authorities as a comfortable *medium*). Therefore, the "Aryan" linguistic identity assumed other, fully historical, implications, although it was based on a tradition, partly original and derived by an ancestral cultural heritage, partly invented, especially in its socio-linguistic and socio-political implications, as normally happens when the power and its legitimacy are strongly involved.

---

[76] This interpretation presupposes a strong impulse towards a universalistic political and religious vision, which we can postulate during the Achaemenid period. The fact that in the Sasanian Empire a titulature in which *ērān* and *anērān* were not only mentioned, but, probably, also opposed each other, seems to counter what has been stated here, in particular if we consider that a certain continuity should be postulated in the use of formulary expressions of ancestral origin. This difficulty can be bypassed considering that the term *ērān* had stronger confessional (and not simply "religious") implications in Sasanian Persia than *ariya-* in the Achaemenid period, in which the Mazdaean identity of the king was not so strongly emphasised in close relation with his "Aryan" status. We do not know of religious persecutions in the earlier periods, but just of political actions of punishment; the same "Daiva-inscription" reflects a political repression of (still) unclear cults and traditions, but we have no arguments to suggest that other religions were persecuted under the Achaemenids just because other non-Aryan peoples were not following a Mazdaean tradition. The status of the Persepolis tablets, on the contrary, shows a situation of religious tolerance, respect and cooperation, which would have been impossible in the Sasanian era. This compels us to suspect that the actions against the daiva-worshipers were perhaps directed against a tradition closer (but different) with respect to that of the royal power. Then, the Sasanian scenario was completely different, so that in this period we cannot postulate the same force for the meaning of the words *ērān* and *anērān*, although a certain heritage exerted an inevitable influence.

BIBLIOGRAPHY

Auberger, J. (2001), *Historiens d'Alexandre*, Paris.

Aujac, G. (2001), *Eratosthène de Cyrène, le pionnier de la géographie. Sa mesure de la circonférence terrestre*, Paris.

Baghbidi, H.R. (2009), Darius and the Bisotun Inscription: A New Interpretation of the Last Paragraph of Colum IV, *Journal of Persianate Studies* 2: 44–61.

Bahari, Kh. (2001), The Oldest Old Persian Text, *Iran & the Caucasus* 5: 209–212.

Bailey, H.S. (1937), Ttaugura, *BSOS* 8: 883–921.

Bailey, H.S. (1967), *Prolexis to the Book of Zambasta*, (Indo-Scythian Studies being Khotanese Texts, vol. VI), Cambridge.

Berger, H. (1880), *Die geographischen Fragmente des Eratosthenes neu gesammelt, geordnet und beschprochen*, Leipzig.

Bernhardy, G. (1822), *Eratosthenica*, Berolini.

Berthelot, M. (1893), *La Chimie au moyen*, tome III: *L'alchimie arabe*, Paris.

Bianchetti, S. (2010), Eratostene autore di Historiai nel lemma della Suda, in: G. Vanotti (a cura di), *Il Lessico Suda e gli storici greci in frammenti. Atti Incontro Internaz. Vercelli*, Roma: 329–343.

Bianchetti, S. (2012), I Greci e il "mare esterno": dalle esplorazioni delle aree estreme alla rappresenta-zione "scientifica" dell'ecumene, in: J. Santos Yanguas, B. Díaz Ariño (a cura di), *Los Griegos y el mar (Vitoria-Gasteiz 12–13/11/07)*, (Revisiones de Historia Antigua VI), Vitoria-Gasteiz: 155–171.

Biffi, N. (2005), *L'estremo Oriente di Strabone. Libro XV della Geografia. Introduzione, traduzione e commento*, Bari.

Bladel, K. van (2009), *The Arabic Hermes. From Pagan Sage to Prophet of Science*, (Oxford Studies in Ancient Documents), Oxford.

Briant, P. (1996), *Histoire de l'Empire perse*, Paris.

CAD (1973), *Chicago Assyrian Dictionary*, vol. 9, Chicago, Illinois–Glückstadt.

Chul-Hyun, B. (2003), Literary Stemma of King Darius's (522–486 B.C.E.) Bisitun Inscription: Evi-dence of the Persian Empire's Multilingualism, *Eoneohag* 36: 3–32.

Degener, A. (1989), *Khotanische Suffixe*, (Alt- und neu-indische Studien 39), Stuttgart.

Degener, A. (1990), Indisches Lehngut im Khotanischen, in: W. Diem, A. Falaturi (Hrsgg.), *XXIV. deut-scher Orientalistentag, vom 26. bis 30. September 1988 in Köln: ausgewählte Vorträge*, Stuttgart: 381–390.

D'jakonov, I.M. (1970), The Origin of the 'Old Persian' Writing System and the Ancient Oriental Epi-graphic and Annalistic Traditions, in: M. Boyce, I. Gershevitch (eds.), *W.B. Henning Memorial Volume*, London: 98–124.

Eggermont, P.H.L. (1975), *Alexander's Campaigns in Sind and Baluchistan and the Siege of the Brah-min Town of Harmatelia*, (Orientalia Lovaniensia Analecta 3), Leuven.

Emmerick, R.E. (1968), *The Book of Zambasta: A Khotanese Poem on Buddhism*, (London Oriental Series 21), London.

Emmerick, R.E. (1983), Buddhism among Iranian Peoples, in: E. Yarshater (ed.), *The Cambridge Hi-story of Iran*, vol. 3, part 2: *The Seleucid, Parthian and Sasanian Periods*, Cambridge (reprinted in 2008): 649–964.

Gershevitch, I. (1979), The Alloglottography of Old Persian, *TPhS*: 114–190.

Gershevitch, I. (1982), Diakonoff on Writing, with an Appendix by Darius, in: *Societies and Languages of the Ancient Near East. Studies in Honour of I.M. Diakonoff*, London: 99–109.

Geus, Kl. (2002), *Eratosthenes von Kyrene Studien zur hellenistischen Kultur- und Wissenschaftsge-schichte*, (Münchener Beiträge zur Papyrusforschung und antiken Rechtsgeschichte 92), München.

Geus, Kl. (2007), Die Geographika des Eratosthenes von Kyrene: Altes und Neues in Terminologie und Methode, in: M. Rathmann (Hrsg.), *Wahrnehmung und Erfassung geographischer Räume der Antike*, Mainz: 111–122.

Gnoli, Gh. (1966a), Airyō.šayana, *RSO* 41: 67–75.

Gnoli, Gh. (1966b), Ἀριανή: Postilla ad *Airyō.šayana*, *RSO* 41: 329–334.

Gnoli, Gh. (1967), *Ricerche Storiche sul Sīstān antico*, (IsMEO Reports and Memoirs 10), Roma.

Gnoli, Gh. (1980), *Zoroaster's Time and Homeland. A Study on the Origins of Mazdeism and Related Problems*, Naples.

Gnoli, Gh. (1983), Le dieu des Arya, *Studia Iranica* 12: 7–22.

Gnoli, Gh. (1985), *De Zoroastre à Mani. Quatre leçons au Collège de France*, Paris.

Gnoli, Gh. (1987), Βασιλεὺς βασιλέων Ἀριανῶν, in: Gh. Gnoli, L. Lanciotti (edenda curaverunt), *Orientalia Josephi Tucci memoriae dicata*, vol. 2, (Serie Orientale Roma 57), Roma: 509–532.

Gnoli, Gh. (1989), *The Idea of Iran. An Essay on its Origin*, (Serie Orientale Roma 62), Roma.

Grillot-Susini, F., Herrenschmidt, Cl., Malbran-Labat, F. (1993), La version élamite de la trilingue de Behistun: une nouvelle lecture, *JA* 281: 19–59.

Harmatta, J. (1966), The Bisitun Inscription and the Introduction of the Old Persian Cuneiform Script, *Acta Antiqua Academiae Scientiarum Hungaricae* 14: 255–283.

Henkelman, W.F.M. (2011), Cyrus the Persian and Darius the Elamite, a Case of Mistaken Identity: The Persian Dynasty of the Teispids Revisited, in: R. Rollinger, B. Truschnegg, R. Bichler (Hrsgg.), *Herodot und das Persische Weltreich / Herodotus and the Persian Empire*, Wiesbaden: 1–57.

Henning, W.B. (1960), The Bactrian Inscription, *BSOAS* 23: 47–55 [= Henning 1977, II: 545–553].

Henning, W.B. (1977), *Selected Papers*, vol. II, Téhéran–Liège.

Herrenschmidt, Cl. (1989), Le paragraphe 70 de l'inscription de Bisotun, in: C.-H. de Fouchécour, Ph. Gignoux (éds), *Études irano-aryennes offertes à Gilbert Lazard*, Paris: 193–208.

Hinz, W. (1942), Zur Behistun-Inschrift des Dareios, *ZDMG* 96: 326–349.

Hinz, W. (1952), Die Einführung der altpersischen Schrift. Zum Absatz 70 der Behistun-Inschrift, *ZDMG* 102: 28–38.

Hinz, W. (1968), Die Entstehung der altpersischen Keilschrift, *AMI* NF 1: 95–98.

Huyse, Ph. (1990), Noch einmal zu Parallelen zwischen Achaimeniden- und Sāsānideninschriften, *AMI* NF 23: 177–183.

Huyse, Ph. (1999), Some Further Thoughts on the Bisitun Monument and the Genesis of the Old Persian Cuneiform Script, *BAI* 13: 45–65.

Junge, [P.]J. (1944), *Dareios I. König der Perser*, Leipzig.

Keith, A.B (1909), *The Aitareya-Āraṇyaka Edited from the Mss. in the Indian Office and the Library of the Royal Asiatic Society with Introduction, Translation, Notes, Indexes and an Appendix Containing the Portion Hitherto Unpublished of the Sankhayana Āraṇyaka*, Oxford.

Kellens, J. (2005), Les *Airiia*- ne sont plus des Āryas: ce sont déjà des Iraniens, in: G. Fussman, J. Kellens, H.-P. Francfort, X. Tremblay (éd.), *Āryas, Aryens et Iraniens en Asie Centrale*, Paris: 233–252.

Konow, S. (1939), The late Professor Leumann's Edition of a New Saka Text, II, *Norsk Tidsskrift for Sprogvidenskap* 11: 5–84.

Kuiper, F.B.J. (1955), Rigvedic Loan-words, in: O. Spies (Hrsg.), *Studia Indologica. Festschrift für Willibald Kirfel zur Vollendung seines 70. Lebensjahres*, Bonn: 137–185.

Kuiper, F.B.J. (1991), *Aryans in the R̥gveda*, Amsterdam–Atlanta.

Lazard, G. (1976), Notes de vieux-perse, *BSL* 71: 175–192.

Lecoq, P. (1974a), La langue des inscriptions achéménides, in: *Commémoration Cyrus. Hommage Universel à l'Iran*, vol. 2 (Acta Iranica 2), Téhéran–Liège: 55–62.

Lecoq, P. (1974b), Le problème de l'ecriture cunéiforme vieux-perse, in: *Commémoration Cyrus. Hommage Universel à l'Iran*, vol. 3 (Acta Iranica 3), Téhéran–Liège: 25–107.

Lecoq, P. (1997), *Les inscriptions de la Perse achéménide. Traduit du vieux-perse, de l'élamite, du babylonien et de l'araméen, présenté et annoté*, Paris.

Leumann, M. (1933/1936), *Das nordarische (sakische) Lehrgedicht des Buddhismus*, Text und Übersetzung von Ernst Leumann. Aus dem Nachlaß herausgegeben von Manu Leumann, (Abhandlungen für die Kunde des Morgenlandes 20), Leipzig (reprint, Nendel 1966).

Mann, R.D. (2011), *The Rise of Mahāsena. The Transformation of Skanda-Kārttikeya in North India from the Kuṣāṇa to Gupta Empires*, Leiden.

Marcotte, D. (2005), Aux quatre coins du monde. La Terre vue comme un arpent, in: D. Conso, A. Gonzales, J.Y. Guillaumin (éd.), *Les vocabulaires techniques des arpenteurs romains*, Besançon: 149–155.

Nattier, J. (1990), Church language and vernacular language in Central Asian Buddhism, *Numen* 37: 195–219.

Panaino, A. (1996), The Year of the Maga Brāhmaṇas, in: *Convegno internazionale sul tema: La Persia e l'Asia Centrale. Da Alessandro al X secolo, 9–12 Novembre 1994*, (Atti dei Convegni Lincei 127), Roma: 569–587.

Panaino, A. (2007), Chronologia Avestica, in: A. Panaino, V. Sadovski (Hrsgg.), *Disputationes Iranologicae Vindobonenses I*, Wien: 7–33.

Panaino, A. (2009), Avestan *daxšta-* and *čiθra-*. I: *The Semantic Field: Female Germen and Menstruation*, in: E. Pirart, X. Tremblay (éd.), *Zarathushtra entre l'Inde et l'Iran: études indo-iraniennes et indo-européennes offertes à Jean Kellens à l'occasion de son 65e anniversaire*, Wiesbaden: 197–220.

Radt, S.L. (2005), *Strabons Geographika*, Band 4, Buch XIV–XVI: *Text und Übersetzung*, Göttingen.

Roller, D.W. (2010), *Eratosthenes' Geography. Fragments collected and translated, with Commentary and Additional Material*, Princeton, New Jersey.

Rossi, A.V. (1981), La varietà linguistica nell'Iran achemenide, *AIΩN – Sezione Linguistica* 3: 141–196.

Rossi, A.V. (1984), Glottonimia ed etnonimia nell'Iran achemenide, *AIΩN – Sezione Linguistica* 6: 39–65.

Rossi, A.V. (1985), La competenza multipla nei testi arcaici: le iscrizioni di Bisotun, *AIΩN – Sezione Linguistica* 7: 191–210.

Rossi, A.V. (2000), L'iscrizione originaria di Bisotun: DB elam. A + L, in: S. Graziani (a cura di con la collaborazione di M.C. Casaburi – G. Lacerenza), *Studi sul Vicino Oriente Antico dedicati alla memoria di Luigi Cagni*, vol. 4, Napoli: 2065–2107.

Rossi, A.V. (2003), Echoes of religious lexicon in the Achaemenid inscriptions?, in: C.G. Cereti, M. Maggi, E. Provasi (eds.), *Religious themes and texts of pre-Islamic Iran and Central Asia. Studies in honour of Professor Gherardo Gnoli on the occasion of his 65th Birthday on 6th December 2002*, (Beiträge zur Iranistik 24), Wiesbaden: 339–351.

Rossi, A.V. (in print), Once again on DB/AE L and DB/OP iv 89–92, in: G.P. Basello, E. Filippone, A. Panaino, A.V. Rossi, V. Sadovski, R. Schmitt, *Achaimenidica*, Vienna.

Samad, A. (2010), *Emergence of Hinduism in Gandhāra. An Analysis of Material Culture*, Thesis zur Erlangung des Doktorgrades eingereicht am Fachbereich Geschichts- und Kulturwissenschaften der Freien Universität Berlin im August 2010; http://www.diss.fu-berlin.de/diss/receive/FUDISS_thesis_000000036928.

Sander, L. (1989), Remarks on the Formal Brāhmī of Gilgit, Bamiyan and Khotan, in: J. Jettmar (ed.), *Antiquities of Northern Pakistan: Reports and Studies*, 1: *Rock Inscriptions in the Indus Valley*, Mainz: 107–130.

Scherrer-Schaub, C. (2009), Copier, Interpreter, Transformer, Representer, ou Des modes de la diffusion des écritures et de l'écrit dans le bouddhisme indien, in: G. Colas, G. Gerschheimer (éd.), *Écrire et transmettre en Inde classique*, (Études Thématiques 23), Paris: 151–172.

Schmitt, H. H. (1964), *Untersuchungen zur Geschichte Antiochos' des Grossen und seiner Zeit*, Wiesbaden.

Schmitt, R. (1990), *Epigraphisch-exegetische Noten zu Dareios' Bisutun-Inschriften*, Wien.

Schmitt, R. (1991), *The Bisitun Inscriptions of Darius the Great: Old Persian Text*, London.

Schmitt, R. (2009), *Die altpersischen Inschriften der Achaimeniden*, Editio minor mit deutsche Über-setzung, Wiesbaden.

Schmitt, R. (2014), *Wörterbuch der altpersischen Königsinschriften*, Wiesbaden.

Sims-Williams, N. (1981), The Sogdian Sound-system and the Origins of the Uyghur Script, *JA* 269: 347–360.

Sims-Williams, N. (1996a), Eastern Iranian Languages, in: E. Yarshater (ed.), *Encyclopaedia Iranica*, vol. 7/6: 649–652 (Costa Mesa, California).

Sims-Williams, N. (1996b), Nouveaux documents sur l'histoire et la langue de la Bactriane, *CRAI*: 633–654.

Sims-Williams, N. (1998), Further Notes on the Bactrian Inscription of Rabatak, with an Appendix on the Names of Kujula Kadphises and Vima Taktu in Chinese, in: N. Sims-Williams (ed.), *Proceedings of the Third European Conference of Iranian Studies held in Cambridge, 11th to 15th September*, part 1: *Old and Middle Iranian Studies*, (Beiträge zur Iranistik 17), Wiesbaden: 79–92.

Sims-Williams, N. (2008), The Bactrian Inscription of Rabatak: A New Reading, *Bulletin of the Asia Institute* 18: 53–68.

Sims-Williams, N., Cribb, J. (1995–1996), A New Bactrian Inscription of Kanishka the Great, *Silk Road Art and Archaeology* 4: 75–142.

Skjaervø, P.O. (1985), Thematic and Linguistic Parallels in the Achaemenian and Sassanian Inscriptions, in: *Papers in honour of Professor Mary Boyce*, vol. 2, (Acta Iranica 25), Leiden: 593–603.

Tarn, W.W. (1938), *The Greeks in Bactria and India*, Cambridge.

Tuplin, C. (2005), Darius Accession in (the) Media, in: *Writing and Ancient Near Eastern Societies. Papers in honour of Alan R. Millard*, New York–London: 217–144.

Vallat, F. (2011), Darius, l'héritier légitime, et les premières Achéménides, in: J. Álvarez-Mon, M.B. Garrison (èd.), *Elam and Persia*, Winona Lake (Indiana): 263–284.

Voigtlander, E.N. von (1978), *The Babylonian Versions of Achaemenian Inscriptions* (*Corpus inscriptionum Iranicarum*, part 1: *Inscriptions of Ancient Iran*, vol. 2, texts 1), London.

Weissbach, F.H. (1911), *Die Keilinschriften der Achämeniden*, (Vorderasiatische Bibliothek 3), Leipzig.

Witzel, M. (2001), Autochthonous Aryans? The Evidence from Old Indian and Iranian Texts, *Electric Journal of Vedic Studies* (*EJVS*) 7/3: 1–93, http://www.ejvs. laurasianacademy.com/ejvs0703/ejvs0703article.pdf.

Zadok, R. (1981), Review of von Voigtlander 1978, *Bibliotheca Orientalis* 38: 657–665.

Zadok, R. (2003), The Representation of Foreigners in Neo- and Late-Babylonian Legal Documents [Eight through Second Centuries B.C.E.], in: O. Lipschits, J. Blenkinsopp, *Judah and the Judeans in the Neo-Babylonian Period*, Winona Lake, Indiana: 471–589.

ELECTRUM * Vol. 22 (2015): 107–114
doi: 10.4467/20800909EL.15.005.3943
www.ejournals.eu/electrum

KING HUVIŠKA, YIMA, AND THE BIRD: OBSERVATIONS ON A PARADISIACAL STATE[1*]

Touraj Daryaee & Soodabeh Malekzadeh

University of California, Irvine

Abstract: This essay discuses the significance of the unique gold coin of the Kushan king, Huviška. The legend on the coin reads Imšao which recalls the ancient Indo-Iranian mythic figure, Yima/Yama. It is contended that the reason for which Yima/Yama is portrayed on the coin with a bird on his hand is not the idea of Glory and his reign, but rather the paradaisical state according to the Wīdēwdād, where Yima/Yama ruled over the world. It is contended that Huviška aimed at presenting himself in this manner to his subjects who were familiar with the Avestan and mythic Indo-Iranian lore.

Key words: Imšao, Huviška, Kushan, Karšiptar, Yima, Yama.

In 1984 Robert Göbl, in his study of the coinage of the Kushan Empire, published a unique gold coin of king Huviška.[2] In the same year, Frantz Grenet published a major article laying out the importance of this coin for king Huviška's religious ideology.[3] This specific coin depicts a standing male figure wearing a sword around his waist and donning a tiara decorated with a ribbon. The figure also holds a spear in his left hand while a bird is shown sitting on his outstretched right hand. Although the legend on the coin is quite clear and readable, the coin and the study of the iconographic representations on it have proven to be quite challenging. In this article it is argued that the standing figure and the bird depicted on the reverse of the coin represents king Yima, the mythological Iranian ruler. We have also argued that the bird on his hand, unlike most cases, is not a falcon, but a lark or *čakāvak*.

In most of Huvishka's coinage, on the obverse, we have the bust of the king[4] and the legend reads: *Šaonanošao Oohški Košano* "Of the King of Kings, Huviška the Kushan."

---

[1] * We would like to thank F. Grenet and O. Bopearachchi for providing the image of the coin of Iamšo. We would also like to thank M. Shenkar and J. Lerner for their help and suggestions.
[2] Göbl 1984.
[3] Grenet 1984.
[4] For Huviška's coinage, see Rosenfield 1967, 93.

While the obverse of his coins do not pose a great challenge, the reverse of Huviška's coin make it's reading uclear. It is suggested that the reverse of most of Huviška's coins depict a deity, a hypothesis that is strengthened by the legend found next to the figures on the reverse. The legends read the names of Indo-Iranian deity such as: Farr, Mithra, Nana, Veš, or a Hellenistic deity, namely Heracles. In this context it is then assumed that the image of the standing figure under discussion should also be interpreted as a deity.[5]

Regarding the Bactrian legend on the reverse of the coin, one hypothesis is that it reads *Iamšo*, which Grenet believes to be an abbreviated spelling for *Iamo šao "King Yama" similar to the Kafirian form for Yama, given as *Imrā* < *Yama rājā. Humbach disagrees with this hypothesis, and suggests that *Iamšo* is a short form of *Iamšēdo (Old Persian *yama xšhaita, i.e, Jamšīd), harkening back to the Avestan Yima Xšaēta (Yima the Brilliant/Majestic).[6] While both of the above arguments are plausible, the overall reading and the representation of this type of coinage produced for king Huviška is not conclusive.

Fig. 1. Gold coin of Huriška

Two main hypotheses have been suggested for the meaning of the figure and legend on the reverse of this gold coin. On one hand, Grenet suggests that the bird on the hand of Iamšo is the Avestan falcon, *Vārəγna*, which is the corporeal form of the element of Glory, *xvarənah-* and also an avatar of the Avestan deity of offensive victory, *Vərəθraγna*.[7] He states that we should be mindful of *Yašt XIX* of the Avesta where Yima lost his *Farr* or Glory to *Miθra*, *θraētaona*, and *Kərəsāspa*.[8] Grenet's suggestion fits well with his comparison of Kafir *Imra* (Yama rājā), which Fussman had once believed to be the third

---

[5] Shenkar 2015, 166–167.

[6] Humbach 2004, 68–69.

[7] Yasht (14.19) of the Avesta describes the transformation of *Vərəθraγna* as: "Ahura-created Werethraghna came driving to him in the form of a falcon, seizing from below (with his talons), crushing (?) from above (with his beak), who is the fastest of birds, the swiftest of those that fly forth" (Malandra 1983, 84).

[8] In the nineteenth yasht of the Avesta it states that: "Then, when he (?) introduced falsehood to his mind, the Xwarenah, visibly in the form of a bird, went forth from him…" "First, the Xwarenah turned away from regal Yima, the Xwarenah went from Yima son of Wiwahwant in the form of a falcon…" Yt. 19.34, 5 (Malandra 1983, 91).

(beside the Indo-Iranian) view of Yama as a deity.[9] He concludes that as all of the reverse types of Huviška coinage show a deity, then we can conclude that Yima depicted on this specific coin must be a divinity as well.[10]

While Gnoli agrees that the figure portrays a king in an Iranian fashion, he disagrees with what he calls Grenet's "historical-religious inferences." This is because the standing figure is connected to the Iranian element of Glory in its most familiar animal shape that is a falcon which shows that the Kushans were familiar with the Avestan Yašts and its iconography. According to Gnoli, the main issue with Grenet's thesis is that he takes Yima to be the god of the world of the dead to who as a divinity sacrifice was made to prolong life, a role that is distinctly different from that of the Zoroastrian tradition. [11] Gnoli believes that in the Iranian world-view, Yima was never viewed as a divinity.[12] The question that rises here is how important Zoroastrianism was in the Kushan Empire. Here again Grenet and Gnoli have varied stances. While, Grenet believes that their version of Zoroastrianism was superficial, Gnoli very much disagrees and believes that coins could be deceiving for their larger meaning of the religious structure. He suggests that it is the Hellenic influence of the anthropomorphic representation of the deities that created a sort of confusion in the religious belief-system of the Kushans. We not only have Ahura Mazda, whom Gnoli aptly calls the Zoroastrian super-deity, but also other deities such as *Oado* (*Wād*), *Orlagno*, and *Šaornoro* (*Šahrēvar*) one of the Bounteous Immortals (*Aməša Spentas*).[13] For Gnoli the Kushan representation of these deities is closely and clearly related to the Zoroastrian tradition of the Avesta and the *Yašts*.[14] Thus, Yima depicted on Huviška's coin is part of the late mytho-epic tradition of *Yima Xšaēta* encapsulated in the *Shahnameh* and cannot be a god of the underworld, because such a concept did not exist in the Iranian world-view. Gnoli concludes that since Huviška as part of the regal ideology favored various forms of iconographic representation of kingly Glory, it is not the figure of Yima himself that is central to the message conveyed through the coinage, but his possession of *Farr*.[15]

The Kushan Iamšo being the god of the underworld dating back to a pre-Zoroastrian tradition is possible as all the coins of Huviška portray a deity, but the importance of Yima may be more pronounced and for another reason which is in line with imperial ideology. Grenet suggests that Yima was the prototype deity of royalty associated with war.[16] However, there is another solution to the controversial reading of the figure on this coin. The first thing worth mentioning is that Iamšo was not a distant and insignificant figure in the region of Bactria. Whatever the association with Iamšo, we know that it was well-known to the late antique world of Balkh. Evidence such as Bactrian documents[17] and a seal published by Sims-William and Lerner,[18] suggest that the name of Iamšo and

---

[9]   Fussman 1988.
[10] Gnoli 1989, 920.
[11] Gnoli 1989, 920.
[12] Gnoli 1989, 921.
[13] Gnoli 1989, 922.
[14] Gnoli 1989, 922.
[15] Gnoli 1989, 923.
[16] Grenet 2012, 88.
[17] Sims-Williams 2010, 167–172, 323, 504.
[18] Lerner/Sims-Williams 2011, 168.

Yima had been popular in that region. The Avestan and later Persianate lore of Yima together with the coinage of Huviška can also suggest another scenario.

Another interesting piece of evidence can be obtained from the chronology of King Huvishka's reign. Although the dating of Kushan coinage and the chronology of the Kushan Empire is a complicated affair (three hypothesis so far), it may be that Huvishka ruled from 155 to 190 CE.[19] King Huviška produced a large variation of coinage, mainly in gold which can point to the prosperity of the Kushan Empire during his reign. Royal propaganda and legitimation also played a central role in Huviška's royal ideology.[20] He was certainly an ambitious ruler who wanted to outdo his predecessor, Kaniška. This is clear from the number of coins produced during his rule. Based on his royal insignia, Bivar believes that Huviška was not a son, but rather a younger brother of Kaniška.[21] In favor of his legitimacy and sense of importance, Huviška must have wished to surpass the great Kaniška. This aim could have been achieved by minting gold coins with different religious themes in order to appeal to his diverse subjects, the Hindus, the Buddhists, and the Zoroastrians. We believe that what we are seeing on this unique coinage is part of the Iranian lore of Yima that had survived in the region. In fact the image of Yima was very much present in memory of the people of the region from the Avestan era to what Gnoli calls the "mytho-epic period." We should remind ourselves that Yima was the Iranian king *par excellence*, as he ruled over a place and time when a state of perfection existed for humanity. Yašt XIX.33 beautifully mentions this paradisiacal state:

> *yeṅhe xšaϑrāδa*
> *nōiṯ aotəm åṅha nōiṯ garəməm*
> *nōiṯ zauruua åṅha nōiṯ mərəiϑiiuš*
> *nōiṯ araskō daēuuō.dātō*

(Yima) under whose reign,
There was neither cold nor heat,
Neither old age nor death,
Nor the envy created by the *daēvas* (demons/fallen deities).[22]

We think that this paradisical state is the aim of Iamšo coinage of Huviška who was trying to promote, harkening to a time of greatness, ease and lack of any hardship or disease[23] and a golden age under the almost perfect king. The continuation of the story of Yima's paradisiacal or golden age, when Yima ruled is not only well-known in the *Avesta*, but also lived onto the time of the *Shahnameh* of Ferdowsi, composed in Khurasan.[24] This shows that Yima lived not only in the religious memory of the people of this region, but also in the popular oral tradition. It is also worth noting that both the *Avesta* and the

---

[19]   Samad 2011, 84.

[20]   Huviška was succeeded by the last of the great Kushan rulers, Vasudeva, before the Sasanians destroyed their power and established the great Kušānšahs of the Sasanian dynasty (Frye 1984, 261).

[21]   Bivar 2009.

[22]   Humbach 2004, 69.

[23]   However, there is also the probability that the catastrophic outbreak of smallpox in Rome in 166 CE which spread through trade lines to the east, also affected the Kushan Empire (Bivar 1970, 19–21) increasing the need for Huviška to project an image of himself as a ruler that can bring about a plague-less era for his subjects.

[24]   For a comprehensive review of Yima, see Skjærvø 2012.

Shahnameh were composed in approximately the same geographical region as that of the Huvishka rule. This paradisiacal state of course takes place with Yima's building of the underground Vara- or enclosure which he rules over. As Jean Kellens has noted, Yima at the Vara- acts as the pastor of the living and the earth[25] and the artisan of the world.[26] Michael Shenakar has observed that the image of Iamšo on the coin matches most closely with the image of King Huviška.[27] Thus, Yima as the first king of the Iranian world,[28] and his lore as the greatest of kings was a model for our Kushan king.[29] This vita of Yima was probably what king Huviška wished to project as the living example in the Kushan Empire.

In a Middle Persian Zoroastrian text, *Mēnōg ī Xrad*, the *Vara-* is described as:

war ī yimkard pad ērānwēz azēr zamīg ēwēnag ud tōm ī hamāg dām ud dahišn ī ohrmazd ī xwadāy az mardōm ud stōr ud gōspand ud wāyendag har čē wehtar ud (pad) wizēntar ō anōh burd ēstādēd.

The enclosure made by Yima was in the home of the Aryas below the earth, and the genus and species of every creature and creation of Ohrmazd the lord, the best and most choice of men and horses and cattle and birds, each were brought there.[30]

This heavenly realm is "a world of perfection, a world without cares in many ways, a paradise."[31] In fact in the Middle Persian translation of the Avestan *Wīdēwdād* (2.41) it is stated that in Yima's *Vara-* such a life existed: *Awēšān-iz mard nēk pad gyān ziwēnd [kū sad panǰāh sal ziwēnd]* "those humans live the happiest life [they live one hundred and fifty years]."[32] It can be assumed that Huviška meant to highlight the heavenly and blissful characteristics of Yima's paradisiacal realm and to make his subjects view him in the same light. It is clear that in the Kushan realm the Avestan tradition was known and this coin clearly suggests such a tradition connected with Yima.[33] The recent work by Kuzmina, based on Viktor Sarianidi's excavations at Bactrian/Balkh cult centers such as Dashly III and Dzharkutan, may be models of our Avestan Vara-, is also of interest for this paper.[34] Also, Pyankov points to the importance of the mythological memory of Yima and his Vara- for the people of this region up until today.[35]

Another important depiction on the gold coin of Huviška is the image of the bird sitting on Yima's hand. If we accept the figure on this coin as Yima and that those who were exposed to this political propaganda were familiar with the Avestan story and the fate of Yima, then it would be safe to assume that associating the bird on this coin with the idea of Glory, that is *farr* or *xwarənah-* would not have been the best choice. The Iranian element of glory in the form of the falcon actually serves as an ill-omened element for Yima

---

[25] Kellens 1984, 278.
[26] Kellens 1984, 279.
[27] Shenkar 2015, 166.
[28] Shaked 1987, 240.
[29] Piras (forthcoming), 10.
[30] Lincoln 1981, 234.
[31] Lincoln 1981, 234.
[32] Moazami 2014, 66–67.
[33] Shenkar 2015, 167.
[34] Kuzmina 2007, 34.
[35] Pyankov 2002, 43–49.

who lost his Glory because of committing a sin. This part of the story of Yima could not have been a point of pride for Huviška's political aims.

Recent studies on the Indo-Iranian Yama/Yima have been helpful in improving our understanding of Yima in the Indo-Iranian and Kafiri tradition and can be useful in helping us see the bird on this coin in new light.[36] Interestingly, *Vārəγna* or the falcon is not the only bird associated with Yima. Another mythical bird associated with the Vara- and with Yima is the mythical Avestan bird *Karšiptar* which makes its appearance in the *Wīdēwdād*, perhaps codified as late as the Parthian/Kushan era. Karšiptar is supposed to have brought the Zoroastrian religion to the Vara- of Yima. However, in the Middle Persian translation of the Wīdēwdād 2.42 Zarathushtra asks Ohrmazd:

> *kē ō ānōh dēn māzdesnān be burd ō awēšān war mānišān ǰam kard, u-š guft Ohrmazd kū way karšift Spitāmān Zarduxšt [čaxrwāk ī pad axw ī mēnōgān abāz šawēd]*

> Who brought the Mazdayasnian religion to these enclosures that Jam (Yima) made? Ohrmazd answered: "the bird *karšift*, O Spitama Zarathushtra! [that is, čaxrwāk who will return to the spiritual world]."[37]

Here we see that the *Karšiptar*[38] is also called *čaxrwāk*.[39] Redard in her excellent contribution studies the bird in the Iranian, Armenian, and Indic tradition and also provides the Sanskrit cognate *čakravāká* for the Middle Persian name of this bird.[40] In Sanskrit Literature, the lark or čakāvak's songs are viewed as a prayer, encompassing both Iranians views regarding the bird, its heavenly songs and its religious connotation as well.[41] Based on the probable roots of this name, she asserts that *caxrawāk* is a sort of "speaking" *–vāka-* bird.[42] What we can add to this is the Persian cognate for the bird which is čakāvak[43] "lark" and associated with heavenly singing. The čakāvak bird is also a well-known and old part of Persian musical tradition. More interestingly, Manuchehri Damghani,[44] an eleventh century Persian poet, in one of his poems mentions the čakāvak in relation to a treasure called *Ganj-e Gāv*, which is said to have been one of Yima's treasures in his Vara.[45] It is also worth noting that this specific line is part of a greater

---

[36] Azarnouche/Redard 2012.

[37] Moazami 2014, 66–67.

[38] Middle Persian: *Karšift.*

[39] On *čaxrwāk*, see Benveniste 1960, 196.

[40] Redard 2012, 198.

[41] Dave 2005, 108.

[42] Azarnouche/Redard 2012, 199.

[43] The čakavak or lark is a bird widely found in the Persian plateau. Twelve species of larks have been recorded in to be native of Iran and Afghanistan (Hüe/Etchécopar 1970, 465–493). However, due to the modern construction of roads this bird is witnessed less than before, as it prefers to run through dirt fields often found across Iran and Afghanistan. See also A'lam 1990, 649–650.

[44] *vaǧt e sahargah čakav xoš bezanad dar takāv / sā'ataki Ganj-e Gāv, sā'ataki Ganj-e Bād.* The line of poetry reads as: "The skill of the poet is in using four central words that create a double entendre." The poem creates a simultaneous atmosphere of sound and space, the first verse translates as "At the break of dawn the lark starts its sweet music / At the break of dawn the lark dashes toward the creek" while the second verse points to two musical genres two of the greatest mythological treasures, the first belonging to Yima and the second to Khusro Parviz (Manuchehri Damghani 1977, 19, v. 281).

[45] It is interesting to note that in the oral tradition, Yima's wealth that is the *Ganj-e Gav* moves in a full circle, from the first beneficent king Yima to Bahram Gur, who is also renowned for the charity and love he bestowed upon his subjects which won great fame (*Shahnameh* VII, 457–463).

poem, which Manuchehri composed in lieu of the Persian New Year, *Nowruz,* a celebration that is also attributed to Yima. In the *Shahnameh* it is stated that Yima proclaimed the first day of Spring as the Persian New Year, which symbolized the end of winter and the beginning of a "new era."[46] In the *Shahnameh* this bird is also portrayed in the context of daybreak and a symbolic messenger whose arrival and singing is followed by the ultimate victory of the Iranian army over their arch enemy Afrasiyab.[47] Moreover, this bird, unlike most birds that have nests on branches and high places, builds its nest in a hollow in the ground, similar to Yima's Vara- which is was an enclosure underground.

If we follow this tradition and take into account that the Kushana king Huviška was not only familiar with the lore of the *Avesta*, but with the Iranian epic tradition (oral or otherwise), we can provide another suggestion for the meaning of this unique Iamšo and the bird coinage. It can be suggested that the image on the reverse of Huviška's coinage represents the mythical king Yima or Jamšīd as the lord of the Vara- with the bird čakāvak. That story is reminiscent of the idea that King Yima/Jamšīd was the ultimate culture-hero and king of the Iranian world, where for 250 year he taught people all that was needed to know and then ruled over a paradisiacal world for another 250 years. This is the paradise now lost, but was the greatest time for the Iranian speaking peoples, and it was remembered in the *Wīdēwdād*. As time passed the tradition became embellished with more details, in the Pahlavi translations of the *Wīdēwdād*, the Middle Persian *Xwadāy-namg* of the Sasanian period and finally in the *Shahnameh*.

BIBLIOGRAPHY

Primary Sources

Ferdowsi, A. (1987), *The Shahnameh*, ed. D. Khaleghi-Motlagh, 8 vols., (Bibliotheca Persica), New York.
Manuchehri Damghani (1977), *Divan*, ed. M. Dabirsiaq, 4th ed., Tehran.

Secondary Literature

A'lam, H. (1990), *s.v.* Čakāvak, in: *Encyclopedia Iranica*, vol. IV, fasc. 6: 649–650.
Azarnouche, S., Redard, C. (eds.) (2012), *Variations on the Indo-Iranian Myth of Yama/Yima*, Paris.
Benveniste, E. (1960), Le nom de l'"oiseau" en iranien, *Paideuma* 7: 193–199.
Bivar, A.D.H. (1970), Hāritī and the Chronology of the Kusanas, *BSOAS* 33: 10–21.
Bivar, A.D.H. (2009), Kushan Dynasty, in: *Encyclopaedia Iranica*, Online Edition.
Dave, K.N. (2005), *Birds in Sanskrit Literature, with 107 Bird Illustrations*, New Delhi.
Frye, R.N. (1984), *The History of Ancient Iran*, München.
Fussman, G. (1988), Kafiristan/Nouristan: Avatars de la définition d'une éthnie, in: J.-P. Digard (ed.), *Le fait ethnique en Iran et Afghanistan*, Paris: 55–64.

---

[46] *Shahnameh* I.
[47] *Čo xoršīd bar zad sar az borj e gāv / ze hāmun bar āmad xoruš e čakāv* (*Shahnameh* I, 44–52).

Gnoli, G. (1989), On Kushan and Avestan Yima, in: L. de Meyer, E. Haerinck (eds.), *Archaeologica Iranica et Orientalia. Miscellanea in Honorem Louis Vandem Berghe*, Gent: 919–927.

Göbl, R. (1984), *System und Chronologie der Münzprägung des Kušānreiches*, Wien.

Grenet, F. (1984), Notes sur le pantheon iranien des Kouchans, *Studia Iranica* 13: 253–262.

Grenet, F. (2012), Yima en Bactriane et en Sogdiane: nouveaux documents, in: S. Azarnouche, C. Redard (eds.), *Yama / Yima: variations indo-iraniennes sur la geste mythique*, Paris: 83–94.

Hüe, F., Etchécopar, R.D. (1970), *Les Oiseaux du Proche et du Moyen Orient: de la Méditerranée aux contreforts de l'Himalaya*, Paris.

Humbach, H. (2004), *Yima / Jamšēd*, in: C.G. Cereti *et al.* (eds.), *Varia Iranica*, Roma: 45–58.

Kellens, J. (1984): Yima, magicien entre les dieux et les homes, in: *Orientalia J. Duchesne-Guillemin emerito oblata*, (Acta Iranica 24), Leiden: 267–281.

Kuzmina, E. (2007), *The Origin of Indo-Iranians*, Leiden–Boston.

Lerner, J., Sims-Williams, N. (2011), *Seals, Sealings and Tokens from Bactria to Gandhara (4th to 8th Century CE)*, Wien.

Lincoln, B. (1981), The Lord of the Dead, *History of Religions* 20: 224–241.

Malandra, W.W. (1983), *An Introduction to Ancient Iranian Religion: Readings from the Avesta and Achaemenid Inscriptions*, Minnesota.

Moazami, M. (2014), *Wrestling with the Demons of the Pahlavi Widēwdād: Transcription, Translation, and Commentary*, Leiden–Boston.

Piras, A. (forthcoming), Xvarənah- and the Garlands. Notes about the Avesta and Manichaean Yima, in: A. Rossi (ed.), *G. Gnoli Memorial Volume*, Roma.

Pyankov, I.V. (2002), Arkaim and the Indo-Iranian Var, in: K. Jones-Bley, D.G. Zdanovich (eds.), *Complex Societies Of Central Eurasia from the 3rd to the 1st Millennium BC: Regional Specifics in Light of Global Model*, Washington, D.C.: 43–52.

Rosenfield, J.M. (1967), *The Dynastic Arts of the Kushans*, Los Angeles–Berkeley.

Samad, R.U. (2011), *The Grandeur of Gandhara: The Ancient Buddhist Civilization of the Swat, Peshawar, Kabul and Indus Valleys*, New York.

Shaked, Sh. (1987), First Man, First King: Notes on Semitic-Iranian Syncretism and Iranian Mythological Transformations, in: S. Shaked, D. Shulman, G.G. Stroumsa (eds.), *Gilgul: Essays on Transformation, Revolution and Permanence in the History of Religions Dedicated to R.J.Z. Werblowsky*, Leiden–Boston: 238–256.

Shenkar, M. (2015), *Intangible Spirits and Graven Images: The Iconography of Deities in the Pre--Islamic Iranian World*, Leiden–Boston.

Sims-Williams, N. (2010), *Bactrian Personal Names*, Wien.

Skjærvø, P.O. (2012), Jamšid. Myth of Jamšid, in: *Encyclopaedia Iranica*, Online Edition.

ELECTRUM * Vol. 22 (2015): 115–142
doi: 10.4467/20800909EL.15.006.3944
www.ejournals.eu/electrum

STOREHOUSES AND STORAGE PRACTICES IN OLD NISA (TURKMENISTAN)

Carlo Lippolis & Niccolò Manassero

Università di Torino, Centro Ricerche Archeologiche e Scavi di Torino per il Medio Oriente e l'Asia

Abstract: The article analyses the body of evidence related to the storage and administration of food in Parthian Nisa, according to the results of the recent excavations of the Italian Archaeological Expedition in Turkmenistan. A new corpus of clay sealings, *khums* (big jars) and ostraka came to light in the so-called SW Building, which, together with the previously known findings from the other buildings of Nisa, gave way to some speculations about the storage and administration practice within the Arsacid citadel. The spatial distribution of the khums gives information on the function of each building and their single rooms; the texts on the ostraka inform us on the nature and quantities of the food stored in the khums; the various ways the sealings were impressed on clay suggest some ideas on the number and roles of the officers involved in the administration of the storehouses, and perhaps on the nature of the goods stored as well. In general, the findings from the latest excavations provide fundamental information on the economic life of the citadel and of the Parthian society as well. Despite the lack of scholarly debate on such issues as related to the Parthian and Central Asian world, the authors try to interpret the evidence from the Nisa excavations, and give a preliminary reading of the data from the new and old excavations in the Arsacid citadel.

Key words: Parthian archaeology, Parthian economical history, Old Nisa, storage and administration practice, sealings.

1. Storehouses at Nisa (C. Lippolis)

Despite the rich archaeological evidence supporting the existence of storehouses, systematic record-keeping and storage practices in Old Nisa (Turkmenistan), to this day there has been no study on the architecture of Nisa's functional building complexes, nor on the storage and distribution practices employed within them.[1] The attention of schol-

---

[1] Diakonoff/Livshits 1976–2001: on more than one occasion, the explanatory notes accompanying the transcriptions refer the reader to a yet-to-be-published "commentary."

ars has always been monopolised by the ceremonial buildings, even though the presence of extensive storehouses and storage areas is, in fact, a meaningful feature of the site.

Andrei N. Bader's precious, albeit preliminary analysis[2] of the historical data contained in Nisa's economic records (ostraka) gives us an idea of the useful information, and seeds of future research, that might be drawn from a deeper philological and historical investigation of these inscriptions in the light of existing and new archaeological data. This paper offers an overview on storage practices in Old Nisa, taking into consideration both the already published material and the new data that has recently come to light in Old Nisa.

The latest Italian archaeological investigations have effectively demonstrated the great significance of the presence at Nisa of large built areas (and possibly "open" areas, as well – see below) used for storing food, both liquids and solids. Excavations all around the central monumental complex (i.e. the Red Building, Tower Building, Round Hall and Square Hall) have identified extensive areas that were used for storing incoming and outgoing foodstuffs. Within this context, it is not our intention to give careful consideration to every single building-phase and destination of the various buildings in Old Nisa. Rather, we will only consider their topographic position and original purpose.

Excavations conducted by the JuTAKE in the northern part of the citadel uncovered part of the so-called *khumkhana*.[3] These structures lie immediately to the east of the Square House,[4] which in a late phase was turned into a storehouse, albeit for furnishings and precious items rather than food products.[5] From this area come the majority of the Nisean ostraka, real "labels" describing the contents of the large jars that were stored there.

The area between the fortification walls and the Square House has never been systematically investigated. The ground surface is here quite flat and apparently free from buildings, a fact that may have contributed to the relative lack of attention given to it by archaeologists. In addition, the entire sector was used as a burial site in the (late?) Islamic period, and the numerous pit graves, which can often be identified on the ground only by the presence of small piles of stones, cut the older Arsacid layers. At the end of the 1950s, the Russian archaeologists opened two small trenches close to the northern section of the fortifications and brought to light large walls (built in mud bricks of the typical "Parthian" size: 41–42 × 41–42 × 12 cm). The considerable thickness of these walls suggests the presence of a building of monumental scale. In 2014, the Italian team opened a further test trench (sector CQ1: around 7.70 m × 6.30 m: Fig. 1) close to the north-eastern corner of the Square House, revealing a large wall in bricks and pakhsa (i.e. beaten clay; the total thickness is around 2 metres) along which hollows for ten or so large storage jars were arranged.[6] We cannot rule out the possibility that these structures

---

[2] Bader 1996.

[3] Or, rather, "khum-buildings," in which the term "khum" – here, and in general in the Russian academic literature relating to Nisa and Central Asia – refers to large storage jars (see below).

[4] Pilipko 2001, 163–171.

[5] For a functional reading of the Square House over the course of its various phases of construction, see Invernizzi 2000.

[6] This trench, too, revealed the presence of numerous Islamic graves, quite feasibly from a late period. In the four graves recently excavated, the body was facing south/south-west (i.e. towards the Ka'aba in Mecca). Unfortunately, the complete absence of grave goods makes a precise dating difficult.

Fig. 1. Old Nisa, general map with excavation areas (elaborated by C. Bonfanti)

originally formed part of the same complex of storehouses, to the east of the Square House (and so-called *severnoe vinohranilišče*) that was partially excavated by the Soviets in the 1950s and '60s. Its "U" shape, the product of subsequent building phases, could in fact represent the southern half of a larger rectangular complex with rooms arranged around an open-air court.[7]

Another area characterised by the presence of numerous khums is that of the "North-East Building" (Fig. 1), so called for its location in relation to the central complex. This area, which has only been partially surveyed, is distinguished by wide courtyards, with buildings along the north/north-east side that displayed large storage jars. These structures were most likely added in a subsequent phase of building.[8]

A third area in which numerous hollows/housings and remains of storage jars have been recorded lies along the south-eastern inner side of the fortification walls, where the Italian team opened test trenches in 2007. Immediately next to the walls (Area A, Figs. 1 & 2), a large number of khum-housings were arranged rather haphazardly into a layer of earth, gravel and blocks of virgin soil. The original purpose of this area remains uncertain, particularly given the apparent absence of walls: only very scant remains of structures in pakhsa have been uncovered in the south-western corner of the excavation. Nevertheless, the large number of khums registered for this area, and its distinctive earthworks (maybe an artificial levelling) seem to suggest a particular function, quite likely storage. Moreover, it cannot be ruled out that there once existed light, perishable structures, of which no traces remain.[9]

During the Italian team's recent excavations (2007–2011), remains of khums – sunk into the ground and again apparently separate from any built structure – were uncovered at the top of the eastern slope of the larger depression in the central part of the site (Area G, Fig. 1) and close to the south-eastern corner of the fortress. In this latter zone (Area E, Fig. 1), several khums – completely sunk into the ground and with blocks of pakhsa bordering their rims[10] – were arranged without any order and apparently were

---

[7]   In fact, the plan that has been proposed for these northern storehouses is unusual, insofar as this type of building normally has a rectangular/square layout. The hypothesis that there might be a "courtyard," to the north of the double row of rooms so far uncovered, has been forwarded before, following the Soviet excavation of a trench (8.5 m × 4 m) that failed to reveal any trace of walls in that area (Pilipko 2001, 165 and 168, Fig. 122).

[8]   Pilipko 2001, 175–185; Pilipko 2008.

[9]   It is important to keep in mind that this sector features no accumulation strata. Immediately below a thin layer of deposits, which is itself just below ground level (in all, between 10 cm and 30 cm in depth), we find the virgin soil or the artificial soil and gravel fill that served to level the area. It is not clear whether the entire south-eastern sector was levelled and cleared by human interventions during a late (?) period (with the consequent removal of any existing structures), or whether the bad state of preservation of the remains can be attributed exclusively to natural erosion. For a preliminary note on this issue, see Lippolis/Messina 2008, 53–55.

[10]   Some of the khums found sunk into the ground were still "sealed" with stones or blocks of pakhsa. Unfortunately, however, analysis has not identified substantial traces of substances that might identify their contents with any certainty. Nor in other areas of the site did analysis of the soil from the inside of the jars provide the expected information. For example, vine pollen was detected in hardly any of the khums, which is very surprising given that the majority of these jars were used for storing wine. It is not currently possible to establish whether this anomaly, which must be investigated further with new samples, is due to particular conditions of conservation, soil composition, subsequent reuse of the vessels, or simply to chance.

Fig. 2. Area A, view from the east

not related to any built structure. A substantial number of these khums had their mouths sealed with stones (Fig. 4). The interiors of these vessels did not yield finds of particular interest, although it is worth noting that one of the jars contained bone material, which was possibly human. This suggests that at least a few of these jars may have been reused in a later period and this area changed into a graveyard.[11] In this case, too, it is important to recognise that a more precise reconstruction is made very difficult by the limited extent of the excavation.

In Area F, further to the north-east (Fig. 1), remains of mud walls have been found together with large jars sunk into the floor.[12] This area, which has yielded a sizeable quantity of Parthian pottery, was revisited in a late period (Islamic) with interventions that certainly disturbed the ancient layers, preventing us from defining an accurate chronology of the unearthed structures.

Finally, we mention Nisa's south-western corner (Figs. 1 & 5), where between 2007 and 2015 Italian excavations brought to light a large, functional complex that included storehouses.[13] The complex was only partially uncovered by the team's investigations, as it extends further east than the excavated area and along the southern walls.

Two main structures can be distinguished here, conventionally known as the "South-Western Building" and the "Eastern Building." These are linked together and form a single complex, which is the result of several phases of building likely dating from the sec-

---

[11]   The southern sector of the site, together with the northern area and the area between the central complex and the Square House, were used during the late Islamic period as graveyards.

[12]   Lippolis/Messina 2008, 59–61.

[13]   For a preliminary report, see Lippolis 2013.

Fig. 3. Area E, view from the south

ond century BC to the first century AD. The quadrangular structure at the south-western corner of the walls – whose interior part, comprising a row of rooms around an open courtyard, presumably corresponds with an older nucleus – had the functional characteristics of a storehouse, although some of the spaces within it must have been used for other productive activities.[14] On the other hand, the structures of the Eastern Building seem to belong to a wing used either for residential purposes or for official functions, though here too, isolated areas have been identified that were used for storing khums.[15]

The area of the South-Western Building housing the storehouses featured a roughly squared plan, with elongated rooms arranged around a central courtyard. A second row of rooms, on the north and east sides, was added during a later phase of construction, effectively increasing the storage space (some of the rooms in the new, eastern wing were

---

[14]   *Ibidem.*

[15]   The hypothesis concerning the building's purpose is based, first and foremost, on the presence – at the southern edges of the building as we currently know it – of a row of three rooms (not visible on the schematic plan of Fig. 5), each of them displaying a pair of column bases. This architectural detail is more fitting for official or even residential purposes than for a storage area. With the exception of two rooms on the eastern side of the building, there is no trace of other housings for jars inside the building.

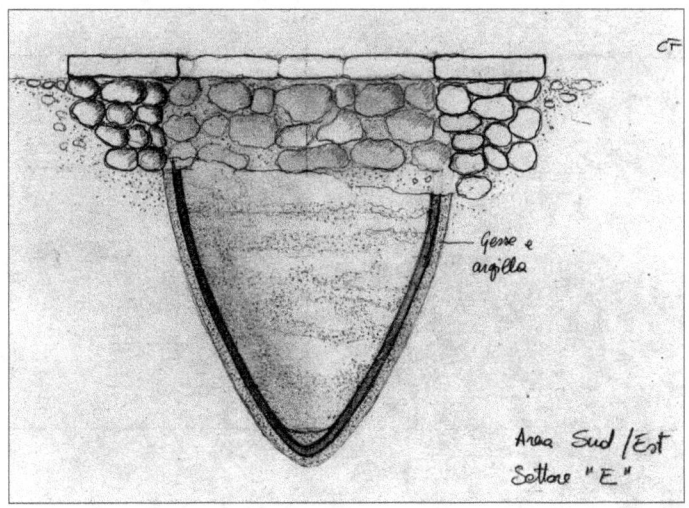

Fig. 4. Area E, section of a khum sunk into the ground (drawing C. Fossati)

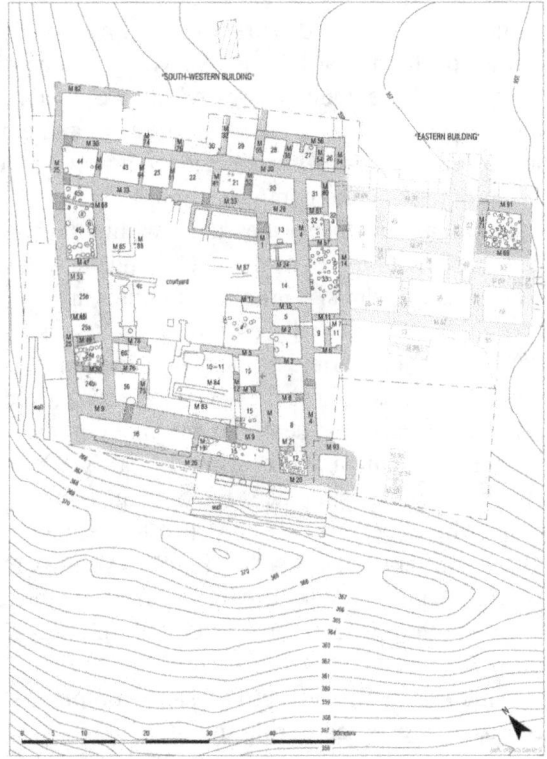

Fig. 5. "South-Western" and "Eastern" Buildings (2007–2014 excavation) with distribution of jars or
housings found in the buildings (drawing C. Bonfanti)

Fig. 6. South-Western Building, room 1: reused khums

used to store khums) and leading to the construction of a new building (it is likely that the Eastern Building was constructed at this point). The presence of two or three floor levels within these rooms, and the evidence here and there of extensive collapses, not to mention frequent repairs and restorations, testify to the long and complex building history of this area of the citadel. This is unsurprising, since it is clear, from its location, that this area served the central monumental complex directly.[16]

It is true that isolated khums have been unearthed, within the building, usually in the corners of the rooms. However, almost all of these are concentrated in just a few areas of the western, southern and eastern wings. A number of khums are also found at the centre, in the courtyard that would later be partially closed off by a subsequent phase of building (still within the Parthian period). Some of these jars contain burnt residues and were placed upside down: a clear clue as to how they were reused. Indeed, it was the top half of the khum that was reused; turned upside down and fixed or supported on the floor, it could be used as an oven for cooking and preparing food (Fig. 6).

Very few complete khums remain in place. We owe this situation in part to the collapse of the buildings and the effects of time, but also to the ancient practice of the recovery and reuse of these jars. Traces of this "ancient" recycling can also be seen in the pits dug alongside the original khum housings (Fig. 7), or where the lower part of the jars is still partially sunk into the floor (their edges level with the floor), the top part having been sliced clean off.

The total number of the khums in the south-western complex is revealing. The sum of the jars and of the housings recorded during the excavations is around 200, although

---

[16]   Based on the most recent excavation data, for all that it may be particularly difficult to identify the remains of structures in this area, parts of wall belonging to the South-Western Building can still be identified just 15 metres from the southern facades of the Round Hall and the Tower Building.

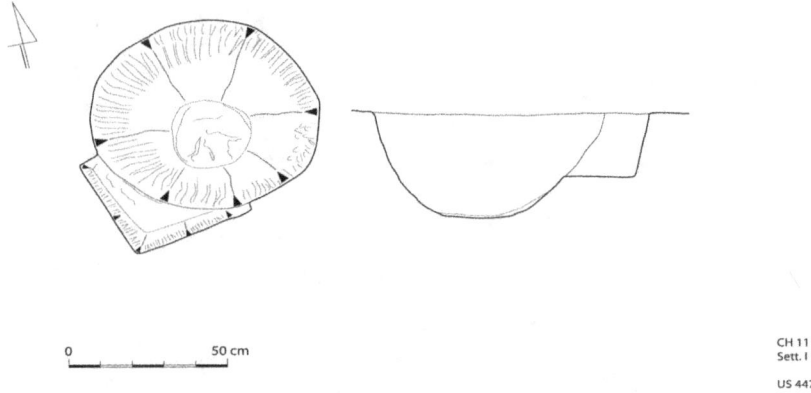

CH 11
Sett. I

US 447

Fig. 7. South-Western Building, room 45a: housing of a khum (plan and section)

this figure obviously relates to the total number of vessels spread across the building's various phases of construction.

The arrangement of khums within the rooms does not seem to strictly follow a particular scheme. In general, they are laid out starting at the corners and/or the sides of the rooms, and continuing inwards. They may even nearly fill a room completely. Fig. 8 shows the arrangement of jars as identified in room 12. The variations in grey tone correspond with the main phases of storing. Other cases, such as room 15, display khums arranged in a less rational manner, with some of them positioned away from the walls.

Given that they are frequently cut into by later pits, damaged by collapses or refilled artificially, attributing the several hollows for housing khums to particular phases of the buildings' use is no easy task. Moreover, the substitution of one vessel with another – with the opening of another hole in the ground, which might cut or simply lie close to a previous hollow – may in fact occur after only a brief interval.

Furthermore, both the shape of the khums and the way they were arranged in a room can vary. For a general classification of these vessels by type and an account of how they were produced, the studies by Masson[17] and Vdovin[18] are still worthy of attention, despite certain aspects of the production process still needing to be clarified. The very nature of the clay used makes it clear that manufacturing such large, heavy vessels in a single piece would have been impossible. On the basis of the observations made by the Russian archaeologists, we can say that the production of a khum would require the use of a composite technique: the central section and "shoulder" were modelled by hand, while the rim was made separately to be attached afterwards. The lower section, in contrast, was always made on a wheel. On that subject, we should bring the reader's attention to the seams that can still be identified on some fragments, indicating where the

---

[17] Masson 1953.
[18] Vdovin 1984.

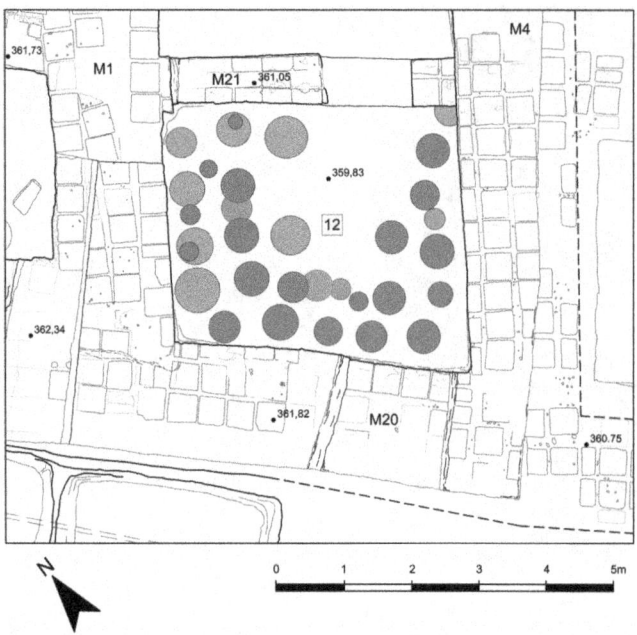

Fig. 8. South-Western Building, room 12 with distribution of jars (drawing C. Bonfanti)

separately prepared sections were joined together.[19] Assembly would take place at a later stage, possibly after the clay had partially dried and hardened but while the edges were still moist, and certainly before the final firing.[20] The seams, which were subsequently masked on the inside with a covering of fine clay (and on the outside using a burnishing or smoothing technique), can be discerned on a number of khum fragments that still fit together perfectly and which bear clear finger impressions and bumps at the points where two sections were brought into contact and joined, using the fingers to press them together (Fig. 9).

We leave out here further details on the technique and the morphological types, considering now the two main ways to store these containers. The khum could be sunk into the floor or on a raised base of clay/bricks (the latter being the case, for example, in the northern *khumkana* sector). Most khums were buried up to about one third of their height, but there are also cases of khums that were sunk in their entirety, with their rims

[19] See G. Ceccarini's forthcoming "Parthian period storage jars from the South-West Building in Old Nisa," in: G. Affanni, C. Baccarin, L. Cordera, A. di Michele, K. Gavagnin (eds.), *Proceedings of Broadening Horizons 4. Conference of Young Researchers Working in the Ancient Near East, Egypt and Central Asia*, BAR International Series, Oxford. The same author proposes a preliminary classification of khums in Nisa Partica. La ceramica dagli scavi della missione italiana 2007–2012, Università degli Studi di Torino (unpublished degree thesis, 2012).

[20] To date, no kiln or other device for firing ceramics has been found at Old Nisa (and this is obvious if we consider that Old Nisa is a ceremonial complex). As such, information regarding this process is entirely lacking.

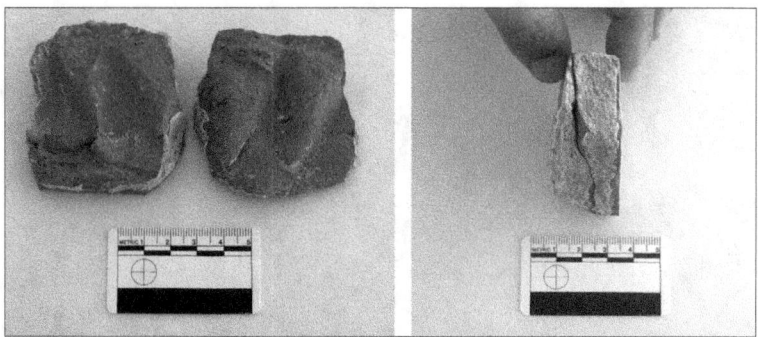

Fig. 9. Seam of a jar with finger imprints

Fig. 10. South-Western Building, room 45a: a jar sunk into the floor and sealed with a baked brick

Fig. 11. South-Western Building, khums in room 45a after the removal of the floor

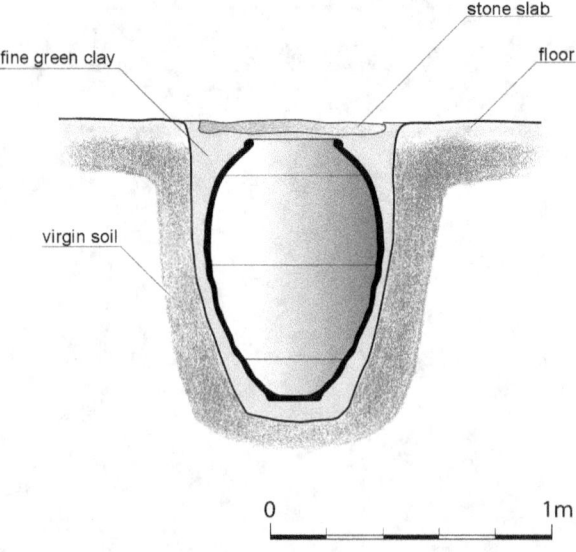

Fig. 12. Section of a khum sunk into the floor (drawing C. Fossati)

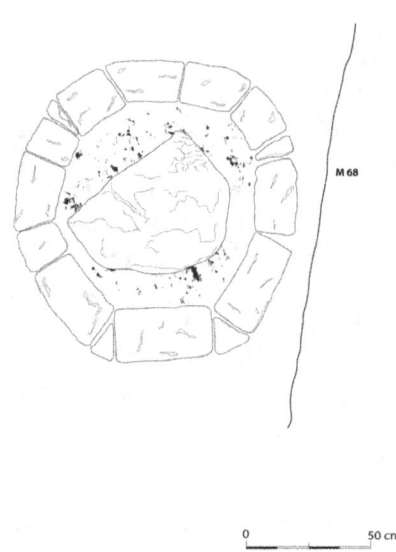

M 68

0   50 cm

Fig. 13. The mouth of a khum sunk into the floor of room 45a, encircled by a ring of mud bricks and sealed with a stone

loosely embedded in the floor (Figs. 10, 11, 12). In both cases, they were stoppered using terracotta elements (bricks, tile fragments or purpose-made round lids[21]) or stones that had been cut to shape and smoothed. The type of stone used for this purpose was a grey-green sandstone largely used at Nisa for architectural elements (plinths, column bases, friezes and so on). It is a soft, rather friable stone, from which thin slabs (2–3 cm), either rectangular or circular, can be cut with relative ease.[22] Fragments of an unbaked clay lid were also discovered in 2014: this was a disc with a rough handle in the shape of a lump of clay with deep finger impressions to provide grip. Furthermore, the use of other materials, such as matting or fabric, to provide a hermetic seal cannot be excluded (remains of a rough fabric were discovered in room 15 beside a group of jars). Lastly, the khum could be sealed with pieces of unbaked clay into which impressions were made with various sorts of seals (see below, part 2).

The hollows housing the khums are round, and just wider in diameter than the walls of the jar. The walls of these cavities often yield traces of a greenish, fine-grained clay, which occasionally contains chalk inclusions. This mixture evidently served to better anchor the container in the ground, and at the same time protect it from damp. In such

---

[21] As in the case of a fragment of a terracotta disc around 50–55 cm in diameter, found in 2011.

[22] There are, however, examples of stones of other types being used; they are roughly shaped and arranged to close up the khums.

cases, when khums were entirely sunk into the virgin soil, the gap around them was wider (even as much as 10–15 cm; Figs. 10, 11, 12), while the mouth of the jar might be surrounded by mud bricks (half-bricks), as was the case of a khum in the oldest floor in room 45a (Fig. 13).

It is not yet possible to establish whether this difference between fully or only partially sunk jars is related to their specific contents (liquid or solid as they might be). Analysis of samples taken from the inside of these containers has not thus far provided clear information indicating with any certainty a single variety of produce for all of the fully buried jars.[23]

The majority of data concerning the contents of these large storage jars and the management of the storehouses comes from ostraka. As is widely known, these usually follow a standard formula (although in reality there is a shorter variation and a longer one) of an essentially economical nature, with an indication of the type of the incoming product, its quantity and the specific estate on which it was produced (with occasional mention of who delivered and recorded it). Infrequently, however, a date or a note on the quality of the produce (particularly in regard to wine), its provenance or destination might also be inscribed (or preserved). The great majority of the ostraka record consignments of wine, which could vary widely in size. Wine came from lands that either belonged to the crown or were obliged to furnish tributes (on an annual basis?), from temple properties, or from private individuals (cavalry commander, treasurer, etc.).

With only a few isolated exceptions, all the ostraka come from storehouses and sometimes are found beside the khums they are related to (at times inside the hollows in which the jars were sunk). It seems possible, on the basis of the actual contents of the jars, that the ostraka were used as temporary labels and subsequently discarded, erased or reinscribed.[24] In some cases, there are additions and corrections to the original text, but these revisions were made only a short time after the original inscriptions, and frequently by the same hand. It is likely, as has already been suggested,[25] that it was the practice in these storehouses to "tidy up" or substitute the ostraka on a regular basis, and perhaps even some of the jars themselves.

In the South-Western Building the ostraka come almost exclusively from storage rooms (Fig. 14). Some of the ostraka coming from its eastern side report a date between the years 141 and 162 of the Arsacid era (i.e. 107–86 BCE), which may well be the period in which these premises were used.[26]

---

[23]   The two samples taken from entirely sunk khums that have been analysed have yielded no trace at all of seeds, nuts or pollen grains, perhaps an indication that this type of vessels was simply used for storing water. All the same, some of the sunk jars at Ulug Depe seem to have been used to store solid foodstuffs: Lecomte 2011, 237.

[24]   There are numerous examples of "labels" describing jars that had been removed from rooms or buildings that had collapsed. It is the text on the ostrakon itself that puts it in this category. There are even "labels" for empty jars.

[25]   Bader 1996, 255.

[26]   Should this be the case, the buildings further to the west (in other words the original nucleus of the South-Western Building) would have to date from before the last decade of the second century BC. For the time being, this remains a hypothesis to be examined in the light of a definitive stratigraphic investigation of the complex as a whole.

Fig. 14. South-Western Building, room 33, view from the north

Even though there has not yet been a systematic investigation of the onomastics and the principal roles of the individuals mentioned on the ostraka, a preliminary analysis[27] identified the toponyms of at least five vineyards, while 45 villages and/or properties around Nisa have also been recognised. Other information concerns the organisation of the storehouses. For example, ostrakon n. 2577 tells us that in the year 72 BC one particular "wine store" contained a total of 6351 *mari* of old wine. In the same year, according to ostrakon n. 2576, a so-called "royal treasury" counted 2933 *mari* of new wine.[28] Another, undated ostrakon (n. 2624) tells us that at Mihrdatkirt, 160 jars of wine were stocked in the so-called "new storehouse," while another 316 jars were to be found in the "second storehouse." Sixteen jars were recorded as being empty, giving a total of 500 jars used for wine alone.[29] Unfortunately, it is not clear which and how many storehouses were being used at the same time within the citadel.

---

[27] Bader 1996.

[28] 1 *mari* is generally held to equal 9.32 litres.

[29] The dimensions of the khums are relatively consistent. However, there are differences, and it is unclear whether these are to be attributed to variations in usage (a few ostraka mentioning jars of oil were recently found beside fragments from medium-large containers), to different producers or to the period of production.

The ostraka also provide occasional indications of the wine's quality. In addition to the familiar references to "old wine" and "new wine," we also find – as might be expected – wine that had turned vinegary ("gone sour"). However, there is also mention of "eatable" wine or wine that was "newly fit to drink,"[30] "inferior" wine, "fortified wine" and wine that may have been set aside for ageing ("intended for store"). Besides, we find here one or more varieties of "colourless" wine (white, rosé?) mentioned.[31] Wine could be transferred (or decanted) from one jar to another, or new wine could be added to old to improve it. The existence of various varieties of wine is not surprising if we consider the significant quantities that flowed into Nisa every year. Furthermore, these same ostraka regularly distinguish between those who simply managed estates and vineyards ("wine-factors"), and the owners of the land ("wine-growers"). Meanwhile, references to a "wine-dresser," and even a "wine-collector" or "vintner" (ostrakon n. 1677) remain more doubtful.

Other types of foodstuff that were present in the storehouses, such as flour, oil (vegetable or animal?), flax seeds, sesame seeds, raisins, wheat and barley,[32] are mentioned more sporadically.

As far as processes of record-keeping, checking and sealing within the storehouses are concerned, from the inscribed ostraka we can infer the presence of scribes,[33] a head-scribe, individuals responsible for applying seals ("seal-setters"), storehouse "keepers" (who are occasionally, but not always, the same people who apply the seals), "cup-bearers" and "accounters." We are lucky in a few instances to know these individuals' names, but we have no further information about the precise nature of their duties. It is possible that individual ostraka occasionally use different names for the same functionary, resulting in a distorted picture of reality.

Indeed, on the basis of the ostraka inscriptions, we might infer that the system of storing and redistributing produce was, in some respects, rather complex, whereas the picture that emerges from the physical data is one of relatively simple record-keeping practices.

In general, the average capacity of these large, pear-shaped containers, which would frequently measure 120–130 cm in height and up to 80 cm in diameter, could be as much as 280–300 litres.

[30] Definitions in inverted commas, such as "eatable" and so on, are taken from Diakonoff/Livshits 1976–2001. Some of these definitions, in fact, seem to be rather unusual. The lexicon on the Nisean ostraka, in effect, is one of those aspects that needs to be more systematically reviewed and investigated, also in light of the new data now available.

[31] It is possible that this is, in fact, a reference to a type of beer.

[32] Barley, for example, is mentioned in a well-known ostrakon that records the coronation of a king (ostrakon n. 2-L): Arsak, the king, son of grandson (2) of Arshak. Accounted (3) this offering – 2000 e(phas) of barley. If the conversion rate of 1 epha to roughly 35 litres is correct, this equates to 70,000 litres, a not insignificant quantity, even considering that the density of barley is substantially lower than that of liquids.

[33] We ought to bear in mind, in addition to this reference to record-keeping scribes, that some ostrakon inscriptions are thought to be scribal exercises.

2. Storage practices (N. Manassero)

At this point, it is necessary to switch our attention to the analysis of the clay sealings brought to light by the Italian excavations of 2007–2014. These were found exclusively in the south-west sector. However, the fact that the other areas excavated by Italian teams have not yielded a single such sealing may be due to the limited extent of the test excavations carried out in these sectors, in addition to the precarious state of the buildings, where the debris is few and the later use probably affected the original stratigraphy.[34]

It is important to point out that identifying such clay sealings in the field presents something of a challenge since, due to their poor state of conservation, they may no longer bear clear seal impressions, and above all, because the clay they are made from is the same type and consistency as that used to make the bricks used at the site. As such, the sealings would be found amongst rubble composed of the same material. We could add that, unlike many other examples of inventories in which fire, at the expense of more perishable documents, actually contributed to the conservation of clay sealings by effectively firing and hardening them,[35] the clay sealings of Nisa have reached us unfired. After all, use of the South-Western Building did not cease because of a fire, but because of the collapse of certain sections – which can, in certain cases, be attributed to earthquakes – and the consequent collapse of the buildings themselves. As a result, the clay sealings from the South-Western Building are especially fragile. They are often broken into pieces and covered with concretions of the same consistency, which makes the process of cleaning them and discerning their shape even more difficult. The seal impressions are invariably faint and indistinct due to the natural erosive effect of the soil in which the clay sealings are deposited, and frequent immersion in water as witnessed by the loamy accretions that are often evident in individual examples. The result is that observations on such objects are largely subject to uncertainty. Readings and interpretations can only be considered definitive in a small number of cases, while much of the remainder is subject to speculation. A number of the iconographic variations found in these seal impressions have been studied elsewhere.[36] Our intention with this paper is rather to gather a few observations on the morphological characteristics of the clay sealings that have been found to date, and to consider their purpose. Thus, we hope to contribute to the study of the methods of produce-storage and administration employed in the building currently being excavated; we believe that only by examining different categories of artefact can these methods be clarified.

In spite of the difficulties we have described, since 2009, 129 specimens of clay sealings, of various shapes and sizes, have been identified in the excavations in the South-Western Building. For the most part, this figure comprises sealings bearing seal impressions. However, there is also a small number of clay fragments that lack seal impressions

---

[34] Outside of areas A, E and F, no seal impressions have thus far been recorded, not even in the small test trench opened north-east of the Square House. Here, khum hollows and khum fragments and various ostraka have been found underneath the Islamic tombs, which leads us to suppose that the vessels must have been sealed at some point.

[35] Boussac/Invernizzi 1996.

[36] Manassero 2010, and Manassero, forthcoming.

but bear imprints of one sort or another – pieces of wood, cord, corners – that confirm their identity as sealings.

At this point, it is worth pausing to offer a brief clarification in regard to terminology, since there are a number of terms that are used in different ways by different authors when discussing similar artefacts. In the following pages, I will use the term *clay sealing* or *sealing* generically to refer to pieces of clay bearing an *imprint* of the sealed object on the reverse, and a *seal impression* on its external surface. In line with the terminology that has prevailed in recent years,[37] we can say that this latest inventory from Nisa does not contain true *bullae*, such as those of the Sasanian period. *Bullae* are globular sealings pierced by a hole, in which the document being sealed would be inserted. Nor are there *tokens*, which is to say clay lumps with a seal impression at the centre that seal the ends of the string with which a document is closed. On the contrary, all of the clay sealings in the "new" inventory, insofar as we can ascertain both shape and function, can be described as sizeable lumps of rough clay, the majority lacking any clear shape, that feature a band of purified clay into which seals would be impressed (see below). These clay blocks are, at times, surprisingly large, and frequently contain gravel inclusions, which are sizeable in their own right (up to 3 cm). This leads us to suppose that such clay sealings might seal objects with large surfaces, and not documents. The fact that they are always found together with a large khum, as discussed earlier, allows us to state with some certainty that they were used almost exclusively as seals on this sort of container, and potentially on other vessels of a more perishable nature. Indeed, it is worth stating that the majority of these clay sealings were found either inside khums, or immediately beside them – next to the base, if the khum was still in place, and in the khum hollow if the jar itself had been removed. Other clay sealings have been found in layers of rubble, but always close to khums.

As far as the reverse side of these clay sealings – that is the side that faced the sealed object itself – is concerned, on more than a third of the specimens (49) it is either missing, or has an indistinguishable imprint. A similar number have a smooth surface with impressions made by a round-sectioned rope (14), are pierced by a hole (17), or bear the imprint of some sort of plant material characterised by a flat shape and distinct, parallel fibres, probably canes or wooden slats. In some cases, however, it is difficult to differentiate between the piercings left by ropes from those made by burrowing insects, after the artefact lay buried. Imprints that appear to have been made by knots have been identified on a number of items – S36/09 and S5/10 for example – but it is unclear to what sort of object these seals might have been attached. Lastly, a sizeable number of specimens (33) bear imprints made by other objects. In some cases, these can be attributed to a very gently curving edge, presumably the rim of a khum, or in rare cases, to the straight edge of some sort of box. In some instances, these imprints suggest a slightly concave surface of considerable size. We cannot offer a more detailed definition of these imprints. They vary in shape, but can all be attributed with some certainty to the walls or rims of khums or their lids. In two specimens (Fig. 15, a photograph of S20/12), a gently curving, stepped outline can be made out. This is undoubtedly the imprint left by the rim of

---

[37]   Cf. Rostovzeff 1932, but also Harper 1973; Göbl 1976; Frye 1977; Huff 1987; Lerner/Skjaervø 1997, and Lerner/Sims-Williams 2011.

Fig. 15. Imprint of a khum's rim on S20/12

Fig. 16. Likely an "appended sealing", S22/12

a khum. Examples of clay sealings thought to have been used to seal doors, or rather to seal locks, are rare and, in any case, usually questionable. Such cases include S22/12, a cone-shaped lump whose purpose is uncertain, but which was certainly not used on a khum. It is more likely that it belongs in the category of "appended sealings" (Fig. 16).

Turning to the outward-facing side of the clay sealings, we see that the majority (79) can be grouped together in the same category. We can figure a process where a large mass of clay is spread out, and in many cases smoothed carefully with a baton, on top of which is applied a flattened band, like a belt, of variable thickness. Impressions are made in this band, using a seal. It is difficult to say how these bands were flattened out, but in one case (S10/12) the band is pierced lengthways, from one end of the preserved part of the band to the other, by a hole left by a piece of rope. It seems feasible that a piece of string made from a perishable material was entirely covered with a paste of clay and chalk, stretched right across the surface to which the seal was being applied, and flattened to make it stick. It is quite reasonable to envision the end section of a rope that held some sort of lid in place on the mouth of the khum. In many cases (31), it appears that the seal was pressed into the mass of coarse clay, rather than the band of purified clay that surrounded the string. We should note, however, that this conclusion is debatable, since occasionally only small portions of the surface around the seal impression are preserved and therefore it is not objectively verifiable that such a band is even present. In only three cases, including the aforementioned S22/12, can we be sure that the clay sealing is globular, and could not have had a flattened band. In these cases, we may wish to place the artefact in the category of "appended sealings."[38] Finally, there are 15 samples of pieces of clay that bear the imprint of a corner, rim or rope on the reverse – from which we can infer that they are the body of a sealing – but on which there is no sign of a seal impression. It should not be forgotten that the statistics are especially subject to variation due to the miserable condition of these artefacts, which are badly fragmented and incomplete. However, careful evaluation of the complete specimens, those that can be assessed with any confidence, does tell us with a degree of certainty that nearly every clay sealing sealed either a broad, concave surface, feasibly that of a khum, or in rare cases a flat surface, which could be that of a wooden box. Only in the cases of the three "appended sealings" might we point to clay sealings from Nisa being used for documents, bags or pegs used for keeping doors closed.

Fortunately, Nisa itself has provided another collection of clay sealings, those from the Square House, which has been known about for some time and its various categories studied in some depth.[39] It is thanks to these very studies that we can carry out meaningful comparisons regarding the issues discussed above, and venture a hypothesis concerning the management of the storehouse in question based on analogous features and differences between the two inventories of artefacts. The type of clay sealing described earlier – a sizeable volume of rough clay crossed by a band of purified clay that bears one or more seal impressions – seems to be exclusive to the South-Western Building. The certainty of this assessment may be undermined by the methods of collection and preservation used during the excavation of clay sealings by the JuTAKE.

---

[38]   In this regard, globular clay sealings of this kind, which in two cases bear simple pinch-marks and finger-imprints, recall another category of artefacts found in the same areas of the South-Western Building and many other parts of Nisa: balls of clay and chalk, whose surfaces bear marks made by fingernails, and impressions made by coins. For a number of observations regarding the possible pertinence of such artefacts to the realm of seals, rather than the ritual sphere to which literature usually assigns them, see Manassero 2013, 47–48: the author will discuss his personal view in greater depth in the final publication of the excavations.

[39]   Mollo 2001.

Time and again, at the Square House, we see only the seal impressions and a minimal portion of the surrounding clay being preserved, giving rise to the suspicion that the additional, more cumbersome parts were discarded. The overriding impression is that the aim, during the excavation phase, was to preserve the smallest portion required to document the seal impression, which is consistent with the overriding interest displayed by the Russian academics in the sealings' outer surface, rather than the inner surface and the imprints left by the sealed objects themselves. All the same, even amongst the Square House sealings there are some discernible examples of flattened bands with rows of seal impressions, although these are smaller than those found at the South-Western Building. In addition, there is greater variation in the imprints left by the sealed objects on the reverse of the clay sealings in the Square House, which bears witness to a wider variety of stored items. Indeed, although a few fragments of plant fibre have been found together with clay sealings in the South-Western Building, sealings bearing the imprint of fabric, and likely, therefore, to have been used on a sack, are entirely absent. Nor are there any of the L-shaped sealings that can confidently be attributed to boxes' sealings, although there is a good number of flat-backed sealings which could feasibly be placed in that category. As such, we may propose, albeit in a preliminary manner, that there was a clear difference in the nature of the objects stored and sealed in the Square House and those stored and sealed in the South-Western Building – various types of container in the former and almost exclusively khums in the latter.

These conclusions are also supported by examining the collection of clay sealings found at Ulug Depe, a site that is close to Nisa physically, although it dates from an earlier period. It is located about 150 km east along the same range of Kopet Dagh mountains at whose feet Nisa was built. Here, recent French excavations have brought to light a significant inventory of clay sealings. As in Nisa, these were always found together with khums.[40] In a number of cases, they bear the clear imprint of the rim of a jar on the reverse, as we have seen in our own examples. The French archaeologists have even managed to make out the micro-stratigraphy of the clay within individual specimens and understand the methods with which the clay was applied. It is clear that the conditions in which the Ulug Depe sealings were preserved were much better than those at Nisa, where similar observations proved impossible.

We can therefore conclude with some confidence that the clay sealings of the new inventory from Nisa were used for sealing khums, and very occasionally wooden boxes or storage sacks stored together with jars. As such, it appears that the seal impressions bear witness to the work of functionaries employed in managing the storage of produce contained almost entirely in khums – namely wine and oil, going by the information provided by the ostraka.

We will now switch our attention to a number of issues that are rarely given consideration in the literature on this subject. We will examine the seal impressions in more detail – with a particular focus on the methods used, their shape, number and arrangement, but with little attention to questions of iconography – with the aim of determining what sort of information they can give us. We hope to learn something not only of the identity of the functionaries charged with the task of applying the seals, but also of the contents

---

[40] Xin/Lecomte 2012.

of the khums and how they were managed. At this point in time, it is possible to take accurate notes on such features, but we can do little more than speculate on their meaning until more complete data from the running excavations or the ostraka inscriptions might provide a key to their interpretation.

For the most part, the seal impressions on the clay bands are arranged in a single row, but they also appear in double, triple and, in very rare cases, in quadruple rows (Fig. 17). They are usually neatly aligned and arranged at regular intervals, but in a few rare cases we find impressions that touch or just barely overlap. Similar arrangements of seal impressions are found in the inventory from Shahr-i Qumis,[41] which is likely the other Parthian capital mentioned by sources as Hekatompylos, and therefore on a similar sociocultural level to Nisa. The arrangement of seal impressions on one specimen (S33/09: Fig. 18) may be boustrophedic, as it has one impression set on a separate row underneath the main one. In this case, it is difficult to find a clear reason for such an arrangement, insofar as it would be obvious that the extended row of impressions would end up filling the width of the band, and the space available to extend the following row would have been enough. The most plausible explanation, to these authors' eyes, is that an arrangement of this sort implies a method of counting, perhaps comparable to the concept of an abacus, but in any case one that communicates quantitative information about the contents of the khum. This theory requires that we consider the very arrangement of the impressions, whether on single, double or multiple rows, together with the number of impressions, as established codes, capable of furnishing detailed information about the contents of the container, without the need to break the sealing to check. For example, it may be that the number of impressions on a single sealing corresponds to the number of units of produce stored in the khum, for instance the *mari* mentioned on the ostraka. If not, it may tell us something about the date the seal was applied.[42]

The impressions on S10/2010 may encourage a similar interpretation. At its centre, it bears a simple groove, made lengthways, which would have been easy for anybody to counterfeit, and which therefore undermines the integrity of the contents, or rather, makes it impossible to detect a break-in and subsequent, counterfeit, resealing. A similar artefact was discovered at Shahr-i Qumis,[43] where, in place of the single rectangular groove, there are two, perpendicular to one another, forming an equally straightforward and falsifiable cross-shaped design. We might surmise, in this case too, that this mark indicates a numeric figure relating to the contents of the container, rather than to the functionary. We should therefore consider whether analogous features of the counting systems used at Nisa and Hekatompylos might exist. From the little information we have on Central Asian practices, it would appear that these might grow out of traditional Iron-Age systems, as attested by the example of Ulug Depe.

One point should be added regarding the lack of sophistication in the images we have just described. The act of sealing does little to hinder the breaking of the seal. At most, it leverages the magical, apotropaic quality inherent to any seal to ward off those who

---

[41] Bivar 1982.

[42] We would also do well to keep Indonesian sealing practices in mind, specifically the fact that the number of repetitions of an impression is in proportion to the importance of the letter's sender, cf. Teh Gallop 2006.

[43] Bivar 1982, 175: Fig. 5: E3.

Fig. 17. Multiple rows of impressions of seals on S3/13

Fig. 18. Particular rows of impressions on S33/09

might break it illicitly. The main purpose of the seal is, rather, to provide evidence of a breach after it has occurred.[44] As such, logic would dictate that a seal should bear clear, unequivocal images that are ideally difficult to counterfeit. However, in the case of the new collection from Nisa, we have found that not only are many images of a sort that would be easy to counterfeit, but the impressed surface is occasionally entirely smooth. In some cases, it could be that the image has been erased by the effects of time and the conditions in which the items were preserved; but in others the surface is perfectly smooth, despite the crisp, precise and unworn edges surrounding it, which leads us to conclude that such smoothness is intentional. The existence of impressions that are either extremely simple or lack any sort of representation at all leads us to suppose that in a given context, it was not necessary to individualise a sealing to identify who applied it. This clearly suggests a situation in which the management and administration of the storehouses was particularly straightforward, with a single functionary dedicated to the task of applying seals. As such, we can also suppose that the only function of the seal impressions was to bear witness to the very act of applying the seal, and therefore to the integrity of a container's contents. It would then seem reasonable to assume, in cases in which seal impressions are applied in an otherwise inexplicably sophisticated arrangement or in excessive numbers (as in the case of S33/09), that these transmit information of another sort. In this case, too, it is tempting to conclude that such information cannot refer to anything if not to the contents of the recipient, or rather, as we have already suggested, to the nature and quantity of the product it contains, or else to the date the seal was applied. Beyond this, we dare not push further into speculative territory.

The idea that the management of the storehouse in the South-Western Building was not excessively complex, and was entrusted to a small group of functionaries, seems to be supported by the fact that very few of the clay sealings found bear impressions made with different seals. We find the same situation at Shahr-i Qumis and Ulug Depe. The process of applying seals was clearly conducted, for the most part, by a single individual who did not require a counterpart to confirm that the task was done correctly. We may wish to consider pushing our speculations further and – assuming that we are correct to suggest that the seal impressions do not refer to the identity of the functionaries but, rather, communicate some kind of quantitative or qualitative information about the sealed contents – suggest that different seal impressions found on the same sealing might, in fact, transmit different pieces of information about the container's contents. For example, we may wonder whether one type of impression refers to the date, while another to the quantity, or even the very nature of the product in question. There is not a single case in which more than two different seal impressions can be effectively identified on the same sealing. As such, we are led to interpret a combination of different seal impressions, as well as the manner in which they are arranged, as an attempt to articulate, on the surface of the clay sealing, whatever information was required in regard to the contents. In this respect, we need to compare the information provided by the ostraka about the nature, characteristics and the quantity of produce contained in the khums, which was discussed in broad terms earlier. That which the ostraka express in words and figures, the sealings might express through the features of the seal impressions mentioned above.

---

[44]   Duistermatt 2012, 12–13.

Fig. 19. Likely the point of an unbaked clay sealing, PO7/12

The shape of the seal impressions might just as easily be interpreted as a sort of code for communicating quantitative or qualitative information about the sealed contents: for example, the nature of the produce, the estates it came from, its age, and many other characteristics that will be discussed in depth when a definitive report of the excavations is published. The seal impressions on the clay sealings of the South-Western Building are, for the most part, circular, but there are also many examples of ovals. Square and rectangular impressions appear more sporadically. In a couple of cases, however, we see rough impressions whose shape is more irregular. These may have been made by fingers or some other, unrecognisable object, but they were certainly not produced with a seal. However, it should be stated that these impressions only appear on more or less globular clay sealings that lack the flattened band described earlier.

The only body of evidence we found of an actual seal – not its impression on a sealing – is a thin "button" of unbaked clay bearing an engraved image, possibly a highly stylised face or a symbol of some sort (PO7/12, Fig. 19). Gliding over the question of iconography, which is not within the scope of this paper, this item is still of particular interest from a typological perspective. The fact that such a thin disc of unbaked clay has reached us with its circular surface in one piece suggests that this is indeed the shape it was designed to have, insofar as it is highly unlikely that it broke off like this accidentally. It is most probably the surface of a seal; it is less likely to be a decorative medallion from a piece of pottery or furniture, since it bears an intaglio image rather than an image in relief. As such, it seems more suited to stamping an impression. It might be tempting to think that this "button" would have been affixed to some sort of object that might be pushed into clay to create such deep impressions, but at this point in time we have no clue to further speculate on the purpose of such a clay object. This is intriguing in itself, insofar as it suggests, once again, that there might have been original sealing practices in use at Nisa that may be of particular interest to us.

Even though we have intentionally avoided the question of iconography, there is one more piece of information we think worth noting. The new inventory of clay sealings does not include a single seal impression that closely resembles any of those found at the Square House. However, even though the iconography is different throughout, certain subject matter does appear in both groups of artefacts, although generally the seal impressions from the Square House appear to be manufactured to a higher standard, at least in some cases. In the collection from the South-Western Building there are no import seal impressions and the intaglio engravings seem overwhelmingly schematic. This is even the case for subjects that are distinctly western in their inspiration,[45] although subjects derived from the local culture, which are unknown in the Greek figurative vocabulary, are in the majority. This group includes the tamga impressions I discussed elsewhere,[46] and other abstract and geometrical impressions that may have local roots or, as suggested earlier, are designed to convey some sort of information, of which we remain ignorant, regarding the contents of a container. The differences between the two collections can certainly be explained by suggesting that the seals belonged to different individual functionaries, although we should bear in mind the doubts already expressed about the possibility that a seal might made exclusive and unequivocal reference to the identity of a particular individual. The possibility that these differences arise from a temporal dislocation seems to be untenable, insofar as the phases of both buildings span the whole life of the citadel. Therefore, they would have been used contemporaneously.

Conclusions

We will put off any further elaboration of these observations on the inventory of the clay sealings in the final report of the Italian excavations at Nisa (2007–2015). This is to say that what we have offered here are preliminary observations which, all the same, note a number of interesting characteristics and demand further comparison with other, perhaps less well-known but equally important collections, in the interests of developing our understanding of the glyptic arts and administrative practices of the Parthian period. The observations we have assembled here show a distinctive range of sealing practices that are, in large part, different from those found in better-known archives and storehouses. The only comparable collections come from Shahr-i Qumis and Ulug Depe, two sites that, in both a geographical and cultural sense, can be said to be close to Nisa. All the same, we must not forget that inventories of this sort are very rare, and either have only been partially published (such as that from nearby Gobekly[47]), or have not been

---

[45] Manassero, forthcoming.
[46] Manassero 2010.
[47] Bader/Gaibov/Koshelenko 1990.

published at all. Furthermore, generally speaking, very little is known about administrative practices in the Central Asian context during this period.

Our observations on the new material evidence from Nisa must therefore be limited in their scope, in anticipation of further confirmation from other inventories and, above all, from the ostraka also found at Nisa, whose commentary would be of particular value, as it would provide an insight into the extent to which the material data matches the epigraphical sources, and as such, deepen our understanding of how the storehouses at Nisa operated.

BIBLIOGRAPHY

Bader, A. (1996), Parthian Ostraca from Nisa: Some Historical Data, in: *La Persia e l'Asia centrale. Da Alessandro al X secolo*, International Conference, Rome, 9–12 November 1994, Atti dei Convegni Lincei, 127, Roma: 251–276.

Bader, A., Gaibov, V., Koshelenko, G. (1990), New Evidence on Parthian Sphragistics. Bullae from the Excavations of Göbekly-Depe in Margiana, *Mesopotamia* 25: 61–78.

Bivar, A.D.H. (1982), Seal-Impressions of Parthian Qūmis (Qūmis Commentaries no. 4), *Iran* 20: 161–176.

Boussac, M.-F., Invernizzi, A. (eds.) (1996), *Archives et sceaux du monde hellenistique, Turin, Villa Gualino, 13–16 January 1993*, (*BCH*, Supplément 29), Athens–Paris.

Diakonoff, I.M., Livshits, V.A. (1976–2001), *Parthian Economic Documents from Nisa*, (Corpus Inscriptionum Iranicarum – Inscriptions of the Seleucid and Parthian Periods and of the Eastern Iran and Central Asia), vol. 1–2 (texts), vol. 1–5 (plates), ed. D.N. MacKenzie, A.N. Bader, N. Sims Williams, London.

Duistermaat, K. (2012), Which Came First, the Bureaucrat or the Seal? Some Thoughts on the Non Administrative Origins of Seals in Neolithic Syria, in: I. Regulsky, K. Duistermatt, P. Verkinderen (eds.), *Seals and Sealing Practices in the Near East. Developments in Administration and Magic from Prehistory to the Islamic Period*, (Orientalia Lovaniensia Analecta 219), Leuven–Walpole–Paris: 1–16.

Frye, R.N. (1977), The Use of Clay Sealings in Sasanian Iran, *Acta Iranica. Textes et Mémoires*, V: *Varia 1976*, Tehran–Leiden: 117–124.

Göbl, R. (1976), *Die Tonbullen vom Takht-e Suleiman: ein Beitrag zur spätsasanidischen Sphragistik*, Berlin.

Harper, P.O. (1973), Physical Characteristics of the Sealings and Forms of the Seals, in: R.N. Frye (ed.), *Sasanian Remains from Qasr-i Abu Nasr: Seals, Sealings and Coins*, Cambridge: 42–46.

Huff, D. (1987), Technological Observations on Clay Bullae from Takht-i Suleyman, *Mesopotamia* 22: 367–390.

Invernizzi, A. (2000), The Square House at Old Nisa, *Parthica* 2: 13–53.

Lecomte, O. (2011), Ulug-Depe: 4000 Years of Evolution between Plain and Desert, in: *Historical and Cultural Sites of Turkmenistan*, Ashgabat: 221–237.

Lerner, J., Sims-Williams, N. (2011), *Seals, Sealings and Tokens from Bactria to Gandhara (4th to 8th Century)*, Vienna.

Lerner, J., Skjaervø, P.O. (1997), Some Uses of Clay Bullae in Sasanian Iran: Bullae in the Rosen and Museum of Fine Arts Collections, in: R. Gyselen (ed.), *Sceaux d'Orient et leur emploi*, (Res Orientales 10), Bures-sur-Yvette: 67–78.

Lindstrom, G. (2003), *Uruk. Siegelabdrücke auf hellenistischen Tonbullen und Tontafeln*, (Ausgrabungen in Uruk-Warka 20), Mainz.

Lippolis, C. (2010), Notes on Parthian Nisa on the Light of New Research, *Problemy istorii, filologii, kul'tury*, 1 (27): 36–46.

Lippolis, C. (2013), Old Nisa, Excavations in the South-Western Area. Second Preliminary Report (2008–2012), *Parthica* 15: 89–115.

Lippolis, C., Messina, V. (2008), Preliminary Report on the 2007 Italian Excavations in Parthian Nisa, *Parthica* 10: 53–61.

Livshits, V.A. (1977), New Parthian Documents from South Turkmenistan, *Acta Antiqua Academiae Scientiarum Hungaricae* 25: 157–185.

Manassero, N. (2010), Tamga-like Images on Sealings from Old Nisa, *Parthica* 12: 17–29.

Manassero, N. (2013), Tamgas and Literacy among the Ancient Iranians, *Remarks, Journal of Signum* 1: 43–61.

Manassero, N. (2014), Marine Monsters in the Desert Sands. Thoughts on Some Sealings from Parthian Nisa, *Parthica* 16: 31–47.

Masson, M.E., Pugachenkova, G.A. (1954), Ottiski parfjanskih pechatej iz Nisy, *Vestnik Drevnej Istorii* 4: 159–169.

Masson, V.M. (1953), Humy Nisy, in: *Trudy JuTAKE II*, Ashgabat: 413–436.

Mollo, P. (2001), Le sigillature da Nisa Vecchia, *Parthica* 3: 159–210.

Nikitin, A.B. (1993/1994), Parthian Bullae from Nisa, *Silk Road Art and Archaeology* 3: 71–79.

Pilipko, V.N. (2001), *Staraja Nisa. Osnovnye itogi arheologičeskogo izučenija v sovetskij period*, Moscow.

Pilipko, V.N. (2008), The Central Ensemble of the Fortress Mihrdatkirt. Layout and Chronology, *Parthica* 10: 33–51.

Rostovzeff, M. (1932), Seleucid Babylonia, Bullae and Seals of Clay with Greek Inscriptions, *Yale Classical Studies* 3: 3–114.

Teh Gallop, A. (2006), One Seal Good, Two Seals Better, Three Seals Best? Multiple Impressions of Malay Seals, *Indonesia and the Malay World* 34 (100): 407–426.

Vdovin, V.Ju. (1984), Humy juznogo Turkmenistana parfjanskogo i sasanidskogo vremeni (Parfieny i Apavartikeny), in: V.M. Masson (ed.), *Problemy arheologii Turkmenistana*, Ashgabat.

Xin, W., Lecomte, O. (2012), Clay Sealings from the Iron Age Citadel at Ulug Depe, *Archäologische Mitteilungen aus Iran und Turan* 44: 313–328.

ELECTRUM * Vol. 22 (2015): 143–154
doi: 10.4467/20800909EL.15.007.3945
www.ejournals.eu/electrum

Laser-scanner Survey at Kong-e Yār 'Alīvand. Research of the Iranian-Italian Joint Expedition in Kūzestān*

Vito Messina

University of Torino

Jafar Mehr Kian

Iranian Center for Archaeological Research, Tehran

Abstract: Between 2008 and 2010, the Iranian-Italian Joint Expedition in Kūzestān conducted research in the area of the modern city of Īda under the co-direction of the authors of this paper. The aim of the expedition was to acquire new data on the Parthian rock reliefs recognised up to now at Kong-e Azdar, Kong-e Yār 'Alīvand and Kong-e Kamālvand by applying the most up-to-date technologies, namely the GPS survey and laser scanning. Indeed, despite the several studies conducted on these works, several aspects, such as the chronology of the represented scenes, their evolution and carving techniques, still need to be clarified.

A preliminary elaboration of the data acquired at Kong-e Yār 'Alīvand allowed us to create a digital 3D model of the sculpted surface consisting of 2,467,745 points. The surface analysis conducted on this digital support revealed traces of an inscription on the upper part of the sculpted scene, which has been deeply eroded and was never reported in previous surveys, and still undetected iconographic details, which shed new light on the sculpted scene, usually interpreted as an investiture.

Key words: rock reliefs, Kong-e Yār 'Alīvand, Kūzestān.

When I met Professor David Sellwood for the last time in 2006, in Florence, he was preparing a revision of a particular series of Parthian "provincial" issues with Alberto Simonetta. We spent almost the whole day looking at ruler portraits through magnifying lenses and, on that occasion, I asked him for his opinion on a project that I was at that time just starting to think about. My intention was to conduct field research in the area

* Acknowledgements: all pictures are courtesy of the "Iranian-Italian Joint Expedition in Khuzestan," held by the Centro Ricerche Archeologiche e Scavi di Torino per il Medio Oriente e l'Asia and the Iranian Center for Archaeological Research.

of the city of Izeh (ancient Mal-e Mir), where several Parthian rock carvings are located, with the aim of acquiring new information and data on their method of manufacture and interpretation. Needless to say, he warmly encouraged me to proceed and kindly gave me precious suggestions on the scientific relevance of these sculptural works. That research started in 2008, with the first campaign of the Iranian-Italian Joint Expedition in Khuzestan, and is still ongoing under the co-direction of myself – the corresponding author – and Jafar Mehr Kian.[1] We would like to honour Professor Sellwood by presenting some of the results of the research conducted at Hung-e Yar-i Alivand, where traces of an inscription unnoticed by previous surveys and new iconographic details have been detected on the surface of a well-known Parthian rock carving.

The Parthian carvings located in the area of the modern city of Izeh belong to the so-called group of rock carvings of ancient Elymais.[2] These works are of particular importance for two main reasons: they constitute the most outstanding group of carvings in Parthian Iran, and their individual characteristics set them apart from other sculptural works found in other regions of the Parthian empire. The carvings dated to the AD centuries appear particularly uniform because of their composition (in which an absolute hieratic frontality of the figures prevails), the choice of iconographic themes (such as scenes celebrating the sovereign, the homage of dignitaries or investiture scenes), and some figurative details (such as the clothing).

However, some carvings are not well understood because of their poor state of preservation, while their method of manufacture and interpretation have never been focused on in recent studies. Indeed, despite the research being carried out by traditional methods, some aspects regarding their iconography, style and carving technique still need to be clarified, for the available documentation is limited to photographs or drawings which, even when of superior quality, do not allow for more in-depth examination.

Our project aimed to acquire new data on these carvings by means of modern technologies and methods, including architectural survey techniques: namely laser scanning and 3D modelling. This technology produces complex information by 3D digital models that are faithful and measurable representations of real objects. Given that 3D models of the carvings might be constructed on a scale of 1 : 1 (both graphically and in a digital medium), previously undetected details might be subjected to analysis. These observations are the result of objective measurements, verifiable by other observers using the same data: for this reason, the 3D surface analysis offers promise of considerable advance in the study of ancient sculptural works, while 3D digital models are innovative means for documenting and sharing both raw and elaborated data.

Three rock carvings in the area of Izeh, dated to the Parthian period, have been selected for this analysis, namely at Hung-e Yar-i Alivand, Hung-e Azhdar and Hung-e Kamalvand. The relief at Hung-e Azhdar is, for several reasons, the most important of them from the historical point of view: indeed, it shows a scene of homage or investiture

---

[1] The expedition operates within the framework of a Memorandum of Understanding signed by the Centro Ricerche Archeologiche e Scavi di Torino per il Medio Oriente e l'Asia and the Iranian Center for Archaeological Research. Other Institutions involved in the project are the University of Turin, Politecnico di Torino, and the Ayapir Cultural Heritage NGO.

[2] At present, 14 Parthian monuments are known to us in the region of Elymais (Mehr Kian 1997, 67–72; Mehr Kian 2011, 293–298).

that has been related to the conquest of Elymais by Mithradates I.[3] The data acquired and elaborated after our laser-scanner acquisition revealed that the scene showing a bearded horseman in profile (often identified as Mithradates I himself) proceeding toward four standing men in a frontal position and lined-up in a paratactic manner, which can be seen there (on the surface of a huge boulder), was executed at two times: its right half, in which the standing men are represented, was re-sculpted in the first decades of the 2nd century AD, having been added to the left half (that of the horseman), which can be dated to the half of the 1st century BC.[4] In any case, the carving appears to have been commissioned and re-sculpted by local rulers, and not by the famous Parthian king.

In the same area, two other rock carvings reveal stylistic and iconographic analogies with the four Hung-e Azhdar standing men: one is located at Hung-e Kamalvand, on the southern slope of a gorge giving access to the highlands of the Bakthiari mountains, and the other at Hung-e Yar-i Alivand, on the mountain slope that follows the modern road leading to the valley of Hung-e Azhdar.

The relief at Hung-e Yar-i Alivand is particularly damaged because of surface erosion: it is indeed completely exposed to wind and rainwater, having been sculpted at about 2 m from ground level on a vertical cliff oriented approximately north-southward.[5] It represents two standing men in a frontal position, paratactically placed side-by-side and dressed in the characteristic Parthian belted (?) tunics and trousers, perhaps with a cloak.[6] Their feet are in profile and slightly turned down. The man on the right has his left hand at his hip, perhaps on the hilt of a sword – almost completely disappeared – and holds an object – usually interpreted as a ring – in his lowered right hand. The man on the left mirrors that on the right, with his right hand on his hip: he seems to hold an object that is interpreted by some scholars as a flask;[7] his left hand seems to be at his chest. The scene is interpreted as an investiture, in which the right man is investing the left man with his authority,[8] and is dated, quite unanimously, to the 2nd century AD.[9] However, one of the most interesting problems related to the Hung-e Yar-i Alivand carving is the debated presence of an inscription below the lower frame of the sculpted surface, under the feet of the two standing men, which allowed the Hungarian scholar J. Harmatta to identify the figure on the left as a god (Ahura Mazda) presenting a diadem to a local ruler (Kamnaskires VI), on the right.[10]

The purpose of our survey was to verify, in the first instance, the presence of this debated inscription. The laser-scanner acquisition was accurately planned before the fieldwork was started and then performed using a high-resolution instrument based on the triangulation principle. This traditional survey technique, which is also the basis of

---

[3] Von Gall 1969–1970, 301–302; de Waele 1975, 60; Vanden Berghe 1983, 120–121; Vanden Berghe/ Schippmann 1985, 32–38; Kawami 1987, 209–213; Mathiesen 1992, 119–121; Invernizzi 1998, 219–259.

[4] Messina and Mehr Kian 2010, 31–45; Messina/Mehr Kian 2011, 215–231.

[5] The rock carving is located at 31°56'12.47"N and 49°50'24.90"E, according to the WGS84 coordinates system.

[6] Hinz 1963, 169–170, pl. 57; de Waele 1975, 65–66, note 4; Vanden Berghe 1983, 48; Vanden Berghe/ Schippmann 1985, 40–41, fig. 2, pl. 7; Kawami 1987, no. 51; Mathiesen 1992, 123–124.

[7] Vanden Berghe/Schippmann 1985, 41.

[8] Hinz 1963, 170; Vanden Berghe/Schippmann 1985, 41; Kawami 1987, 127.

[9] Mathiesen 1992, 124 and selected bibliography.

[10] Harmatta 1984, 174–175.

other metric survey techniques such as photogrammetry, allows very high accuracy (less than 0.2 mm) and resolution (1 point every sq mm). The instrument selected is a third-generation handyscan, a laser scanner device that fixes the coordinate system directly on the object, allowing the acquisition phase also in critical field conditions. Markers have to be placed randomly on the object's surface at a distance of no more than 5 cm from each other, in order to allow the scanner to recognise its position in a 3D model: these are reflective circular targets, with a diameter of about 5 mm, that can be removed after acquisition. The surveyed surfaces may be subdivided into small portions in order to fit the memory capacity of the laptop used for recording data.

The handyscan seems particularly suited to the acquisition of the irregular surface often characterising rock carvings. The natural, and generally irregular, conformation of a carved rock requires careful detection, because of the presence of blind angles or protruding parts that could hinder the objective measurement and analysis of the sculpting depth. The handyscan is moved like a brush, at about 10–15 cm from the acquired surface, and it follows the natural conformation or irregular surface of a rock carving perfectly, avoiding the problems of blind angles or loss of information in post-processing. Each of the acquired sectors overlaps adjacent sectors by about 10%, in order to guarantee the stability of the geometry of the whole object and an average of 1 point every 2 mm, with an estimated accuracy of 0.15 mm.

The 3D model provides a geometric description and in many cases this is not sufficient to allow a correct interpretation of both semantic and geometric contents. To overcome this limit, high-resolution true colour images may be acquired and oriented in a photogrammetric way on the 3D laser scanner model to allow a correct mapping of the images on the 3D model itself.

At the end of the data treatment many instruments of analysis were produced in order to provide various information: realistic 3D models, true orthophotos and solid images. While 3D realistic models and orthophotos are well-known products, solid images are a new investigation instrument realised thanks to the integration of laser scanner and photogrammetry: they are high-resolution digital RGB files (perspective and non-orthorectified) integrated by a numerical matrix of the same resolution and providing tridimensional data of the scanned surface, in which all the pixels contain x, y and z coordinates. In this way, experts may obtain sections, profiles and points in order to verify their hypothesis and to outline new investigation strategies. The use of controlled lighting conditions, infrared or macro photography for the carving at Hung-e Yar-i Alivand was initially taken into consideration for verifying the data acquired by laser scanning; however, the preliminary results of raking light and infrared photography, showing a very faint relief, left us doubtful of achieving a good result, and discouraged us from pursuing those techniques, notwithstanding their reliability, because of the poor state of preservation of the sculpted surface.

Acquisition by laser scanning at Hung-e Yar-i Alivand was conducted in March 2009 and lasted two days. The 2.2 sq m sculpted surface was divided into nine squared sectors, each of 60 × 60 cm. About 3,000 markers were placed on the surface for the laser tracker and completely removed after acquisition. Even the rock below the carving's lower frame, under the feet of the standing men, was acquired down to ground level, with the purpose of verifying the presence of an inscription. Each sector was separately scanned and the instrument was handled at about 15–20 cm from the rock surface: several frames were acquired as digital files at the highest resolution (1.95 mm), and an overlap band was saved between adjacent sectors, with a tolerance of 10%. The scanner never touched the surface during the operation. The acquisition of several sectors was repeated when the relevant acquired frames needed to be completed or integrated.

Images with a digital photogrammetric camera were also acquired in order to update the information provided by the laser scanning: several frames were photographed twice, at a distance of 5.3 and 1.3 m (for details) and the used lens was calibrated before the image acquisition in order to bypass radial and tangential geometric distortions.

The vertices were located on the ground by a traditional topographic method, while 15 control points, placed on the sculpted surface, were located by a total station, in order to define a georeferenced network. This allowed us to relate the numerical and tridimensional nature of the acquired information to a known reference system. The accuracy of the grid was verified by triangulation of each vertex, and intersections of the control points were measured from two vertices. Some of the markers (less than 0.1% of those placed on the sculpted surface) were surveyed by using a total station from two different stations, whose coordinates were surveyed by using a GNSS static positioning. The coordinates of the total station points were estimated with an accuracy of 1 mm, but the survey scheme adopted for the markers – namely forward intersection from known points – provided an accuracy of less than 0.5 mm for the markers and less than 1 mm for the global coordinate system.

The frames acquired at Hung-e Yar-i Alivand were elaborated in the laboratory of the Politecnico di Torino, and allowed us to create a 3D digital model of the rock carving consisting of 2,467,745 points, with an accuracy of approximately 0.2 mm. The images acquired by the digital photogrammetric camera were elaborated to obtain digital ortho-photos and solid images of the scanned surfaces. Software was created for the analysis of these data: the user can follow lines, locate points, define areas on the image and recover metric information.[11]

All the elaborated files – the 3D models, orthophotos and solid images – were merged on a single digital platform, and precise and objective measurements of the sculpted surfaces were taken in a virtual three-dimensional space. Given that the numerical and three-dimensional nature of the acquired information, namely the point cloud, is related to a known reference system, the anomalies evidenced by the software basic tools (progressive sections, distances, angles, areas and volumes) are nothing but the graphic rendering of equations, whose result can be mathematically verified at any time. Consequently, the detected anomalies cannot be ascribed to the subjective interpretation of anyone observing the 3D model and/or using the software tools, but rather to the objective situation of the carving and/or the conformation of the rock.

The preliminary elaboration of the data acquired at Hung-e Yar-i Alivand demonstrated that there is no inscription below the carving's lower frame, under the feet of the standing men. If this inscription existed, it has now completely disappeared. The 3D model rather revealed traces of a previously unreported inscription on the upper part of the sculpted scene, between the heads of the standing men: this is invisible to the naked

---

[11] Bornaz/Rinaudo 2004, 514–519.

eye as it has been deeply eroded, and only scant traces of some letters became detectable in the grey-scale post-processed 3D frame of the carving.

It is an Elymaean inscription in Aramaic of the south Mesopotamian group, arranged on two lines, which can be read as follows:[12]

line 1.   [.] 'š(m)b(p)[.](n/k)[…]
line 2.   br k[.](n/k)[..]k[…]

These can be translated as:

line 1.   […]
line 2.   son of […]

The letters are typologically similar to those that compose the much clearer inscription already recognised on the rock carving at Hung-e Kamalvand, which appears to be read as "Phraates, the priest, son of Kabneshkir" and has been dated, by comparison with similar inscriptions on the carvings at Tang-e Sarwak, to the end of the 1st/beginning of the 2nd cent. AD.[13] As far as palaeography is concerned, the letters of the Hung-e Yar-i Alivand inscription appear to be of the same type and, if the date proposed for the former is accepted, it seems possible to date the Hung-e Yar-i Alivand carving to the same period, for it was surely sculpted when the letters were incised on the surface between the men's heads. In the second line of the Hung-e Yar-i Alivand inscription, after the word "son (of)," one could be tempted to read the dynastic name "Kbnshyr," in the light of the Hung-e Kamalvand inscription; however, only two letters out of six – or seven (?) – are clear, and this name – that of the father or ancestor of one of the standing men – remains obscure. In any case, the scene composition, arranged on two paratactic figures with an inscription running on the top of it, and the type of the inscription itself, which is a statement made by "someone, son of someone," appear quite similar to those on the Hung-e Kamalvand carving. It is generally assumed that this carving depicts an investiture:[14] it shows a man, on the right, wearing a belted tunic and trousers, pouring liquid (probably water) from a small jug, flask or pitcher held in his right hand, and standing in front of a horseman proceeding toward him. It is also assumed that the inscription refers to the horseman and claims his royal descent, while the standing figure remains unidentified; however, the possibility that the inscription refers to the standing man cannot be completely ruled out. In any case, if this scene represents an investiture, it must be placed in a religious context, because of the reference to a priest made in the inscription and the action of pouring liquid made by the standing man. According to T.S. Kawami, who also considers the religious milieu, this relief may depict a member of the Kamnaskirid dynasty who retained some power, perhaps religious, rather than political, in the region.[15]

The religious milieu already attested for the Hung-e Kamalvand carving could help in the interpretation of the Hung-e Yar-i Alivand sculpted scene, especially in the light of the observations that can be made on the 3D model and post-processed false-colour image obtained after our laser scanner acquisition. Indeed, the preliminary surface analysis

---

[12] Moriggi 2011, 109.

[13] W. Hinz translated the Hung-e Kamalvand inscription and proposed dating it to c. AD 100 (Hinz 1963, 171–172).

[14] Mathiesen 1992, 122–123 and selected bibliography.

[15] Kawami, 1987, 72–73.

revealed first of all that the left hand of the left figure is undoubtedly at his chest (his arm being folded), that no flasks are clearly detectable in his right hand, which seems indeed to rest on his hip (maybe on the hilt of a sword, like the mirroring figure), and that the object held in the right man's right hand appears oblong in shape rather than circular. This said, it seems improbable that the right man holds a ring, which should appear circular, and even that the left man is receiving it, for his left arm is folded. The oblong shape of the object held by the right man is closer to that of the small vessel held by the left figure sculpted at Hung-e Kamalvand, and even the arm gesture is similar, the hand being lowered to pour liquid from the vessel. On the basis of these observations, it seems that the scenes at Hung-e Yar-i Alivand and Hung-e Kamalvand have been sculpted following the same composition scheme: this is based on two paratactic figures (one of which is identified by an inscription on the top), of whom the figure on the right makes a symbolic gesture – of purification (?) – in front of the figure on the left (a standing man at Hung-e Yar-i Alivand, a rider at Hung-e Kamalvand). Furthermore, the head of the left man at Hung-e Yar-i Alivand seems surrounded by a kind of halo, which could be interpreted as either what remains of curly hair or else a crown of rays (judging by the points that can still be seen beside the figure's left ear): if the latter interpretation is valid, the left man could be even identified as a sun god or – more probably – a deified person. It must be admitted, however, that this hypothesis cannot be definitively demonstrated, for the left figure's head is deeply eroded, especially on the top. In any case, the analogies between the two carvings outlined above, if considered correct, lead us to assume that both represent a scene of homage rather than an investiture; a homage paid, in a religious milieu, by a high-ranking personage, perhaps a sovereign (who is always represented on the right), to a figure majestically standing in front of him (and always on the left), which can be defined as an ancestor, possibly deified, of his own dynasty: the line of descent is indeed traced in both inscriptions by the occurrence of the word "son (of)."

The religious nature of the Elymaean rock carvings in fact also seems to be confirmed by the discovery, in front of the sculpted boulder at Hung-e Azhdar, of a cult place, far older than the Parthian relief sculpted, in two times, onto its surface, where particular objects (most of all arrowheads) were offered close to a platform in undressed stones, laid at the feet of the boulder itself.[16]

BIBLIOGRAPHY

Bornaz, L., Rinaudo, F. (2004), Terrestrial Laser Scanner Data Processing, in: M. Orhan Altan (ed.), *International Archives of the Photogrammetry, Remote Sensing and Spatial Information Sciences. Proceedings and Results XXXV, Istanbul (2004) XX ISPRS Congress*, Istanbul: 514–519.

De Waele, E. (1975), La sculpture rupestre d'Elymaïde. Deux fragments inédits d'époque parthe, *Revue d'Assyriologie et d'Archéologie Orientale* 69: 59–79.

---

[16]   Messina/Mehr Kian 2011, 215–231.

Harmatta, J. (1984), King Kabneshkir Son of King Kabneshkir, *Acta Antiqua Academie Scientiarum Hungaricae* 30: 167–180.

Hinz, W. (1963), Zwei neuentdeckte Parthische Felsreliefs, *Iranica Antiqua* 3: 169–172.

Invernizzi, A. (1998), Elymaeans, Seleucids, and the Hung-e Azhdar Relief, *Mesopotamia* 33: 219–259.

Kawami, T.S. (1987), *Monumental Art of the Parthian Period in Iran*, Leiden.

Mathiesen, H.E. (1992), *Sculpture in the Parthian Empire. A Study in Chronolgy*, Aarhus.

Mehr Kian, J. (1997), The Elymaian Rock-Carving of Shavand, Izeh, *Iran* 35: 67–72.

Mehr Kian, J. (2001), Trois bas-reliefs parthes dans le monts Bakhtiari, *Iranica Antiqua* 36: 293–298.

Messina, V., Mehr Kian, J. (2010), The Iranian-Italian Joint Expedition in Khuzistan. Hung-e Azhdar. 1st Campaign (2008), *Parthica* 12: 31–45.

Messina, V., Mehr Kian, J. (2011), Ricognizione dei rilievi partici d'Elimaide. La piana di Izeh-Malamir, *Vicino & Medio Oriente* 15: 215–231.

Moriggi, M. (2011), An Aramaic Inscription in the Hong-e Yar-'Aliwand rock relief (Elymais), *Parthica* 13: 107–109.

Vanden Berghe, L. (1983), *Reliefs rupestres de l'Irān ancien*, Bruxelles.

Vanden Berghe, L., Schippmann, K. (1985), *Les reliefs rupestres d'Elymaïde (Iran) de l'époque parthe*, Gent.

Von Gall, H. (1969–1970), Beobachtungen zum arsakidischen Diadem und zur parthischen Bildkunst, *Istanbuler Mitteilungen* 19–20: 299–318.

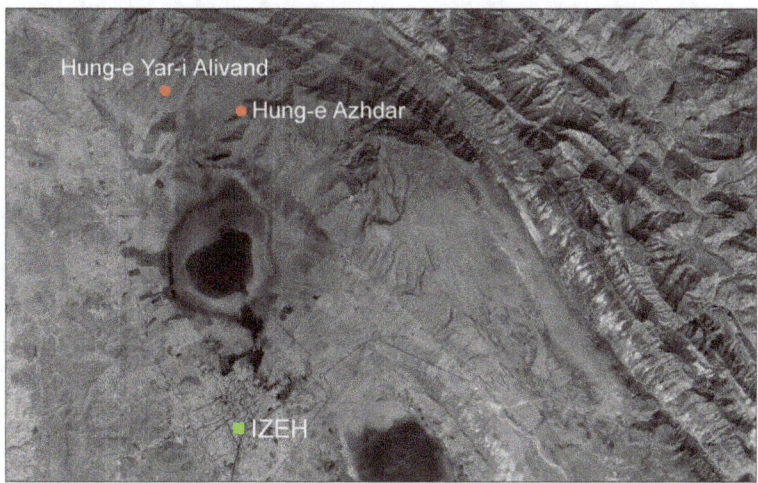

Fig. 1. The Area of Izeh in modern day Khuzestan (south-western Iran)

Fig. 2. Location of the Hung-e Yar-i Alivand rock carving

Fig. 3. The rock carving at Hung-e Yar-i Alivand

Fig. 4. Hung-e Yar-i Alivand. Acquisition of the rock carving by handyscan

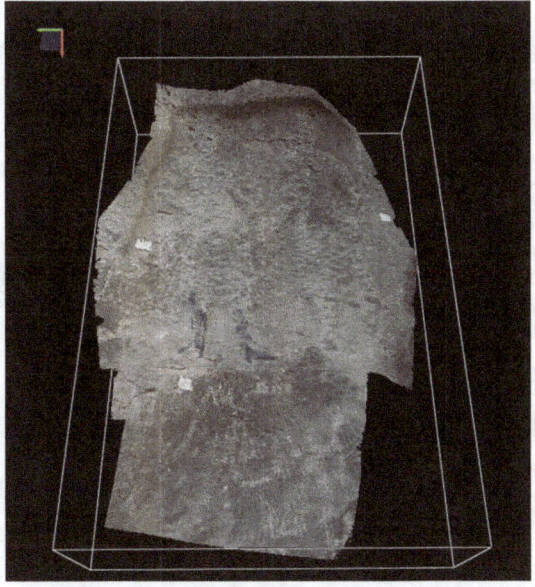

Fig. 5. 3D model of the Hung-e Yar-i Alivand carving

Fig. 6. False-color image Hung-e Yar-i Alivand carving. Chromatic nuances correspond to different sculpting depth

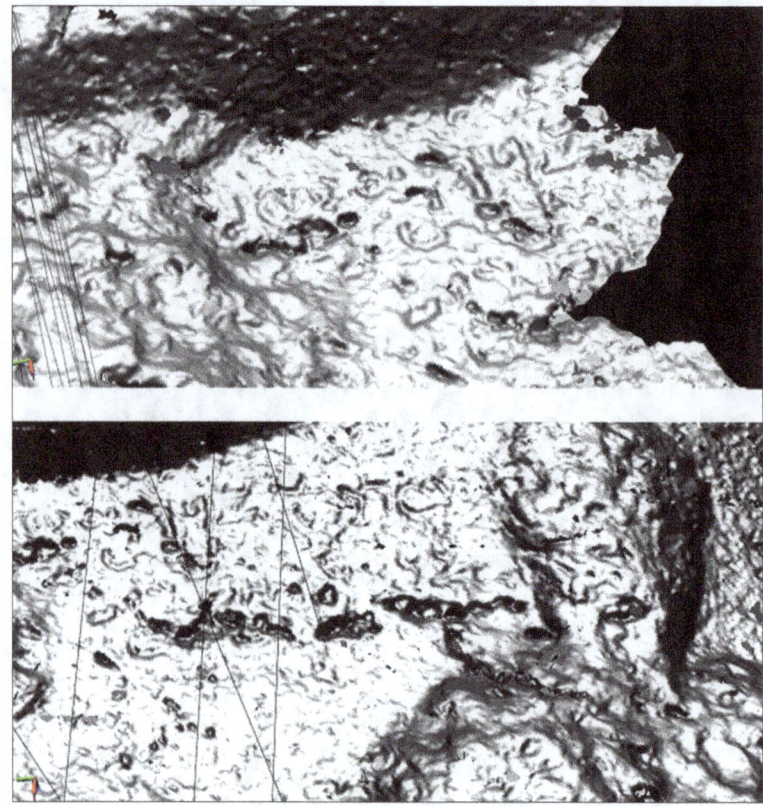

Fig. 7. Grey-scale 3D model of the Hung-e Yar-i Alivand Parthian carving. Detail of the inscription in the upper part of the sculpted scene

ELECTRUM * Vol. 22 (2015): 155–158
doi: 10.4467/20800909EL.15.008.3946
www.ejournals.eu/electrum

CRÉPUSCULE DE L'EMPIRE PARTHE – LES DERNIÈRES DRACHMES

Alain Chenevier

Abstract: The silver drachms issued for the two competing Arsacid brothers Vologases VI and Artabanus V may be conveniently divided into two distinct groups. However, the ensuing political instability from the rivalry between the two sons of Vologases V was not without numismatic consequence. It has, in fact, left its marks on some very rare and important outputs from the turbulent period c. AD 208–224 of Parthian history. We have several « mule » or « hybrid » drachms that are struck from different obverse and reverse dies, each belonging to one of the two brother kings. These testify to the political confusion that persisted up until the fall of the Arsacid dynasty.

Key words: Vologases VI, Artabanus V, Arsacids, Parthian numismatics, Parthian history.

A la mort de Vologèses V, en 208, son fils aîné Vologèses VI monte sur le trône. Une partie de la noblesse lui préfère pourtant son frère Artaban V. Ces querelles de succession affaiblissent une fois de plus le royaume. Après plusieurs années de guerre civile Artaban finit par l'emporter, mais laisse malgré tout à Vologèses l'administration d'une partie des provinces orientales du royaume.[1]

En 216, Caracalla spécule sur les divisions entre les successeurs de Vologèses V pour mener une offensive contre les Parthes. Après quelques mois de pillage sans gloire les Romains sont contraints de s'enfuir devant les forces regroupées des Parthes. Caracalla est assassiné et c'est Macrin qui est amené à signer une capitulation désastreuse pour Rome, après une terrible bataille.

Pourtant la cohésion fragile qui avait permis aux Parthes de vaincre les forces romaines se brise sitôt la guerre terminée. C'est d'autant plus dramatique qu'Artaban n'a pas pris la mesure de la rébellion qui se fomente contre l'autorité centrale parthe, depuis qu'en 208 Ardashir a placé son père Papak sur le trône de Perside. En 223 et 224 Ardashir franchit une nouvelle étape en s'emparant facilement de l'Elymaïde, de la Characène et de la Susiane, sans véritable réaction d'un pouvoir parthe exsangue.[2]

---

[1] A. Verstandig, *Histoire de l'Empire parthe* (-250–227), Bruxelles 2011, 338.

[2] *Ibid.*, 350.

Artaban V se décide enfin à réagir en avril 224, mais l'affrontement tourne à l'avantage d'Ardashir. Artaban est tué au combat à la bataille d'Hormizdgan. C'est la fin des Arsacides et l'avènement d'une nouvelle dynastie, les Sassanides.[3]

Toutes les drachmes de Vologèses VI sont actuellement classées sous la même référence, S.88, pourtant celles-ci se subdivisent en deux groupes bien distincts. Sur le type principal, frappé en abondance, figurent derrière l'effigie deux caractères qui correspondent au début du nom du Roi.

A l'intérieur de ce type principal, le graphisme des deux caractères derrière le buste et l'aspect du monogramme du revers permettent de différencier les drachmes S.88.18 (Fig. 1) à S.88.20,[4] pendant que le très rare type S.88.22 se singularise par la forme recourbée des oreillettes de la tiare. De nombreuses variantes, actuellement non inventoriées, concernent l'aspect du trône, quand il est matérialisé, et la représentation du collier du Roi.

Fig. 1   Fig. 2

Le type S.88.23 (Fig. 2) se distingue par l'absence des deux lettres derrière le buste propres aux autres drachmes de Vologèses VI. La tiare décorée d'un croissant et les oreillettes démesurément longues en sont deux autres caractéristiques.[5] Toutes ces particularités font que ce type n'est pas une simple variante et qu'il mérite d'être considéré comme une émission à part entière.

Sur l'ensemble des drachmes de Vologèses VI, quel que soit le type, le nom du souverain apparaît en totalité sur la première ligne du revers (Fig. 3). L'inscription se lit de droite à gauche.

---

[3]   La chronologie reste incertaine. Selon les sources la date de la mort d'Artaban V varie de 224 à 227. Concernant Vologèses VI, Séleucie émet des tétradrachmes à son nom jusqu'en 221/222, mais pas au-delà. L'unique exemplaire avec la date ΘΛΦ (soit 227/228), conservé à la B.N.F., n'est pas un élément suffisant pour considérer que le règne de Vologèses VI s'est prolongé jusqu'à cette date.

[4]   L'existence du type S.88.21 n'est pas avérée. Un caractère imparfaitement réalisé, par un graveur malhabile, a pu être interprété comme une volonté délibérée d'inscrire une lettre différente à la place d'un des deux caractères placés derrière le buste.

[5]   On trouve de rares exemplaires « intermédiaires », avec le style des drachmes S.88.23, en particulier les oreillettes très longues, mais avec les deux caractères derrière le buste et pas de croissant pour orner la tiare.

Fig. 3 wlgšy MLK' (Roi Vologèses)   Fig. 4 'rtbnw MLK' (Roi Artaban)

Les drachmes d'Artaban V portent elles aussi le nom du Roi sur la première ligne du revers (Fig. 4). Ces drachmes, beaucoup moins courantes que celles de Vologèses, se répartissent également en deux groupes, S.89 (Fig. 5) et S.90 (Fig. 6).

Les types S.89.1, S.89.2 et S.89.3[6] sont presque identiques et ne se différencient entre eux que par le monogramme. A l'avers s'inscrivent les deux lettres du début du nom d'Artaban derrière le buste, ce qui incite donc à rapprocher ces trois variantes du type principal de Vologèses VI.

Les drachmes S.90, sans lettres derrière l'effigie et avec une étoile au centre de la tiare, sont le pendant des drachmes S.88.23, ce qui laisse penser que ce sont deux émissions parallèles.

Fig. 5   Fig. 6

Depuis Orodes II le croissant et l'étoile prennent place régulièrement sur les drachmes parthes. On peut supposer qu'à un moment donné, dans la rivalité qui oppose Vologèses et Artaban, le croissant indique sans ambiguïté qu'il s'agit d'une monnaie de Vologèses, pendant que l'étoile, présente sur le type S.90, désigne une monnaie d'Artaban.

L'existence de quelques exemplaires S.88.23 avec le croissant volontairement effacé (S.88.24, Fig. 7) confirme qu'il faut voir, dans ce contexte, une signification politique à ces symboles.

David Sellwood répertorie, sous le type S.89.5, une drachme hybride Vologèses VI / Artaban V, avec un avers S.88.18 et un revers S.89.1. Si la réalité de cette drachme est très peu probable, on trouve en revanche une drachme hybride avec un avers S.88.18 et un revers S.89.3 (Fig. 8). Une autre variante de ce type provient elle aussi d'un avers de

---

[6] La rarissime S.89.4, où la deuxième ligne de la légende porte le nom « Tiridates », est sans doute la drachme parthe la plus tardive. Toutefois, ce type n'appartient pas *stricto sensu* au monnayage d'Artaban V, cette drachme ayant probablement été frappée après la mort de ce dernier, par un de ses partisans, témoignage d'une ultime tentative de s'opposer à la mainmise d'Ardashir sur la totalité de l'Empire.

type 88.18, mais d'un revers, d'après l'examen de la deuxième ligne de la légende,[7] de type 90.1 (Fig. 9).

Le cas de figure d'une drachme hybride Artaban V / Vologèses VI existe également. Sur cette monnaie (Fig. 10), non référencée, l'avers est de type S.89 et le revers de type S.88.19.

Fig. 7   Fig. 8

Fig. 9   Fig. 10

Les drachmes S.88.24 où le croissant qui désigne Vologèses VI est volontairement effacé et ces différentes monnaies hybrides ont très probablement été frappées à la fin du règne d'Artaban. Bien que très peu communes, elles sont un important témoignage de la confusion qui règne alors dans l'Empire parthe, prélude à l'extinction de la dynastie arsacide.

Crédits photographiques :

Fig. 1, 2, 5, 9 : Collection A.C.
Fig. 6, 8, 10 : Collection G.R.F. Assar
Fig. 7 : Classical Numismatic Group, Inc.

---

[7] Les revers des types S.89.3 et S.90.1 portent le même monogramme, mais se différencient après observation de la légende : sur l'ensemble des drachmes du type S.89 le « N » de la deuxième ligne de la légende est rétrograde, alors qu'il a toujours une forme normale sur les drachmes S.90.1.

ELECTRUM * Vol. 22 (2015): 159–171
doi: 10.4467/20800909EL.15.009.3947
www.ejournals.eu/electrum

THE SYRIAC *BOOK OF THE LAWS OF THE COUNTRIES*, EUSEBIUS' *PREPARATION FOR THE GOSPEL*, AND THE *CLEMENTINE RECOGNITIONS*: EARLY WITNESSES FOR CHRISTIANITY IN CENTRAL ASIA?*

Nathanael Andrade

University of Oregon

Abstract: In a key passage of the Syriac *Book of the Laws of the Countries*, Christians are de-scribed as residing among the Medes, Persians, Parthians, and Kushans. This statement has some-times encouraged scholars to accept that Christianity had penetrated the Iranian plateau and cen-tral Asia by the early third century CE. But this testimony does not necessarily reflect the actual state of contemporary Christianity in such regions. Instead, it is based on a text that had been circulating in the eastern Mediterranean and upper Mesopotamia during the late second and early third centuries CE. This text, now lost, had ascribed the evangelization of such regions to the apostle Thomas.

Key words: *Book of the Laws of the Countries*, Eusebius, *Clementine Recognitions*, the apostle Thomas, central Asia, the Parthian empire, Christianity.

According to a certain passage from the Syriac *Book of the Laws of the Countries*, oth-erwise known as *On Fate*, contemporary Christians resided in the Iranian plateau and central Asia.[1] Since the Syriac *Book* (as it is hereafter called) is intimately associated with the school of Bardaisan and is generally deemed to have been composed in its sur-viving form c. 225 CE,[2] scholars have sometimes treated the passage as testimony for the movement of Christianity to these regions by the early third century. But whether the

---

* I am grateful to the Department of History at the University of Oregon, to the Institute for Advanced Study (School of Historical Studies) at Princeton, NJ, and to the Andrew W. Mellon Foundation Fellowship for Assistant Professors. Their support made the research for this article possible.

[1] *The Book of the Laws of the Countries*, in Drijvers 1964, 60 and Ramelli 2009a, 196–198.

[2] Ramelli (2009a, 18–32 and 2009b, 54–60) treats date and the relationship to the text described by Eusebius (as *on Fate*) and attributed to Bardaisan by him. Eusebius' citations are represented by *Preparation for the Gospel* (*Praeparatio Evangelica*) 6.9.32–6.10 in Mras 1982/1983 and *HE* 4.30 in Schwartz/Mommsen 1999.

text is referring to the actual state of Christianity is in fact unclear, and the sources for the *Book*'s information have yet to be thoroughly explored.

This article accordingly examines the nature of the source material informing how the key passage of the Syriac *Book* represents the state of Christianity in central Asia. As it maintains, the key passage does not reflect actual knowledge that Edessenes or Upper Mesopotamians possessed regarding Christian communities that dwelled in the region. Instead, it is based on the fiction of a text that had been circulating in the eastern Mediterranean and upper Mesopotamia during the late second and early third centuries CE: the lost Parthian *Acts of Thomas*. While eclipsed by the surviving *Acts of Thomas*, which celebrated the putative ministry of Judas Thomas in India,[3] the tradition regarding Judas Thomas' evangelization of Parthia clearly preceded it, and it generated the belief among contemporary Christians that coreligionists inhabited the Iranian plateau and central Asia. As a result, the Syriac *Book* has little value as a source for Christianity in central Asia; its treatment relies on the fictive *Acts of Thomas* in Parthia.

The Testimony of the *Book of the Laws of the Countries*

According to a passage from the Syriac *Book*, as well as the Greek variation notably transmitted by Eusebius about a century later, Christians dwelled in Media, Persia, Parthia proper, and the Kushan empire. By the time of the *Book*'s composition, the Kushan empire had spanned central Asia and north India, and writers of Greek often defined its inhabitants as "Bactrians." The Syriac *Book* in fact notes that "Kushans" and "Bactrians" were different names for the same basic people.[4] The Syriac text and the Greek variation provided by Eusebius for the relevant passage read as follows:

> (*Book of the Laws*): Those (our Christian brothers) who are in Parthia do not take two wives. Those who are in Judea are not circumcised. Our sisters among the *Gelaye*[5] and among the Kushans do not couple with foreigners. Those who are in Persia do not marry their daughters. Those who are in Media do not flee their dead, bury them while living, or give them as food for dogs. Those who are in Edessa do not kill their wives or sisters who have committed adultery.[6]

> (Eusebius, *Preparation for the Gospel*): The Christians in Parthia do not engage in polygamy, while happening to be Parthian. Those in Media do not throw corpses to dogs. Those in Persia, while being Persian, do not marry their daughters. Among Bactrians and Gelians, they do not kill their spouses.[7]

As narrated immediately above, the key passage from the Syriac *Book* asserts that Christians lived in the Iranian plateau and central Asia by the time that the *Book* was composed (c. 225 CE). The variation of Eusebius entirely replicates this perspective,

---

[3] In Wright 1871 and Bonnet 1903, 99–291. For translation and extended commentary, see Klijn 2003.

[4] *The Book of the Laws of the Countries*, in Drijvers 1964, 46 and Ramelli 2009a, 182.

[5] In Syriac *gelaye* is sometimes rendered *'elaye*. The single manuscript of the *Book of the Laws of the Countries*, in Drijvers 1964, 44 and 60 and Ramelli 2009a, 180 and 198, with n. 179, accordingly features both forms. See also the single Syriac manuscript of the surviving *Acts of Thomas* containing the *Hymn of the Pearl*, line 6 in Poirier 1981, 330–236 and Ferreia 2002, 39–65.

[6] *The Book of the Laws of the Countries*, in Drijvers 1964, 60; Ramelli 2009a, 196–198.

[7] Eusebius, *Praeparatio Evangelica* 6.10.46: Mras 1982/1983. Also see *FGrH/BNJ* 710, Fr. 3.

even if it omits certain material and associates with the Kushans and *Gelaye* the characteristics that the *Book* attributes to Edessenes (the killing of wives, as opposed to promiscuity with foreigners). As a result, scholars have sometimes assumed that Christian communities populated the regions in which the passage situates Christian brethren: Parthia, Fars/Persis, Media, the territory inhabited by the *Gelaye* of the Caspian sea coast, and the Kushan empire of central Asia and north India.[8] The implication of such an interpretation is that the writer of the *Book* had actual knowledge of Christians living in such regions and that some meaningful contact between Christians in Iran and central Asia and those residing in Edessa existed. This view receives ostensible support from the Syriac *Book*'s accurate description of laws at the Mesopotamian city of Hatra.[9]

But this viewpoint poses problems, and as this section argues, it is most probable that the *Book*'s testimony was based on a fictive literary tradition. This tradition was encapsulated by a text, now lost, that narrated how the apostle Judas Thomas had evangelized Parthia. This text was eventually eclipsed by the surviving work known as the *Acts of Thomas*, which narrates how Judas Thomas had evangelized India. During the third century, the Indian *Acts* circulated in both Greek and Syriac versions within the eastern Roman empire and Sasanian Persia, but a prior version of the *Acts* that described Judas Thomas' evangelization of Parthia was receiving the attention of eastern Roman readers decades and perhaps even generations earlier, certainly by the early third century. Moreover, Judas Thomas' alleged missionary activity in "Parthia" apparently referred to his itinerary in the Parthian empire, not merely to the region of north Iran known as Parthia in antiquity.

The third-century circulation of Thomas' Parthian *Acts* is certain. Eusebius' *Ecclesiastical History* indicates that the theologian Origen (who died c. 255 CE) had referred to a narrative in which the apostle Thomas evangelized Parthia. Origen had done so in his commentary on Genesis, which he had begun c. 225.[10] In Eusebius' rendering, the apostle is described simply as Thomas and not as Judas Thomas, as Greek authors commonly depicted him. As Eusebius' citation of Origen states, it was according to tradition (*paradosis*) that Thomas had engaged in such activity.[11] Origen could have been referring to an oral tradition here, but it is more reasonable to surmise that Origen was indexing a recent written tradition that had been ascribed a putatively oral origin and whose author was anonymous. This is because the earliest cited oral traditions regarding Judas Thomas or Thomas, which were recorded in writing by patristic authors in the late second century, indicate that he had not suffered martyrdom or evangelized any remote region at all.[12] The *Acts of the Apostles* and *The Gospel of Thomas* similarly bear no mention of Judas

---

[8] Jullien/Jullien 2002, 128–136; Baum/Winkler 2003, 7–8; Baumer 2006, 19; Nedungatt 2008, 111–112.

[9] *The Book of the Laws of the Countries*, in Drijvers 1964, 46 and 60 and Ramelli 2009a, 182 and 196–198. Kaizer 2006 treats Hatra's laws and the *Book*'s depiction of them.

[10] Eusebius, *HE* 3.1.1–3: Schwartz/Mommsen 1999. Myers 2010, 27–52 provides key discussion regarding the composition of the Indian *Acts* and its potential relationship with previous traditions, including the Parthian *Acts* (47–48). Nedungatt 2008: 177–222 compiles ancient attestations for Thomas' Parthian and Indian ministry. For dating of the commentary on Genesis, see McGuckin 2004a: 12.

[11] Eusebius, *HE* 3.1.1–3, with the Latin translation of Rufinus, *HE* 3.1: Schwartz/Mommsen 1999. Likewise, Socrates, *HE* 1.19, in Hansen 1995. For discussion of Eusebius' citation of Origen, see Nedungatt 2008, 182–186.

[12] Clement of Alexandria, *Strom*. 4.9.71.3–4, citing Heracleon, in Stählin/Früchtel 2011.

Thomas' martyrdom or evangelization of faraway lands.[13] It seems, then, that the written account of the Parthian *Acts* reflects a later second-century fiction influenced by the belief that the apostles had apportioned the known world for evangelization and had then suffered martyrdom.[14] Thomas' Parthian itinerary and martyrdom, even if ascribed to an older, anonymous oral tradition (*paradosis*), were accordingly the product of a textual agenda that can be traced to c. 175–200 CE. Since it is cited by both the Syriac *Book* and Origen and constituted the antecedent to the surviving Syriac and Greek *Acts of Thomas*, the Parthian *Acts* apparently circulated in the eastern Mediterranean and upper Mesopotamia during the late second and early third century, in both Greek and Syriac forms.

The premise that the testimony of the Syriac *Book* and Eusebius' variation are ultimately derived from the Parthian *Acts of Thomas* is supported by a vital article of evidence dating to the early fourth century. The *Clementine Recognitions*, which survives in Rufinus' Latin translation, contains yet another variation of the key passage from the Syriac *Book*.[15] While its narrator purports to be the voice of the first-century figure Clement, it explicitly associates the putatively contemporary preaching of the apostle Thomas with the state of Christianity in Parthian territory. The relevant passage states:

> Finally, most among the Parthians (*apud Parthos*) are no longer scattered into numerous marriages, just as Thomas, who is proclaiming the gospel among them, has written to us (*sicut nobis Thomas, qui apud illos evangelium praedicat, scripsit*). Most among the Medes do not throw corpses to dogs. The Persians do not take pleasure in wedlock with mothers or impure marriage with daughters. Susian women do not conduct permitted adultery.[16]

To be certain, this statement from the *Clementine Recognitions* is derived either from the key passage of the Syriac *Book* or an overlapping source tradition, even if its author misconstrued the Kushans as the Susians.[17] It is unclear how the reference to the promiscuity of "Kushan" women was transformed into a characterization of licentious "Susian" women, but the similar lexical appearances of the terms in a Syriac or Greek antecedent to the passage that Rufinus translated may have prompted it. Whatever the precise relationship between the versions of the key passage from the Syriac *Book* and the *Recognitions* might be, it is evident that the author(s) who composed the variation from the *Recognitions* assumed that its reference to Christians in the Iranian plateau and central Asia was inspired by the tradition of Judas Thomas' Parthian travels, as narrated by the lost Parthian *Acts*. The passage from the *Recognitions* thereby explicitly linked Thomas to "Parthia" (whether it was referring to the Parthian empire or Parthia proper) and, by extension, to Media, Fars/Persis, and the Kushan empire. Even though the *Recognitions* was composed in its surviving form in the early fourth century, the

---

[13] The relationship among the various early Christian texts that feature Judas Thomas is still uncertain. Drijvers 1991, 324–325 and van Rompay 2008, 369–370 explore the scholarly tradition. Sellew 2001, 11–35 and Piovanelli 2010, 443–462 critique the premise of a "Thomasine" Christianity that can be formulated on the basis of these texts. Most 2005 explores the various permutations of the Thomas figure in early Christian literature.

[14] In *Acts of the Apostles* 1:8, the Holy Spirit bids the apostles to be witnesses of their faith throughout the earth and to its uttermost ends. The various apocryphal acts depict apostles who continue with this theme: Klauck 2008, 1–14; Spittler 2013, 353–375.

[15] Jones 2012 provides treatment of this work.

[16] *Clementine Recognitions* 9.29.1–2: Rehm/Streker 2011.

[17] Jones 2012, 3–5, 8, 21–22, and 68–71 treats the *Clementine Recognitions* and the Syriac *Book*.

narrator, purporting himself to be the first-century figure Clement, even claimed that Thomas had corresponded with him about his contemporary exploits. Other statements to this effect should be treated in a similar light. When Arnobius of Sicca (writing c. 305) likewise situated Christians, among other places, in the land of the Persians, Medians, and the Parthians, his mental geography was in this instance most probably shaped by a tradition that had its origin in the Parthian *Acts*.[18]

Literary Traces of the Lost Parthian *Acts of Thomas*

As emphasized in the previous section, the key passage from the Syriac *Book* does not present reliable evidence for where Christianity had actually traveled by c. 225 CE. It is in fact derived from fictive information imparted by the Parthian *Acts*, which described the various peoples of the Parthian empire that Judas Thomas had putatively evange-lized.[19] But the key passage has value because it provides some indication of what the lost Parthian *Acts* contained. When it describes the regions of the Iranian plateau and central Asia that allegedly housed contemporary Christian populations, it gives some meager indication of the regions that Judas Thomas evangelized in the Parthian *Acts*.

The skeletal outline for the itinerary of Judas Thomas in the Parthian *Acts* that can be reconstructed from the key passage of the Syriac *Book* is amplified further by sources that describe the Parthian itinerary of the apostle. For instance, early medieval lists of ap-ostolic itineraries that clearly derived from traditions originating in late antiquity recount his Parthian travels. References to these appear in the Latin works of Isidore of Seville, and they exist in early medieval Greek texts attributed spuriously to earlier patristic au-thors, along with an insertion into a later Greek translation of Jerome's *Illustrious Men*. While their specifics vary to a certain degree, these texts reflect in generic outline a rela-tively common engagement with earlier traditions for the itineraries of various apostles. These collections of itineraries were circulating in aggregate before the sixth century and perhaps as early as the fourth, but the itineraries for certain apostles are based on traditions that originated even earlier. For Thomas in particular, the texts convey an itinerary that most reasonably had its ultimate origin in the Parthian *Acts*.[20] While they contain some minor variations, the texts generally state that Thomas had preached to the Parthians, Medes, Persians, Karmanians, Hyrcanians, Bactrians, and either Magians or Margians. He then died and was interred at an Indian site called Kalamene, Kalame, Calamina or similar permutations thereof in Greek or Latin.[21]

---

[18] Arnobius, *Ad nat.* 2.12: Reifferscheid 1875; Simmons 1995, 47–94 treats date.

[19] Koshelenko/Bader/Gaibov 1995, 55–70 nonetheless endow the Parthian *Acts* with a certain measure of historical validity, as do Ellerbrock/Winkelmann 2012, 273–274 (by conflating the missionary field of the Parthian and Indian *Acts*).

[20] For recent synthesis and assessment, see Dolbeau 2005, 455–480 (on 462–463), also Leloir 1992, 2: 713–716. Isidore of Seville, *De ortu et obitu patrum* 73, in Gómez 1985, claims that Thomas preached to the Parthians and Medes Persians, Hyrcanians, and Bactrians before dying in "Calaminica, a city of India." On Jerome/ps. Sophronius, see von Gebhardt 1896, vii–x and 2–13 (esp. 7–8); Dolbeau 1994, 97; Tubach 2002, 105–110.

[21] Greek texts are in Schermann 1907, 111, 155–156, and 166, along with the Latin *Breviarium apos-tolorum* (207–212); the Latin for the ps. Epiphanius and ps. Dorotheus passages are found in Dolbeau 1986,

In regards to such apostolic itineraries, the following clarifications should be noted. First, they are characterized by some variation regarding whether they depict Thomas as having evangelized "Margians" or "Magians." The rendering of "Magians" probably reflects a distortion of "Margians" produced by the late antique tradition that Judas Thomas had converted the Magi of Persia. According to this narrative, which is attested in the eighth-century *Zuqnin Chronicle* and an anonymous sermon that survives in Latin but was probably written in Greek, Thomas was responsible for converting the same Persian Magi who had visited Jesus in the Gospel of Matthew and had settled in "Shir" (arguably a reference to China). Apparently originating as a third-century CE pseudepigraphon told from the perspective of the Magi, this narrative was redacted in the late third or fourth century to include the activity of Judas Thomas, as narrated by his character.[22] Such a tradition may have influenced the apostolic lists that presented Thomas as evangelizing the Magi instead of Margiana.

Second, an issue is raised by the Indian site in which the apostolic itineraries often depict Thomas' relics as having been interred. The site that these itineraries describe as Kalamene, Kalame, Calamina or a similar variation has hitherto been unknown. It is not mentioned in the surviving text of the Indian *Acts of Thomas*, in which Judas Thomas dies in an anonymous location.[23] A recent argument maintains that it represents how Greek- and Latin-speaking Romans of late antiquity rendered a Tamil (or otherwise south Asian) term for the Coromandel coast of India, where Thomas' relic cult was at some point established and maintained by Christians located in south India.[24] Whatever this site may have been, the link between Thomas and "Kalamene" was certainly not part of Thomas' Parthian *Acts*. It should be stressed that the traditions of Thomas' Parthian travels (among the Parthians, Medes, Persians, Karmanians, Hyrcanians, Bactrians, and Margians) and of his Indian travels (with his death at Kalamene) appear to have circulated separately in different apostolic itineraries during late antiquity before being merged c. 600.[25] It is most reasonable to infer that the itineraries had acquired their information

---

299–314 (text on 308–309) and Dolbeau 1990, 50–70 (68–70 for text). Likewise, a manuscript dating to 874 CE in van Esbroeck 1994: 141 and 188–189 and a tenth-century manuscript from Mt. Sinai: Lewis 1896: 7 contain Syriac references. Barhebraeus, *Ecclesiastical Chronicle* 1: 33–34 and 3: 4–11, in Abbeloos/Lamy 1872/1877, refers to both the Parthian and Indian traditions. Leloir 1992, 2: 740–742 and 755 contains the Armenian texts that refer to the Parthian or Indian travels of Thomas. For further comments and bibliography, see Jullien/Jullien 2002, 80–81. For recent synthesis and assessment, see Dolbeau 2005, 455–480 (esp. 462–463).

[22] Landau 2010, 18–26 treats the complex genealogy of the pseudepigraphon, with Landau 2008, 22–136 containing a critical edition and translation. The *Chronicle of Pseudo-Dionysius* (also known as *Zuqnin*) 1: 86–90, in Chabot 1927/1949, contains the episode, with Landau 2010, 82–86 (English) and 2008: 67–71 (Syriac). The relevant lines from the *Incomplete Work on Matthew* 2.2.2 are in PG 56, col. 637–638 in Migne 1857/1866.

[23] Wright 1871, 1: šl' provides the Syriac text; the *Acts of Thomas* 168, in Bonnet 1903, provides the Greek.

[24] Nedungatt 2010, 181–199 and 2008, 151–173. Also, Tubach 2002, 106–107.

[25] The fifth-century Latin *De ortu et obitu prophetarum et apostolorum* and an early "Greco-Syrian" list from roughly the same time associate Thomas with India and Calamina, but not Parthia. See Dolbeau 1994, 91–107 (esp. 101–102 and 106); Schermann 1907: 172, with Dolbeau 2005, 468, who provides corrections. The general Parthian and Indian itineraries are merged in the testimony of Isidore of Seville, *De ortu et obitu patrum* 73 and 80, in Gómez 1985. Likewise, much later, Barhebraeus, *Ecclesiastical Chronicle* 1: 33–34

regarding the Parthian travels of Thomas from an ultimate point of origin in the material of Judas Thomas' Parthian *Acts*, even if citing it by proxy. All told, the references to Thomas' Parthian activity and his Indian travels, while eventually merged in the apostolic itineraries, had their origins in two distinct traditions, and these traditions ultimately can be traced to two different texts (the lost Parthian *Acts of Thomas* and the surviving Indian *Acts of Thomas*).

Along with such evidence, the testimony of Origen regarding Christianity's presence in Asia corresponds with the citations of the narrative of Thomas' evangelization of Parthia made by the Syriac *Book*, the *Clementine Recognitions*, and the later apostolic itineraries. In a somewhat lacunose passage of his commentary on the Gospel of Matthew, which survives principally in Latin translation and was composed late in his life, Origen apparently claims that Christianity had not yet arrived among (*apud*) the Ethiopians, Seres, and "Ariacin."[26] The last term clearly refers to Ariake, the Greek name for a region of India that the *Periplus of the Red Sea* and Claudius Ptolemy locate immediately south and east of the region encapsulating the Indus river valley, specifically the coast of the Gulf of Barygaza and its interior.[27] As noted previously, Origen was aware of Thomas' Parthian *Acts* (as stated by Eusebius), and it is most reasonable to conclude that his information regarding Christianity in north India relies on it.[28] Apparently accepting the premise that Thomas had traveled to Media, Parthia, Fars/Persis, Margiana, Hyrcania, Karmania, and Bactria, he placed Christians in the various regions of Iran, central Asia, and north India that were in his lifetime part of the Parthian/Sasanian or Kushan empires.[29] For him, Christianity had stopped short of the Pamir mountains (which separated Bactria or central Asia and the Seres in Greek thinking) and the territory beyond the Indus river (the threshold of Kushan north India and Ariake).[30] By implication it had nonetheless penetrated as far as Bactria, which for Greek authors included both Kushan central Asia and north India.[31] Origen's testimony provides further indication that the Parthian *Acts* was influencing how Christians in the Mediterranean littoral and upper Mesopotamia conceived of the evangelization of the Iranian plateau, central Asia, and parts of north India under Kushan control.

In composite, the testimony of Origen and the medieval itineraries described above significantly indicate that in the Parthian *Acts* (composed c. 175–200), Judas Thomas evangelized the very regions in which the Syriac *Book* locates the presence of Christian communities. These, namely, were Media, Persis/Fars, Parthia proper, Hyrcania,

---

and 3: 4–11, in Abbeloos/Lamy 1872–1877, and an Armenian treatment contained in Bayan 1910: 415–417 and 420–421.

[26]   Origen, *Comm. Matt.* 24.9–14, in Klostermann 2012. For date, see McGuckin 2004b, 30. For discussion, see Nedungatt 2011, 418–420 and 2008, 107–111.

[27]   *Periplus of the Red Sea* 6 and 41–42, in Casson 1989; Ptolemy, *Geog.* 7.1.6, in Stückelberger/Graßhoff 2006/2009. Nedungatt 2011, 418–420 and 2008, 107–111 emphasizes the importance of Ariake but interprets its significance differently.

[28]   Eusebius, *HE* 3.1.1–3, in Schwartz/Mommsen 1999.

[29]   For a different interpretation, see Nedungatt 2011, 418–420 and 2008, 107–111.

[30]   Ptolemy, *Geog.* 1.11–12 and 6.13–17 in Stückelberger/Graßhoff 2006/2009; de la Vaissière 2009, 527–536.

[31]   Clement, *Strom.* 1.15.71.3–6, in Stählin/Früchtel, describes Buddhists (*Sarmanai* and *Samanaioi*) as inhabiting India and Bactria, and his reference to Bactria seems to include north India.

Karmania, Margiana, and Bactria. In reference to these territories, the Syriac *Book* describes the inhabitants of Media, Persis, Parthia proper, and Bactria/the Kushan empire by name. The Syriac *Book* also mentions Christians among the *Gelaye* of the west Caspian sea littoral; the source for this may have been the Parthian *Acts*, but this is not certain. The Syriac *Book*, however, does not mention the presence of Christians in Hyrcania, Margiana, or Karmania. This can be explained by the premise that the *Book* does not convey a comprehensive list of regions in which Christian communities putatively existed; it instead presents a few illustrative examples for Iran and central Asia (Media, Persis/Fars, Parthia, and the Kushan empire). Finally, Origen's treatment of Christians as inhabiting regions as remote as Ariake in India (but not Ariake itself) suggests that the Parthian *Acts* depicted Thomas as evangelizing the Indus river valley of north India, which the Syriac *Book* too implicitly includes in its reference to the territory of the Kushans.

Geographic and Chronological Clarifications

The premise that the scope of Judas Thomas' activity in the lost Parthian *Acts* extended into Kushan central Asia and north India begs for a certain measure of clarification. After all, the Parthian *Acts* depicted Judas Thomas as evangelizing the first-century territories of the Parthian empire and not of Kushan imperial space, and the Parthian empire is not known to have governed north India directly. Moreover, the precise areas of governance exerted by the Parthian Arsacid dynasty and the Kushans in central Asia during the first and second centuries CE are sometimes difficult to determine with precision. This difficulty is amplified by the fact that relatively autonomous dynasts of apparent Parthian origin, as opposed to the Parthian empire, governed parts of central Asia and north India at various times. Accordingly, a clarification must be made regarding why the relevant passage of the Syriac *Book* seems to rely on the apostle's Parthian itinerary, as depicted in the Parthian *Acts*, in its rendering of Christians as living in contemporary Kushan territory, which included central Asia and north India during the late second century.

During the mid-first century CE, when Judas Thomas or Thomas was allegedly active, the Kushan empire was only in its incipient stages, and the Parthian empire controlled much of the Iranian plateau. But various parts of central Asia and north India were governed by dynasts who, while being of Parthian background, nonetheless exercised various degrees of autonomy from the Parthian empire. Accordingly, the Parthian empire or otherwise the realms of certain Parthian dynasts extended beyond the Iranian plateau and into central Asia, and they controlled places such as Merv (Antioch Margiana), Herat (Areia), and Sistan (Gedrosia/Drangiana).[32] Likewise, in north India, a dynasty of "Indo-

---

[32] Merv was in fact often deemed "little/lesser Parthia" by Chinese sources. See *Hou Hanshu* 88 in Leslie/Gardiner 1996, 45; Hill 2009, 23; Hackl/Jacobs/Weber 2010, 3: 498. For Merv and Herat in Parthian space, see Ellerbrock/Winkelmann 2012, 93. Dąbrowa 2012, 175–176 and Pyankov 2012 describe the Parthian presence in central Asia and its relationship with the Kushan empire. Ellerbrock/Winkelmann 2012, 114 comment on the Kushan empire's expansion into central Asia. Frye 1984, 197–204 and Kaim 2012, 154–155 provide useful discussion of (semi-)autonomous Parthian dynasties. The notable treatment of Pliny, *NH* 6.112–13, in Jahn/Mayhoff 1870–1906, extends the *regna Parthorum* into central Asia.

Parthian kings," governed the region of the Indus valley and a substantial part of central Asia and Sistan.[33]

Because such regions were governed either by the Parthian empire or relatively autonomous dynasts of Parthian background during the first century CE, the late second-century Parthian *Acts* apparently treated Judas Thomas' first-century zone of evangelization as consisting of the putatively aggregate "Parthian" regions that had extended east of Iran into central Asia at that time. The text also located the apostle among the "Indo-Parthian" kings of the Indus river region; his encounter with an "Indo-Parthian" king described as Gudnaphar in Syriac and Goundaphores in Greek, as it exists in the surviving Indian *Acts of Thomas*, was probably derived from the Parthian version.[34] The notion that the Parthian *Acts*, composed c. 175–200 CE, either imprecisely or simplistically framed the Parthian empire as controlling a significant portion of central Asia and rendered north India as governed by an "Indo-Parthian" king is inherently plausible. In a similar manner, the third-century *Life of Apollonius of Tyana* by Philostratus, itself characterized by severe geographical inaccuracy, depicts first-century Parthian territory as extending to the Hindu Kush. The text then describes an "Indian" king with the Iranian name of "Phraotes," one commonly held by members of the Parthian Arsacid dynasty, as ruling at Taxila in north India.[35]

After 200 CE, however, the presence of the Parthian empire or Parthian dynasts in central Asia had been compromised by the formation and expansion of the Kushan empire. Likewise, the governance of Indo-Parthian kings in north India had long since ended amid the consolidation of Kushan authority in the region. The Parthian empire of the Arsacids at best maintained an insecure grasp over east Iran and Margiana at the time that the Arsacids were overthrown by the Sasanians, and in the decades that followed, Kushan control over central Asia was largely ceded to the Sasanians too.[36]

As noted previously, the present form of the Syriac *Book* was composed c. 225, and its treatment of various societies in Iran and central Asia apparently was not shaped by the Sasanians' overthrow of the Parthian Arsacids or their subsequent conquests of Kushan territories. Accordingly, the Syriac *Book*'s treatment follows the premise that the territory controlled by the Kushans (whom Eusebius, like many Greek-speakers, describes as Bactrians) currently included much of central Asia and the north Indian territories once ruled by Parthian or "Indo-Parthian" rulers.[37] In other words, much of

---

[33] For general synthesis on the Indo-Parthians, see Bopearachchi 1998, 389–406; Puri 1999a, 191–207.

[34] Luke 1995/1996, 433–450 and Tubach 2002, 72–98 discuss the figure, whose reign is attested by coins and a Prakrit inscription of north India (Luke 1995/1996, 448–450; Tubach 2002, 80–82). For the Iranian etymology of the name "Gudnaphar," a misspelled variation of Gundaphar/Vindafarna(h), see Justi 1895, 368–369; Luke 1995/1996, 438–439; Gignoux/Jullien/Jullien 2009, 76. For the king's name as rendered in the Indian *Acts*, see Wright 1871, q'g (Syriac, Gudnaphar) and *Acts of Thomas* 2 in Bonnet 1903 (Greek, Goundaphores).

[35] Philostr., *VA* 2.20 in Jones 2006 depicts Parthian authority as extending to the Hindu Kush (the "Caucasus" mountains), even if he erroneously claims that Media adjoins it. Philostr., *VA* 2.26 provides the Indian king's name, on which Justi 1895, 101–102; Gignoux 1986, 86; Gignoux/Jullien/Jullien 2009, 72. For geographical inaccuracies, see Jones 2002.

[36] For a general survey of the Kushan empire, see Puri 1999b. The first Sasanian monarch Ardashir I therefore had to reintegrate Margiana, Karmania, and Sistan: Puri 1999b, 255; Litvinsky 1999, 476–481.

[37] For areas of Kushan control, see Puri 1999b, 254–263.

the "Parthian" territories of central Asia and north India evangelized by the putative first-century figure of Judas Thomas in the Parthian *Acts* had fallen under Kushan sway by the time that the Syriac *Book* was written. If the Parthian *Acts* had treated the first-century Parthian empire or various Parthian dynasts as controlling central Asia and north India, the Syriac *Book* rendered these regions as being under contemporary Kushan control, even as it implicitly sustained the premise, as espoused by the Parthian *Acts*, that Christians to whom Judas Thomas had preached lived there.

Conclusion

In a key passage of the Syriac *Book*, composed c. 225 CE, Christians are described as residing among the Medes, Persians, Parthians, and Kushans, and this statement has sometimes encouraged scholars to accept an early date for Christianity's penetration of the Iranian plateau and central Asia. But this testimony does not reflect actual knowledge that Edessenes or Upper Mesopotamians possessed regarding Christian communities in the Kushan empire. Instead, it is based on the fiction of a text that had been circulating in the eastern Mediterranean and upper Mesopotamia during the late second and early third centuries CE: the Parthian *Acts of Thomas*, which is now lost. Because the lost *Acts* generated the belief among contemporary Christians that coreligionists inhabited central Asia, the value of the Syriac *Book* as a source for Christianity in central Asia is very limited. Its treatment relies on the fictive *Acts of Thomas* in Parthia.

ABBREVIATIONS

BNJ – *Brill's New Jacoby*, ed, by I. Worthington, edition online, Leiden 2007–
FGrH – F. Jacoby *et al.*, *Die Fragmente der griechischen Historiker*, Berlin–Leiden 1928–

BIBLIOGRAPHY

Abbeloos, J.-B., Lamy, T.J. (1872–1877), *Gregorii Barhebraei Chronicon Ecclesiasticum. The Ecclesiastical Chronicle of Barhebraeus*, 3 vols., Paris.
Baum, W., Winkler, D. (2003), *The Church of the East. A Concise History*, London.
Baumer, Chr. (2006), *The Church of the East. An Illustrated History of Assyrian Christianity*, London.
Bayan, G. (1910), Le Synaxaire Arménien de Ter Israel, *Patrologia Orientalia* 5: 344–556.
Bonnet, M. (1903), *Acta Apostolorum Apocrypha*, part 2, vol. 2, Leipzig.

Bopearachchi, O. (1998), Indo-Parthians, in: J. Wiesehöfer (ed.), *Das Partherreich und seine Zeugnisse/the Arsacid Empire: Sources and Documentation*, Stuttgart: 389–406.

Casson, L. (1989), *Periplus maris Erythraei. Text with Introduction, Translation, and Commentary*, Princeton, NJ.

Chabot, J.-B. (1927–1949), *Chronicon anonymum Pseudo-Dionysianum vulgo dictum*, 3 vols., Louvain.

Dąbrowa, E. (2012), The Arsacid Empire, in: T. Daryaee (ed.), *The Oxford Handbook of Iranian History*, Oxford: 164–187.

Dolbeau, F. (1986), Une liste ancienne d'apôtres et de disciples, traduite du grec par Moïse de Bergame, *AB* 104: 299–314.

Dolbeau, F. (1990), Une liste latine de disciples et d'apôtres, *AB* 108: 50–70.

Dolbeau, F. (1994), Nouvelles recherches sur le *De ortu et obitu prophetarum et apostolorum*, *Augustinianum* 34: 91–107.

Dolbeau, F. (2005), Listes d'apôtres et de disciples, in: P. Geoltrain, J.-D. Kaestli (eds.), *Écrits apocryphes chrétiens*, vol. 2, Paris: 455–480.

Drijvers, H.J.W. (1964), *The Book of the Laws of the Countries: Dialogue on Fate of Bardaisan of Edessa*, Assen.

Drijvers, H.J.W. (1991), *The Acts of Thomas*, in: W. Schneemelcher, R. McLachlan Wilson (eds.), *New Testament Apocrypha*, vol. 2: *Writings Related to the Apostles. Apocalypses and Related Subjects*, Rev. ed., Cambridge: 322–411.

Ellerbrock, U., Winkelmann, S. (2012), *Die Parther: die vergessene Großmacht*, Mainz.

Ferreia, J. (2002), *The Hymn of the Pearl. The Syriac and Greek Texts with Introduction, Translation, and Notes*, Sydney.

Frye, R. (1984), *The History of Ancient Iran*, München.

Gebhardt, O. von. (1896), *Hieronymus de viris inlustribus in griechischer Übersetzung (der sogenannte Sophronius)*, Leipzig.

Gignoux, Ph. (1986), *Iranisches Personennamenbuch*, vol. 2, fasc. 2: *Noms propres sassanides en moyen-perse épigraphique*, Wien.

Gignoux, Ph., Jullien, Chr., Jullien, F. (2009), *Iranisches Personennamenbuch*, vol. 7, fasc. 5: *Noms propres syriaques d'origine iranienne*, Wien.

Gómez, C.C. (1985), *Isidoro de Sevilla: de ortu et obitu patrum*, Paris.

Hackl, U., Jacobs, B., Weber, D. (eds.) (2010), *Quellen zur Geschichte des Partherreiches. Textsammlung mit Übersetzungen und Kommentaren*, 3 vols., Göttingen.

Hansen, G.C. (1995), *Kirchengeschichte: Sokrates*, Berlin.

Hill, J. (2009), *Through the Jade Gate to Rome. A Study of the Silk Routes during the Later Han Dynasty (1st to 2nd Centuries CE)*, Charleston, SC.

Jahn, L., Mayhoff, K. (1870/1906), *Naturalis historiae libri XXXVII*, 6 vols., Leipzig.

Jones, C.P. (2002), Apollonius of Tyana's Passage to India, *GRBS* 42: 185–199.

Jones, C.P. (2006), *Apollonius of Tyana: Philostratus*, 2 vols., Cambridge, MA.

Jones, F.S. (2012), *Pseudoclementina Elchasaiticaque inter Judaeochristiana*, Leuven.

Jullien, Chr., Jullien, F. (2002), *Apôtres des confins: processus missionnaires chrétiens dans l'empire iranien*, Bures-sur-Yvette.

Justi, F. (1895), *Iranisches Namenbuch*, Marburg.

Kaim, B. (2012), Serakhs Oasis at the Crossroads of Communication Routes, *Parthica* 14: 149–160.

Kaizer, T. (2006), Capital Punishment at Hatra. Gods, Magistrates, and Laws in the Roman-Parthian Period, *Iraq* 68: 139–153.

Klauck, H.-J. (2008), *The Apocryphal Acts of the Apostles. An Introduction*, trans. B. McNeil, Waco, TX.

Klijn, A.F.J. (2003), *The Acts of Thomas. Introduction, Text, and Commentary*, Leiden.

Klostermann, E. (2012), *Origenes Werke*, vol. 11: *Origenes Matthäuserklärung*, vol. 2, 2nd ed., Berlin.

Koshelenko, G.A., Bader, A., Gaibov, V.A. (1995), The Beginnings of Christianity in Merv, *Iranica Antiqua* 30: 55–70.

Landau, B. (2008), *The Sages and the Star-Child. An Introduction to the Revelation of the Magi, an Ancient Christian Apocryphon*, DTh Dissertation, Harvard University.

Landau, B. (2010), *Revelation of the Magi. The Lost Tale of the Three Wise Men's Journey to Bethlehem*, New York.

Leloir, L. (1992), *Écrits apocryphes sur les apôtres: traduction de l'édition arménienne de Venise*, 2 vols., Turnhout.

Leslie, D.D., Gardiner K.H.J. (1996), *The Roman Empire in Chinese Sources*, Rome.

Lewis, A.S. (1896), *Catalogue of the Syriac Mss. in the Convent of S. Catherine on Mount Sinai*, London.

Litvinsky, B.A. (1999), The Rise of Sasanian Iran, in: J. Harmatta (ed.), *History of Civilizations of Central Asia*, vol. 2: *The Development of Sedentary and Nomadic Civilizations, 700 BC to AD 250*, Paris: 473–484.

Luke, K. (1995/1996), Gondopharnes, *The Harp* 8–9: 433–450.

McGuckin, J. (2004a), The Life of Origen, in: J. McGuckin (ed.), *The Westminster Handbook to Origen*, 1–24, Louisville, KY.

McGuckin, J. (2004b), The Scholarly Works of Origen, in: J. McGuckin (ed.), *The Westminster Handbook to Origen*, 25–44, Louisville, KY.

Migne, J.-P. (1857/1866), *Incomplete Work on Matthew* (*Opus imperfectum in Matthaeum*), Paris.

Most, G. (2005), *Doubting Thomas*, Cambridge, MA.

Mras, K. (1982/1983), *Eusebius: Werke*, vol. 8: *Die Praeparatio Evangelica*, 2nd ed., Berlin.

Myers, S. (2010), *Spiritual Epicleses in the Acts of Thomas*, Tübingen.

Nedungatt, G. (2008), *A Quest for the Historical Thomas. A Re-Reading of the Evidence*, Bangalore.

Nedungatt, G. (2010), Calamina, Kalamides, Cholamandalam: Solution of a Riddle, *OCP* 76: 181–199.

Nedungatt, G. (2011), Christian Origins in India according to the Alexandrian Tradition, *OCP* 77: 399–422.

Piovanelli, P. (2010), Thomas in Edessa? Another Look at the Original Setting of the Gospel of Thomas, in: J. Dijkstra, J. Kroesen, Y. Kuiper (eds.), *Myths, Martyrs, and Modernity. Studies in the History of Religions in Honor of Jan Bremmer*, Leiden: 443–462.

Poirier, P.-H. (1981), *L'Hymne de la Perle des Actes de Thomas. Introduction, Text-Traduction, Commentaire*, Louvain.

Puri, B.N. (1999a), The Sakas and the Indo-Parthians, in: J. Harmatta (ed.), *History of Civilizations of Central Asia*, vol. 2: *The Development of Sedentary and Nomadic Civilizations, 700 BC to AD 250*, Paris: 191–209.

Puri, B.N. (1999b), The Kushans, in: J. Harmatta (ed.), *History of Civilizations of Central Asia*, vol. 2: *The Development of Sedentary and Nomadic Civilizations, 700 BC to AD 250*, Paris: 247–264.

Pyankov, I. (2012), Romano-Parthian Merchants on the Silk Road, *Parthica* 14: 145–148.

Ramelli, I. (2009a), *Bardesane di Edessa: Contro il fato, κατὰ Εἱμαρμένης*, Bologna.

Ramelli, I. (2009b), *Bardaisan of Edessa: A Reassessment of the Evidence and a New Interpretation*, Piscataway, NJ.

Rehm, B., Streker, G. (2011), *Die Pseudoklementinen*, vol. 2: *Rekognitionen in Rufins Übersetzung*, 2nd ed., Berlin.

Reifferscheid, A. (1875), *Arnobii Adversus nationes libri VII*, Wien.

Schermann, Th. (1907), *Prophetarum vitae fabulosae: indices Apostolorum Discipulorumque Domini Dorotheo, Epiphanio, Hippolyto, aliisque vindicata*, Leipzig.

Schwartz, E., Mommsen, Th. (1999), *Die Kirchengeschichte*, 3 vols., 2nd ed., Berlin.

Sellew, Ph. (2001), Thomas Christianity: Scholars in Quest of a Community, in: J. Bremmer (ed.), *The Apocryphal Acts of Thomas*, Leuven: 11–35.

Simmons, M.B. (1995), *Arnobius of Sicca. Religious Conflict and Competition in the Age of Diocletian*, Oxford.

Spittler, J. (2013), Christianity at the Edges: Representations of the Ends of the Earth in the Apocryphal Acts of the Apostles, in: C. Rothschild, J. Schröter (eds.), *The Rise and Expansion of Christianity in the First Three Centuries of the Common Era*, Tübingen: 353–375.

Stählin, O., Früchtel, L. (2011), *Clemens Alexandrinus*, vol. 2: *Stromata, Buch I–VI*, 4th ed., Berlin.

Stückelberger, A., Graßhoff, G. (2006/2009), *Klaudios Ptolemaios: Handbuch der Geographie*, 3 vols., Basel.

Tubach, J. (2002), Historische Elemente in den Thomasakten, *Beiträge zur Orientwissenschaft* 33 (*Studien zu den Thomas-Christen in Indien*): 49–116.

Van Esbroeck, M. (1994), Neufs lists d'apôtres orientales, *Augustinianum* 34: 109–199.

Van Rompay, L. (2008), The East: Syria and Mesopotamia, in: S. Ashbrook Harvey, D.G. Hunter (eds.), *The Oxford Handbook of Early Christian Studies*, Oxford: 365–386.

Vaissière, É. de la (2009), The Triple System of Orography in Ptolemy's Xinjiang, in: W. Sundermann, A. Hintze, F. de Blois (eds.), *Exegisti monumenta: Festschrift in Honour of Nicholas Sims-Williams*, Wiesbaden: 527–536.

Wright, W. (1871), *Apocryphal Acts of the Apostles*, 2 vols., London.

ELECTRUM * Vol. 22 (2015): 173–199
doi: 10.4467/20800909EL.15.010.3948
www.ejournals.eu/electrum

I Am Your Father! Dynasties and Dynastic Legitimacy on Pre-Islamic Coinage between Iran and Northwest India*

Omar Coloru

Pisa – UMR 7041 ArScAn-HAROC

Abstract: The present paper intends to explore the way in which the new kingdoms born from the dissolution of the Greco-Macedonian powers east of the Tigris employed coinage in order to promote kingship ideology based on kinship and family relationships. At the same time, it will try to show the interplay as well as the differences between Greco-Macedonian and local cultures in using family as a tool of propaganda.

Key words: kingship ideology, Seleucids, Bactria, India, Arsacids, Persis, Elymais, Characene, Sakas, Indo-Scythians, Kushans, Sasanians.

1. Coins and communication

Aside from being a financial instrument, coinage has always been an important means of spreading messages related to ideology from a central power towards subjects. This practice became all the more widespread from the Hellenistic period onwards,[1] when the dynasties emerging from the disintegration of Alexander's empire had to claim their legitimacy to rule in the face of their opponents. Thus, coins were a suitable way of communicating basic concepts of kingship, legitimacy and even ethnic identity. This kind of communication operated at several levels: the most immediate was the use of a particular iconography, which included the portrait of the ruling king, images recalling the myths of foundation of the dynasty, military victories, gods or personification of virtues protecting the king and his family. At a regional level, iconography would refer to indigenous features and traditions such as local shrines and deities. A second level was represented by written communication, which was intended for all those people

---

* I wish to thank Joe Cribb (The British Museum), Alex McAuley (McGill), Michele Napolitano (Cassino), and Andrea Piras (Bologna) for sharing information and useful comments with me during the preparation of this paper. Any errors and omissions in the present text remain my responsibility alone.

[1] For a recent discussion, see Meadows 2014, 169–195.

capable of reading the messages carved on one or both the faces of the coin. Apart from giving more technical details such as the location of the mint, the weight of the coin and the name of the magistrate charged with the task of supervising the mintage, coin legends provided information about the identity of the ruler, the royal titles he bore and, accordingly, the ideology of his kingship. Those who were able to understand both the non-written and the written messages of a coin could then access a small but effective compendium of the public image a sovereign wanted to show to his subjects (as well as to those living outside his kingdom).

Eastern civilisations under the rule of the Persian Empire were not accustomed to coins; rather, they used weighted metal bars for their commercial and fiscal needs or had recourse to other form of exchanges such as payments in kind or barter. Once these regions became part of the Seleucid Empire, this new means of exchange spread throughout the large area between Mesopotamia and Afghanistan and was not discarded after the Seleucids lost control of the Upper Satrapies. In fact, the new powers succeeding the Seleucids in the East continued striking coins and using them to convey messages on dynastic ideology.

2. Looking for a model. Greco-Macedonian coinage in the East

In order to detect the model(s) which may have exerted a certain influence in the creation of dynastic messages on the coinage of the new rulers, our survey will begin from the Seleucid coinage struck or likely to have circulated in the areas under study here. We will then take into account the issues struck by the Greco-Macedonian dynasties of Bactria and India.

The Seleucids

In 294 BC, Antiochos, the young son of the Bactrian princess Apama and Seleukos I, was appointed joint king by his father and entrusted with the government of the Upper Satrapies. In this period coins do not feature particular signs ascribable to an intention of promoting the dynasty and his rightful heir. Coin legends insist on the names of the joint kings rather than on the relation which identified them as father and son (see e.g. ΒΑΣΙΛΕΩΣ ΣΕΛΕΥΚΟΥ ΚΑΙ ΑΝΤΙΟΧΟΥ, "Of King Seleukos and Antiochos" or ΒΑΣΙΛΕΩΝ ΣΕΛΕΥΚΟΥ ΚΑΙ ΑΝΤΙΟΧΟΥ, "Of the kings Seleukos and Antiochos", etc.).[2] Likewise, the iconography neither reveals nor suggests any family relation between the two kings.

We have to wait until the beginning of the second century BC to find examples of promotion and/or commemoration of members of the royal family on Seleucid coins.

---

[2]   See also an issue, possibly from Western Arachosia, with the reverse legend R/ ΑΝΤΙΟΧΟΥ ΣΕΛΕΥΚΟΥ ΒΑΣΙΛΕΩΣ, "of Antiochos (and) King Seleukos": *SC* 1, no. 235.

The veiled portrait of Queen Laodike, (second?) wife to Seleukos IV,[3] makes its appearance on the obverse of Antiochene royal bronze issues in association with a reverse image showing an elephant head, a tripod or a prow.[4] These coins, a specimen of which was also found in excavations at Dura Europos, were meant to serve military purposes, possibly a *sitarchia*,[5] even if the reasons for pairing Laodike with such iconography is not yet clear. This series continued to be struck during the first part of the reign of Antiochos IV. Other Seleucid queens were portrayed in this way, as is the case, for example, with Cleopatra, wife of Alexander Balas, who was associated with the reverse image of a cornucopia because of her royal epithet, i.e. *Thea Eueteria*, "goddess of the good harvest," and accordingly goddess assuring prosperity to the kingdom.

If we come back to Laodike, wife of Seleukos IV, we may see that she is also present on a series of gold octadrachms in the name of his young son Antiochos V which were struck in the autumn of 175 BC, in the period between the murder of Seleukos IV and the accession of the latter's brother Antiochos IV. The jugate busts of the king's widow (put into the foreground) and her son were meant to promote the role of Laodike as regent against the plots of the prime minister, Heliodorus, who had murdered the king and wanted to rule through the tutorship of Antiochos. However, this figurative typology was not an innovation of the Seleucids, but was already customary in the coinage of the Ptolemaic kingdom and later adopted by other non-Greek Hellenistic monarchies such the Artaxiads of Armenia (attested for Tigranes IV and his sister-queen Erato)[6] or the Pontic house (Mithridates IV and his sister-queen Laodike).[7] A similar portrait of Laodike, this time with Antiochos IV, is attested by a quasi-municipal bronze issue from Tripolis.[8] Coins depicting jugate busts of members of the royal family were issued throughout the history of the Seleucid dynasty; the prominence in the representation depends on which of the pair held the real power or more political influence. Thus, we have portraits with kings in the foreground (Demetrios I and Laodike[9]), queens (Cleopatra Thea and Alexander Balas[10]), queen-mothers acting as regent for their sons (Cleopatra Thea and Antiochos VIII Grypos[11] – see Fig. 1; Cleopatra V Selene and Antiochos XIII[12]), and brothers reigning jointly (Antiochos XI and Philip I[13]).

---

[3]   The identification of Laodike IV was proposed by Hoover (2002), 81–87; see also *SC* 2, pp. 4, 13. However, the akkadian sources clearly state that the queen died in the summer of 182 BC, cf. del Monte 1997, 70. One could suppose, as Savalli-Lestrade 2005, 193–200 suggests, a second marriage of Seleukos IV with a woman who possibly took the dynastic name of Laodike (V) after her accession. See also *IGIAC*, no. 13 and 14.

[4]   *SC* 2, no. 1318, 1407, 1421–1422 (imitations), 1477.

[5]   Hoover 2002; *SC* 2, p. 17.

[6]   Kovacs 2008, 339–341.

[7]   Callataÿ 2009, 77–78. The stater presenting the portrait of Laodike alone is probably a modern forgery, see again Callataÿ 2009, 83–84.

[8]   *SC* 2, no. 1441.

[9]   *SC* 2, no. 1683, 1684, 1686–1688, 1689.2, 1691.

[10]   *SC* 2, no. 1841, 1843–1846, 2258.1b.

[11]   *SC* 2, no. 2259–2260, 2261b, 2262.1d, 2265, 2267.2a, 2268–2269, 2270-AV, 2271.1, 2271.2, 2272.3a, 2273, 2276.1, 2277.1a.

[12]   *SC* 2, no. 2484–2486.

[13]   *SC* 2, no. 2435.2, 2436–2439.

Fig. 1. Tetradrachm with jugate busts of Cleopatra Thea and her son Antiochos VIII Grypos;
© CNG Inc.

The adoption by a king of official epithets recalling the memory of a member of the royal family was another common form of conveying legitimacy. Among the Seleucids it is possible to enumerate several examples: the title *Eupator*, "he whose father is good," borne by Antiochos V, appears on most of the monetary legends of his coinage.[14] The choice of such a title honouring the late Antiochos IV should be ascribed to the prime minister and tutor of the young king, Lysias, in the attempt to support the cadet branch of the dynasty – originating from Antiochos IV – against the claims of Demetrios I.[15]

The same Antiochos IV is remembered through the epithet of his alleged son and successor Alexander Balas, *Theopator*, "He whose father is a god," or maybe "The one who deified his father."[16] This title focuses attention on the divinisation of Antiochos IV and put the king in a position of pre-eminence when compared to the *Eupator* of Antiochos V.

As for the title of *Philopator*, "Father-Loving," it not only expresses feelings of affection from the son towards his father, but also conveys the message that the son was the heir designated for succession.[17] Even though this epithet is not attested on coins, we know from other sources that it was attributed to Seleukos IV. Neither was this usage unique to this generation of Seleucid monarchs: Antiochos IX, for his part, adopted it on his coinage in order to commemorate his father Antiochos VII.[18] Antiochos X did the same for his father Antiochos IX, while the members of the other branch of the family, namely Demetrios III and Antiochos XII,[19] likewise employed the same title in reference to Antiochos VIII.

---

[14] *SC* 2, no. 1572–1576, 1578, 1582–1583, 1585–1586. On *Eupator* and its significance, see Muccioli 2013, 236–242.

[15] Muccioli 2013, 236–239.

[16] See Muccioli 2013, 297–298. The epithet *Theopator* was accompanied by *Euergetes*, "Benefactor." Among the Seleucid mints only that of Ecbatana struck coinage of all metal bearing this monetary legend; see *SC* 2, 213.

[17] See Muccioli 2013, 220–236.

[18] *SC* 2, 524; Muccioli 2013, 227–228.

[19] Antiochos X see SC 2, 567; Muccioli 2013, 228. For Demetrios III and Antiochos XII, see *SC* 2, 583 and 608; Muccioli 2013, 229.

On the other hand, the epithet *Philometor* – "Mother-Loving" – was less common in the early stages of the Hellenistic age, when the transfer of power according to a pat-rilineal system was practically the rule. But later, from Laodike IV onwards (as for the Seleukids), and Cleopatra Syra (as for the Ptolemies), we observe a growing importance of matrilineality in these dynasties. Accordingly, it was assumed when there was the in-tention of honouring and/or stressing the prominence of a female member of the family, especially when she acted as a tutor and/or coregent for a young prince.[20] Antiochos VIII used this title during his joint rule with his mother Cleopatra Thea and even after her death; Demetrios III, in turn, appealed to the authority of his mother Cleopatra Selene on coins struck at Seleukeia Pieria and possibly Tarsos. The same Cleopatra Selene is honoured in the joint coinage showing the jugate busts of the queen and her son Antiochos XIII, the latter bearing the epithet *Philometor*.[21]

Finally, the official title of *Philadelphos*, "Brother-Loving,"[22] has a complex range of nuances which varies from dynasty to dynasty. As a general rule – but not one set in stone – *Philadelphos* denotes, in a dynastic framework, the intention of celebrating brotherly concord. For instance, it may appeal to feelings of unity and loyalty between two broth-ers who are joint kings, or an endogamous union between brother and sister; or again, the respect the cadet has towards the elder brother and vice versa. In the Seleucid dynasty, *Philadelphos* occurs quite late on coinage under the first reign of Demetrios II (145–139 BC) and should be seen as an homage to his younger brother, the future Antiochos VII.[23] Other Seleucid kings assumed this epithet on coins: in this way, Antiochos XI[24] paid homage to his twin brother Philip I – who was also joint king before Antiochos' death – and probably his elder brother Seleukos VI. The same Philip later kept the title in the coinage of his sole reign.[25]

Greek kings of Bactria and India

After the death of Demetrios I (ca. 185 BC), the kingdom of Bactria witnessed a period of dynastic strife between different houses leading to a gradual and irreversible crisis, which in the end brought the loss of Greek sovereignty over Central Asia and Northwest India. However, this crisis gave the various contenders the opportunity to promote their legitimacy to rule through coins. I am referring here to the so-called *pedigree coins* issued by Antimachos I and Agathokles. It is by this name that numismatists refer to the series struck during the reign of Antimachos I or Agathokles but presenting the portraits and the

---

[20] Muccioli 2013, 242–243.

[21] I leave apart the discussion concerning the identification of the son of Cleopatra Selene as Antiochos XIII or Seleukos Cybiosactes, see *SC* 2, 615–616; Muccioli 2013, 248–249.

[22] See Muccioli 2013, 203–220.

[23] Other possibilities are his brother Antigonos or his bride Cleopatra Thea, who, like other Seleucid queens, had the honorific title of "sister" of the king; see Muccioli 2013, 213–214.

[24] *SC* 2, 574.

[25] *SC* 2, 597.

monetary types of former kings of Bactria.[26] While only two kings are commemorated by Antimachos, i.e. Diodotos I and Euthydemos I, Agathokles instead follows a fairly precise chronological order celebrating Alexander the Great and Antiochos II, the two Diodoti, Euthydemos I (Fig. 2), Demetrios I and finally Pantaleon, who might be Agathokles' brother and was king for a short period before him. The choice of Alexander the Great and the Seleukid Antiochos II should be interpreted in an ideological sense, in that these two sovereigns were probably seen as the ideal founders of the kingdom: in a sort of dynastic passing of the baton, Agathokles wanted to link his reign to the memory of the conqueror of Central Asia and India as well as to the last Seleukid king ruling over Bactria. It is also interesting to note that the only Bactrian king not to be celebrated by Agathokles was Euthydemos II, young heir of Demetrios I, who reigned for a few years before Antimachos I in Bactria, and Pantaleon and Agathokles in Northwest India, seized power. The absence of Euthydemos II from the *pedigree coins* of Agathokles might be explained by a lack of recognition of his sovereignty. As for Antimachos I, his limited choice can perhaps be attributed to an attempt to emphasise what Tarn called a "Bactrian local patriotism"[27] in order to assert his ideal (and real?) ties with the founders of the two dynasties of independent Bactria.

Fig. 2. "Pedigree coin" of Agathokles commemorating Euthydemos I; © Numismatica Ars Classica

The immediate ruler who succeeded in unifying under his control the whole of the kingdom was Eukratides I (ca. 171–145 BC). He too asserted his right to rule by striking four series portraying the jugate busts of his parents, Heliocles and Laodike (Fig. 3), accompanied by the composite coin legend:

Ob/ ΒΑΣΙΛΕΥΣ ΜΕΓΑΣ ΕΥΚΡΑΤΙΔΗΣ
R/ (Ο ΥΙΟΣ ΤΟΥ) ΗΛΙΟΚΛΕΟΥΣ ΚΑΙ ΛΑΟΔΙΚΗΣ
"The Great King Eukratides, (the son) of Heliokles and Laodike"[28]

---

[26] For the pedigree coins as well as the political history of the kingdom of Bactria during the reigns of Antimachos I and Agathokles, see Holt 1984, 69–91; Bernard 1985, 152; Bopearachchi 1991; Coloru 2009, 195–203.

[27] Tarn 1951, 451.

[28] Bopearachchi 1991, *Eucratide I*, sér. 13–16.

Fig. 3. Tetradrachm of Eukratides I commemorating his parents Heliokles and Laodike;
© Numismatica Ars Classica

It seems clear that such a precise statement of kinship must have had a consider-able weight in Eukratides' assertion of legitimacy. What is more, his mother Laodike wears a diadem, a clue indicating that she belonged to a royal family.[29] Other examples of jugate busts featuring a member of the royal family may be found in the coinage dating to the joint rule of Queen Agathocleia (ca. 130–125 BC), widow of the Indo-Greek king Menander I Soter, and her son Strato I,[30] as well as on the first two series of the coins struck by King Hermaios (ca. 90–70 BC), who is portrayed together with his wife Calliope. Moreover, the name of the queen is also present in the obverse legend ΒΑΣΙΛΕΩΣ ΣΩΤΗΡΟΣ ΕΡΜΑΙΟΥ ΚΑΙ ΚΑΛΛΙΟΠΗΣ, "Of King Hermaios the Sa-viour and Calliope."[31]

Among the official epithets relating to kinship or dynastic ties, the only one we can find is *Philopator*. As a matter of fact, there are only two cases dating to a later phase of the Greek presence in Northwest India: Apollodotos II (ca. 80–65 BC), who ruled over an area that stretched between Gandhara and the Eastern Punjab, adopted this title after he managed to regain the kingdom from the Indo-Scythian king Maues (ca. 90–80 BC). Quite probably Apollodotos chose this epithet in order to link himself to the memory of his father[32] while at the same time proclaiming dynastic continuity. The second case is that concerning Strato II (ca. 25 BC–10 AD),[33] the last Greek king to rule in India. From his coin legends we learn that he had associated his son Strato III on the throne and the latter had taken up the title of *Philopator* in homage to his father:

---

[29] For discussion and bibliography on the identity of Eukratides' parents, see Coloru 2009, 209–212.

[30] Bopearachchi 1991, *Agathocleia et Straton*, sér. 5–6; Coloru 2009, 246.

[31] This portrait could celebrate the dynastic union between the house of Hermaios and that of another Indo-Greek king, Philoxenos, who would also be the father of Calliope, see Bopearachchi 1991, *Hermaios*, sér. 1–2; Coloru 2009, 256. A reference to Calliope would be detectable, even if implicitly, in the representation of an Amazon queen on horseback on the obverse of a series struck in the name of Hermaios, see Bopearachchi 1991, *Hermaios*, sér. 6.

[32] According to Bopearachchi 1991, 139–141 Apollodotos' father was Strato I; on the contrary, Coloru 2009, 259 thinks that Archebios may be more likely.

[33] Bopearachchi 1991, *Straton II et son fils Straton*, sér 6–7; Coloru 2009, 260–261.

Ob/ ΒΑΣΙΛΕΩΣ ΣΩΤΗΡΟΣ ΣΤΡΑΤΩΝΟΣ ΚΑΙ ΦΙΛ(ΟΠΑΤΩΡΟΣ) ΣΤΡΑΤΩΝΟΣ
"Of King Strato the Saviour and Strato the Father-Loving"

Finally, we should mention the peculiar case of King Artemidoros, who ruled in the area of Taxila around 85 BC. For want of more evidence, Artemidoros was usually considered a Greek monarch both on onomastic grounds and in terms of the iconography of his coinage until the discovery of a silver hemiobol,[34] whose reverse legend in prakrit states the following:

R/ *Rajatirajasa Moasa putrasa Artemidorasa*
"Of Artemidoros son of the King of kings Maues"

As we have seen, Maues was the Indo-Scythian chief who seized power in Gandhara. What is worth noting here is that Artemidoros does not claim his (half-?)Scythian origins in the obverse Greek legend – which is in fact quite customary in style and phraseology – but in the legend intended for the local population. This choice cannot be casual, and might be understood as an attempt to appeal to his Indian-speaking subjects by drawing attention to his direct familial ties with Maues. A new specimen[35] has been found inside a hoard allegedly discovered by local people in Barikot (Swat, Pakistan). The town occupies the site of the ancient Barygaza, which during the Indo-Greek rule knew a period of urban expansion, here including the building of a massive defence system designed according to Hellenistic techniques of military architecture.[36] In comparison with the first specimen, the reverse legend of this new coin seem to be more readable and different in meaning owing to the presence of the conjunction *cha*, i.e. "and." R.C. Senior proposes the following reading and translation:

R/ *Rajatirajasa Moasa putrasa cha Artemidorasa*
"Of the King of kings Maues and his son Artemidoros"

If the above reading proposed by Senior is correct, this should mean that Artemidoros had been reigning jointly with his father for a certain period. As the obverse legend still mentions Artemidoros alone, the hypothesis that the message concerning his lineage was only intended for Indian-speaking subjects seems to be strengthened. We can only speculate about the reasons for such a choice. In my opinion, the most plausible scenario could be that Artemidoros wanted to style himself as a Greek ruler to gain the support of the Greek aristocracy of the Gandhara region, so he preferred to use the reverse legend of a bronze series with very limited circulation in order to show the not irrelevant detail that he was the son of a Saka king responsible for the overthrowing of the former dynasty of Greek sovereigns. Of course, his relationship to Maues must be known, and we have to expect that a certain number of Greek settlers in the Swat valley were also bilingual, and therefore capable of understanding the message written in the legend. Thus, Artemidoros could have tried to keep a Greek style and appearance while revealing his real origins "in a low voice."

---

[34] MacDonald/Senior 1998, 55–56; Coloru 2009, 258–259.
[35] *ICH* 2, XI, 151–152.
[36] For an overview on the archaeological findings, see Callieri 2007, 133–164.

3. Appropriation of a paradigm

We must now turn to the coinage of local dynasties in the area under study and see in which ways messages on kinship were transmitted in order to put forward claims of legitimacy or strengthen a dynasty through the promotion of familial affection and unity.

The Arsacids

As an absolutistic and hereditary monarchy, the proclamation of a successor to the kingdom of Parthia depended solely on the decision of the king. The heir was usually the elder son, but this tradition was not always followed, because the king's will was the only rule which mattered in the end. Thus, it was not unusual for a younger son or even a brother of the king to be proclaimed sovereign in his own right.[37]

Among the Parthian kings, the habit of stating dynastic and family ties on coins makes its appearance by the second half of the second century BC with Phraates II (138–127), for whom the epithets[38] *Philopator* and *Theopator* are attested in order to recall the memory of his father Mithradates I (ca. 171–138). As Federicomaria Muccioli points out,[39] these titles became all the more frequent in the period of dynastic conflict and scarcity of documentation known as the *Dark Age* of the Parthian Empire (first century BC). It was then that a group of sovereigns, namely Gotarzes I (95–87), Orodes I (90–77), Sinatruces (77–70), Phraates III (70–57) and Orodes II (57–38), adopted these titles on their coinage to claim their legitimacy and filial piety towards their fathers. To these rulers we have to add Mithradates III (57–54) and Phraates IV (38–2), who also bore the epithet *Eupator*.[40]

The representation of other members of the royal family besides the king occurs only once in Parthian coinage, specifically in the joint reign of Musa[41] and her son Phraatakes (2 BC–4 AD). A gift to Phraates IV (38–2 BC) from Augustus, Musa soon became the favourite concubine of the king, to whom she gave birth to Phraatakes. Taking advantage of her sway on Phraates, Musa persuaded the king to send his other sons to Rome as hostages, and then poisoned her husband and married her own son in order to hold power, although she did so under the appearance of a joint rule. Unlike the Greek precedent, the couple is not depicted together, but separately on either side. Edward Dąbrowa[42] explains that sometimes Parthian queens seem to have enjoyed the recognition of their status as public persons, even if the available evidence prevents us from having a clearer picture of their specific condition. The way Musa gained power was exceptional, and possibly the separate portrait instead of a jugate one might suggest her position of queen not subject to her husband but on an equal level with him. In fact, in jugate portraits one of

---

[37] For a study on Parthian kingship, see Dąbrowa 2010, 124–126.

[38] On the official epithets of the Arsacids, see Muccioli 2013, in particular 171, 192, 195, 199, 219, 232–233, 257–258, 314–315, 320–326, 341–342, 346, 403–407, 419–420.

[39] Muccioli 2013, 232.

[40] Muccioli 2013, 232–233, 239 and n. 496.

[41] For a biography of this queen, see Strugnell 2008, 275–298.

[42] Dąbrowa 2010, 126.

the members of the couple is more prominent than the other, and this position is usually held by the one who holds real power, as we have already seen in the case of Cleopatra Thea. Musa's status must have been high, if we consider that her image is accompanied by the title of *Thea Ourania* – "Heavenly Goddess."[43] To a Greek audience, this epithet recalled Aphrodite, but in the Iranian world it was connected to Anahita, a warlike goddess also tied to the water element and fertility who occupied an important place in Iranian religion.

Fig. 4. Separate portraits of Phraatakes and Musa; © Roma Numismatics Ltd.

The *frataraka* of Persis

In the first decades of the second century BC, Persis was made independent from the Seleukids thanks to a dynasty of local rulers bearing the old Persian title *frataraka*, or "leader, governor," (literally "before/ahead of us").[44] After Mithradates I's conquest of Parthia in 140 BC, these dynasts continued to reign in the region as vassal kings of the Parthians, but the title *frataraka* disappeared from their set of titles. Baγdād (second century BC), one of the last *paratarakas* before the Parthian conquest, states his lineage on the Aramaic legend: *bgdt prtrk' zy 'lhy' br bgwrt*, "Baγdād the frataraka of the gods, son of Bagawart." This statement is justified by the fact that Baγdād may have been in need of legitimacy against a rival, possibly Wādfradād I.[45]

It is also noticeable that the coin inscriptions of the *frataraka* Ardašir and Wahbarz add to their personal name the phrase *br prs*, i.e. "son of a Persian," clearly with the scope of emphasising their ethnic lineage.[46]

To once again find a reference to the ruler's ancestry one must go to a later period of the history of Persis, between the first century AD and the rise of the Sasanian dynasty in the third century AD. The coin legends are usually standardised, so I will limit myself to quoting, for the sake of example, that of Dārāyān II, the first king of Persis to put his father's name in the coin legend:

---

[43]   On this title and bibliography, cf. Muccioli 2013, 325–326.

[44]   On the translation of the title *frataraka*, see Skjærvø 1997, 102; on the phrase *prtrk' zy 'lhy'*, see Panaino 2003.

[45]   Sarkhosh Curtis 2010, 388.

[46]   Klose 2005, 96; Klose/Müseler 2008, 25.

R/ *d'ryw MLK' BRH wtprdt MLK'*
"King Dārāyān, son of King Wādfradād"

In addition, two other rulers of Persis, Manūčihr I and Ardašir III, seem to have had joint rule with an individual called Mihr in the first half of the second century AD.[47] Who exactly was Mihr, and was he somehow related to those rulers? The problem remains unresolved, although Frye thought the existence of such a king questionable.[48]

The Kingdom of Elymais

A small kingdom that emerged in the second century BC from the gradual disintegration of the oriental possessions of the Seleukids, Elymais covered the area of the modern Iranian province of Khuzestan. Throughout its history, the status of Elymais was often that of a vassal state to the Parthians. Elymaean coinage begins to exhibit statements of family ties under the reign of Kamnaskires III (82–75 BC): the king is represented with his wife Anzaze,[49] (Fig. 5) and both their names are expressed in the reverse legend:

R/ ΒΑΣΙΛΕΩΣ ΚΑΜΝΑΣΚΙΡΟΥ ΚΑΙ ΒΑΣΙΛΙΣΣΗΣ ΑΝΖΑΖΗΣ
"Of King Kamnaskires and Queen Anzaze"

Fig. 5. Tetradrachm with jugate busts of Kamnaskires III and Anzaze; © Roma Numismatics Ltd.

His son Kamnaskires IV might have been put on the throne by the Parthian king Phraates III in 61 BC as a reward for his reconciliation with Pompey. This is hardly a verifiable hypothesis, owing to the lack of more data.[50] What we can say, judging by the coin legends, is that he wanted to put emphasis on his ascendance from Kamnaskires III:

R/ ΒΑΣΙΛΕΩΣ ΚΑΜΝΑΣΚΙΡΟΥ ΤΟΥ ΕΓ(γόνου) ΒΑΣΙΛΕΩΣ ΚΑΜΝΑΣΚΙΡΟΥ

"Of King Kamnaskires, born of King Kamnaskires"

That is the general reading of the legend, and to my knowledge it has always been referred to under this form: if this is the case, then the legend is worth noting for the

---

[47]　See Alram 1986, no. 627 and 629.
[48]　Frye 1984, 272, note 5.
[49]　Alram 1986, 143–144, no. 454–455; van't Haaf 2007, 63–67.
[50]　See Shayegan 2011, 118, 325.

choice of the word ἔκγονος instead of the more common υἱός. However, there is no need to think of ΕΓ as an abbreviation for ἔκγονος, given that the expression "Χ τοῦ ἐγ βασιλέως Y," denoting a pronominal function of the article, is well attested in the Greek language in both literary and documentary sources,[51] so there is no reason for an abbreviated word here. As a consequence, one may read the legend simply as it is: ΒΑΣΙΛΕΩΣ ΚΑΜΝΑΣΚΙΡΟΥ ΤΟΥ ΕΓ ΒΑΣΙΛΕΩΣ ΚΑΜΝΑΣΚΙΡΟΥ.

The same coin legend is attested for another namesake who ruled in the first century AD, Kamnaskires V.[52] By the second half of the first century, the ancient Elymaean dynasty was replaced by a new line, possibly of Arsacid descent if we have to rely only on the onomastics of these individuals, who nevertheless also seem to have kept the name Kamnaskires as a royal title. The coin legend attesting the king's lineage is no longer in Greek, but rather in Aramaic characters, and it occurs in the issues by Orodes III[53] (R/ *wrwd MLK' BRY wrwd*, "King Orodes, son of Orodes") Kamnaskires-Orodes[54] (*kbnhzkyr wrwd MLK' BR wrwd MLK'*, "King Kamnaskires Orodes, son of king Orodes"). Another king Orodes (third century AD)[55] not only mentions his queen Ulfān in the coin legend (Ob/ *wrwd MLK'*, "King Orodes; R/ *ulp'n*, "Ulfān"), but she is also portrayed in the reverse. The disposition of the portraits recalls that of the issues by Musa and Phraataces, although the role of Ulfān seems less stressed than that of Musa, as her portrait is accompanied neither by the title of queen nor by any other court epithet.

The Kingdom of Characene

The history of this southern Mesopotamian kingdom[56] centred on its capital of Spasinou-Charax (a former Alexandria founded by Alexander the Great, then re-founded as Antioch by Antiochos IV)[57] on the Persian Gulf, was established by a king of Iranian descent, Hyspaosines, around 127/126 BC. References to familial relations on coins can be observed only in the short reign of Artabazos I (49/48 BC),[58] who presents the title of *Philopator* among his royal epithets. This is the only reference to kinship in Characenian coinage until the reign of Meredates (ca. 130/131–150/151 AD),[59] who in the coin legend refers to his father Pacoros II, king of Parthia:

R/ ΜΕΡΕΔΑΤΗΣ ΥΙ[ΟΣ] ΦΟ[ΚΟΡΟΥ] ΒΑΣΙΛΕΩΣ ΒΑΣΙΛΕΩΝ ΒΑΣΙΛΕΥΣ ΟΜΑΝΑΙΩΝ
"Meredates, son of the King of kings Pacoros, king of the Omani"

---

[51] See e.g. *IDélos* 1542, *ll.* 2–3 or *CIRB* 3, 356, *ll.* 1–4.

[52] See Alram 1986, no. 463.

[53] Orodes II in Alram 1986, no. 477.

[54] Kamnaskires-Orodes III in Alram 1986, no. 479.

[55] Orodes IV in Alram 1986, no. 488.

[56] For the history of Characene, see Schuol 2000.

[57] Schuol 2000, 108–109; Cohen 2013, 109–117.

[58] Schuol 2000, 223–224.

[59] Alram 1986, no. 506; Schuol 2000, 232–233; Wiesehöfer 2005, 169–170. Apart from his coinage Meredates is known from a bilingual Greek-Parthian inscription carved on a statue of Heracles discovered in 1984 at Seleukeia-on-the-Tigris. This source celebrates the victory of Vologases IV of Parthia over Meredates in 151 AD, see Bernard 1990, 3–68.

King Orabazes II may have mentioned his father in the reverse legend, provided that the word ΠΡΑΤΑ (or ΠΑΤΑ) is intended as an abbreviation of the patronymic Phraata or Phraataphernes.[60] Finally, the last ruler of Characene, Māga (ca. 195–210 AD),[61] mentions his father Attambelos VIII in the coin legend in Aramaic script: R/ *m'g zy 'tmb'y'z MLK'*, "Māga, the son of king Attambelos." Māga does not bear any royal title, probably because of his status as a vassal of the Parthians. However, the reference to Attambelos is meant to stress clearly his belonging to a royal lineage.

Sakas and local dynasties between Seistan and Northwest India

Coins are often the only source by which we might gain some understanding of the history of Central Asia and India during the troubled and poorly documented period following the fall of the Greek kingdom of Bactria in the second half of the first century BC. Nomadic people gradually occupied Bactria, Drangiana (whose name changed into Sakastan, "Land of the Sakas" after the Scythian tribes who settled in the region), Arachosia and Northwest India, and created their own dynasties. Those tribal chiefs struck coinage imitating Greek, Indo-Greek as well as Parthian models, but also introduced new features in style, and of course in kingship ideology.[62]

According to Strabo,[63] the migration of the Scythian tribe of the Sakaraukae together with other Central Asian nomads was the cause of the fall of the Greco-Bactrian kingdom. In the first century BC, Tanlis Maidates,[64] possibly a tribal chief belonging to the Sakaraukae, struck a series of coins representing himself and his wife Raggodeme (Fig. 6). The linguistic analysis conducted by Weber[65] on this ruler's name suggests that the first part, Tanlis (of unknown etymology), might be considered as a title, whereas the second one is more certainly an Iranian personal name which can be translated as "Given by the Moon." The model adopted by Tanlis Maidates closely recalls that attested for Musa of Parthia: the helmeted head of Maidates occupies the obverse of the coin, while the veiled portrait of Raggodeme, accompanied by the Greek title KYPIA, i.e. "the Lady," is represented on the reverse. Raggodeme's Greek title is often related to deities, and in this particular case it could stand for an honorific epithet denoting the divine status of the queen as already attested for Musa *Thea Ourania* or Cleopatra *Thea Eueteria*. The same title would later become part of the Sasanian court ceremonial, since it is attributed to a Princess Chashmak as well as to Myrrōd, mother of Šabuhr I.[66]

---

[60] See Schuol 2000, 234.
[61] Schuol 2000, 235–237.
[62] See *ICH*; Frölich 2008.
[63] Strabo, XI.8.2.
[64] Alram 1986, no. 1269; Weber 2004, 247–250.
[65] Weber 2004, 248–249.
[66] *Res Gestae Divi Saporis* (ed. Huyse 1999) 37.4; 37.6.

Fig. 6. Separate portraits of Tanlis Maidates and Raggodeme; © CNG Inc.

Almost at the same time as Tanlis Maidates, in a chronological span ranging from 50 BC to 30 AD, but in an area located between Kandahar and Peshawar, we find Naštēn, another local chief of Iranian origins who states his lineage on the coin legend.[67] This ruler is known from one tetradrachm discovered in 1992 in the mountainous region of Badakhshan (Northeast Afghanistan). Naštēn was probably a member of the local Iranian aristocracy, but the engraver used Greco-Bactrian and Indo-Greek models to carve his portrait. The reverse legend states the following:

R/ ΝΑΣΤΗΝΗΣ / [Ξ]ΑΤΡΑΝΝΟ[Υ]
"Of Naštēn, (the son) of Xatrannos"

Unlike his contemporaries, the Indo-Scythians, we can observe that this Iranian prince does not have any title to specify the nature of his rule: the patronymic seems sufficient to convey his noble lineage as well as his right to reign.

The Sakas who settled in Arachosia and India, the so-called Indo-Scythians, provide remarkable examples about the representation of family relations. Following chronological order, we can begin with the aforementioned Maues, father of Artemidoros. In the coinage of this Saka king we can find a tetradrachm where the obverse legend mentions his wife M/Nachene (the reading of the first letter is uncertain) accompanied by the same royal epithet, *Theotropos*, already borne by Agathocleia during her regency for Strato I.[68] The name of Maues, on the contrary, appears on the reverse: this specimen is all the more interesting if one considers that the obverse of the coins is usually reserved for the king. Should this fact suggest that M/Nachene held a significant position at court even more important than her husband's? We do not have enough data to support this view; nevertheless this joint issue, as isolated as it may be, attests the high status a woman of the royal family could attain among the Indo-Scythians.

Also noteworthy are the joint issues of the Indo-Scythian king Vonones, who at the beginning of the first century AD controlled the area between the Kabul valley and Taxila. He was helped in this task by his brothers Spalahores and Spalirises, and his nephew Spalagadames, Spalahores' son[69] (Fig. 7). All of them are mentioned in Vonones coin

---

[67]   Bopearachchi 1993, 609–611; Bopearachchi/Grenet 1993, 299–307. On the contrary, Muccioli 2013, 421 reads Xatrannos as *tyrannos* and suggests understanding the word as a title of Naštēn rather than a patronymic.

[68]   Le Rider 1967; Widemann 2003, 95–125; *ICH* 2, type 4.

[69]   See *ICH* 2, types 65–71.

legends, which also state their familial relation to the king. They were probably joint kings entrusted with the government of a particular area. In addition, Spalahores had a joint issue with his son Spalagadames, while Spalirises gained increasing autonomy and struck coins of his own – although still stating his being brother to Vonones, until he proclaimed himself King of kings.

Tab. 1. Coin legends mentioning family ties in the Vonones dynasty

Authority	Ob/ legend (in Greek)	R/ legend (in prakrit)
Vonones + Spalahores	ΒΑΣΙΛΕΥΣ ΒΑΣΙΛΕΩΝ ΜΕΓΑΛΟΥ ΟΝΩΝΟΥ, "The Great king of kings Vonones"	*Maharajabhrata dhramikasa Spalahorasa*, "Of Spalahores the Just, brother of the king"
Vonones + Spalirises	ΒΑΣΙΛΕΥΣ ΒΑΣΙΛΕΩΝ ΜΕΓΑΛΟΥ ΟΝΩΝΟΥ, "The Great king of kings Vonones"	*Maharajabhrata dhramikasa Spalarishasa*, "Of Spalirises the Just, brother of the king"
Vonones + Spalagadames	ΒΑΣΙΛΕΥΣ ΒΑΣΙΛΕΩΝ ΜΕΓΑΛΟΥ ΟΝΩΝΟΥ, "The Great king of kings Vonones"	*Spalahoraputrasa dhramiasa Spalagadamasa*, "Of Spalagadames, son of Spalahores the Just"
Spalahores + Spalagadames	ΣΠΑΛΥΡΙΟΣ ΔΙΚΑΙΟΥ ΑΔΕΛΦΟΥ ΤΟΥ ΒΑΣΙΛΕΩΣ, "Of Spalahores the Just, brother of the king"	*Spalahoraputrasa dhramiasa Spalagadamasa*, "Of Spalagadames, son of Spalahores the Just"
Spalirises	ΒΑΣΙΛΕΩΣ ΑΔΕΛΦΟΥ ΣΠΑΛΙΡΙΣΟΥ, "of Spalirises the Just, brother of the king"	*Maharajabhrata dhramiaasa Spalarishasa* , "Of Spalirises the Just, brother of the king"

As we can see from the above table, kinship with Vonones is always stated as a means to suggest the subordinate role of his brothers towards him. Apparently, the only exception is that of the joint issue of Vonones and Spalagadames, for whom only the name of his father is specified, while that of his uncle, which should be more relevant in terms of legitimacy, is omitted. This is not a secondary detail, as in the next pages we will see that other rulers in Northwest India preferred to state their position as nephews of a powerful uncle instead of recalling their father's memory.

a   b

Fig. 7. a) tetradrachm of Vonones + Spalahores; b) hemiobol of Spalahores + Spalagadames;
© CNG Inc.

The crisis of the Indo-Greek kingdoms in the first century BC gave rise to several local states ruled by powerful families and dynasts. They adopted a plethora of titles in order to define their rank, such as the old Persian *satrap* or a mixed Indo-Persian *mahasatrap*, i.e. "great satrap" or Indian *raja*, which denotes a king of lesser status in the face of a *maharaja*, lit. "great king" – which is also the Indian translation of the Greek term *basileus*. The highest title was *King of kings*, which was quite popular among Iranian people, because it was borne by the Achaemenid monarchs. In time, titles such as "satrap" lost their original meaning and in turn acquired the connotation of an independent sovereign: in several dynasties like that of the Western Satraps, *mahasatrap* was employed to define the status of a king in his full right, while satrap was reserved for his heir.

The Apracharajas. The Indo-Scythian dynasty of the kings of Apracha, or Apracharajas, ruled the Bajaur area in Pakistan between the last decades of the first century BC and the first century AD.[70] As was the case with other dynasts, they struck coinage bearing legends with an indication of the king's lineage. Among the issues we can quote are those by Indravasu (ca. 32–33 AD):

> R/ *Vijayamitraputrasa Itravasusa apracharajasa*
> "Of Indravasu king of Apracha, the son of Vijayamitra"

On the other hand, Vijayamitra's grandson Aspavarma (ca. 30–60 AD) bore the Greek military title of *strategos*. He struck coins[71] jointly with the Indo-Scythian king Azes II, for whom he may have controlled a certain district in Northern India:

> R/ *Imtravarnaputrasa Aspavarmasa strategasa*
> "Of Aspavarma the *strategos*, son of Indravarma"

The Northern and Western Satraps. Saka rulers bearing the title of satrap or mahasatrap are attested in several parts of the north-western side of the Indian subcontinent between the second half of the first century BC and the fourth century AD, when the expansion of the Gupta kingdom put an end to their rule. Depending on their area of political influence, modern historians divide them into the Northern Satraps and Western Satraps.

Northern Satraps: they controlled the regions of Northwest India and Mathura. These dynasties were sometimes related by means of intermarriage. Zeionises (ca. 10 BC–10 AD),[72] satrap of Chukhsa – possibly Chach in modern Pakistan – mentions his father Manigula on the bilingual coin legends:

> Ob/ (M)ΑΝΝΙΟΛΟΥ ΥΙΟΥ ΣΑΤΡΑΠΟΥ ΖΕΙΩΝΙΣΟΥ
> R/ *Manigulasaputrasa chatrapasa Jihuniasa*
> "Of Zeionises the satrap, son of Manigula"

On the other hand, the satrap Kharaostes,[73] a contemporary of Zeionises in Gandhara, remembers his father Arta:

---

[70] Salomon 1996a, 233–246; Falk 1998, 85–108; *ICH* 1, 89–94; *ICH* 2, 136–143; Salomon 2007, 267–282.

[71] *ICH* 2, type 182–185.

[72] *ICH* 2, type 130–135.

[73] Salomon 1996b, 353–358; *ICH* 1, 95–100; *ICH* 2, type 143.

Ob/ ΧΑΡΑΗΩΣΤΕΙ ΣΑΤΡΑΠΟΥ ΑΡΤΑ ΥΙΟΥ
"Of Kharaostes the satrap, son of Arta"

R/ *chatrapasa pra Kharaostasa Artasaputrasa*
"Of Kharaostes the satrap, son of Arta"

Kharaostes, in turn, was mentioned on the issues of his son Hajatria.[74] By doing so, these rulers could show their subjects a dynastic sequence which strengthened their claims of legitimacy:

R/ *chatrapasa Kharaostaputrasa Hajatriasa*
"Of Hajatria the satrap, son of Kharaostes"

Western Satraps. The satraps based in the coastal area of Gujarat and Saurashtra acquired wealth and power because they held control on the maritime trade routes between Rome and India. One of the ruling dynasties, the Kshaharatas, gained momentum under Nahapana (first half of the first century AD), the king Mambanos mentioned by the *Periplus of the Erythrean Sea*, 47. Another important member of the Western Satraps was Chastana, ruler of Ujjain, who was reported by Ptolemy[75] as Tiastanos. The Kshaharatas were defeated by King Gautamiputra Satakarni, a member of the Satavahanas family, who subsequently established his own dynasty. As was the case after the demise of the Kshaharatas, the coin legends usually report the name of the king's father and always follow the same syntactical structure. For the sake of brevity, I limit myself to citing those of Chastana and Rudradaman:

- Chastana
  R/ *rajno kshatrapasa Ghsamotikaputrasa Chastanasa*
  "Of Chastana king and satrap, son of Ghsamotika"

- Rudradaman
  R/ *rajno kshatrapasa Jayadamasaputrasa rajno Rudradamasa*
  "Of Rudradaman king and satrap, son of King Jayadaman"

Pārata kingdom. In the period between the second and fourth century AD, the northeastern part of Baluchistan was controlled by the Pāratarajas, i.e. kings of the *Pāratas* (or *Pāradas*), a tribe of Iranian origin whose history is almost unknown, even if we can grasp some amount of information by the issues they struck. The kingdom was established by a certain Bagareva, of whom no coin has been found so far. To our knowledge, the Pāratarajas coinage begins under Bagareva's son and successor Yolamira. The Pāratarajas used to provide the name of their fathers in the coin legends, meaning that we have a good knowledge of their genealogical tree, especially after the analysis led by Pankaj Tandon.[76] Once again, I will mention just a few of them:

- Yolamira (ca. 125–150 AD)
  R/ *Yolamirasa Bagarevaputrasa pāratarāja*
  "Of Yolamira the Parataraja, son of Bagareva"

---

[74] *ICH* 2, type 145–148.
[75] Ptolemy, VII.1.63: Ὀζηνὴ βασίλειον Τιαστανοῦ.
[76] Tandon 2006; Tandon 2009; Tandon 2010. See also *ICH* 2, 190–193.

- Kozana (first quarter of the third century AD)
  R/ *Kozanasa Bagavharnaputra pāratarāja*
  "Of Kozana the Parataraja, son of Bagavharna"

The Indo-Parthians

In the first decades of the first century AD (ca. 20–45),[77] a prince possibly from the noble house of Suren, known by his Iranian title of Gondophares (o. P. *Vindapharna*, "May he find glory"), left his home in Seistan to begin a series of campaigns towards the east which finally made him master of a large area between Seistan and Gandhara. With Gondophares began the Indo-Parthian dynasty, which lasted until the third century AD.[78] The king managed to hold his conquests partly by letting local rulers remain in their place as vassals, while also putting his relatives in command of certain regions. The latter aspect is significant in that it will form the basis of the claims to legitimacy of some of Gondophares' successors. In fact, after the death of Gondophares some of his heirs (Sases, Orthagnes, Hybouzanes and Sarpedones) took the name of the founder of the dynasty as a royal title, like Arsaces among the Parthians and Caesar in the Roman Empire.[79] In addition, they stated their kinship with Gondophares, such as Abdagases I, the king's nephew, as we can read on the coin legends of his bilingual series issued in Gandhara:[80]

Ob/ ΒΑΣΙΛΕΥ ΑΒΑΔΑΓΑΣ ΥΝΔΙΦΕΡΟ ΑΔΕΛΦΙΔΕΩΣ
"Of King Abdagases the nephew of Gondophares"

R/ *Guduvharabhrataputrasa maharajasa tratarasa Avadagashasa*
"Of King Abdagases the Saviour, nephew of Gondophares"

It is interesting to note that Abdagases' kinship is stated on issues from the Gandhara area, but it is absent from specimens circulating in northern Arachosia as well as the Kabul valley, which seems to demonstrate his need for obtaining more recognition in northern India.

On the other hand, the Indo-Parthian king Hybouzanes claimed to be the son of Orthagnes,[81] one of Gondophares' subkings and successors in Seistan and Southern Arachosia:

R/ ΒΑΣΙΛΕΥΣ ΥΒΟΥΖΑΝΗΣ ΥΙΟΣ ΟΡΘΑΓΝΟΥ ΒΑΣΙΛΕΩΣ
"King Hybouzanes, the son of King Orthagnes"

---

[77] The majority of the scholars tend to place Gondophares' reign in the first half of the first century AD, see Frölich 2002, no. 173; *contra* R.C. Senior in *ICH* 1, 123–126 who proposes an earlier date in the last decades of the first century BC (ca. 20 BC) for the beginning of his rule.

[78] *ICH* 1, 108–128; Frölich 2004, 100–103; Bivar 2007, 26–36.

[79] Cribb 1985, 295; MacDowall 1991, 246; MacDowall 2007, 106.

[80] *ICH* 2, types 226–230. Several variants exist because of the corrupt legend and the bad state of preservation of the coins, see e.g. Alram 1986, no. 1148: ΑΒΔΑΚ; *ICH* 2, type 226: ΑΒΑΔΑΚΑΣΟΥ; type 228: ΑΒΔΑΓΑΣΟΥ.

[81] Alram 1986, no. 1176; *ICH* 2, type 259.

King Sases, on the contrary, points to his relationship with an individual named Aspa.[82] The latter could be an abbreviated form of Aspavarma, the Indo-Scythian commander in Bajaur (Pakistan) who, as we have already seen, bears the Greek title of *strategos* in his coin legends:[83]

R/ *Maharajasa Aspabhrataputrasa tratara Sasasa*
"Of King Sases the Saviour, nephew of Aspa"

In 1999 the discovery of a new golden coin struck by Abdagases II (ca. 90 AD) sheds more light on the genealogy of the Indo-Parthians.[84] In fact, the Pahlavi inscription reports:

Ob/ *'bdgšy MLKYN MLK' BRY s'nbry MLK'*
"Abdagases King of kings, son of King Sanabares"

Kinship with Sanabares is also stated on the composite coin legend of the last Indo-Parthian ruler of which we are aware, Farn-Sasan (third century AD),[85] whose reign was limited to the Seistan area:

Ob/ *prssn BRY 'twrssn*
R/ *BRY BRY tyrdty BRY npy s'nbry MLKYN MLK'*
"Farn-Sasan, son of Adur-Sasan, grandson of Tiridates / great-grandson of Sanabares King of kings"

The Kushans

Founded by Kujula Kadphises (ca. 40–90/95 AD) around 40 AD, the Kushan Empire ruled over an area stretching from modern Uzbekistan to Northwest India. On the obverse, Kushan coins have quite standardised legends mentioning the title *King of kings* (ΒΑΣΙΛΕΥΣ ΒΑΣΙΛΕΩΝ in Greek, then *shaonaoshao* in Bactrian, after the reform of Kanishka I in the second century AD), the king's name followed by the clan denomination, i.e. *Kushan*. The reverse, on the contrary, depicts a number of deities of various origins (Greek, Iranian and Indian) accompanied by a legend stating their names. No members of the royal family are present, except in two cases. The first one is formed by a commemorative series struck by Wima Kadphises (100/5–127 AD) in honour of his father Wima Taktu (90/95–100 AD):[86]

Ob/ ΒΑΣΙΛΕΥΣ ΟΟΗΜΟ ΚΑΔΦΙΣΗΣ
R/ ΒΑΣΙΛΕΩΣ ΟΟΗΜΟΤΑΚΤΟΟΥ ΚΟΡΡΑΝΟΥ ΥΙΟΣ
"King Wima Kadphises, son of King Wima Taktu the Kushan"

According to Osmund Bopearachchi,[87] the commemoration of Wima Taktu by his son served the purpose of celebrating the end of the usurpation of the anonymous ruler

[82]   Alram 1986, no. 1203; *ICH 2*, type 245.
[83]   *ICH 2*, types 182–185.
[84]   Bopearachchi/Grenet 1999, 73–82.
[85]   Nikitin 1994, 67–69.
[86]   Bopearachchi 2006, 1433–1447; Bopearachchi 2008, 3–56.
[87]   Bopearachchi 2006, 1438–1445; Bopearchchi 2008, 43–52.

(92/97–110 AD), known only by his Greek epithet of Soter Megas, "The Great Saviour." Furthermore, it seems that the general pattern of these coins followed the model of the *Pedigree coins* by Agathokles.

The second case is more enigmatic. Apparently, it was issued for a Kushan ruler named Kanishka, who seems to have exerted some rule in India between the second and third century AD. In fact, a unique specimen in copper discovered in the district of Mathura in 1973 specifies Kanishka's lineage in the combined legend in brāhmi:[88]

Ob/ *Huvishkasya-*
R/ *-pūtra Kaṇikasa*
"Of Kanishka, son of Huvishka"

We know that a king Huvishka (ca. 153–191 AD) – renowned for his beautiful gold coinage representing Iranian, Indian and Greco-Roman deities – was especially active in the area of Mathura, as attested by numerous epigraphical records.[89] If the Huvishka mentioned in the coin legend is the same king, we should infer that Kanishka was a royal prince exerting some authority in the region.[90] As Huvishka's successor to the throne was Vasudeva, it is hard to say whether or not Kanishka should be identified with Kanishka II, who was king in the third century AD. In the coin legend neither Kanishka nor Huvishka is qualified with any titles, but as we are dealing with a local issue with a very limited circulation we may not expect a strict compliance of the official court titles. Unfortunately, there is not enough information we can ascertain from this unique specimen, not to mention that Kushan genealogy after the reign of Kanishka I is practically impenetrable.

The Sasanians

In Sasanian coinage, the depiction of other members of the royal family is quite unusual, and coin legends generally do not mention individuals other than the king himself. The only two exceptions to which we can refer with any certainty are 1) the coins belonging to the period of the rise of the Sasanian dynasty, and 2) the issues struck for Wahrām II (276–293 AD). Around 211/212, Ardaxšīr I and his brother Šabuhr started fighting each other for supremacy in Fārs:[91] both struck coins with their portrait on the obverse (Fig. 8), while the reverse displayed the image of their father Pābag. Their composite legends read as follows:

Ob/ *bgy šhpwhly* (or *'rthštr*) *MLK'*
R/ *BRH bgy p'pky MLK'*
"The divine Šabuhr (or Ardaxšīr) the king, son of the divine Pābag, the king"[92]

---

[88] Göbl 1984, 984; Gupta 1985, 201–205; Alram 1986, no. 1347; Gupta 1989, 124–139, n. 6, pl. 14.1.

[89] See e.g. Konow 1931/1932, 55–61; Lüders 1912, no. 56; Lüders 1961, 68.

[90] Gupta 1989, 124–139 suggests that Kanishka might have been an otherwise unknown son of King Huvishka.

[91] See Daryaee 2010, 245–246, 249–250.

[92] Alram 1986, n° 653–659; Alram 2008, 17–18; Daryaee 2010, 236–255, especially 243–245.

Fig. 8. Hemidrachm of Šabuhr commemorating his father Pābag; © Paul-Francis Jacquier – Numismatique Antique

As for Wahrām II, he is portrayed in jugate busts together with his queen, Shapur-dukhtak.

Fig. 9. Drachm with jugate busts of Wahrām II and his wife; © Paul-Francis Jacquier – Numismatique Antique

Apart from these examples, the depiction and/or mention of other relatives in Sasanian issues is still a matter of debate. This is mostly the case of the small figure appearing in front of the ruler's portrait on the obverse of issues of Ardaxšir I (d. 242), Wahrām II (276–293 AD), Šabuhr III (383–388) and Jāmāsp (496–498), whose identification is far from certain (Fig. 9). Part of the extent scholarship tends to see a portrait of the crown prince, while other commentators are more inclined to identify it with a god, possibly Ahura Mazdā, and Anāhitā in the case of Wahrām II.[93] Be that as it may, this particular iconography could have drawn inspiration from the many specimens of Roman coins showing the opposite portraits of members of the imperial house. For instance, we could compare a bronze coin struck at Edessa (Mesopotamia), thus in an area close to the Sasanian Empire, representing Alexander Severus and his mother Julia Mamea (Fig. 10),

---

[93] On the main features of the Sasanian coinage, see Göbl 1971; Schindel 2005. For a discussion on the identification of the small busts, see Göbl 1971, 42–45; Choksy 1989, 117–135; Alram/Gyselen 2003, 101–103, 178; Schindel 2004, 64, 261–263, 266, 450–451; Schindel 2009, 49–50.

with a bronze issue of Ardaxšir I and an individual that might be identified with his son and heir Šabuhr I (Fig. 11):

Fig. 10–11. Alexander Severus and Julia Mamea; Ardaxšir and an individual
(deity? His son Šabuhr I?); © CNG Inc.

There is not enough space to examine the question in depth, but we can conclude with an open hypothesis: if Ardaxšir adopted this iconographical model from Rome, he could also have adopted the message of dynastic legitimacy profoundly connected to the representation of the members of a ruling house. If so, the mysterious individual facing the Sasanian king might well be identified with a crown prince.[94]

4. An appraisal

Reflecting on the possibility of family connections between the Indo-Parthian dynasty and the Sasanians, the late Richard N. Frye once wrote, "Family connections always have been more important in the East than in Europe, and certainly America, so the continuation in station and influence of the noble Parthian families, such as the Suren and Karen, in Sasanian times is not surprising. It is purely conjecture but not unusual to suggest that when the Suren liege lord of Sistan heard that another liege lord of the Parthian king, Ardaxšir in Fars, had overthrown the Parthian king it was easy to transfer allegiance to the new emperor. This was especially true because of the previous connections between the East and Fars."[95] One might discuss the alleged importance which should be assigned to family connections by eastern populations in comparison with Europeans who are perhaps less interested in the matter. Nevertheless, at the end of this quick survey, I think we can detect some differences in how messages concerning kinship and dynastic propaganda were transmitted through coinage by Greco-Macedonian kingdoms in the East and local dynasties. Family held an important place in both the groups, but they chose different strategies of communication which were not limited to coins but included other means such as inscriptions, literary works, works of art, etc. Coins, however, had the advantage of holding multiple functions concentrated in one item, as they were not only a means of exchange, but also an official document from the

---

[94]   On this hypothesis, see Göbl 1971, 43–45.
[95]   Frye 2004, 131.

court and a work of art. Entrusting explicit and implicit messages about kingship to the coins allowed them to be disseminated more quickly and widely than any other form of official communication.

As for coinage, the Seleucids seem to have preferred suggesting family ties in two ways: on the one hand, through a series of royal epithets recalling messages of affection and unity between father/son, mother/son, and brother/brother, and on the other hand by portraying the ruler together with another member of the family in jugate busts or reserving the coin reverse for the portrait of the family member that the king intended to honour.

The Seleucid coinage has without a doubt exerted a direct influence on the Arsacid dynasty as well as the petty kingdoms based in Southern Mesopotamia and on the coasts of the Persian Gulf. As for the Greco-Bactrian and Indo-Greek coins, their influence can be detected particularly in areas closer to Central Asia and India. Because of the manner in which they found themselves in-between different cultures, the kings of Bactria and India could thus represent a sort of unifying link between different traditions. In fact, one can notice the use of iconographic features such as the jugate busts and the use of royal epithets related to family, but it is also possible to notice written statements about a king's kinship.

Nevertheless, the non-Greek dynasties studied in this paper adapted their coinage to their own culture, creating new ways of communication using kinship-based propaganda. From an iconographic point of view, we may see that the jugate bust (e.g. Kamnaskires and Anzaze) was not the most popular form of acknowledging the importance of the role played by a certain individual within a family: Parthian and Saka rulers, for example, opted for separate portraits on either side (e.g. Phraataces and Musa, Tanlis Maidates and Raggodeme). And this detail betrays the intention of marking a distinction in the prominence of individuals on the basis of the position occupied by their portrait. However, the most interesting feature of the oriental issues concerning messages on family relationships is the overwhelming preference for written statements via coin legends rather than visual depictions of the members of the family. While among the Seleucids this option is almost absent – except for the royal epithets belonging to the sphere of familial harmony – oriental coinages present a varied set of solutions not only in Greek, but in local languages too. As a result, we can observe a vocabulary expressing different degrees of kinship. Moreover, messages illustrating a ruler's lineage could be entrusted to a particular language and not to another. In my opinion, the evidence suggests that different languages could be used in order to convey different messages for a different audience. While the bilingual coinage of the Indo-Greek kings usually showed a uniform version in both Greek and its prakrit translation, the situation was different for the non-Greek rulers who took over the power in Northwest India. For instance, in the case of the joint coinages of Vonones and his family, kinship of his co-rulers and relatives is stated only in prakrit in the reverse legend, while the obverse, in Greek, is reserved for the only Vonones. But once Spalahores and Spalirises gained more independence and struck their own coinage, their relationship to Vonones was stated in Greek on the obverse, which was the most important side of the coin. Whereas the case of the brothers and nephew of Vonones may be ascribed to considerations of priority in visibility, in other situations such as the coinage of Artemidoros, information on his familial ties with the Indo-Scythian king Maues appears to be intentionally directed to his Indian-speaking subjects, and most limited in terms of the circulation of the message. Even if the Greek and Indian legends expressed distinct contents, this does not mean that the messages were false. On the contrary, they could coexist without any problem as they provided complementary information; for instance, the combined message of the bilingual legends of Vonones' coins is that the latter is the King of Kings; Spalahores and Spalirises are rulers, but only because they are nephews of Vonones. From this point of view, coins were the ideal tool to keep these different messages together. Bilingual individuals could learn more about the partition of powers among the members of the dynasty of Vonones. On the other hand, subjects proficient in only one language could nonetheless understand the basic message, i.e. Vonones was the highest in command.

In many cases, the mention of kinship was due to the presence of rivals or usurpers aiming for the throne (see e.g. Ardaxšīr and Šabuhr), while in other situations it was just a means of asserting his right to rule by inscribing himself in an established lineage. In this framework, written messages about family relationships may have been perceived as more explicit and immediate than a portrait or an epithet. Although the evidence I have surveyed may at first sight appear less interesting compared to more detailed categories of documents such as inscriptions, papyri and parchments, I am nevertheless convinced that it retains a wealth of untapped potential for further research. At the same time, once again it bears witness to the complexity of the cultural interactions which sprang from the encounter of Greek and Eastern civilisations in the Hellenistic period and its aftermath.

Summary table of the expressions of kinship on Eastern coinages in Antiquity (Iran – Northwest India)

Words denoting father/son relationship	Words denoting brother/ brother relationship	Words denoting other familial relationships (uncle/nephew; grandfather/grandson)		Royal epithets denoting father/son; brother/ brother relationship	Iconography
ΥΙΟΣ	ΑΔΕΛΦΟΣ	ΑΔΕΛΦΙΔΟΥΣ		*Eupator*	Jugate busts
BRY = Parth. *puhr* (son); *BRH* MPers. = *pus*		*BRY BRY* = Parth. *puhrēpuhr*; MPers. *nab* (grandson)	*BRY npt* = Parth. *puhrēnapāt* (great-grandson)	*Philopator*	Separate portrait on either side
-putra (son of)	*-bhrata* (brother of)	*-bhrataputra* (nephew of)		*Theopator*	Busts facing each other (*uncertain*)
				Philadelphos	

ABBREVIATIONS

AD II – A.J. Sachs, H. Hunger (1989), *Astronomical Diaries and Related Texts from Babylonia*, vol. II: *Diaries from 261 B.C. to 165 B.C.*, Wien

CIRB – B. Latyschev (1965), *Corpus Inscriptionum regni Bosporani Graecae et Latinae*, Hildesheim

ICH – R.C. Senior (2001–2006), *Indo-Scythian Coins and History*, vol. I–IV, Lancaster–London

IDélos – P. Roussel, M. Launey (1937), *Inscriptions de Délos, nos. 1497–2879 : décrets, dédicaces, listes, catalogues, textes divers, postérieurs à 166 av. J.-C.*, Paris

IGIAC – G. Rougemont (2012), *Inscriptions grecques d'Iran et d'Asie Centrale*, (Corpus Inscriptionum Iranicarum II, 1, 1), London

SC 1 – A. Houghton, C. Lorber (2002), *Seleucid Coins. A Comprehensive Catalogue*, part I: *Seleucus I through Antiochus III*, New York

SC 2 – A. Houghton, C. Lorber, O. Hoover (2008), *Seleucid Coins. A Comprehensive Catalogue*, part II: *Seleucus IV through Antiochus XIII*, New York

BIBLIOGRAPHY

Alram, M. (1986), *Nomina propria iranica in nummis*, Wien.

Alram, M. (2008), Early Sasanian Coinage, in: V. Sarkhosh Curtis, S. Stewart (eds.), *The Age of the Sasanians*, London–New York: 17–30.

Alram, M., Gyselen, R. (2003), *Sylloge Nummorum Sasanidarum Paris–Berlin–Wien*, Band I: *Ardashir I.–Shapur I.*, Wien.

Bernard, P. (1985), *Les monnaies hors trésors. Questions d'histoire gréco-bactrienne*, Paris.

Bernard, P. (1990), Vicissitudes au gré de l'histoire d'une statue en bronze d'Héraclès entre Séleucie du Tigre et la Mésène, *Journal des Savants*: 3–68.

Bivar, A.D.H. (2007), Gondophares and the Indo-Parthians, in: V. Sarkhosh Curtis, S. Stewart (eds.), *The Age of the Parthians*, London–New York: 26–36.

Bopearachchi, O. (1991), *Monnaies gréco-bactriennes et indo-grecques. Catalogue raisonné*, Paris.

Bopearachchi, O. (1993), Naštēn, un prince iranien inconnu entre Grecs et Kouchans, *CRAI*: 609–611.

Bobearachchi, O. (2006), Chronologie des premiers rois kushans : nouvelles données, *Comptes rendus de l'Académie des inscriptions et belles-lettres*: 1433–1447.

Bopearachchi, O. (2008), Les premiers souverains kouchans : chronologie et iconographie monétaire, *Journal des Savants*: 3–56.

Bopearachchi, O., Grenet, F. (1993), Naštēn, un souverain iranien inconnu entre Grecs et Kouchans, *Studia Iranica* 22: 299–307.

Bopearachchi, O., Grenet F. (1999), Une nouvelle monnaie en or d'Abdagases II, *Studia Iranica* 28: 73–82.

Callataÿ, F. de (2009), The First Royal Coinages of Pontos (from Mithridates III to Mithridates V), in: J.M. Højte (ed.), *Mithridates VI and the Pontic Kingdom*, Aahrus: 63–94.

Callieri, P. (2007), Barikot, an Indo-Greek Urban Center in Gandhāra, in: D.M. Srinivasan (ed.), *On the Cusp of an Era. Art in the Pre-Kuṣāṇa World*, Leiden: 133–164.

Choksy, J.K. (1989), A Sasanian Monarch, His Queen, Crown Prince, and Deities: The Coinage of Wahram II, *American Journal of Numismatics* 1: 117–135.

Cohen, G.M. (2013), *The Hellenistic Settlements in the East from Armenia and Mesopotamia to Bactria and India*, Berkeley–Los Angeles.

Coloru, O. (2009), *Da Alessandro a Menandro. Il regno greco di Battriana*, Pisa–Roma.

Cribb, J. (1985), New Evidence of Indo-Parthian Political History, *Coins Hoards* 7: 282–300.

Daryaee, T. (2010), Ardaxšīr and the Sasanian Rise to Power, *Anabasis* 1: 236–255.

Dąbrowa, E. (2010), The Parthian Kingship, in: G.B. Lanfranchi, R. Rollinger (eds.), *Concepts of Kingship in Antiquity*, Padova: 123–134.

Del Monte, G. (1997), *Testi dalla Babilonia ellenistica. Volume I. Testi cronografici*, Pisa–Roma.

Falk, H. (1998), Notes on Some Apraca Dedicatory Texts, *Berliner Indologisches Studien* 11/12: 85–108.

Frölich, Ch. (2002), Dating Gondophares, *Oriental Numismatic Society Newsletter* 173: 11–15.

Frölich, Ch. (2004), Indo-Parthian Dynasty, *Encyclopaedia Iranica*: http://www.iranicaonline.org/articles/indo-parthian-dynasty-1.

Frölich, Ch. (2008), *Monnaies indo-scythes et indo-parthes. Catalogue raisonné*, Paris.

Frye, R.N. (1984), *The History of Ancient Iran*, München.

Frye, R.N. (2004), Parthians in the East, *Parthica* 6: 129–132.

Göbl, R. (1971), *Sasanian Numismatics*, Braunschweig.

Göbl, R. (1984), *System und Chronologie der Münzprägung des Kušanreiches,* Wien.

Gupta, P.L. (1985), Kuṣāṇas in the Yamuno-Gangetic Region. Chronology and Date, *Annali dell'Istituto Universitario Orientale di Napoli* 45: 199–222.

Gupta, P.L. (1989), Early Coins of Mathura Region, in: D.M. Srinivasan (ed.), *Mathurā: The Cultural Heritage*, Columbia (Mo): 124–139.

Holt, F.L. (1984), The so-called "Pedigree Coins" of the Bactrian Greeks, in: W. Heckel, R. Sullivan (eds.), *Ancient Coins of the Graeco-Roman World. The Nickle Numismatic Papers*, Waterloo (Ontario): 69–92.

Hoover, O. (2002): Laodice IV on the Bronze Coinage of Seleucus IV and Antiochus IV, *American Journal of Numismatics* 14: 81–87.

Huyse, Ph. (1999), *Die dreisprachige Inschrift Šābuhr I. an der Ka'ba-i Zardušt (ŠKZ)*, 2 vols., London.

Klose, D.O.A. (2005), Statthalter, Könige, Rebellen, *Numismatisches Nachrichtenblatt* 54: 93–103.

Klose, D.O.A., Müseler W. (2008), *Statthalter und Rebellen Könige. Die Münzen aus Persepolis von Alexander dem Grossen zu den Sasaniden*, München.

Konow, S. (1931/1932), Mathura Brahmi Inscription of the Year 28, *Epigraphia Indica* 21: 55–61.

Kovacs, F.L. (2008), Tigranes IV, V, and VI: New Attributions, *American Journal of Numismatics* 20: 337–350.

Le Rider, G. (1967), Monnaies de Taxila et d'Arachosie: Une nouvelle reine de Taxila, *REG* 80: 331–342.

Lüders, H. (1912), *A List of Brāhmī Inscriptions from the Earliest Times to about A.D. 400 with the Exception of those of Aśoka*, Appendix to *Epigraphia Indica* 10, 1909–1910, Calcutta.

Lüders, H. (1961), *Mathurā inscriptions*, Göttingen.

MacDonald, D., Senior, R.C. (1998), *The Decline of the Indo-Greeks. A re-appraisal of the chronology from the Time of Menander to that of Azes*, Athens.

MacDowall, D.W. (1991), The Interrelation between Indo-Parthian and Kushan Chronology, in: P. Bernard, F. Grenet (eds.), *Histoire et Cultes d'Asie Centrale préislamique*, Paris: 243–250.

MacDowall, D.W. (2007), Numismatic Evidence for a Chronological Framework for Pre-Kaniṣkan Art, from Kalchayan to Gandhāra, in: D.M. Srinivasan (ed.), *On the Cusp of an Era. Art in the Pre-Kuṣāṇa World*, Leiden: 95–117.

Meadows, A. (2014), The Spread of Coins in the Hellenistic World, in: P. Bernholz, R. Vaubel (eds.), *Explaining Monetary and Financial Innovation. A Historical Analysis*, Heidelberg: 169–195.

Muccioli, F. (2013), *Gli epiteti ufficiali dei re ellenistici*, Stuttgart.

Nikitin, A.K. (1994), Coins of the Last Indo-Parthian King of Sakastan (A farewell to Ardamitra), *South Asian Studies* 10: 67–69.

Panaino, A. (2003), The baγān of the Fratarakas: Gods or 'Divine' Kings?, in: C.G. Cereti, M. Maggi, E. Provasi (eds.), *Religious Themes and Texts of Pre-Islamic Iran and Central Asia. Studies in Honour of Professor Gherardo Gnoli on the Occasion of his 65th Birthday on 6th December 2002*, Wiesbaden: 265–288.

Salomon, R. (1996a), Five Kharosthi Inscriptions, *Bulletin of the Asia Institute* 10: 233–246.

Salomon, R. (1996b), An Inscribed Silver Buddhist Reliquary of the Time of King Kharaosta and Prince Indravarman, *Journal of the American Oriental Society* 117: 353–358.

Salomon, R. (2007), Dynastic and Institutional Connections in the Pre-and Early *Kuṣāṇa* Period. New Manuscript and Epigraphic Evidence, in: D.M. Srinivasan (ed.), *On the Cusp of an Era. Art in the Pre-Kuṣāṇa World*, Leiden: 267–282.

Sarkhosh Curtis, V. (2010), The Frataraka Coins of Persis. Bridging the Gap between Achaemenid and Sasanian Persia, in: J. Curtis, S. St John (eds.), *The World of Achaemenid Persia. History, Art and Society in Iran and the Ancient Near East*, London–New York: 379–394.

Savalli-Lestrade, I. (2005), Le mogli di Seleuco IV e di Antioco IV, *Studi Ellenistici* 16: 193–200.

Schindel, N. (2004), *Sylloge Nummorum Sasanidarum Paris–Berlin–Wien*, Band III: *Shapur II.–Kawad I./2. Regierung*, Wien.

Schindel, N. (2005), Sasanian coinage, *Encyclopaedia Iranica*, http://www.iranicaonline.org/articles/sasanian-coinage.

Schindel, N. (2009), *Sylloge Nummorum Sasanidarum Israel*, Wien.

Schuol, M. (2000), *Die Charakene. Ein mesopotamisches Königreich in hellenistisch-parthischer Zeit*, Stuttgart.

Shayegan, M.R. (2011), *Arsacids and Sasanians. Political Ideology in Post-Hellenistic and Late-Antique Persia*, Cambridge.

Strugnell, E. (2008), Thea Musa, Roman Queen of Parthia, *Iranica Antiqua* 43: 275–298.

Tandon, P. (2006), New Light on the Pāratarājas, *Numismatic Chronicle*: 1–37.

Tandon, P. (2006), The Coins of the Pāratarājas. A Synthesis, *Journal of the Oriental Numismatic Society* 205, Special Supplement: 1–30.

Tandon, P. (2009), Further Light on the Pāratarājas. An Absolute Chronology of the Brāhmī and Kharoṣṭhī Series, *Numismatic Chronicle*: 137–171.

Tarn, W.W. (1951), *The Greeks in Bactria and India*, 2nd ed., Cambridge.

Van't Haaf, P.A. (2007), *Catalogue of Elymaean Coinage, ca. 147 B.C.–A.D. 228*, Lancaster–London.

Weber, D. (2004), The Coin Legend *TANLISMAIDATES* and Related Problems, *Parthica* 6: 247–250.

Widemann, F. (2003), Maues King of Taxila. An Indo-Greek Kingdom with a Saka King, *East and West* 53: 95–125.

Wiesehöfer, J. (2005), *Ancient Persia. From 550 BC to 650 AD*, Düsseldorf.

ELECTRUM * Vol. 22 (2015): 201–225
doi: 10.4467/20800909EL.15.011.3949
www.ejournals.eu/electrum

THE DEITIES ON THE KUSHANO-SASANIAN COINS

Fabrizio Sinisi

Österreichische Akademie der Wissenschaften, Wien

Abstract: This article deals with Kushano-Sasanian coins, aiming to interpret the images of deities used on their reverses. The topic has occasionally been discussed in numismatic studies on the
Kushano-Sasanian series, and some images have also been examined in archaeological literature
on Central Asia. Yet Kushano-Sasanian religious imagery has never really been the subject of
specific treatment. In fact, such series provide extremely interesting evidence of the religious imagery of the Sasanian period, due to the conventions which governed typological selection, since
these allowed a more varied iconographic repertoire in comparison with what we can see on the
imperial issues. Contrary to previous hypotheses of the phenomenon of syncretism produced by
the supposed Bactrian religious specificity, the analysis results in a picture showing a fully Zoroastrian imagery, which absorbed iconographic features of Sasanian and Kushan derivation against
the background of the presence of the new Sasanian power.

Key words: Kushano-Sasanians, Kushanshahs, Sasanians, numismatics, religious iconography,
Iranian deities, Zoroastrian imagery.

The coin series struck by the governors of the former Kushan lands conquered by the
Sasanians in the third century represent an extremely interesting phenomenon from several points of view. Their most prominent characteristic is the mixture of Sasanian and
Kushan features, which provides researchers with material for various kinds of enquiries
– from numismatics to history, to iconographic studies and the history of religions – that
have so far only been explored in part.

Due amongst other things to the objective difficulties in the historical reconstruction
and to the priority given to the analysis of the coin sequence and the resulting issue of
attributing the series to specific rulers, Kushano-Sasanian coinage has been the subject of
various studies that have always been of a strictly numismatic nature.[1] These have mainly dealt with relative as well as absolute chronology – the latter in the framework of the

---

[1] Herzfeld 1930; Bivar 1956; 1979; Brunner 1974; Carter 1985; Cribb 1990; Schindel 2005.

debate on the eras used in Central Asia[2] – and have only cursorily tackled other aspects. Among the latter, a topic of some interest is the religious imagery displayed by such series, namely the depictions of deities on coins of various denominations. The importance of this documentation lies in the fact that, contrary to standard Sasanian practice, the reverses of Kushano-Sasanian coins regularly display anthropomorphic depictions of gods, sometimes associated with the standard device of the fire altar of Sasanian derivation, sometimes together with the kings or even merely on their own. While largely due to the legacy of the Kushan coin tradition maintained by Kushano-Sasanian series,[3] this translates into an unparalleled possibility for the study of Sasanian period religious imagery, which is notoriously less common on coins of the main dynasty.

Within the framework of a wider ranging work on Kushano-Sasanian coin finds to be published by Nikolaus Schindel,[4] the typology of the Kushano-Sasanian copper series – which is especially rich in iconographic variety – is currently under investigation by the present author, the aim being a detailed treatment carried out applying a systematic approach. The results achieved so far have produced material for further elaboration, part of which is presented here, with account also taken, where necessary, of the gold and silver series.

According to the general reconstruction of the sequence of rulers determined by Schindel,[5] the Kushano-Sasanian coinage begins with the series of Ardashir 2 and Ardashir 1,[6] which constitute a group of their own to be dated around the 290s. They issued only copper series, all with striking reverse types showing two of the main yazatas of the Zoroastrian pantheon, Anahita and Mithra.[7] A hiatus of several years was followed by the main group of Kushano-Sasanian issues, beginning with the Peroz series.[8] The production assumed a more regular character, with copper series accompanying gold denominations, occasionally joined by silver drachms in the very early stages. The main mints were Balkh, where most of the series in gold were struck, and Kabul, both mints also accounting for the coining of copper series. Only occasionally were they joined by Merv and Herat.[9]

Indeed, this pattern of mint distribution is mirrored in the employment of specific types, at least as a general norm. Balkh is accordingly characterised by a reverse type that portrays a male god with trident standing in front of a bull, known also on coppers but mainly dominating the gold coinage. The standard typology of the copper reverses presents two variants of the basic type of the altar of Sasanian derivation with a human

---

[2] Above all thanks to the *Zeitschranke* defined by Robert Göbl, see 1984; 1993, 77–86; 1999. Cribb (1990, 176–177) also used the absolute chronology of the Kushanshahs to date the era of Kanishka. See also Schindel 2005.

[3] Cf. Brunner 1974, 145.

[4] Whom I would like to take the opportunity to thank here. All the attributions as well as the chronological reconstruction here follow Schindel, forthcoming.

[5] Forthcoming, already proposed in Schindel 2005; 2012; 2014.

[6] Here the custom of numbering the Kushano-Sasanian rulers with Arabic numbers is followed (cf. Göbl 1984, 80; 1993, 44). Types are referred to according to Göbl 1984, abbreviated as MK.

[7] In Merv and Balkh respectively.

[8] A single ruler with this name, whose series were previously conventionally ascribed to Peroz 1, 2, and 5.

[9] All mints are attested by direct reference on some of the series, with the exception of Kabul, whose identification is a convention introduced by Göbl 1984 for a mint certainly located south of the Hindukush.

bust emerging from flames: apart from other differences, in Balkh the figure is normally seen in left profile, while in Kabul the bust is shown full on.

Beside these common types, there are also unique images, mainly belonging to the category of the so-called investiture scenes involving the ruler and a deity. Altogether these types bear depictions of no less than three different gods, in various figurative compositions.

The first such image is also the earliest Kushano-Sasanian reverse type, since it occurs on the coppers of Ardashir 2 struck in Merv (Fig. 1b).[10] The ruler, immediately recognisable on the left thanks to his diademed crown,[11] is being presented with a diademed tiara by a standing goddess. She holds a globe-topped staff in her left hand, and is clad in a long robe reaching to her ankles, the shoulders covered by a cloak. While her body is depicted frontally, the diademed head is fully turned to the left in order to look towards the king, showing in profile the three-pronged rendering of the goddess' headgear, which must be identified as a mural crown. A Middle-Persian inscription surrounds the image, perhaps also mentioning the name of the deity,[12] but it has not yet been deciphered.

a–b. Ardashir 2 (Merv)

c–d. Ardashir 1 (Merv)   e–f. Ardashir 1 (Balkh)

Fig. 1

---

[10] MK 1029.

[11] Shaped like a bird, as used by Ardashir on his obverses.

[12] The inscription is long enough to include a reference to both the ruler and the deity, as is generally the case with similar types.

The same deity appears to be depicted on the reverses of copper series again struck in Merv by the following Kushanshah, Ardashir 1 (Fig. 1d).[13] This time the goddess is portrayed frontally, seated on a high-backed throne with railings on the side and surmounted by a circular canopy, which suggests a temple setting.[14] The deity holds the same staff in the left hand, and with the right offers a ribbed diadem. She wears earrings and bracelets on her wrists, and displays the long robe reaching to her ankles, its heavy folds emphasised on the lower legs. While no cloak is visible, the three-pronged headgear appears to be the same displayed by the goddess on the coppers of Ardashir 2, this time seen from the front and on a larger scale, which allowed the engraver to better reproduce the crenellated battlements composing the main elements of the mural crown.[15] Here too a Middle-Persian inscription is visible around the image, even if the part engraved in the right-hand field has not been deciphered. In the left-most part, running roughly from 11 o'clock to 7 o'clock in an anti-clockwise direction, the words 'n'ḥyt MR'T', "Lady Anahita," are legible, providing a clear key to an identification that, given the role of Anahita as a Sasanian royal deity, would already have been possible on an iconographic basis alone.

A second enthroned deity (Fig. 1f),[16] this time a male one, is used on coppers struck by Ardashir 1 in Balkh.[17] The figure is seen in an almost frontal view, slightly turned three-quarters to the right, sitting on a throne very similar to that of the seated Anahita used in Merv, with high back and side railings, although no arched frame is visible above. In his left hand the god holds the hilt of his sword, held vertically between his legs, which are clad in the pleated trousers typical of Sasanian iconography. The right hand is stretched forward to offer a conspicuous diadem, whose ties show the ribbed treatment ubiquitous in Sasanian imagery and that was also to be seen in the two previously described types depicting Anahita. The god has a moustache and a beard, while his hair is gathered on the sides in two spherical bunches, also common in images from Sasanian Iran. Finally, the diademed head is framed by a large rayed halo, the deity's main iconographic mark, which identifies the god as Mithra. In addition, an explicit legend in Bactrian can be read around the figure, ΒΟΓΟ ΜΙΥΡΟ, "God Mithra."

The resumption of the Kushano-Sasanian coinage under Peroz after a break of several years[18] brings a different pattern. Alongside a single issue of silver drachms struck in Herat,[19] gold is introduced with dinars minted in Balkh,[20] accompanied by an isolated series from an unidentified mint located south of the Hindukush.[21] Copper series appear to be produced in both Balkh and Kabul.

---

[13] MK 1028.

[14] Cf. Göbl 1984, 40, followed by Cribb 1990, 159, 186. Also Carter 1985, 225, 230.

[15] Needless to say, the crown appears three-pronged or with just three battlements due to the perspective of the image, but the full complement was of four battlements, one each on front and rear and the two lateral ones.

[16] MK 1114.

[17] The very same type is employed on a unique gold dinar of Ardashir published by Cribb 1990, 186, no. 14. The authenticity of this coin has been questioned, see Göbl 1993, 47; Schindel, forthcoming.

[18] Peroz 1 = 2 = 3 = 5, see Schindel, forthcoming.

[19] MK 1030. See Schindel, forthcoming.

[20] MK 702, 703–706.

[21] MK 555.

All denominations bear interesting types on their reverses. The dinars introduce the type that was to dominate gold production throughout the Kushano-Sasanian series, namely the standing god with bull (Fig. 2). The full-size deity is depicted in frontal view, with a bull seen in left profile standing behind him. The god holds a trident in his left hand and offers a diadem with his right. He has a full beard and long hair, with the hair on top of his head being depicted as dishevelled, while a circular halo is visible around the head. The clothing consists of a belted long-sleeved tunic reaching to above the knees, and baggy trousers pleated on the sides. The image is surrounded by a Bactrian inscription reading OOPZOANΔO IAZAΔO, corresponding to the Middle Persian *bwrz'wndy yzdty* legible on other Kushano-Sasanian series and variously translated as "exalted god" or "the god who acts in the high regions."[22] In the last version the appellative has been regarded as recalling Avestan, "(the one) who acts in the superior region" borne by the god of the atmosphere Vayu, i.e., *Vaiiuš Uparō.kairiiō*, "the Wind who acts in the high region." Accordingly, the legend has been interpreted as a reference – more or less direct – to the deity depicted, and in particular to its Kushan forebear, the Bactrian Vayu, Wesh, explicitly named on Kushan coins as Oesho.[23] Indeed the main iconographic mark of the Kushano-Sasanian deity, the trident, perfectly matches the imagery of Oesho, as do the bull and the dishevelled hair. Yet there are differences, since no multiple heads or arms are associated with the Kushano-Sasanian type, and other features of the Kushan Oesho are also missing, such as the Indian style clothing,[24] the secondary attributes and the erect linga.

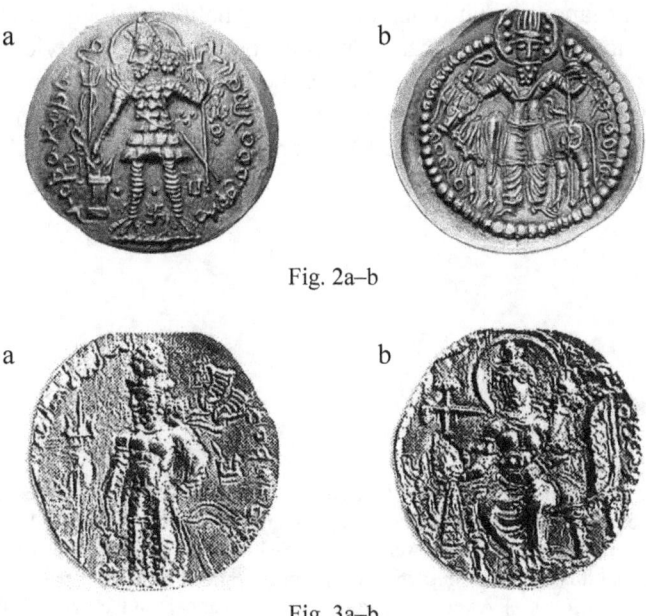

Fig. 2a–b

Fig. 3a–b

[22] Bivar 1956, 16; 1979a, 746; Humbach 1975, 408; Tanabe 1991/1992, 59.

[23] Tanabe 1991/1992, 61–62; Grenet 1994, 43; cf. also Cribb 1997, 29–30.

[24] Cf. Bivar 1956, 15.

In addition to such standard series, a further gold issue from another mint is attributed to Peroz, of which only one specimen is known,[25] and which shows the combination of a rather peculiar rendering of the ruler's image on the obverse with a unique reverse type. The latter depicts an enthroned Ardokhsho-type goddess of Kushan style (Fig. 3b), closely imitating the images of the enthroned goddess of the late Kushan series. The deity is portrayed frontally, with a circular halo around her head and her main iconographic attribute, the cornucopia, held in the left hand. The only significant difference to the Kushan model is that with her right hand the deity offers not a diadem, but a diademed mitre similar to those worn by late Kushan kings.

Another rather unusual type is used by Peroz on the reverses of silver drachms struck in Herat (Fig. 4b),[26] reproducing one of the so-called investiture scenes. The king, recognisable by all his standard paraphernalia, is visible on the left, as seen in the type with Anahita on coppers of Ardashir 2. He is pouring offerings on a small fire burner with his right hand and addressing a figure in front of him with the gesture of the bent left forefinger well known in Sasanian imagery. The figure on the right appears to be a male deity, despite the long robe reaching to the ankles,[27] and sits in a three-quarter view on a high-backed throne with side railings similar to those of Anahita and Mithra already seen on coppers of the first two Kushanshahs. In his left hand the god holds a spear, and offers a diadem to the king with his right. The god is short haired,[28] and in all likelihood fully bearded, as evidenced by comparing the image of these coins with other depictions of the same figure. The head, in full left profile, is surrounded by a halo of flames, and comparable types also show a crescent-shaped element on the forehead, apparently supported by a sort of triangular shaped feature probably held by a ribbon around the head. It is not clear if the dots on top of the head render a close cropped hairstyle or a tight-fitting tiara-like headgear.[29] In addition to mentioning the ruler by his name and titles, the Middle Persian legend surrounding the image refers to the god, calling him *bwrz'wndy yzdty*, *burzāwand yazad*, the equivalent of the Bactrian OOPZOANΔO IAZAΔO that accompanies the standing god with bull.

---

[25]   MK 555.

[26]   MK 1030.

[27]   The engraving of the muscular masses of the chest may suggest that the deity is bare-chested, but this might not be the case, as can be inferred by comparing the image with that of the standing god with bull, or even with the royal portraits, where figures wearing tunics still display a rather emphasised chest musculature. A confirmation that it is a sleeved dress that is worn might indeed come from the silver drachms struck in Merv by Ohrmazd 1 (MK 1031). A very well-preserved specimen kept in the BM and illustrated in Cribb 1990, no. 59 shows a circular border at the neck of the deity as well as similarly engraved lines at the wrists. These might be interpreted as a necklace and bracelets respectively, but it seems more likely that they could represent the border of the neck and the sleeve edges of a dress covering the whole body of the deity.

[28]   The ear is visible, and neither long hair nor hair bunches are engraved.

[29]   Cribb 1990, 187, no. 24 described "a crescent adorned tiara type crown," and Tyler-Smith 1997, 7 "a domed headdress."

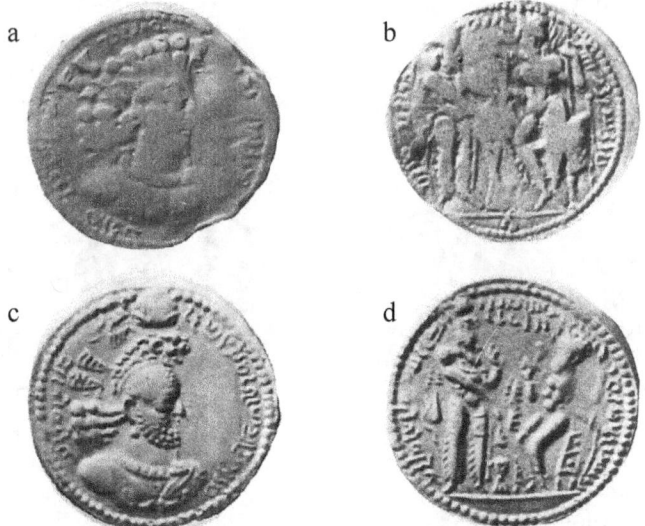

Fig. 4a–d

The copper series bear two basic types showing different sources of inspiration. The first is the same standing god with bull of the gold dinars, regularly used in Balkh and only shortly, at the very beginning,[30] in Kabul. The second (Fig. 5b), employed only in Kabul, very closely recalls the standard reverse type of Sasanian imperial series, namely the altar on which the dynastic fire burns. Similarly to the issues of the founder of the dynasty Ardashir I,[31] the altar is decorated with feline throne legs, as well as diadem ribbons on its sides. Instead of the flames, a human bust emerges from the altar, as can be seen in the reverse types of Sasanian imperial coinage from the series of Ohrmazd II.[32] The bust is depicted in frontal view, breast and shoulders just above the altar upper slab and arms not visible. It is not clear if the bust is bareheaded or if some kind of headgear is worn,[33] but at any rate the long hair falls behind the head. Indeed the image closely recalls the frontal busts typical of Sasanian art that can be seen at Paikuli or Hajiabad. A Bactrian inscription frames the type, read as ΒΑΓΟ ΒΟΡΖΑΝΟ by J. Cribb[34] and accordingly connected to the "exalted god" of the drachms.

---

[30] Schindel, forthcoming.

[31] The throne legs were first used in Type 2 and the ribbons in Type 3a, i.e. from the pre-imperial phase throughout the whole coinage of Ardashir, see Alram/Gyselen 2003, 117–132. The feline throne legs reappear in Sasanian imperial coinage only with Type 2a of Shapur II (used on gold issues alongside the silver series), see Schindel 2004 (I), 215–217; 2004 (II), 14, 22.

[32] Throughout all his series, see Alram/Gyselen 2012, 362–365, 380–393. In fact, the busts in the Kushano-Sasanian types appear larger, almost completely hiding the flames.

[33] On some specimens (cf. for example, Cribb 1985, no. 4.82, here Fig. 5b) the top of the head shows some lines departing from the centre, perhaps in order to depict hair. Cribb (1990, 188, no. 132) described the bust with "flaming hair," which supported his connection to the deity with flaming halo and the epithet "exalted god."

[34] In Cribb 1985, 309, 319.

A less common type,[35] also minted in Kabul, shows the same frontal view with a different bust, this time female, since the Bactrian legend has been read as ΒΑΓΑ ΝΑΝΑ (Fig. 6b).[36] The deity appears bareheaded, the hair closely framing the face and a conspicuous crescent decorating the forehead. A large circular halo is visible behind the bust.

a   b   a   b

Fig. 5a–b   Fig. 6a–b

The basic typological choices of Peroz were largely inherited by his successors, starting with Ohrmazd 1, with some variations. The standing god with bull was to remain standard on gold series minted in Balkh,[37] making his last appearance on copper, struck in the same mint, under Ohrmazd 1 himself. Ohrmazd was also to copy the Herat drachms of Peroz with the investiture scene (Fig. 4d),[38] coining drachms with the same reverse type even in Merv (Fig. 7b),[39] and exporting it on coppers minted in Balkh.[40]

In this phase of systematisation under the second ruler of the main group, unique types can still occasionally be found, like the reverse image of Ohrmazd's gold dinars from Merv (Fig. 8b). Two standing male figures face each other on either side of a burning fire on a ribboned altar of Sasanian derivation. Indeed, the basic scheme of the type clearly owes much to Sasanian imperial issues as developed under the king of kings Ohrmazd I.[41] On the left, the Kushanshah, portrayed in a stance closely resembling that of the ruler in the "investiture scenes" already described, is recognised by his diademed and lion-headed crown. The bearded figure on the right is identified as a deity by the combination of the diadem he offers to the king and the rayed halo surrounding his

---

[35]   MK 1117.

[36]   Apparently written retrograde, see Cribb 1985, 311, 319–320; 1990, 188, no. 31, followed by Tanabe (1991/1992, 60).

[37]   Only shifting to a slight three-quarters to left view, instead of the fully frontal depiction used on the coins of Peroz. This is especially visible in the rendering of the head. Furthermore, unlike the right leg, the left one shows the lateral pleating of the trousers only on the inner side, meaning that the leg was not supposed to be depicted as seen from the front. From Ohrmazd onwards as a general norm the head of the god acquires Sasanian-style hair bunches in lieu of the long hair rendered as a fringe.

[38]   MK 1031.

[39]   Cribb 1990, no. 59.

[40]   MK 1042–1048.

[41]   Cf. Schindel 2012, 69. While the type of the fire with two attendants was introduced by Shapur I, its elaboration into an "investiture scene" is due to Ohrmazd I, cf. his reverse Types 2a–b, Alram/Gyselen 2012, 117–119, 128–130.

head, clearly identifying the god as Mithra even if no mention of him is included in the legend.[42]

Fig. 7a–b

Fig. 8a–b

Fig. 9a–d

The typology of the copper series is also subject to a degree of change due to the demise of the standing god with bull under Ohrmazd 1. Alongside the "investiture scene," modelled after the type used on the drachms, a new variant of the altar with human bust is introduced, destined to become canonical in the Kushano-Sasanian copper series from Balkh. The male human figure is portrayed as a bust seen from the front with the head

---

[42] Cf. Bivar 1979a, 745–746; Tanabe 1991/92, 60. The god's left hand rests on the hilt of his sword, which is well in evidence exactly as in the type with the enthroned Bago Miuro of Ardashir 1.

looking left (Fig. 9b), emerging from the altar at the waist. Both arms are fully visible, allowing the figure to show specific identifying features, such as the spear held in the left hand and a ribboned diadem in the right. In addition, flames are visible around the figure's head, and there is a crescent on the forehead, clearly connecting the image to the "exalted god" of the "investiture scenes" on the drachms of Peroz and Ohrmazd 1 from Herat and Merv. Indeed, the Middle Persian legend appears to read as *bwrz'wndy yzdty* (Fig. 9d).

This type is used by Ohrmazd 1 on coppers struck in Balkh as well as in Kabul, but under the following kings a sort of division between the two mints can be observed: the fully facing bust employed in Kabul and that with the head seen in profile view in Balkh.

The last innovations are due to Ohrmazd 2. A unique type reproducing an "investiture scene" appears on a gold dinar from Balkh (Fig. 10b),[43] alongside the standard series with the standing god with bull. Since the deity is sitting on a throne, the basic scheme closely recalls analogous types with enthroned deities on the coins of Peroz and Ohrmazd 1. The king is depicted standing on the right in the same posture, pouring offerings on a small altar with his right hand while raising his left. On the right, a diademed goddess is sitting on a throne with side railings as already seen in similar types, offering a diadem to the king with her right hand. All around the image there is a Middle Persian inscription, identifying the deity as "Anahita the Lady." Yet there are several peculiarities. The first is the small altar upon which the king is pouring offers, since it has the shape of a bird, with smoke rising from it. Such unusual rendering of the fire burner is indeed strictly paralleled by the analogous bird-shaped burner, complete with rising smoke, upon which the king pours offerings recently detected on the obverses of some coppers of Ardashir I Kushanshah.[44] Even more striking, nonetheless, is the fact that the deity wears a completely different crown from the mural one displayed by Anahita elsewhere. The headgear is low, flat and slightly flared towards the top, with a patterned decoration on the side, resembling in the design of its base element similar royal crowns commonly employed by the Kushanshahs on their obverses from Peroz onwards. These in turn reproduce the motif of "arcades" inaugurated on the imperial issues by Narseh.[45] In addition, the goddess holds a bow with her left hand, a unique occurrence for Anahita, even if in accordance with the warrior traits which were also part of the complex religious physiognomy of this deity.[46]

---

[43] Cribb 1990, 184, no. 5, where the only known specimen was first published: Göbl 1993, Pl. 11, no. 746A.

[44] Schindel 2014.

[45] His first crown, see Type I of Narseh in Alram/Gyselen 2012, 295–300. Cf. also Schindel 2012, 71.

[46] Owned also by Nana, portrayed in an Artemidean version – with bow – in a type employed by Huvishka, see Göbl 1984, Pl. 167, Nana 2.

Fig. 10a–b

A different type employs the same iconographic variant of the goddess on coppers of Ohrmazd 2 minted in Balkh (Fig. 11b), where it alternates with the god with flaming halo and spear.[47] Like the latter, the deity, once again directly mentioned as "Anahita the Lady" in Middle Persian, is depicted emerging from an altar at the waist, her bust portrayed frontally and the diademed head in left profile. Also identical are the arms, with a spear held in the left hand, and the ribbed diadem offered with the right. The crown is the same flat-topped one with patterned side decoration visible on the gold dinar from Balkh.

Fig. 11a–b

As shown by this survey, a significant group of divinities can be seen on the reverses of the Kushano-Sasanian series. Some of them have clear antecedents, some not; some are directly mentioned by their name, others in a more indirect way.

Among the former, Mithra is clearly recognisable thanks to his iconographic physiognomy alone, characterised by the conspicuous rayed halo around his head. The god is depicted in two types, one from Merv and one from Balkh, the former instance closely recalling standard Sasanian imagery as known from the so-called "investiture scenes" of the rock reliefs, despite the fact that Mithra appears there only much later and only in a single occurrence at Taq-e Bostan. In fact, similar images already appear on Sasanian imperial coins under Ohrmazd I,[48] and of the two figures accompanying the king at the reverse of his coins, one is marked by a radiate crown and accordingly easily identifiable as Mithra.[49] While the identification of these figures is related to the general interpreta-

---

[47] Cf. Tyler-Smith 1997.

[48] Alram/Gyselen 2012, 128–130.

[49] Despite the doubts, cf. the discussion of the possible hypotheses in Alram/Gyselen 2012, 143–144. Indeed, the god with radiate halo at Taq-e Bostan is identified (as Mithra) on a mere iconographic basis, so

tion of such images, the typological kinship with the Kushano-Sasanian type is objective and could provide further evidence to be included in the wider discussion.[50]

More unusual is the enthroned Mithra from Balkh. In Bactria the imagery of Mithra has a tradition going back at least to Kushan times, when the god was frequently employed on the reverses of the coins of Kanishka and Huvishka. Yet the visual rendering of the Kushan Mithra clearly owes much to the original iconography of Helios-Apollo, as made explicit even by the Greek version of the god's name, Helios, used before the passage to Bactrian for Kushan coin legends. Indeed, even if his costume is modified according to local taste, the Kushan Mithra is always depicted as a youthful, beardless figure. The only exception so far known is represented by the appearance of the deity, immediately recognisable thanks to the rayed halo, on the so-called "Kanishka reliquary" from Shāh-jī-kī-dherī, where the god is portrayed as bearded and wearing a pointed cap.[51] At any rate, no enthroned images of the Kushan Mithra are known. In fact, even Western Iranian imagery has kept a record of a double tradition in the iconography of this very popular deity, since the image of the Sasanian official, dynastic Mithra at Taq-e Bostan, i.e. a fully bearded figure, is contrasted with the documentation provided by glyptics. On a few Sasanian period seals where Mithra is depicted,[52] he is regularly portrayed beardless according to the Helios imagery of Greek derivation,[53] and the only connection with the bearded version of the god's image is the rayed halo, in fact Mithra's primary iconographic mark. This double tradition indeed seems to be attested also in the East in earlier times. While the type of Helios on his chariot appears on coins of the Graeco-Bactrian Plato,[54] providing us with a direct antecedent in the area for the later image of the Sun-god, as can be seen for example at Bamiyan as well as in Sogdiana,[55] a very interesting iconographic case is presented by an unusual obverse type employed on coins of the Indo-Greek kings Amyntas and Hermaeus. On some of

---

it is not clear from a methodological point of view why a similar figure on coins should raise doubts over its identity.

[50] In fact, the possible contribution of Kushano-Sasanian evidence to the debate on more general Sasanian issues is too often neglected: with the explicit mention of his name, the Kushano-Sasanian Bago Miuro provides an indisputable comparison for Mithra with sword in a Sasanian context (cf. Alram/Gyselen 2012, 143), for example.

[51] Thus providing two features elsewhere unknown for the Kushan Mithra. For a recent treatment of the reliquary, strangely enough regularly ignored in the literature dealing with the iconography of Mithra (with the only exception of Callieri 1990, 92), see Errington 2002, where the casket is dated to the period of Huvishka.

[52] See Callieri 1990 for a survey of the occurrences known at the time, then Grenet 2001; cf. also Gubaev/Loginov/Nikitin 1996, 58, no. 1.3. Some of these seals explicitly mention Mithra in the inscription accompanying the image.

[53] Grenet 2001, 37, note 3, interpreted the facing Mithra on several seal impressions from Ak Depe (all from the same seal, see Gubaev/Loginov/Nikitin 1996, 58, no. 1.3) as bearded, but in no case is the face of the god clearly impressed. On the basis of the comparison with the other depictions of the facing Mithra on seals (particularly Gignoux 1978, 62, 6.84, Pl. XXII, illustrated in Callieri 1990, 87, Fig. 7), the somewhat bulging lower face of the impressions from Ak Depe, which could appear as a beard on the worn surface, could also be explained as a stylistic trait without requiring the presence of a beard.

[54] Bopearachchi 1991, 220–221, Platon s. 1–3 (Pl. 24, 1–C). A fourth issue by the same king (s. 4, Pl. 24, D) depicts Helios standing with no chariot, holding a sceptre in his left hand (and apparently making a gesture of blessing with his right).

[55] Grenet 2001, 38–44.

their copper series, the obverse depicts a bearded bust facing right, wearing a pointed cap and showing rays emanating from the head.[56] On one of the two series issued by Amyntas, a spear-shaped sceptre is also visible resting on the figure's shoulder. The combination of attributes, namely rays and pointed beret, indeed leaves few doubts that this is a depiction of Mithra, even if the background for the use of his image on the coins of two late Indo-Greek kings remains rather obscure. The same set of attributes appears to be employed by another reverse image commonly used by Hermaeus and on some of his posthumous imitations: an enthroned deity, holding a staff in one hand and making a gesture of blessing with the other.[57] While in terms of posture and clothing the figure is clearly inspired by the imagery of Zeus, who appeared in that very same type on coins of various Indo-Greek kings,[58] the transformation of the laurel wreath of Zeus in rays and the bashlyk apparently visible on top of the head seem to speak in favour of the possibility that this is Mithra.[59] This has indeed led to postulate the iconographic assimilation of Zeus to Mithra,[60] a peculiarly eastern Iranian synthesis of the two gods in lieu of the expectable equation of Zeus with Ahura Mazda, attested in the West of the Iranian world up to Commagene. Such a particular development would allegedly be due to the status of Mithra in the East and his role there of supreme deity similar to that of Ahura Mazda in western Iran. The acquisition of Jovian features connected to sovereignty by the figure of the Indo-Greek series with rays and bashlyk should be seen in this light, as further hinted at by the staff held by the deity both in the bust version and in its rendering as an enthroned figure. Indeed, it is exactly this enthroned version of the Zeus-Mithra that would provide the only attestation so far known of an enthroned Mithra before the Kushano-Sasanian type of Ardashir 1.[61]

---

[56] Bopearachchi 1991, 303–304, Amyntas, s. 14–15 (Pl. 47, K–L), and 329–330, Hermaios s. 9 (Pl. 54, 16–F).

[57] Bopearachchi 1991, 326–329, Hermaios s. 1–5, 7–8 (Pl. 52–54). See also pp. 330–334, s. 10–13, Pl. 54–56, for the imitation series, commonly attributed to the Yuezhi expanding south of the Hindukush from c. 70 BC onwards: bashlyk and rays seem to disappear with s. 14 at the latest (cf. Bopearachchi 1991, 122, 334).

[58] The most famous instance being the type depicted on the reverse of the double decadrachms of Amyntas (Bopearachchi 1991, 299, Amyntas s. 1, Pl. 46, A–B). See Bopearachchi 1991, 380 for an index of the occurrences of the variants of this basic type on coins of several Graeco-Bactrian and Indo-Greek kings.

[59] Coins of Heliocles I have been adduced as further evidence (Grenet 1991, 149), due to the pointed dots appearing around the head of the god on coins of this king which depict a standing Zeus with thunderbolt and sceptre on the reverse (see Bopearachchi 1991, Pl. 24–26). In fact, the vast majority of the coins of Heliocles I seem to show no discernible feature around the head of the deity. The case is different with Heliocles II (Bopearachchi 1991, Pl. 42, series 1–6), but here one should take into account the possibility that it is the laurel wreath of Zeus that is depicted: if the more or less elongated dots around the head of Zeus must always be interpreted as rays, then we have "Zeus-Mithra" even on coins of Archebios, for example (Bopearachchi 1991, Pl. 50–52). Yet his series provide us with a different possibility, since some coppers depict the profile bust of Zeus (series 13), and clearly no rays are visible. Unless we postulate a rather unlikely Herakles-Mithra, the standing Herakles of Zoilus I (Bopearachchi 1991, Pl. 34) in fact shows that the laurel wreath around the head could be depicted in the same way as the "rays" on coins of Heliocles II. A good comparison is finally provided by some coppers of Philoxenus (Bopearachchi 1991, Pl. 44, series 12), where real rays, depicted as long strokes rather than more or less elongated dots, are visible around the head of a Helios-like deity.

[60] First by Newell 1938, then followed by all other studies.

[61] Cf. Bivar 1956, 22.

The discussion on such possible antecedents is important due to the scholarly hypotheses on the background to the typological and iconographic choices of the Kushano-Sasanian series, which are mostly based on the notion of some continuity with previous periods. Accordingly, the Kushano-Sasanian enthroned Mithra has been seen as involved in a wider process of syncretism that, through the concept of Zeus-Mithra, brought together Mithra and the "exalted god."[62] The latter's differing iconographic renderings, i.e. the Oesho-style standing god with bull and the deity with flaming head, would connect the shivaite element of Oesho and that deriving from Mithra, since the flames would indeed represent the rayed halo of the sun-god in an updated rendering of the Jovian Mithra.[63] Needless to say, the aim of such a synthesis by the Kushano-Sasanians would have been the strengthening of their legitimacy. However, the different explanations put forward by scholars highlight the difficulties of such interpretations, as well as their importance due to the possible impact on general reconstructions. Within the basic framework of a struggle between the Sasanian main imperial house and the Kushano-Sasanians, Martha L. Carter has proposed that the latter could have promoted the retrieval of older formulas to obtain the support of a group of local population of Saka stock.[64] From a different point of departure, Frantz Grenet has instead merely stressed the appeal to Indian as well as Iranian subjects in the then Sasanian eastern regions, where the Kushanshahs had to cope with Iranian beliefs "non conforme au zoroastrisme codifié."[65]

We are here faced with an interesting case of method in iconographic analysis, since the concept of iconographic assimilation, i.e. the borrowing by an eastern god of the iconographic physiognomy of a western deity, seems to a certain extent to overlap with that of religious syncretism. While this may appear as a mere terminological issue, in fact the two notions should be kept clearly separated,[66] and the possibility that Mithra could be given visual rendering thanks to the image of Zeus in no way translates into the existence of a Zeus-Mithra. If we accept the reconstruction of the process from its first Graeco-Bactrian or Indo-Greek stages – and if we dispense here with the problematic aspects[67] – we should merely speak of Mithra,[68] precisely as, for example, we do not speak of a Kushan Helios-Mithra, but only of the Iranian god. Indeed the analysis of the Kushan coinage, which provides the most conspicuous documentation in this regard, eloquently shows that the deities' Greek names were just translations of the *names* of gods that had always been conceived and felt to be local: Mioro was Mithra even when labelled Helios.[69] An analogous occurrence – and a rather significant one in the context

---

[62]   Bivar 1979a, 747; Carter 1985, 238; Grenet 1991, 149; cf. also Grenet 2001, 43.

[63]   Bivar 1979a, 746; Grenet 2001, 43–44, along the same basic lines as Carter 1981, 96–98.

[64]   Carter 1985, 229, synthesising the arguments already put forward in Carter 1981.

[65]   Grenet 1991, 150; 2001, 44.

[66]   Cf. the remarks in a similar context in Callieri 2007, 78.

[67]   Cf. in this regard Martinez-Sève 2010, 206, where the presence of the Zeus-like statue in the main temple of Ai Khanum is explained in connection to the cult of the Oxus.

[68]   As indeed did Grenet in the title of his seminal article of 1991. Cf. also MacDowall 1979, 562.

[69]   Cf. Göbl 1960. The case of Mao is even more illuminating: the Zoroastrian god Mah is given anthropomorphic rendering by re-elaborating the figure of Helios used for Mithra, thanks to the substitution of the rayed halo with a large crescent behind the shoulders. The in fact male figure is then provided with the female name of Salene in the series of Kanishka inscribed in Greek only because the Greek moon deity is female. As

of this discussion – is provided by the name of Zeus in the Greek caption of the image of Ahura Mazda on the relief of Ardashir at Naqsh-e Rostam.[70]

In fact, even qualifying Mithra's aspects of sovereignty as Jovian is more a scholarly construct than anything else, a tool that we may use to define specific features but that can possibly reveal itself also to be misleading: the sceptre held by the Zeus-like figure of the Indo-Greek coins is often well in evidence even in the Helios-inspired Kushan Mithra, for example.[71] Yet the assessment of these traits is crucial as they are at the basis of the interpretation of the iconographic evidence of the Kushano-Sasanian period, with quite important implications: besides the hypothesised synthesis of the *burzāwand yazad* with the Jovian Mithra, i.e. the enthroned and bearded Bago Miuro, this eastern bearded Mithra, having allegedly survived in Bactria thanks to cult images from the Greek period, would have provided the model of the bearded image of the god as seen at Taq-e Bostan.[72]

This is why all such considerations must be set in a broader analysis, i.e. an examination of the typology of the Kushano-Sasanian coin system as a whole rather than of mere single images. Indeed, the picture is made complex by the presence of several different levels. On the one hand deities are depicted with more than a single iconographic identity, like Anahita with her two sets of headgear; then, a coexistence can be seen between Iranian deities of western and eastern derivation, like Anahita and Nana, due to the two legacies – Sasanian and Kushan – which were used for the Kushano-Sasanian repertoire. All this is accompanied by the inconsistent pattern of the legends, which sometimes mention the gods by their name, sometimes only by appellatives.

The point of departure is that the impact of Sasanian imagery may be clearly detected.[73] This is evident in the adoption of Sasanian types like that of the reverse altar, for example, as well as in the royal effigies on the obverses, whose crowns were conceived on the pattern of the imperial ones, despite the presence of peculiar features of local origin. This Sasanian influence is visible even in the images of the reverse deities. The very presence of Anahita is in itself quite telling, since she is a religious figure of specifically Persian derivation. Apart from the unusual version seen in the series of Ohrmazd 2, the image on the coins of Ardashir 2 is perfectly in line with her iconography from Sasanian Iran known from rock reliefs at Naqsh-e Rostam and Darabgird,[74] the mural crown providing a very clear link. In fact, the Ardashir 2 type is the earliest instance in which an

---

a matter of fact, there was no iconographic confusion, but just a "free translation," so to say, of the *name* of the deity, based – as was normally the case – on a merely functional equivalence.

[70] Back 1978, 282. This – fortunately – has never translated in theories on a Zeus-Ahura Mazda in Sasanian Fars. Needless to say, the differences in how problems are approached in dealing with the same issues against an imperial Sasanian as opposed to a "provincial" Sasanian background show well, albeit indirectly, how conditioning scholarly prejudices can be.

[71] Göbl 1984, Pl. 116–117, types Miiro 2, 4–6, 8–10.

[72] Grenet 2001, 36–37.

[73] Cf. Schindel 2005.

[74] Cf. Shenkar 2013, where the female figure of the relief of Narseh at Naqsh-e Rostam is re-examined in the framework of a discussion on Anahita and identified as a depiction of the goddess.

explicit and indisputable connection is made between the name of Anahita and the image distinguished by the mural crown.[75]

With regard to male deities, leaving aside the god with flaming halo, the figures are consistently dressed according to typical Sasanian canons, i.e., with sleeved tunic and trousers, as noted by all authors. This is most striking in the case of the standing god with bull, who is markedly "sasanised" in comparison with his previous iconography of Indian inspiration. Among the new iconographic features displayed by this figure there is also the beard, completely unknown in images of the Kushan Oesho. This is indeed a crucial detail, to be associated with conventions for the rendering of the hair typical of Sasanian iconography, like the hair bunches commonly seen in the images of this god from Ohrmazd 1 onwards.[76] If we are to follow the hypothesis that the Sasanian official Mithra of Taq-e Bostan inherited his beard from eastern images of the god like the Kushano-Sasanian enthroned Bago Miuro, then an eastern source must also be found for the beard of the standing god with bull. Yet, contrary to the case of Mithra, the visual documentation available across the various media for the Shiva-inspired image of this god clearly excludes a bearded image at any period. Therefore, if we accept that the god with flaming halo actually represents (a Jovian version of) Mithra, the only possibility is that the competition for supreme god between Mithra and the Shiva/Wesh identified with the figure of the god with bull[77] – which would in a way be synthesised by the use of the appellative *burzāwand yazad* for both – could produce a transfer of iconographic details between the figures of the two deities.

Such a scenario already appears unlikely without tackling specific issues, as even its premises are debatable, based as they are on a number of gods, Mithra as well as Vayu, disputing the role of supreme god with Ahura Mazda in a context, i.e. Bactrian religion, that was in fact still Zoroastrian. It definitely becomes too contradictory when individual features are analysed: while they are both bearded, no common *distinctive* iconographic attribute can be found between the images of the enthroned Mithra and that of the god with bull, exactly in the same way as no iconographic link exists between the latter and the god with flaming halo, despite the fact that they share the appellative of "exalted god."

The proposal of an even deeper osmosis producing a real wider syncretism that involved all these figures, i.e. Shiva/Vayu in their "oeshoite" rendering as well as Mithra in an updating of his alleged Zeus-Mithra forebear,[78] is likewise, if not more, difficult to accept. Leaving aside the too extreme iconographic oscillation, it would be even harder to account for the inconsistencies just mentioned. For example, the standing god with bull linked to the god with flaming head by the appellative does not display any solar character at all.[79] His plain circular halo cannot be considered relevant, since the original background of this image, Kushan iconography, clearly shows that it had no solar con-

---

[75]   With a definitive impact on the debate about the identification of this figure, cf. above note 50 and the discussion in Alram/Gyselen 2012, 141–143.

[76]   Cf. above, note 37. In fact even the fringe hairstyle previously displayed by the god's image is of clear Sasanian derivation.

[77]   Cf. Grenet 2001, 43.

[78]   Carter 1985, 238.

[79]   Rather the contrary, if one takes due account of the poseidonic features of his iconography.

nection whatsoever, as plain halos were commonly used for several Kushan deities.[80] Indeed, the Kushano-Sasanian Nana on the coppers of Peroz exhibits exactly this kind of plain halo (cf. Fig. 6b).

In fact, we would have a syncretistic religious phenomenon visually translated by excessively disparate features such as the moon crescent and the radiate halo, or the bull of Oesho, an animal elsewhere associated with Mah in Sasanian imagery,[81] somehow connected to the solar god instead of his horses.

Finally, a specific analysis is necessary for the halo around the head of the figure that for the time being we can define only as "exalted god," since we do not know its real name. This halo is actually not made of rays, like the radiate nimbus of Mithra, but of flames, an element of crucial importance for all our discussion. Once again the Kushan series provide fitting comparisons to properly assess the character of the iconographic devices under discussion: while Mioro customarily displays a nimbus of rays and never of flames, the figure of Atsho, for example, has flames emerging from his shoulders, not rays; this clearly implies that the craftsmen who engraved such images had a clear understanding of the difference and of the differing meanings these iconographic marks were supposed to transmit.

This means that there are no real links even between the god with flaming halo and Mithra, despite the sharing of attributes like the throne, which in fact must be understood as a secondary iconographic attribute for both figures. Indeed, the two deities are perfectly recognisable thanks to their primary marks – flaming halo and radiate nimbus respectively – in those Kushano-Sasanian series where they both appear without throne. In addition, the throne is used in the analogous function of accessory device even in the type of Ardashir 2 depicting Anahita.

What, then, is the sense in the use of the appellative *burzāwand yazad*, and how should one deal with the possible problems created by its shared use by the god with standing bull and the one with flaming halo? The answer was already available at least a couple of decades ago, when Katsumi Tanabe explicitly wrote that this appellative "does not represent the name of a particular god. It is an epithet of Zoroastrian deities."[82] Here a very straight and consequential approach is necessary, as we cannot simply state a concept without really taking due consideration of all its implications: once we properly understand that the appellative was not tied to a specific deity and could refer to completely different gods, it becomes clear that its use was not meant to hint at some kind of overlapping of discrete religious physiognomies. While the use of legends on the reverses of Kushano-Sasanian coins is surely less direct in this regard when compared to Kushan series, in fact there is no reason to imagine the Kushano-Sasanian minting authorities making a deliberate choice to produce an ambiguous picture of their religious policy as transmitted by coin imagery.

Therefore, there is no need to imagine any link, either explicit or alluded to, between the standing god with bull and the god with flaming halo, and between this and Mithra. In

---

[80] As well as for the royal images.

[81] As shown by the image of the chariot of Mah drawn by bulls on a seal in the Staatliche Münzsammlung in Munich (Göbl 1973, Pl. 6, no. 7d) and on one of the silver plates from Klimova (Vanden Berghe 1993, 212–213, no. 66), regardless of its post-Sasanian dating.

[82] Tanabe 1991/1992, 59.

fact this leaves room for a more harmonious reconstruction that does not require imagining more or less complex syncretism phenomena. While the figure with rayed halo is the only one to effectively depict Mithra, in the two types of the enthroned Bago Miuro and of the investing deity beside the fire altar on the gold coins of Ohrmazd 1 from Merv, the standing god with bull can be comfortably identified in straightforward accordance with its iconography as an updated version, i.e. sasanised, of the Bactrian Wesh, the Zoroastrian Vayu.

Apart from these two yazatas, only the figure with flaming halo still needs to be identified. The inherent difficulties have been repeatedly stressed,[83] since the iconography of this deity does not have real parallels, in contrast to the other instances. A feature that in fact clearly sets it apart from other figures is the clothing, since the outfit comprising tunic and trousers is replaced by a robe reaching to the ankles as normally associated with female deities. Indeed, combined with the rendering of the chest and the sceptre-spear, this is probably what led Göbl to identify the figure as Anahita.[84] Yet traces of a beard are visible on better-preserved specimens. Moreover, the rendering of the chest is actually that of a male figure, the muscular masses enhanced exactly as visible in the depictions of the king, or that of the standing Wesh with bull (Fig. 12).

a. "Exalted god"   b. Wesh with bull   c. King

Fig. 12

In fact, these parallels also show that the treatment of the chest musculature is not meant to depict a bare-chested figure. Actually the deity wears a long-sleeved robe, whose circular edge is indeed visible at the base of the neck.[85] The main identifying features are nonetheless the spear and the flaming halo, perhaps accompanied by the diminutive moon crescent visible on the forehead.

Once the identifications with Anahita or with a figure synthesising aspects of Vayu and Mithra in order to render the Jovian Mithra have been discarded, we might proceed by exclusion. A first possibility that immediately comes to mind is Ahura Mazda, which

---

[83]   Bivar 1956, 16; Tanabe 1991/1992, 61; Cribb 1997, 187.

[84]   Göbl 1984, 46, and Pl. 172 (under reverse type Investiture 1).

[85]   Consequently negating another alleged trait of continuity between the figure of the Indo-Greek Mithra, bare-chested as for its Jovian model, and that of the Kushano-Sasanian deity.

was indeed proposed by Christopher J. Brunner.[86] To a certain extent this hypothesis appears strengthened by the peculiarity of the image, and the spear could well refer to the sphere of sovereignty embodied by Ahura Mazda, as noted by Tanabe for the type of Ooromozdo already seen on Kushan coins.[87] Yet Tanabe himself rejected Brunner's proposal, aptly commenting on the impossibility of reconciling the Kushano-Sasanian deity with the imagery of Ahura Mazda that we know from Sasanian Iran: Sasanian reliefs regularly depict Ahura Mazda holding the barsom and not a spear, and the flaming halo is completely unknown. Tanabe's arguments may be further expanded if we take due account of the wider context, i.e., that of a clear Sasanian influence on Kushano-Sasanian imagery even in religious iconography. In the Sasanian rock reliefs, the image of Ahura Mazda is clearly modelled on that of the king, betraying no element of other, i.e. earlier, iconographic models. This does not imply that we can exclude the existence of previous images of the god, of course. Yet a clear approach by the new dynasty to visual communication can be seen, which is translated into a rendering of the god immediately recognisable as manifestly local, with no concessions to the imagery of Greek origin shared by western and eastern Iran, which in Kushan Bactria, for example, produced an image of Ooromozdo of clear Graeco-Roman derivation. A constitutive element of the Sasanian approach to religious imagery, which indeed sheds light on how the gods' images were conceived, is that of the role of distinctive headgear, clearly indebted conceptually to the Sasanian royal crowns system. That is why deities connected to the sphere of royalty, like Ahura Mazda or Anahita, normally wear mural crowns. When all this is given due consideration, it appears extremely unlikely that the Sasanian governors of Kushanshahr could depict on their coins an Ahura Mazda that has nothing in common with the image of the god seen on the visual monuments of the main dynasty in western Iran, not even for the single most important identifying feature represented by the crown.

Once Ahura Mazda is also excluded, it seems that hardly any connection can be made between the god with flaming halo and most of the deities depicted in Sasanian official art. Yet Sasanian coinage offers a fine comparison, since a series of Khusraw II bears on the reverse the frontal bust of a deity surrounded by a halo of flames.[88] The bust is beardless, and accordingly has long been identified as Anahita.[89] Rika Gyselen has already rejected this interpretation, instead putting forward the hypothesis that the bust could depict either Adur or Xwarrah, rightly stressing the identifying character of the iconographic attribute represented by the flames surrounding the head of the deity.[90] The context of the use of the image could favour the identification as Xwarrah, perhaps partly overlapping with a personification of Adur. A similar interpretation could indeed be proposed for the Kushano-Sasanian image. The presence of Xwarrah on the series of a new dynasty is very understandable, and is well paired with the frequent depictions on

---

[86]   Brunner 1974, 148.

[87]   Tanabe 1991/1992, 61.

[88]   Göbl 1971, Pl. XII, Xusrō II reverse type 4 and 5. See Gyselen 2000 for a specific study of the series (where similar images on Sasanian seals are also listed). Mosig-Walburg 2009, 192–193, opted for a depiction of Adur as an explicit reference to the "good Religion."

[89]   Since Göbl 1971, 20.

[90]   Gyselen 2000, 302–308.

Kushano-Sasanian coins of fire altars with feline legs.[91] These are clearly modelled on the similar reverse types of Ardashir I, and must be understood in similar terms, namely as referring to the establishment of royal fires,[92] in this instance hinting at the creation of the Kushano-Sasanian dynasty by the main imperial house of Iran. In fact, despite the peculiarity of the iconography of the god with flaming head, both Xwarrah and Adur have a Kushan antecedent, and in both instances the fire is often well in evidence in their anthropomorphic rendering. Occasionally the Kushan Pharro also shows a staff similar to a spear in lieu of the caduceus,[93] not to mention that he is depicted enthroned on rare coppers of Kanishka.[94] On the other hand it is true that the god with flaming head is quite distant from these hypothetical Kushan antecedents, unlike – for example – the Kushano-Sasanian Wesh, which is only a sasanised version of the Kushan Oesho.

It seems that the iconographic physiognomy of the god with flaming halo has a sort of experimental character, at the same time being distinctly less Sasanian-looking than the other two male deities and completely new in the local iconographic tradition of Bactria, at least for what is known so far.[95] Similarly peculiar is the presence on Kushano-Sasanian coins of Bactrian deities already known from Kushan coinage, which, unlike Mithra and Wesh, have no direct counterpart – or, it is perhaps better to say, cannot be straightforwardly assimilated – in Persian Zoroastrianism, like Nana and the isolated occurrence of the Ardokhsho-like goddess. The appearance of Nana is especially remarkable, since her royal function in Bactrian Zoroastrianism is exactly the same as that of Anahita in western Iran, essentially providing the Kushano-Sasanian "monetary pantheon" with a functional duplicate of the Persian goddess. This can only be the result of a planned choice: with the depiction of Nana the Kushanshahs appear to have aimed to integrate the Kushan royal goddess into their visual propaganda, and the direct mention of the goddess' name cannot be more explicit. Yet this is set – unsurprisingly – in a clearly Sasanian context, as Nana is emerging from a Sasanian-inspired fire altar.

Indeed, what must be properly addressed is the nature of the Sasanian contribution to the imagery displayed by the Kushano-Sasanian coins, for, significant as the inheritance from the local tradition might have been, the influence of the new Persian conquerors was greater than was generally supposed. Indeed what is visible on coins is a strong impact of Sasanian iconography, and the fact that the local tradition was not wiped out but integrated does not make such impact lighter. Religious iconography was sasanised like royal imagery, and in the same way as Kushan tiaras and mitres were substituted by Sasanian-style crowns with princely *korymboi* on the obverses, so were the reverse im-

---

[91]   All in connection with the types with facing bust minted in Kabul: MK 1115–1119 and 1123 (for Peroz), MK 1122, 1124 (Kavad), MK 1125 (Peroz 4).

[92]   Cf. Schindel 2004, 217 with reference to the employment of this type by Shapur II (his Type 2a).

[93]   Göbl 1984, Pl. 171, Pharro 4–5, 7, 9, 11. Other types (Pharro 1–2, 6, 12) depict the deity with a scepter with a spherical ending.

[94]   Göbl 1993, 125, no. 163 (Pl. 43).

[95]   In fact this deity is marked by some of the attributes borne on Kushan coins by Manaobago, i.e. Vohu Manah: the throne as well as the lunar connotations, symbolised by the crescent behind the shoulders of Manaobago and on the forehead of the Kushano-Sasanian god. Yet there seem to be too many differences, especially when the role of single features is addressed, since no connection with fire is detectable in the images of Manaobago. Moreover, the throne does not appear to have been a primary mark of the god with flaming halo.

ages of deities, which were thoroughly re-clothed in Sasanian outfits. Even the hairstyle was sasanised, and long braid-looking fringes as well as hair bunches were introduced. It is this process which led to bearded gods, for Wesh as well as for Mithra: the enthroned Bago Miuro is not bearded in continuity with the Indo-Greek bearded Mithra, but as a result of the contribution of Sasanian iconographic canons to Kushano-Sasanian imagery. Connected to this, the idea that the bearded Mithra of Taq-e Bostan might be dependent on the bearded Bago Miuro must definitely be discarded: the Kushano-Sasanian Mithra is bearded like the Ahura Mazda of Ardashir I at Naqsh-e Rostam or Firuzabad. Against this background it is easy to explain the presence of all those typically Sasanian features, from ribbed diadems and pleated trousers to so-called investiture scenes.[96]

This degree of influence of Sasanian imagery on Kushano-Sasanian series can be explained only with the presence in Sasanian Kushanshahr of craftsmen in close contact with western Iran. They probably worked together with local personnel, but Kushano-Sasanian typology, on both obverse and reverse, owes too much to Sasanian concepts to be conceivable without a direct western Iranian contribution. While a shared artistic vocabulary between western and eastern Iran surely existed,[97] Kushano-Sasanian imagery seems to attest to something more circumstantial: in order to renew the repertoire of the local coin tradition to the extent shown by the Kushano-Sasanian series, pattern books must have been brought from Sasanian Iran by personnel with the mastery necessary for adapting standard Sasanian imagery to include, or to merge with, Kushan features. Indeed, this might find possible parallels in other media, as the Sasanian rock relief of Rag-i Bibi would suggest: while the style of the relief seems to imply a local sculptural craftsmanship distinct from artistic centres of western Iran,[98] its imagery shows Sasanian features not only in the subject and iconography of major features, but also in details like the pleating of the king's trousers.[99] While in theory coins could be copied from coins, this is obviously not the case with rock reliefs, and it requires the import of models from Sasanian Iran that could reach Bactria only with specialised personnel who knew how to use them. The rather unlikely alternative would be to imagine that Bactrian craftsmen all of a sudden, and above all completely on their own, became aware of the semantics of Sasanian imagery, from general features to details, from composition to iconography. Therefore we must assume that at least part of the personnel – probably those in charge of the direction of the works – came directly from Sasanian Iran,[100] coordinating the work of local sculptors who gave the relief its distinctly Bactrian stylistic rendering.

Indeed, this is the most plausible scenario even with regard to coin engravers or mint masters, and Merv is of course a most likely place to depart from, especially when the role of its mint for both imperial Sasanian and Kushano-Sasanian series is taken into ac-

---

[96] In their explicit formulation. The same subject is hinted at on Kushan coins, but in a more indirect way, as king and deity appear on the two faces of the coin (due to the conventions of the previous coin tradition of Greek derivation). Only a single Kushan reverse type, employed by Huvishka on rare coppers, reproduces the full image of the king paying homage to a deity, see Göbl 1984, Pl. 167, Nana 5.

[97] Cf. Cribb 1990, 162–163.

[98] Grenet/Lee/Martinez/Ory 2007, 249; Callieri forthcoming, dealing with centres of artistic production in Sasanian Iran.

[99] Grenet/Lee/Martinez/Ory 2007, 257.

[100] All the more so if the high chronology proposed by Grenet/Lee/Martinez/Ory 2007 (the late years of Shapur I) is accepted.

count.[101] In Balkh itself, imperial series were minted under Wahram I,[102] and Herat also struck both imperial and Kushano-Sasanian series, even if the production of imperial issues is certain only from Shapur II onwards.[103] The close connection of the Kushan-shahr mints with Sasanian Iran is further strengthened by the possible cases of motifs moving from East to West, like the upper ribbons of the korymbos inaugurated by the Kushanshah Ohrmazd 1 and the reverse base line appearing in imperial series with coins of Shapuhr II from Merv.[104]

Even within the framework of the activity of Kushano-Sasanian mint workshops, the merging of Sasanian and Kushan features may be better explained by the joint work of Sasanian and local craftsmen, at least in the early stages. The most telling instances are exactly those provided by religious iconography, since phenomena like the sasanidisa-tion of Wesh require the knowledge of the values transmitted by his image both from the point of view of its original environment and from that connected to its re-elaborated version seen on Kushano-Sasanian coins. One must only remember that the deity nor-mally associated with a bull in western Iranian imagery is Mah, not Wesh, in order to appreciate the degree of conceptual elaboration behind the images. The same is true for Nana, taken directly from Kushan imagery to be connected with a Sasanian style fire altar.

In fact, this seems to draw a picture of the interaction between the new Sasanian power and the local context based on notions of close integration, rather than independ-ence or hostility.[105] This appears to be the only possible background in order to imagine the Kushano-Sasanian mints set in a network connecting them to centres of production in western Iran.[106] Needless to say, this does not imply that there could not be local innova-tions or that the interaction with the Iranian West must be rigidly understood as always of the strictest nature at every moment of Kushano-Sasanian history. Yet a reconstruc-tion based on a sort of dialectic within the Sasanian sphere of power in the East between the imperial house and the Kushanshahs does not appear to be supported by the study of the semantics of the Kushano-Sasanian imagery used on coins. There were original choices, but within formulas essentially consistent with Sasanian visual culture, without fractures. As a matter of fact, on coins the Kushanshahs appear for what they were, i.e. governors of the former Kushan lands on behalf of the Sasanian kings of kings, not in-dependent rulers.

From the point of view of the religious background of the imagery used and the possible inferences on the religious policy lying behind it, a flexible approach seems to be apparent. Once faced in their East with a previous imperial tradition, the Sasanians aimed at presenting themselves as the new masters in an immediately recognisable way.

---

[101]   Cf. Schindel 2012, 72.

[102]   Nikitin 1999; cf. Alram/Gyselen 2012, 47.

[103]   A group of drachms could have been struck in Herat by Narseh: Alram/Gyselen 2012, 326–327, 351; Schindel 2012, 72.

[104]   Schindel 2012, 69–70. Cribb 1990, 166 attributed to Kushano-Sasanian models the adoption of the facing view for the bust on altar designs on coins of the king of kings Hormizd II.

[105]   Cf. for example Grenet/Lee/Martinez/Ory 2007, 259–260, fn. 16, stating that "Hormizd I Kushan-shah temporarily seized Merv..." and that the Kushanshahs were a semi-independent dynasty.

[106]   But this is valid in the same terms for other media, as shown by the case of rock sculpture.

Yet this did not imply a rejection, but rather what appears as the elaboration of a message essentially based on the claim to the inheritance of that legacy. The definition of Kushan was expressly kept as part of the titulature. The deities that played a prominent role in Kushan visual propaganda make their appearance, of special significance among them the royal deities, which are depicted in an explicit way, as shown by the type of Nana on altar or even by that of Ardokhsho employed by Peroz. They do not play the main role, yet they are there, included among the gods who legitimate Sasanian rule in the formerly Kushan lands.

Of course this could happen on the basis of a common religious background, i.e. Zoroastrianism, and these gods were largely common to western and eastern Iran. It is therefore no surprise that the Bactrian Wesh became the standard reverse deity for Kushano-Sasanian gold series. This leaves no room for an unorthodox variant of Zoroastrianism. While adapted to the context, the message of Kushano-Sasanian coin legends and imagery was perfectly summarised in the appellative of *mazdēsn* that the Kushanshahs imported from Sasanian titulature.

BIBLIOGRAPHY

Alram, M., Gyselen R. (2003), *Sylloge Nummorum Sasanidarum, Paris–Berlin–Wien*, Bd. 1: *Ardashir I.–Shapur I.*, Wien.

Alram, M., Gyselen R. (2012), *Sylloge Nummorum Sasanidarum, Paris–Berlin–Wien*, Bd. 2: *Ohrmazd I.–Ohrmazd II.*, Wien.

Back, M. (1978), *Die sassanidischen Staatsinschriften*, (Acta Iranica 18), Tehran–Liège.

Bivar, A.D.H. (1956), The Kushano-Sassanian Coin Series, *Journal of the Numismatic Society of India* 18: 13–42.

Bivar, A.D.H. (1979a), Mithraic Images of Bactria: Are They Related to Roman Mithraism?, in: U. Bianchi (ed.), *Mysteria Mithrae. Proceedings of the International Seminar on the "Religio-Historical Character of Roman Mithraism, with Particular Reference to Roman and Ostian Sources", Rome and Ostia 28–31 March 1978*, Leiden: 741–750.

Bivar, A.D.H. (1979b), The Absolute Chronology of the Kushano-Sassanian Governors in Central Asia, in: J. Harmatta (ed.), *Prolegomena to the Sources in the History of Pre-Islamic Central Asia*, Budapest: 317–332.

Bopearachchi, O. (1991), *Monnaies gréco-bactriennes et indo-grecques. Catalogue raisonné*, Paris.

Brunner, C.J. (1974), The Chronology of the Sasanian Kushanshahs, *American Numismatic Society Museum Notes* 19: 145–164.

Callieri, P. (1990), On the Diffusion of Mithra Images in Sasanian Iran. New Evidence from a Seal in the British Museum, *East and West* 40: 79–98.

Callieri, P. (2007), *L'archéologie du Fārs à l'époque hellénistique. Quatre leçons au Collège de France, 8, 15, 22 et 29 mars 2007*, Paris.

Callieri, P. (forthcoming), *Architecture et représentations dans l'Iran sassanide* (Conférences d'études iraniennes Ehsan et Latifeh Yashater).

Carter, M.L. (1981), Mithra on the Lotus, a Study of the Imagery of the Sun God in the Kushano-Sasanian era, in: *Monumentum Georg Morgenstierne*, (Acta Iranica II, VII), vol. 1, Tehran-Liège: 74–98.

Carter, M.L. (1985), A Numismatic Reconstruction of Kushano-Sasanian History, *American Numismatic Society Museum Notes* 30: 215–281.

Cribb, J. (1985), New Evidence of Indo-Parthian Political History, in: *Coin Hoards* 7, New York: 282–300.

Cribb, J. (1990), Numismatic Evidence for Kushano-Sasanian Chronology, *Studia Iranica* 19: 151–193.

Cribb, J. (1997), Shiva Images on Kushan and Kushano-Sasanian coins, in: K. Tanabe, J. Cribb, H. Wang (eds.), *Studies in Silk Road Coins and Culture. Papers in Honour of Professor Ikuo Hirayama on his 65th Birthday*, Kamakura: 11–66.

Gignoux, Ph. (1978), *Catalogue des sceaux, camées et bulles sasanides de la Bibliothèque Nationale et du Musée du Louvre*, II : *Les sceaux et bulles inscrits*, Paris.

Göbl, R. (1960), Zwei Neufunde in der Numismatik der Kuschan, *Mitteilungen der Österreichischen Numismatischen Gesellschaft* 11: 94–96.

Göbl, R. (1971), *Sasanian Numismatics*, Braunschweig.

Göbl, R. (1973), *Der sāsānidische Siegelkanon*, Braunschweig.

Göbl, R. (1984), *System und Chronologie der Münzprägung des Kušānreiches*, Wien.

Göbl, R. (1994), *DONUM BURNS, die Kušānmünzen in Münzkabinett Bern und die Chronologie*, Wien.

Göbl, R. (1999), The Rabatak Inscription and the date of Kanishka, in: M. Alram, D. Klimburg-Salter (eds.), *Coins, Art and Chronology. Essays on the pre-Islamic History of the Indo-Iranian Borderlands*, Wien: 151–175.

Grenet, F. (1991), Mithra au temple principal d'Aï Khanoum?, in: P. Bernard, F. Grenet (èd.), *Histoire et cultes de l'Asie centrale préislamique. Sources écrites et documents archéologiques, Actes du colloque international du CNRS, Paris, 22–28 novembre 1988*, Paris: 147–151.

Grenet, F. (1994), The Second of Three Encounters between Zoroastrianism and Hinduism: Plastic Influences in Bactria and Sogdiana (2nd–8th c. A.D.), *Journal of the Asiatic Society of Bombay* 69 [*James Darmesteter (1849–1894) Commemoration Volume*]: 41–57.

Grenet, F. (2001), Mithra, dieu iranien : nouvelles données, *Topoi* 11: 35–58.

Grenet, F., Lee, J., Martinez, Ph., Ory, F. (2007), The Sasanian Relief at Rag-i Bibi (Northern Afghanistan), in: J. Cribb, G. Herrmann (eds.), *After Alexander. Central Asia before Islam*, Oxford–New York: 243–267.

Gubaev, A.G., Loginov, S.D., Nikitin, A.B. (1996), Sasanian Bullae from the Excavations of Ak-Depe by the Station of Artyk, *Iran* 34: 55–59.

Gyselen, R. (2000), Un dieu nimbé de flammes d'époque sassanide. Avec une note additionnelle par Ph. Gignoux, *Iranica Antiqua* 35: 291–314.

Herzfeld, E. (1930), *Kushano-Sasanian Coins,* (Memoirs of the Archeological Survey of India, No. 34), Calcutta.

Humbach, H. (1975), Vayu, Śiva und der Spiritus Vivens im ostiranischen Synkretismus, in: *Acta Iranica* 4, 2nd Series: *Monumentum H.S. Nyberg*, vol. 1, Leiden: 397–408.

MacDowall, D.W. (1979), Sol Invictus and Mithra. Some Evidence from the Mint of Rome, in: U. Bianchi (ed.), *Mysteria Mithrae. Proceedings of the International Seminar on the "Religio-Historical Character of Roman Mithraism, with particular Reference to Roman and Ostian Sources", Rome and Ostia 28–31 March 1978*, Leiden: 557–569.

Martinez-Sève, L. (2010), À propos du temple aux niches indentées d'Aï Khanoum: quelques observations, in: P. Carlier, Ch. Lerouge-Cohen (èd.), *Paysage et religion en Grèce antique. Mélanges offerts à Madeleine Jost*, Paris: 195–207.

Mosig-Walburg, K. (2009), Sonderprägungen Khusros II. (590–628): innenpolitische Propaganda vor dem Hintergrund des Krieges gegen Byzanz, *Res Orientales* 18: 185–208.

Newell, E.T. (1938), *Miscellanea numismatica. Cyrene to India, American Numismatic Society Notes and Monographs* 82, New York (n.v.).

Nikitin, A. (1999), Notes on the Chronology of the Kushano-Sasanian kingdom, in: M. Alram, D. Klimburg-Salter (eds.), *Coins, Art, and Chronology. Essays on the pre-Islamic History of the Indo-Iranian Borderlands*, Wien: 259–263.

Schindel, N. (2004), *Sylloge Nummorum Sasanidarum, Paris–Berlin–Wien*, Bd. 3: *Shapur II.–Kawad I./2. Regierung*, Wien.

Schindel, N. (2005), Adhuc sub iudice lis est? Zur Datierung der kushanosasanidischen Münzen, in: H. Emmerig (Hrsg.), *Vindobona docet. 40 Jahre Institut für Numismatik und Geldgeschichte der Universität Wien, 1965–2005*, Wien [= *Numismatische Zeitschrift* 113/114]: 217–242.

Schindel, N. (2012), The Beginning of Kushano-Sasanian Coinage, in: M. Alram, R. Gyselen, *Sylloge Nummorum Sasanidarum, Paris–Berlin–Wien*, Bd. 2: *Ohrmazd I.–Ohrmazd II.*, Wien.

Schindel, N. (2014), Zur kushano-sasanidischen Münzprägung, in: M. Alram, H. Emmerig, R. Harreither (Hrsgg.), *Akten des 5. Österreichischen Numismatikertages Enns, 21.–22. Juni 2012*, Enns–Linz: 133–142.

Schindel, N. (forthcoming), *Schatzfunde spätkushanischer und kushano-sasanidischer Kupfermünzen und ihr Beitrag zur Kenntnis von Prägesystem und Geldumlauf im kushano-sasanidischen Herrschaftsbereich*, (Fundmünzen aus Usbekistan I), Wien.

Shenkar, M. (2013), A Goddess or a Queen? On the Interpretation of the Female Figure on the Relief of Narseh at Naqš-e Rostam (in Russian), in: *Scripta Antiqua, Ancient History, Philology, Arts and Material Culture. Edward Rtveladze Felicitation Volume*, Moscow: 614–634.

Tanabe, K. (1991/92), OHÞO: Another Kushan Wind God, *Silk Road Art and Archaeology* 2: 51–71.

Tyler-Smith, S. (1997), Kushano-Sasanian Small Bactrian Copper Coins: Some Refinements, *Oriental Numismatic Society Newsletter* 151: 5–7.

Vanden Berghe, L. (1993), *Splendeur des Sassanides. L'empire perse entre Rome et la Chine [224–642], 12 février au 25 avril 1993*, Bruxelles.

List of illustrations (all images are enlarged at 170%):

ELECTRUM * Vol. 22 (2015): 227–248
doi: 10.4467/20800909EL.15.012.3950
www.ejournals.eu/electrum

Sakastan in the Fourth and Fifth Century AD. Some Historical Remarks Based on the Numismatic Evidence

Nikolaus Schindel

Österreichische Akademie der Wissenschaften, Wien*

Abstract: This article discusses the Sasanian coinage from the region of Sakastan during the latter part of the 4th and the 5th century AD. Only through a comprehensive collection of material and a detailed re-evaluation of already examined coins was it possible to reconstruct a continuous series of Sakastan coins stretching from Ardashir II (379–383) to Wahram V (420–438). The implications of this numismatic evidence for our understanding of the history of Sakastan in this period are discussed in some detail, also taking into account further numismatic data from Eastern Iran.

Key words: Sasanian history, Sasanian numismatics, Sakastan, Eastern Iran.

Introduction

Having already dealt with the Sasanian mints in Khurasan during the 5th century,[1] a closer look at the neighbouring region of Sakastan not only completes the picture, but also – as I hope to be able to show – adds to the larger picture of Iranian and Eastern Iranian history in several respects. To separate the material presentation which, as it is, rests on a safe (even if small) material basis, represented by Sasanian coins, from the necessarily more hypothetical historical conclusions, I will first present and discuss the numismatic material available to me, and then consider what we can learn from it for our knowledge of Eastern Iran in the 4th and 5th centuries AD.

---

*   I have to thank Michael Alram and Fabrizio Sinisi for valuable discussion, and Sherwin Farridnejad for helping me to find a journal.
[1]   Schindel 2006.

Sasanian issues from Sakastan in the 3rd and 4th centuries[2]

To understand the monetary history of Sakastan during the late 4th and the 5th century AD, a short overview on its numismatic role during the 3rd and 4th century is advisable.[3] With a very high degree of probability, we can state that Sasanian coins were first struck in Sakastan already under Ardashir I (224–241).[4] Although unsigned, a group of drachms as well as large copper coins featuring an additional, unbearded bust[5] on the obverses seems to belong to Sakastan. The main argument for this attribution is the chemical composition of the latter: it is similar to that of local issues of the Indo-Parthian ruler Farn-Sasan,[6] and markedly different from Ardashir I's Western bronzes,[7] as are the weights, which also show close similarities with Farn-Sasan's issues.[8] The bust on the obverse, often interpreted as that of Shapur I as crown prince,[9] probably did not depict him after all, since the future king is already shown bearded on the early rock relief of Firuzabad,[10] and certainly was already mature in the late period of Ardashir's reign when these coins were produced.[11] They can often be found overstruck by Shapur I;[12] it therefore seems more likely that a local ruler of Sakastan was depicted, whose memory Shapur tried to obliterate[13] by overstriking (although one must admit that Farn-Sasan, too, is shown fully bearded on his own coins). Some of these copper coins are stored in the Kandahar Museum,[14] and this might be another indication that they circulated locally in Sakastan.[15] Two of Shapur I's style groups are attributed by Gyselen to Sakastan, even if it is impossible to attain certainty for the silver drachms due to the absence of mint signatures.[16] As yet, no Sakastan issues are attested for the short reign of Ohrmazd I (271/2–273).[17] Under his successor, Wahram I (273–276), the first signed drachms from Sakastan are known; we are now on safe grounds as regards the minting place.[18] At the same time, a star (un-

---

[2] A general overview on this topic can also be found in Schindel 2011, 82–84; additionally, this article contains ample pictorial documentation which is not repeated here. It can also be viewed online at https://www.academia.edu/4220238/Die_M%C3%BCnzst%C3%A4tte_Sakastan_unter_Shapur_II._in_Schweizerische_Numismatische_Rundschau_90_2011_S._79_110 (access: 23.12.2014).

[3] Nowadays the basic literature is Alram/Gyselen 2003; Schindel 2004 (= SNS 3); Alram/Gyselen 2012; for additional coins and discussion Schindel 2009a; Baratova/Schindel/Rtveladze 2012; Schindel 2014a.

[4] Alram 2007, 238; already Alram/Gyselen 2003, 176–177 hints at a probable provenance from Sakastan.

[5] For the typology Alram 2003, 132 (obverse type VIII).

[6] Alram 2007, 237–238 with tab. 1; for the seemingly correct reading of the name Farn-Sasan, see Nikitin 1994; Alram 2007, 234–235.

[7] Alram/Gyselen 2003, 80–81.

[8] Alram 2007, 238.

[9] For discussion Alram/Gyselen 2003, 101–103; Alram 2007, 235–237, 238, 240.

[10] Alram/Gyselen 2003, pl. 42, fig. 2 (drawing).

[11] Alram/Gyselen 2003, 160; Alram 2007, 236.

[12] Alram/Gyselen 2003, 277–278, pl. 20, no. 4, 5, A8.

[13] Alram/Gyselen 2003, 177; Alram 2007, 237.

[14] MacDowall/Ibrahim 1978, 69, 74, no. 145–147 (no. 148 is in reality of Shapur II); Alram/Gyselen 2003, 277–278.

[15] Alram/Gyselen 2003, 277–278.

[16] Alram/Gyselen 2003, 284, 286–287, pl. 20, no. 4–A8; 28, no. A31–108.

[17] Alram/Gyselen 2012, 144.

[18] Alram/Gyselen 2012, 162, 188–189, pl. 12, no. A52–A54, all using the full form SKSTN.

der Wahram I eight-pointed)[19] is added on the obverse, a feature not seen anywhere else, which was to become characteristic of this region until Shapur II.[20] The star enables us to also attribute a group of unsigned drachms to Sakastan.[21] Further evidence is provided by the hybrid combination of a Sakastan-style obverse of Wahram II, which is combined with a signed Sakastan reverse of his predecessor Wahram I.[22] Under Narseh, Sakastan's issues seem to become more numerous;[23] no large copper coins are attested. Some of the drachms featuring the peculiar Sakastan style bear the Pehlevi letter S on the altar shaft, thus providing an indication (even if, strictly speaking, no absolute proof) of the provenance.[24] This letter can also be seen on some issues of Ohrmazd II.[25] Under this ruler, the large copper denomination which we have already observed under Ardashir I and Shapur I reappears.[26] Other than Alram,[27] I am convinced that the large copper coins of Ohrmazd II featuring his bust to the left[28] also belong to Sakastan: on the one hand, the only other Sasanian coins featuring a regular left portrait[29] are issues of Shapur, which I am certain, were struck in this region.[30] They bear the very letter S, which led Alram to attribute the Narseh coins discussed above to Sakastan.[31] In addition, the line in front of all the left-facing Ohrmazd II copper coins which might represent an arrow or a lance[32] – a unique feature in Sasanian numismatics – can to some degree be linked with the lily sceptre shown on rare Sakastan drachms of Narseh.[33] An even closer parallel exists, however, with copper coins of Farn-Sasan holding an arrow or spear,[34] which leads me – unlike Alram, who assumes possible Roman influence[35] – to believe that the depiction on the copper coins of Ohrmazd II can be traced back to a local Sakastan model, even if the Sasanian die cutter apparently did not fully understand it. I cannot conceive of stylistic reasons to rule out the attribution of these two groups of left-facing coins to the same mint. Additionally, the denomination as such is an uncommon one, and to claim that two different mints issued coins of the same heavy weight, with the same highly unusual

---

[19]   The number of rays varies, Schindel 2011, 82–83; apparently the star as such, and not any concrete variant of it, was regarded as being typical of Sakastan.

[20]   Alram/Gyselen 2012, 159, tab. 3a, pl. 12, no. A52–A54.

[21]   Alram/Gyselen 2012, 266, pl. 23, no. 62–A77.

[22]   Alram/Gyselen 2012, pl. 23, no. 62.

[23]   Alram/Gyselen 2012, 329–331, pl. 40–42, no. A94–A107.

[24]   Alram/Gyselen 2012, 310, pl. 40, no. A94 f.

[25]   Alram/Gyselen 2012, 412–413, pl. 66, no. 49.

[26]   Alram/Gyselen 2012, pl. 66, no. 50 f., A146; on the metrology Alram/Gyselen 2012, 423.

[27]   Alram/Gyselen 2012, 407–408.

[28]   Alram/Gyselen 2012, pl. 62 f., no. A117–A120.

[29]   For an overview of left-facing Sasanian coins which owe their existence to die cutters' mistakes see Schindel 2014a, 17–18 with tab. 6.

[30]   Schindel 2004 (1), 230; Schindel 2011, 85–86.

[31]   Schindel 2004, (2), pl. 7, no. A15; Schindel 2014a, pl. 21, no. 234–236; one left-facing copper coin was among the pieces published by MacDowall/Ibrahim 1978, 74, no. 148 (wrongly attributed to Shapur I). These coins are said to have been found in Kandahar and its environs, MacDowall/Ibrahim 1978, 67.

[32]   Alram/Gyselen 2012, 359, 392 (there classified as a "Beizeichen").

[33]   Schindel 2011, 83.

[34]   Alram 1986, pl. 38, no. 1214.

[35]   Alram/Gyselen 2012, 359.

obverse type, and with – to my eye – a broadly speaking similar style means to multiply things without cogent necessity.

We arrive now in the reign of Shapur II, whose Sakastan coinage I have described in some detail.[36] I will avoid repeating all the minutiae here; suffice it to say that four different style groups can be distinguished, which are attested by altogether 89 coins.[37] Without aiming at completeness (which as yet it is impossible to achieve), I was able to collect 49 silver drachms, as well as 40 large copper coins. In the first style group, the letter S known already under Narseh and Ohrmazd II is common.[38] Always in style group 3,[39] and also on one unique drachm of style group 4,[40] the full mint name SKSTN is indicated, which means that the attribution of all these issues to Sakastan is very well founded. The internal chronology of the different types of Shapur II, too, is no longer the subject of serious doubt.[41]

Sakastan between Shapur II and Kawad I: the new picture

In SNS 3, I declared that no Sasanian coins were struck in Sakastan between Shapur II and Kawad I.[42] At the time of writing, this statement was correct; nowadays, with the emergence of some important new coins, and re-evaluation coins which have already been published, things have changed drastically. Let us start with an overview of those coins which can today, in my opinion, be attributed to Sakastan; all pieces are listed in the catalogue below.

Tab. 1. Overview of Sakastan issues from Ardashir II to Wahram V

King	Drachms	Copper coins
Ardashir II		1
Shapur II		2
Wahram IV	10	1
Yazdgerd I	3	3
Wahram V	4	
Total	17	7

---

[36]   Schindel 2011.

[37]   Leaving aside an imitation and a large copper coin of Sakastan style, but bearing the otherwise unattested signature LWH: Schindel 2011, 92, note 58.

[38]   Schindel 2011, 85.

[39]   Schindel 2011, 88.

[40]   Schindel 2011, 89.

[41]   Göbl 1984, 49–51; Schindel 2004 (1), 211–219.

[42]   Schindel 2014a (1), 230.

Two things have to be emphasised: first, the degree of probability of the attribution to Sakastan varies from issue to issue; secondly, while hopefully offering a representative image, these numbers are not even close to being complete.[43]

Before discussing each individual issue in detail, the single most important coin type has to be introduced, because it is the only one to bear a mint indication, and therefore proves beyond doubt the existence of Sakastan coinage in the period discussed here: no. 8.[44] On the altar shaft, where the Pehlevi word *l'st* ("just")[45] is normally placed, one can read SKSTN, i.e. the full version of the mint name Sakastan in Middle Persian, already well known. Once one is aware of this reading, it is possible to make out faint traces of the same inscription also on the heavily corroded no. 9. Thus, without any doubt there is a group of Sasanian coins from the late 4th century struck in Sakastan. As Tab. 1 shows, these two drachms of Wahram IV are not isolated; there are other issues from other kings as well, which I now believe have to belong to this region, thereby giving it a much more active role in Sasanian monetary production than I had previously thought. Let us now look closely at them, king by king and issue by issue.

Ardashir II

The numismatic material clearly shows that Sakastan remained active until the later years of Shapur II.[46] For his successor Ardashir II (379–384), no silver drachms which could possibly be attributed to Sakastan have turned up so far. There exists, however, a rather strange copper coin in the Schaaf collection (no. 1). Its high weight of 5.68 g is atypical of the period; we remember that heavy copper coins were primarily struck in Sakastan up to the later reign of Shapur II.[47] It is very difficult to distinguish the stylistic details, since this unique coin is not only overstruck on an unidentifiable earlier issue, but also heavily double struck; because of this, the images on both sides are fairly obscure. I hesitated to attribute this Ardashir II copper coin to Sakastan in SNS Schaaf. It seems probable, though, that some of the typical features of the Sakastan style – notably, the elongated facial features – might be present on this coin. Now, having trained my eye for the peculiarities especially of the style of the legends in Sakastan, I believe that on the one hand due to the strong similarities in the rounded, very delicate letter forms of this coin with e.g. no. 5, and on the other hand due to the differences from all other Ardashir II coins known to me so far, this piece does not only represent a mint different from

---

[43] My material basis was, as always, the Numismatische Zentralkartei (NZK) at the Institute for Numismatics and Monetary History, University of Vienna, as well as Paruck 1928; Göbl 1971; Mochiri 1977; Amini 1359 [= 1981]; Sellwood/Whitting/Williams 1985; Gyselen 2004; Schindel 2004; Schindel 2009a; Curtis/Askari/Pendleton 2010; Gariboldi 2010; Nelson 2011; Baratova/Schindel/Rtveladze 2012; Schindel 2012; Schindel 2014a; www.britishmuseum.org; www.amnumsoc.org; www.zeno.ru; www.coinarchives. com. Even if certainly far from complete in absolute terms, this compilation at least can be labelled fairly comprehensive at the current state of affairs.

[44] Schindel 2014a, 31, tab. 9.

[45] Schindel 2004 (1), 218.

[46] Schindel 2011, 93.

[47] Schindel 2011, 94–95.

those listed in SNS 3,[48] but can also in fact be attributed to Sakastan. Still, this attribution is less certain than that of e.g. the signed Wahram drachms (no. 8, 9), but still appears to me sufficiently plausible to at least serve as a working hypothesis.

Shapur III

For the next king, Shapur III (383–388), I know two copper coins which can be attributed to Sakastan so far. Other than under Ardashir II, there are several silver drachms which I have as yet not been able to allocate to any of the well-established mints,[49] but none of them seems to be a likely candidate for an equation with Sakastan. One copper coin, held in the Schaaf collection (no. 2),[50] displays a style very similar to that of the latest style group under Shapur II in Sakastan. A typical feature is the use of the Pehlevi letter Š in front of the bust on the obverse. It goes without saying that this is a little strange: wherever the mint name of Sakastan is spelled out in full, it always begins with a Pehlevi S, and not with a Š. Therefore, it seems problematic to claim that this isolated letter directly refers to the mint in the same way as the S on the early issues of Shapur II. Still, the same letter Š can also be found on two copper coins of Shapur II which due to stylistic reasons definitely belong to the same style group as the drachm with the mint name SKSTN. Therefore, on the basis of the parallels with Shapur II, I feel confident in attributing this Shapur III copper coin to Sakastan.[51] Considering how rare copper issues of Shapur III are,[52] it fits well with the typical Sakastan patterns now already familiar to us that this mint is attested by a copper, rather than by a silver coin. At 2.81 g, no. 2 weighs only half of the Ardashir II coin discussed above.

A second Sakastan bronze coin of Shapur III can be reconstructed; this is the undertype of an overstruck Yazdgerd I coin (no. 3; for the overtype no. 18): to the right of the portrait on the obverse, the typical arcaded crown of Shapur III as worn by the right reverse attendant is visible; on the reverse, at 6 h a large "taurus"-symbol which was placed in front of Shapur's bust can be made out. Since this coin had an additional mark in front of the bust, rather than the letter Š as with no. 2, Shapur III apparently had at least two different sub-types issued during his reign.

Wahram IV

As stated above, the Sakastan issues of Wahram IV are of great importance since no. 8 and, less clearly legibly, also no. 9 bears the mint name SKSTN on the altar shaft, and thus prove beyond doubt that this entire style group in fact belongs to Sakastan, rather

---

[48]   Schindel 2004 (1), 256–259; 2004 (2), pl. 22–24.

[49]   Schindel 2004 (2), pl. 31.

[50]   Schindel 2011, 93; Schindel 2014a, 30.

[51]   Thus already Schindel 2014a, vol. 1, 30 with tab. 8.

[52]   In SNS 3 I was able to locate less than half a dozen specimens (Schindel 2004 (1), 269), not counting the find coins from Marw: Loginov/Nikitin 1993.

than to the phantom mint of Yazd.[53] As far as I can see, the use of a mint signature is a peculiarity of the drachms with reverse type 2. Since this is in chronological order, Wahram's second variant, but the first on which mint signatures are commonly used, it is obvious that the Sakastan mint was fulfilling an instruction from the central administration in doing so. Later on, for reasons unknown to us, the employment of a signature was discontinued. We should bear in mind that unsigned drachms are still very common under both Wahram IV and Yazdgerd I, and occur until Yazdgerd II; only from Peroz onwards do all Sasanian drachms canonically bear a mint indication. A copper coin which is fairly corroded (no. 10) shows the same basic reverse type, the peculiar Sakastan style, and a crescent as an additional mark on the obverse in front of the royal bust. Whether or not the mint name was placed on the altar shaft remains uncertain.

These signed drachms provide us with enough stylistic clues that we can also – safely, I believe – attribute coins featuring reverse types 1 and 3 to Sakastan. Let us briefly list them. On the obverse, the head is generally shown rather thin and elongated. The mural element above the forehead is also rather high and thin. The korymbos can be very small, a feature that becomes more and more relevant. The twisting of the altar ribbons is shown in a rather unstructured fashion. On the reverses, the main criteria are the shirts the attendants seem to wear. On reverse 3 – more specifically what should now be labelled variant 3b[54] – the altar shaft is still square, as indicated by its three vertical lines; this seems to be a takeover from the early reverse 1. However, these descriptions can never replace a careful study of the coins themselves. The legends on both sides are also very typical: on the one hand, they are written with fine, delicate letters, which are more rounded than is usual at this time. On the other hand, the legends are often written inwards, and not outwards, as is the rule under Wahram IV.[55]

As can be seen from Tab. 1 above, this king's Sakastan issues are by far the most common ones in the period under discussion. Even more interesting is their typological distribution: four bear the earliest reverse type 1, three the consecutive variant 2, and four the latest reverse 3. The internal chronology of these three reverse types can be regarded as firmly established.[56] The unusual feature of Wahram's Sakastan issues is the fact that reverse 1 is generally rather rare; it was obviously issued only for a rather limited period of time. In SNS 3, I have listed 17 drachms with reverse 1, compared with 126 with type 2, and 122 with reverse 3.[57] Despite the small numbers attested by Tab. 1, it seems that these rather strange distribution patterns are not merely a result of chance, but that another explanation is possible. We will return to this topic below in the chapter on the historical conclusions which can be drawn from the numismatic material.

A short remark might be required on no. 13. The altar flames are shown in a rather peculiar way; therefore, one might suspect that originally a bust in the altar flames (typical for reverse type 2) was depicted. However, the altar shaft shows faint traces of the

---

[53] On this see below.

[54] Not in SNS 3 because the only possible attestation then known to me (Schindel 2004 (2), pl. 44, no. A65 = no. 13) was too badly struck to recognise this feature.

[55] The only coin featuring an obverse legend 6 (written inward) in SNS 3 is Schindel 2004 (2), pl. 44, no. A65 = no. 13, which also belongs to Sakastan.

[56] Schindel 2004 (1), 288–290.

[57] Schindel 2004 (1), 294, tab. 15 (which only covers silver drachms attributable to a specific mint).

three vertical lines typical of reverse 3, rather than the mint name. Therefore, it seems very probable that the die as such was produced only when reverse 3 had already been introduced.

Yazdgerd I

While no signed Sakastan coins of this king are known to date (and, considering the lack of such issues on two of the three reverse types of his predecessor, they may never turn up), on stylistic grounds the attribution of drachms, as well as copper coins, to that mint seems very probable to me. The respective coins show the same elongated facial outlines, the same prominence of the mural element (on Yazdgerd's crown, in the centre), and also the peculiar treatment of the attendants, which seem to wear shirts that could already be observed under Wahram IV. The obverse legend, too, is of typical Sakastan style; there is no reverse legend, and the thin altar shaft certainly did not allow the mint name to be placed there. Strangely enough, all drachms known to me so far bear the very rare reverse type 3 (no. 15–17),[58] while the copper coins of the same style bear the common variant 1 (no. 18–20).[59] Despite the rather bad state of preservation, at least some of these copper coins show enough detail to ensure that the stylistic link with the Sakastan drachms can be regarded as certain. Like the Ardashir II copper coin discussed above (no. 1), the best-preserved Yazdgerd I bronze (no. 18) is overstruck; the undertype (as already discussed) is a Sakastan issue of Shapur III. The number of copper pieces known so far is the same as that of the drachms, a typical feature of the monetary circulation in Sakastan.

Wahram V

He is the last king to employ the peculiar Sakastan style well attested under Wahram IV and Yazdgerd I. Both main reverse types (1 and 2 according to SNS 3) are each represented by two coins (no. 21, 22 and no. 23, 24 respectively). All the stylistic peculiarities, such as the elongated faces and the shirts of the attendants, are still present.[60] In 2004, I thought that these coins belonged to the mint of Yazd. I had based this assumption on Mochiri's reading of the inscription at 3 h on one of these coins.[61] Nowadays, this reading cannot be upheld. The alleged mint signature is just one or two garbled letters which permit no certain reading. The second specimen of reverse 2 also does not show any legible letters, due to corrosion.[62] More puzzling are the reverse inscriptions on the coins with the earlier reverse type 1: other than the later type 2 drachms, they definitely do not

---

[58] Schindel 2004 (1), 323–324; 2004 (2), pl. 57.
[59] Thus already Schindel 2004 (1), 324. I concluded from this fact that the Yazdgerd I drachms with reverse 3 are official issues, and not unofficial imitations.
[60] For a discussion already Schindel 2004 (1), 360.
[61] Mochiri 1998, 10, fig. 2.
[62] Schindel 2004 (2), pl. 66, no. A36.

bear inscriptions at 3 h and 9 h, but they feature some letters on the altar shaft, in the case of no. 22 also to the left of the altar flames. On no. 21, the letters on the shaft seem to read G/Y-D-N/K-B/Z-Y, whereas on no. 22, two small and unclear letters are placed to the left of the altar flames, and on the shaft, a wavy line which in this form does seem to correspond to any Pehlevi (even if combined) can be seen. I have to admit that after consulting Pehlevi dictionaries,[63] as well as the literature on historical and administrative geography,[64] I cannot offer any reading. One would certainly wish to read the mint name SKSTN here, too; but this, I am afraid, is too hypothetical. While one might try (not without doing some violence to the material) to read the beginning of the word as SK (thus combining what rather looks like two letters into one, viz. S), it seems impossible to read the remainder as STN. With the other coins, we are in an even more desperate situation: not only is it impossible to read this inscription; it also seems highly improbable that no. 21 and 22 bear the same inscription. Since neither of the two legends openly contradicts my attribution to Sakastan (as a reading as, say, Herat or Armenia would), with due caution I believe that the stylistic evidence in combination with the unequivocal reading of the reverse legend on the altar shaft of no. 8 as SKSTN still enables us to attribute the entire group to this region. One certainly would have preferred these Wahram V drachms to support this in a clear and unequivocal manner. Given the position of the letter on the shaft, the absence of a reverse legend citing the king, and the fact that on neither coin can the inscription be read as the usual l'st, it seems plausible that both pieces provide a mint name. Especially in the case of no. 21, one cannot even blame the problems of interpreting it on the preservation, since both the coins as such, as well as the photo, are fairly nice; it is the ambiguity of the Pehlevi script, as well as our still insufficient detail knowledge of Sasanian Iran, which cause these problems.

From Yazdgerd II onwards

The typical Sakastan style is no longer attested under Yazdgerd II; it is impossible to tell whether any of his numerous unsigned drachms were issued in Sakastan. There is, to my eye, no proof, or even any hint of this. There are also no Peroz issues which can be associated with Sakastan; all his drachms bear mint signatures, and apart from a few stray specimens, they can all be read and equated with a high degree of probability.[65] A rare issue earlier attributed to Herat and discussed in SNS Schaaf cannot be localised with certainty today;[66] still, there are no obvious clues for assigning it to Sakastan.

Under Walkash, a so far unique drachm seemed to attest the mint signature YZ, and thus to serve as a backbone for my earlier attribution of the entire series now localised in Sakastan to Yazd.[67] However, new photos of the same coin showed that the first letter has two vertical strokes, and therefore looks like a Pehlevi A, rather than a Y;[68] the reading as

---

[63] MacKenzie 1971.
[64] Gyselen 1989; Gyselen 2002.
[65] Schindel 2004 (1), 409; 2004 (2), pl. 97, no. 228–229.
[66] Schindel 2004 (1), 408–409; 2004 (2), pl. 88; Schindel 2014a, 40.
[67] Schindel 2004 (1), 432; vol. 2, pl. 104.
[68] Schindel 2014a, 41, pl. 48.

YZ is therefore no longer valid. In passing, one should add that this is classic example of how misleading photos can be, and that no picture can ever replace the reliability which can be gained from having the actual coin in one's hands. Anyway, there is at present no indication for minting activity in the YZ mint – I became slightly sceptical about its equation with Yazd – during the 5th century; it is first attested safely only under Khusro I. Since this Walkash drachm does not belong to YZ, also the last potential argument in favour of an attribution of the entire earlier style group to Yazd becomes obsolete.

No Sakastan issues are known for the first reign of Kawad I, or for Zamasp. The earliest indication of a resumption of monetary production in this area is drachms bearing the mint name BŠT (for Bist in Sakastan),[69] which are attested from regal year 40 of Kawad I onwards.[70] Under his successor Khusro I, two new mint signatures for Sakastan occur: in his regal years 8, 15, 16, and 18, drachms were struck in ZL,[71] which in all probability refers to the provincial capital Zarang.[72] Like BŠT, the use of this variant was short-lived; from regal year 27 of Khusro I onwards, we can observe the new variant SK, citing the name of the region rather than some specific city. SK is attested, with interruptions certainly due to our insufficient material basis, until the end of Khusro's reign. However, in my SNS 4-database, out of a total of 3096 coins I have only recorded 50 SK specimens. This puts Sakastan in 22nd place among Khusro's mints. Also under Ohrmazd IV, its attestations are not very common; there are 22 SK drachms out of 2956 pieces altogether, dated to the regal years 2, 3, 6, 9, 10, 11 and 12. During the 2nd reign of Khusro II, SK remains of secondary importance; in hoards, it is normally attested by c. 0.5% of all Khusro II drachms.[73] In the Late Sasanian period, i.e. after the death of Khusro II, Sakastan suddenly becomes the most productive mint; but these developments and their historical implications are beyond the scope of the present contribution.

Results: coins and history

Having presented the numismatic basis of this study in some detail, let us see what the coins can tell us about the monetary, economic, and general history of Sakastan in the late 4th and 5th centuries.

Dies

In Tab. 1 above, I have listed the Sakastan coins known to me so far. From a methodological point of view, mere numbers of specimens are never as relevant as the number of dies involved in producing them. Therefore, I have analysed the dies of all known specimens. It has to be stated that the emergence of digital photography has made this

---

[69] Schindel 2004 (1), 133 (reading), 156 (localisation).

[70] Schindel 2004 (1), 470, tab. 47; 2004 (2), pl. 123, no. A9.

[71] Data from my database for SNS 4 (Khusro I–Ohrmazd IV).

[72] On the signature earlier read as ZL or ZR, which in fact denotes YZ: Schindel 2004 (1), 146, 174.

[73] Akbarzadeh/Schindel (forthcoming), tab. 73.

job considerably easier; with the old 1:1 scale, black-and-white images, it is sometimes not possible to reach a definite answer, especially when one or both coins in question are either badly struck, worn, or both (e.g. no. 23, 24). Apart from those cases where the same actual coin was depicted in different sources (indicated in the catalogue below), I was able to find out only a limited number of die identities. No. 5 and 6, as well as no. 11 and 12, were struck from the same pair of dies; no. 15 and 17 might share the same obverse die, but due to the rather worn condition of no. 15, it is impossible to be certain. Even more problematic is the case of no. 23 and 24: it seems likely that they share the same obverse die; both coins are corroded, have broken edges, and are attested only in rather mediocre black-and-white images, so a definite answer to this question is simply not possible. Accepting die identities in these two dubious cases too, the total number of dies attested by the 24 coins listed in Tab. 1 is as follows (Tab. 2):

Tab. 2. Obverse and reverse die distribution

King	Obv. Dies	Rev. dies
Ardashir II	1	1
Shapur II	2	2
Wahram IV	9	9
Yazdgerd I	5	6
Wahram V	3	4
Total	20	22

The 24 coins assembled here were therefore struck by a minimum of 20 obverse and 22 reverse dies; if one does not accept the die identity of no. 15 and 17 on the one hand, and no. 23 and 24 on the other, then the total of obverses rises to 22. As so often in Sasanian numismatics, die links are so rare that we obviously have only a tiny fraction of the original coin and die population at our disposal.

Metrology

As one would actually expect, there is no indication that the silver drachms differ in weight from the imperial norms.[74] While some underweight coins (e.g. 7, 9, 11, 12, 16, 22) occur there, there are also several specimens very close to the ideal weight of c. 4.20 g (e.g. 4, 5, 6, 21). The copper coins show (with due caution owing to the small number of coins attested so far) a tendency of falling weight, a trend recognisable already under Shapur II:[75] no. 1 of Ardashir II weighs 5.68 g, no. 2 of Shapur III almost exactly half of this (2.81 g.), no. 3 just 1.46 g. Since the diameters are also markedly different (30 mm vs. 24 mm), it seems obvious that the differences are not merely the

---

[74]   Schindel 2004 (1), 103–113.
[75]   Schindel 2011, 94–95.

result of chance – weight fluctuations in ancient base-metal coinage can be quite heavy. No. 10 of Wahram IV weighs 2.13 g, whereas the two Yazdgerd I copper issues for which I know the weights (no. 18, 19) show markedly lower values (1.46 g, 1.27 g). It therefore seems that the ideal weights of the copper coins in Sakastan declined heavily during the approx. 40 year-period on which this paper focuses. While in the beginning the coppers were untypically heavy, and represented a local peculiarity of Sakastan, by the end of this period the weights are basically the same as those of the other base-metal coins from the central parts of the Sasanian Empire.[76]

Monetary circulation and its historical implications

As clearly indicated in Tab. 1, copper coins from Sakastan are common: their numerical relationship with the drachms is c. 1 : 2.5 (7 : 17), a truly remarkable value considering that the overall data among the coins depicted in SNS 3 is 27 : 1 for Ardashir II, 83 : 5 for Shapur III, 136 : 7 for Wahram IV, 156 : 9 for Yazdgerd I, and finally 102 : 18 for Wahram V.[77] Amazingly enough, for the last king mentioned here, when copper coins generally become more common, no base-metal coins from Sakastan are attested so far.

Our knowledge of the actual monetary circulation in Sakastan is quite limited, to say the least, due primarily to the absence of larger numbers of coins from archaeological excavations. Some minor insights can be gained from local museum collections: in the Kandahar Museum, one local copper coin of Ardashir I is catalogued, three (or seven, including four uncertain specimens) heavy bronzes of Shapur I, thus in all probability also of local Sakastan mintage, and one left-facing Shapur II.[78] Since the descriptions are not very detailed, and most coins not depicted in the plates, the attribution of two drachms of Shapur II, and one silver coin of Wahram IV has to remain uncertain. Two issues of the Indo-Parthian ruler Gondophares, three of Pakores, and six of Farn-Sasan (then still labelled Ardamitra) should also be mentioned.[79] From the Herat Museum, Alram has published five Indo-Parthian coins (four Pakores, one Farn-Sasan), two Sakastan copper coins of Shapur I, as well as two copper tetradrachms of Kanishka I.[80] Even if Herat lies in Arachosia, and not in Sakastan, this evidence is interesting since it offers one of the few glimpses at the merger of Sasanian, Indo-Parthian, and Kushan coins in the local monetary circulation of the 3rd century AD.

However, the Sakastan copper coins can possibly give us important insights into the monetary conditions and connections during the 3rd, 4th, and 5th centuries, even if much of what follows necessarily has to be quite hypothetical for the time being. First and foremost, the metrological basis of the Sasanian copper coins from Sakastan needs to be addressed. Ardashir's heaviest base-metal issues from Western Iran ("Ctesiphon"

---

[76]   It should be emphasised that we do not yet really understand the metrological basis of Sasanian copper coins in the 5th and 6th century: Schindel 2004 (1), 116–118.

[77]   Schindel 2004 (1), 48, tab. 2.

[78]   MacDowall/Ibrahim 1978, 74, pl. 2.

[79]   MacDowall/Ibrahim 1978, 73–74, pl. 1.

[80]   Alram, forthcoming.

and "Ecbatana") weigh between 14.82 g and 17.85 g.[81] His Sakastan copper coins, on the contrary, show a different weight distribution, between 7.58 g and 11.85 g.[82] Alram has noticed this difference,[83] and also cited the allegedly similar weights of some of Farn-Sasan's coins as a possible model.[84] The majority of them, however, display the same averages as Pakores and the later Indo-Parthian copper coins showing Nike on the reverse, i.e. around 7–8 g.[85] A weight standard of c. 11 g may be attested on some coins of Farn-Sasan, but only in a rather shadowy fashion, and apparently not in a consistent way. However, such weights around 11 g are very common on Kushan coins from group 3 of Huvishka to the earlier types in the name of Vasudeva I.[86] This is a slightly unexpected observation. According to the modern orthodoxy, Year One of Kanishka I equates to 127 AD. According to this theory (and a theory it is, not an established fact), Vasudeva I's reign began around 191 AD; he is last attested in inscriptions dated to year 98 of the Kanishka Era, which would correspond 225 AD. However, there can be no doubt that by the end of his reign, the weights of Kushan copper coins had dropped markedly; for his rival Kanishka II, basically no coins heavier than 8.5 g are attested.[87] One might certainly claim that Farn-Sasan created the weight standard of c. 11 g independently, even if this seems unlikely to me. An alternative explanation is that coins were issued in Sakastan the metrological basis of which was already obsolete in the Kushan Empire; but this too is a rather unconvincing assumption, since one wonders why Ardashir did not simply introduce the imperial Sasanian weight standard, once the Kushan model had become obsolete. If one looks at the metrology of Sasanian Sakastan in a totally unbiased fashion, then it seems logical to date at least the beginning of the use of this 11 g weight standard roughly to the same time as its existence in the Kushan Empire; then, however, the reign of Huvishka falls into the 3rd century AD. It is of great importance that in the Kandahar Museum, Kushan coins were by far the most common group: MacDowall and Ibrahim listed six coins of Kujula Kadphises, ten of Soter Megas, three of Vima Kadphises, twelve of Kanishka I, 58 of Huvishka, 15 Oesho-type and four Ardokhsho-type Late Kushan copper coins.[88] This proves that Kushan copper coins had a huge impact on the monetary circulation of Sakastan in the 3rd and 4th centuries; it is therefore certainly plausible that these numerous issues had an influence on the local minting practices of the late Indo-Parthians as well as those of the Sasanians. The fact that the majority of the Huvishka coins listed above are lightweight unofficial issues does not change this. This is not to say that an isolated metrological observation can serve as an argument for an alternative solution of the complex question of Year One of Kanishka I. Still, considering that a lacuna of some 35 years (a full generation) exists between the end of the use of the 11 g weight standard in the Kushan Empire (c. 200 AD), and the approximate date of Ardashir I's heavy Sakastan copper issues (c. 235 AD), that in the Kushan Empire during

---

[81] Alram/Gyselen 2003, 166.
[82] Alram/Gyselen 2003, pl. 17–18.
[83] Alram 2007, 238.
[84] Alram 2007, 235.
[85] Senior 2001 (2), 184–189.
[86] Göbl 1984, pl. 89–104.
[87] Göbl 1984, pl. 110–112.
[88] MacDowall/Ibrahim 1978, 72–74.

these years markedly lighter coins were issued, and that lightweight Kushan coins are common in the Kandahar Museum, it seems at least a little doubtful whether the current generally accepted view on Kushan chronology really holds true. I have expressed this scepticism previously.[89]

Further historical conclusions

At the beginning, an obvious fact should be stated: due to the almost continuous series of Sasanian coins from the later reign of Ardashir I to the later reign of Wahram V (with the only lacuna so far in the short reign of Ohrmazd I), there can be hardly any doubt that Sakastan was firmly under Sasanian control for this period of approx. 200 years. Admittedly, if there had been an interruption, say, for some years under Shapur II, we would probably be unable to recognise it from the numismatic evidence; in theory it might lie behind one of the stylistic changes. Still, in my opinion the stylistic continuity from the late reign of Shapur II to Shapur III, and then up to Wahram V, argues for a continuous, undisturbed Sasanian control of Sakastan, or at least of its main mint, which we can in all probability locate in the provincial capital Zarang.[90] Considering the lack of direct historical sources on Eastern Iran in the 4th and 5th centuries, this in itself is already a relevant result. However, looking at coinage in Sakastan from a broader perspective, we can go even farther than this.

Let us start with administrative geography.[91] We are in the fortunate situation of knowing approximately the area ruled by at least one Sasanian governor of Sakastan, namely Shapur, son of the great king Ohrmazd, who left an inscription in Persepolis. There, he is styled "king of the Sakas, king of Hindustan, Sakastan and Turan up to the sea-shore."[92] This inscription is dated to regal year 2 of Shapur II; another inscription from Persepolis, composed by a certain Slok, "judge of Yawed-Shapur and Kawar" (Kabul?), is dated to regal year 18 of the same King of Kings, and strongly implies that at that date, Shapur Sakanshah was still in power.[93] Because of the stylistic and typological evidence, there can be no doubt that, during Shapur Sakanshah's tenure, coins of Shapur II's early types, which belong to his Sakastan style group 1, were struck in this region; they definitely belong to the same period of c. 17 years during which Shapur Sakanshah is epigraphically attested. Thus, even when a high-ranking member of the royal dynasty ruled Sakastan with the royal title, coin production was carried out in the name of the great king. As shown some years ago by Nikitin,[94] the Sakanshah did not strike coins in his own name; the only local governor to do so was the Kushanshah (more accurately, a main governor and a sub-governor, in changing geographical settings).

Looking in detail at the coins presented above, one certainly wonders why there are so many specimens of the otherwise rare reverse type 1 of Wahram IV. One possible

---

[89] Schindel 2005; Schindel 2009b; Schindel 2012; Schindel 2014b.
[90] Schindel 2004 (1), 167.
[91] Of fundamental importance for this topic: Gyselen 1989; Gyselen 2002.
[92] Back 1978, 492–494; Schindel 2004 (2), 461.
[93] Back 1978, 495–497; Schindel 2004 (2), 461; Schindel 2011, 94.
[94] Nikitin 1999.

explanation is that this king, who had ruled Kerman before becoming Shahanshah,[95] paid money not only to his local supporters in this region (his KL issues are unusually common),[96] but also to people in Sakastan. These payments definitely took place after he had established his power over the entire Sasanian Empire, since they already bear his imperial crown, and display a reverse type attested throughout the entire Sasanian Empire. The comparatively large output of these early drachms might represent money produced locally to be handed over, in all probability, to members of the military establishment of Sakastan, either for services rendered when Wahram ascended the throne, or to ensure their continuing support. While this interpretation is certainly hypothetical, it might open new possibilities for learning about local alliances and policy-making from a careful, detailed analysis of the numismatic material.[97]

Another, equally hypothetical, but potentially more important topic is the end of Sakastan coinage under, or after, Wahram V. It is certainly problematic to argue *ex silentio*, especially in numismatics, since it may be that tomorrow some Sakastan coins of Yazdgerd II turn up, which then completely change the hypothesis formulated below. Still, in the current state of research, there are no Sakastan coins of this king. What is more, there are also no longer silver drachms from Marw: a continuous, stylistically coherent group of precious-metal as well as copper coins can be observed stretching from Ardashir II to Wahram V;[98] its distribution patterns are thus very similar to Sakastan. While there are local copper coins issued in the name of Yazdgerd II in Marw,[99] I doubt that the few gold and silver coins bearing his image are official Sasanian issues.[100] Under Peroz, there are definitely no Marw issues known so far.[101] The situation in Herat, the second important Sasanian mint in Khurasan, is slightly different: here, the continuous style group starting – in its most obvious form – under Wahram IV comes to an end during the reign of Wahram V; his later coins show a completely different style. Under Yazdgerd II, the signature HLYDY is still attested, featuring the same style as in the later reign of Wahram V. While there are twelve Herat drachms of Wahram IV in SNS 3,[102] 14 of Yazdgerd I,[103] and seven of Wahram V,[104] under Yazdgerd II only a single Herat drachm was listed.[105] Under Peroz, too, only one Herat drachm was attested in SNS 3.[106] Another coin listed under Herat in SNS 3 cannot in fact be attributed to a specific mint.[107]

This means that the number of coins attested for the three Easternmost Sasanian mints (Marw, Herat, and Sakastan), which form a line running from the North to the

---

[95] Schindel 2004 (1), 313–314.

[96] Schindel 2004 (1), 308.

[97] Compared e.g. with the highly problematic (to put it politely) book by Pourshariati 2008, this approach has the advantage that it is connected to actual contemporary sources.

[98] Schindel 2004 (1), 495–501; 2004 (2), pl. 142; Schindel 2008.

[99] Loginov/Nikitin 1993; Schindel 2004 (1), 382; 2004 (2), pl. 72.

[100] Schindel 2004 (1), 382.

[101] Schindel 2004 (1), 402.

[102] Schindel 2004 (1), 294.

[103] Schindel 2004 (1), 327.

[104] Schindel 2004 (1), 351.

[105] Schindel 2004 (1), 376.

[106] Schindel 2004 (1) 408; 2004 (2), pl. 88.

[107] Schindel 2004 (1), 408–409; 2004 (2), pl. 88.

South, greatly declines under Yazdgerd II. After the defeat of Peroz by the Hephthalites in 484, to repeat it once again, all Khurasan was lost to the Sasanians; it was regained, on the basis of coinage, only in the 20s of the 2nd reign of Kawad I.[108] The new evidence from Sakastan seems to hint at the possibility that even before the disaster of 484, the East of the Sasanian realm suffered some instability; I guessed at something like this already in SNS 3, when I raised – with due caution – the possibility that, for example, the stylistic change in Herat under Wahram V might bear witness to a temporary loss of this mint to external enemies.[109] Nowadays, I feel even more confident that the Sasanians had to struggle to control the Eastern parts of their empire in the middle of the 5th century; reports about protracted warfare, which was not necessarily always successful, are available for both Wahram V[110] and Yazdgerd II,[111] not to mention Peroz.[112] Without discussing all the details and all the minor source problems here, it seems that during much of the second and third quarters of the 5th century, both Khurasan and Sakastan were in turmoil; the nadir of Sasanian power was brought about by the defeat of 484, as was the loss of Khurasan (and, one might guess, probably also of Sakastan).[113] Interestingly enough, the imperial recovery under Kawad I has so far attracted little interest, despite the fact that – according to the present reconstruction – he managed not merely to undo the effects of one single unfortunate battle, but to put a definite end to almost half a century of political and military problems in the East. The re-emergence of a powerful enemy in the East (the Turks under Ohrmazd IV) dates to the late 6th century; and nowhere in the numismatic material can we trace a similar cessation of coin production as is recognisable in the 5th century, especially after 484.

Catalogue

The catalogue is arranged by ruler, type (according to SNS 3), and falling weights. If available, weight (in grams), diameter (in millimetres), die axis (according to the watch), as well as any noteworthy technical peculiarities are listed. The location and earlier publication are also given. Coins marked with * are shown on the plates; I have concentrated on pieces for which I had high-quality photos at my disposal, and avoided reproducing images which are already of mediocre resolution.

Ardashir II (379–383)

Type Ic/1a

1*.   AE. 5.68 g. 30 mm. 3 h. Schaaf coll.; Schindel 2014a, pl. 27, no. 307

---

[108]   Schindel 2004 (1), 426, 489–491; Schindel 2006.

[109]   Schindel 2004 (1), 357–358.

[110]   Schindel 2004 (1), 365.

[111]   Schindel 2004 (1), 386.

[112]   Schindel 2004 (1), 414–418.

[113]   Also the evidence of the Sasanian-type coinage in Sind hints at this: Schindel 2004 (1), 507–509; 2004 (2), pl. 145.

Shapur III (383–388)

Type Ib1/1c
2*.   AE. 2.81 g. 24 mm. 4 h. Schaaf coll.; Schindel 2014a, pl. 29, no. 324
3*.   AE. 1.46 g. 29 mm 3 h. CNG electronic auction 321, 26.02.2014, no. 278 (undertype) (= no. 3)

Wahram IV (388–399)

Type Ia3/1a
4.   AR. Δ. 4.21 g. 24 mm. 3 h. CNG Electronic Auction 201, 17.12.2008, no. 202 = http://www.zeno.ru/showphoto.php?photo=50726.
5*.   AR. Δ. 4.17 g. 26 mm. 3 h. CNG Mail Bid Sale 79, 17.09.2008, no. 548 = Schaaf coll.; Schindel 2014a, pl. 33, no. 363 (same obv. die as no. 6)
6.   AR. Δ. 4.15 g. 24 mm. 3 h. CNG Electronic Auction 207, 25. 03.2009, no. 272 (same obv. die as no. 5)
7.   AR. Δ. 3.75 g. 24 mm. 2 h. Berlin/Löbbecke (7079); Schindel 2004, vol. 1, pl. 41, no. 64

Type Ib1/2a
8*.   AR. Δ. Gurnet coll.; Schindel 2014a, p. 31, tab. 9
9.   AR. Δ. 3.81 g. British Museum 1894.0506.1285 = http://www.britishmuseum. org/research/collection_online/collection_object_details.aspx?objectId=905250&partId =1&searchText=1894,0506.1285+&page=1.

Type Ib3/2a
10*.   AE. 2.13 g. 22 mm. 3 h. CNG Electronic Auction 314, 6.11.2013, no. 235

Type Ic/3b[114]
11.   AR. Δ. 3.87 g. 22 mm. Nelson 2011, 365, no. 893 (same obv./rev. die as no. 12)
12*.   AR. Δ. 3.66 g. 22 mm. 3 h. CNG Electronic Auction 217, 26.08.2009, no. 248 = Schaaf coll.; Schindel 2014a, pl. 33, no. 364 (same obv./rev. die as no. 11)
13.   AR. Δ. 23 mm. NZK; Schindel 2004 (2), pl. 44, no. A65
14.   AR. Δ. Mitchiner 1978, 163, no. 936

Yazdgerd I (399–420)

Type Ia1/3
15*.   AR. Δ. 4.05 g. 25 mm. 3 h. Triton 14, 4.01.2011, no. 505; Schindel 2004 (2), pl. 57, no. A69 (same obv./rev. die as no. 17?)
16*.   AR. Δ. 3.66 g. 22 mm. 3 h. Schaaf coll.; Schindel 2014a, pl. 37, no. 401
17.   AR. Δ. Göbl 1971, pl. 9, no. 149 (same obv./rev. die as no. 15?)

---

[114]   Not in Schindel 2014a; the type numbering is continued.

Type Ia1/1a (SNS)
18*.   AE. 1.46 g. 29 mm 3 h. CNG Electronic Auction 321, 26.02.2014, no. 278 (= no. 3)
19.   AE. 1.27 g. 19 mm. Private coll.
20.   AE. 14 mm. NZK; Schindel 2004 (2), pl. 58, no. N4

Wahram V (420–438)

Type Ib2/1
21.   AR. Δ. 4.14 g. 27 mm. 3 h. NZK; Schindel 2004 (2), pl. 66, no. A35
22.   AR. Δ. 2.92 g. 24 mm. Nelson 2011, 369, no. 921

Type Ib1/2
23.   AR. Δ. 26 mm. NZK; Schindel 2004 (2), pl. 66, no. A36 (same obv. die as no. 24?)
24.   AR. Δ. Mochiri 1998, 11, no. 1 (same obv. die as no. 23?)

ABBREVIATIONS

CNG – Classical Numismatic Group, Inc., Lancaster, Pennsylvania – London, England
NZK – Numismatische Zentralkartei at the Institute for Numismatics and Monetary History, University of Vienna
SNS – *Sylloge Nummorum Sasanidarum*

BIBLIOGRAPHY

Alram, M. (1986), *Nomina Propria Iranica in Nummis. Materialgrundlagen zu den iranischen Perso-nennamen auf antiken Münzen*, Wien.
Alram, M. (2007), Ardashir's Eastern Campaign and the Numismatic Evidence, in: J. Cribb, G. Herrmann (eds.), *After Alexander. Central Asia before Islam*, London: 227–242.
Alram, M., Gyselen, R. (2003), *Sylloge Nummorum Sasanidarum Paris–Berlin–Wien*, Bd. I: *Ardashir I.–Shapur I.*, Wien.
Alram, M., Gyselen, R. (2012), *Sylloge Nummorum Sasanidarum Paris–Berlin–Wien*, Bd. II: *Ohrmazd I.–Ohrmazd II.*, Wien.
Amini, A. (1359) [= 1981], *Sassanian Coins*, Teheran.
Back, M. (1978), *Die sassanidischen Staatsinschriften. Studien zur Orthographie und Phonologie des Mittelpersischen der Inschriften zusammen mit einem etymologischen Index des mittelpersischen Wortguts und einem Textcorpus der behandelten Inschriften*, Leiden.

Baratova, L., Schindel, N., Rtveladze, E. (2012), *Sylloge Nummorum Sasanidarum Usbekistan: Sasanidische Münzen und ihre Imitationen aus Bukhara, Termes und Chaganian*, Wien.

Curtis, V.S., Askari, M.E., Pendleton, E.J. (2010), *Sasanian Coins in the National Museum of Iran*, vol. 1: *Ardashir I–Hormizd IV*, London.

Gariboldi, A. (2010), *Sasanian Coinage and History. The Civic Numismatic Collection of Milan*, Costa Mesa.

Göbl, R. (1971), *Sasanian Numismatics*, Braunschweig.

Göbl, R. (1984), *Münzprägung des Kušānreiches*, Wien.

Gyselen, R. (1989), *La géographie administrative de l'empire sassanide. Les Témoignages sigillographiques*, (Res Orientales 1), Paris.

Gyselen, R. (2002), *Nouveaux matériaux pour la géographie historique de l'empire Sassanide: Sceaux administratifs de la collection Ahmad Saeedi*, Paris.

Gyselen, R. (2004), New Evidence for Sasanian Numismatics. The Collection of Ahmad Saeedi, *Res Orientales* 15: 49–140.

Loginov, S.D., Nikitin, A.B. (1993), Sasanian Coins of the Late 4th–7th Centuries from Merv, *Mesopotamia* 25: 271–296.

MacDowall, D.W., Ibrahim, M. (1978), Pre-Islamic Coins in Kandahar Museum, *Ancient Afghanistan* 1: 67–77.

MacKenzie, D.N. (1971), *A Concise Pahlavi Dictionary*, London.

Mochiri, M.I. (1977), *Étude de numismatique iranienne sous les Sassanides et Arabe-Sassanides*, Tome II, Teheran.

Mochiri, M.I. (1998), The Mint Signature of the Mint Place of Yazd, *Oriental Numismatic Society Newsletter* 155: 10–11.

Nelson, B.R. (2011), *Numismatic Art of Persia. The Sunrise Collection*, Part I: *Ancient – 650 BC to AD 650*, Lancaster–London.

Nikitin, A.B. (1994), Die Münzen des letzten indo-parthischen Königs von Sīstān: Ein Abschied von "Ardamitra", *Numismatische Zeitschrift* 102: 167–170.

Nikitin, A.B. (1999), Notes on the Chronology of the Kushano-Sasanian Kingdom, in: M. Alram, D.E. Klimburg-Salter (eds.), *Coins, Art and Chronology. Essays on the pre-Islamic History of the Indo-Iranian Borderlands*, Wien: 259–263.

Paruck, F.D.J. (1924), *Sāsānian Coins*, 2 vols., Bombay.

Pourshariati, P. (2008), *Decline and Fall of the Sasanian Empire. The Sasanian-Parthian Confederacy and the Arab Conquest of Iran*, New York.

Schindel, N. (2004), *Sylloge Nummorum Sasanidarum Paris–Berlin–Wien*, Bd. III: *Shapur II.–Kawad I. / 2. Regierung*, 2 vols., Wien.

Schindel, N. (2005), Adhuc sub iudice lis est? Zur Datierung der kushano-sasanidischen Münzen, in: H. Emmerig (ed.), *Vindobona docet. 40 Jahre Institut für Numismatik und Geldgeschichte der Universität Wien, 1965–2005*, Wien (= *Numismatische Zeitschrift* 113/114): 217–242.

Schindel, N. (2006), The Sasanian Eastern Wars in the 5th Century. The Numismatic Evidence, in: A. Panaino, A. Piras (eds.), *Proceedings of the 5th Conference of the Societas Iranologica Europaea*, vol. I: *Ancient & Middle Iranian Studies*, Milano: 675–689.

Schindel, N. (2008), Die Münzstätte Marw von Ardashir II. bis zur Mitte des 5. Jahrhunderts n. Chr.: Ein Nachtrag, *Numismatische Zeitschrift* 116/117: 249–251.

Schindel, N. (2009a), *Sylloge Nummorum Sasanidarum Israel*, Wien.

Schindel, N. (2009b), Ardashir 2 Kushanshah and Huvishka the Kushan: Numismatic Evidence for the Date of the Kushan King Kanishka I, *Journal of the Oriental Numismatic Society* 198: 12–14.

Schindel, N. (2011), Die Münzstätte Sakastan unter Shapur II., *Schweizer Numismatische Rundschau* 90: 79–110.

Schindel, N. (2012), The Beginning of Kushano-Sasanian Coinage, in: M. Alram, R. Gyselen, *Sylloge Nummorum Sasanidarum Paris–Berlin–Wien*, Bd. II: *Ohrmazd I.–Ohrmazd II.*, Wien: 65–73.

Schindel, N. (2014a), *Sylloge Nummorum Sasanidarum Schaaf*, Wien.

Schindel, N. (2014b), Ardashir 1 Kushanshah and Vasudeva the Kushan. Numismatic Evidence for the Date of the Kushan King Kanishka I, *Journal of the Oriental Numismatic Society* 220: 27–30.

Sellwood, D., Whitting, P., Williams, R. (1985), *An Introduction to Sasanian Coins*, London.

Senior, R.C. (2001), *Indo-Scythian coins and history*, 3 vols., Lancaster.

Fig. 1

Fig. 2

Fig. 5

Fig. 8

Fig. 10

Fig. 12

Fig. 15

Fig. 16

Fig. 17

REVIEW

ELECTRUM * Vol. 22 (2015): 251–254
doi: 10.4467/20800909EL.15.013.4302
www.ejournals.eu/electrum

Paul J. Kosmin, *The Land of the Elephant Kings: Space, Territory, and Ideology in the Seleucid Empire*, Harvard University Press, Cambridge, MA–London 2014, pp. 423, b/w ill., 9 maps, ISBN 978-0-674-72882-0

After many years of stagnation, we are observing a huge interest in the history of the Seleucid Empire. This revival can be attributed to at least several factors, including the publication of Babylonian astronomical diaries written in the Hellenistic period and containing information about previously unknown historical events in Mesopotamia,[1] as well as finds of new inscriptions,[2] numerous studies on the numismatics of the Seleucids[3] and, to a limited extent, archaeological discoveries. To these, we should also add scholars' extensive interest in the political history of the Hellenistic world and those aspects of its past which had previously not been the object of much attention: the structure of power and its operation, the role of social elites, ideology and propaganda in the service of the Hellenistic rulers, the place of the cultural legacy of the civilisations that the Greeks conquered in the structures of the states they created, etc.[4]

Owing to these factors, the history of the Greeks in Central Asia, Mesopotamia and Iran also came to interest scholars. This interest is shown by the rapidly growing number of publications in recent years. One of the latest of these is Paul J. Kosmin's book, which tackles a problem previously given scant attention in studies on the Seleucids.

---

[1] A.J. Sachs, H. Hunger, *Astronomical Diaries and Related Texts from Babylonia*, vol. 1–3, Wien 1988–1996; G. del Monte, *Testi dalla Babilonia Ellenistica*, vol. 1: *Testi cronografici*, Pisa–Roma 1997.

[2] See H.M. Cotton, M. Wörrle, Seleucus IV to Heliodoros. A New Dossier of Royal Correspondence from Israel, *Zeitschrift für Papyrologie und Epigraphik* 159, 2007, 191–205; D. Gera, Olympiodoros, Heliodoros and the Temples of Koile Syria and Phoinike, *Zeitschrift für Papyrologie und Epigraphik* 169, 2009, 125–155; C.P. Jones, The Inscription from Tel Maresha for Olympiodoros, *Zeitschrift für Papyrologie und Epigraphik* 171, 2009, 100–104.

[3] See A. Houghton, C. Lorber, *Seleucid Coins. A Comprehensive Catalogue*, Part I: *Seleucus I through Antiochus III*, 2 vols., New York–Lancaster, PA–London 2002; A. Houghton, C. Lorber, O. Hoover, *Seleucid Coins. A Comprehensive Catalogue*, Part II: *Seleucus IV through Antiochus XIII*, 2 vols., New York–Lancaster, PA–London 2008.

[4] Cf. G.G. Aperghis, *The Seleucid Royal Economy. The Finances and Financial Administration of the Seleucid Empire*, Cambridge 2004; V. Chankowski, F. Duryat (eds.), *Le roi et l'économie. Autonomies locales et structures royales dans l'économie de l'empire séleucide. Actes des rencontres de Lille (23 juin 2003) et d'Orléans (29–30 janvier 2004)* (= Topoi. Orient – Occident, Suppl. 6), Lyon 2004; L. Capdetrey, *Le pouvoir séleucide. Territoire, administration, finances d'un royaume hellénistique (312–129 avant J.-C.)*, Rennes 2007; A. Primo, *La storiografia sui Seleucidi. Da Megastene a Eusebio di Cesarea*, Pisa–Roma 2009; Chr. Feyel, L. Grraslin-Thomé, *Le projet politique d'Antiochos IV*, Nancy 2014; R. Strootman, *Courts and Elites in the Hellenistic Empires: The Near East after the Achaemenids, c. 330 to 30 BCE*, Edinburgh 2014.

In what way, the author asks, did they build the foundations of their rule in areas that were extremely diverse culturally and geographically? He is interested in the symbols and propaganda tools they used to legitimise their government and in how they used the geographical realities of the various lands and organised the space over which they ruled (pp. 4–5), taking as his starting point Megasthenes' work *Indica*. Kosmin is aware that the conclusions his research leads to only refer to the limited geographical area that constitutes the object of his interest.[5]

Notably, the author uses interesting and innovative research methodology, in which he combines the historical approach standard in most previous studies of the Hellenistic era with an anthropological one that allows him to look at the problems that interest him from a different research perspective. The book is divided into four parts, titled "Border", "Homeland", "Movement" and "Colony", each of them containing two chapters. These are complemented by a fairly extensive introduction (pp. 1–27) with information designed to familiarise readers with the sources, geography and history of the region to make it easier to follow the arguments made in the various chapters.

In the section entitled "Border" (pp. 31–76), Kosmin demonstrates how important a place in the policy of the first Seleucids was held by the question of marking the borders of their state, and how this fundamentally changed the way in which the Greeks perceived the world that surrounded them. He uses two examples to discuss this issue: the stretch of the border between the Seleucid territory and the dominions of the Maurya kingdom, and the northern border in Central Asia. Kosmin argues that marking the border with the Maurya kingdom, which took place under the rule of the first Seleucids, meant that from this time the Greeks began to perceive the country of their eastern neighbour in terms of real political geography, rather than, as had previously been the case, legendary and utopian reality. The Seleucids encountered much greater difficulties in their efforts to delineate the border of their influences in Central Asia. Owing to the lack of major political partners, they were forced to employ a different strategy there, marking the symbolic – religious – border of their dominions and the world of the barbarians. According to the author, the expedition of Demodamas and Patrocles to Central Asia and towards the Caspian Sea, supported by the Seleucids, served to demarcate this border. Bearing in mind the actions that accompanied the marking of the eastern and northern borders of their state by the first rulers from the Seleucid dynasty, it is hard to disagree with his conclusion that they contributed to a thorough test of the Greeks' knowledge of the geography of significant areas of Central Asia. Confirmed facts filled the place previously occupied by fantastic ideas and untested information.

Kosmin uses the "Homeland" section (pp. 79–125) to discuss the formation of the western borders of the Seleucid state. His thesis is that Seleucus I's expedition to Europe was not dictated exclusively by his personal ambitions, but was an endeavour to attain an important part of his ideological conception – to regain power over his homeland. Rule over this homeland was of fundamental significance for the shape of the state that he was building. The failure of Seleucus I's plans forced his successors to create another justification for the rule of the Seleucids over the East, which, even though it disassociated

---

[5] "The work has its particular focus – the land of elephant kings – and makes no claim to being a total history of the Seleucid empire" (p. 6).

itself from their claims to rule over Macedonia, still contained many references to the dynasty's Macedonian lineage. The complex ideological programme they created served to justify and legitimise the Seleucids' claims to call themselves rulers of Asia, and their own state the "kingdom of Asia."

The section titled "Movement" (pp. 129–180) employs an array of examples concerning the first Seleucids' internal policy and diplomatic relations with their neighbours to demonstrate how they treated the borders of their state as an indicator of the range of the authority they exercised. Kosmin also uses this section to explore the issue of the Syrian rulers' travels through the territory of their state and the importance of these journeys for propaganda purposes. Considering the role of the royal trips, he writes, "In part, the answer may lie in the language of displacement, peregrination, and journeying that rose to a general prominence in the Hellenistic period. More directly, traveling kings were integral to a coherent and specifically Seleucid system of kingship ideology and governmental practice" (p. 176). He also notes that the vastness of the Seleucid Empire, and its ethnic and cultural diversity, made it a necessity for the rulers to have direct contact with their subjects, in order to secure their loyalty. The importance of these personal relations between the Seleucids and the population is proven by the fact that as many as nine of the dynasty's rulers bore the title Epiphanes. This was justified by the unexpected "revelation" to the subjects. Aptly, Kosmin also notes that this name was also often used by the rulers of those states that grew from the ruins of the Seleucid state, including the kings of the Greco-Bactrian state and the Arsacids, the rulers of Parthia. Their imitation of the practice created by the rulers of Syria means that they appreciated its huge political and propaganda importance (cf. pp. 176–180).

The final section of the book, "Colony" (pp. 183–251), examines the colonising activity of the Seleucids within Asia, understood as a useful tool for transforming the landscape of various regions. The urbanisation that resulted from this activity was a visible testimony to the Seleucids' suzerainty, but it also led to the establishment of the standard administrative structures, for which it was easier to administer efficiently and control effectively. The author emphasises the fact that this colonisation had a distinct ideological objective. This can be perceived through the system by which the new colonies were named. The names they received usually referred either to the names of Macedonian cities or to those of members of the ruling family. In this way, the Seleucids transformed the "spear-won" territories into their own dynastic heritage. The assimilation was also helped by legends and founding narratives invoking the figures founder kings fabricated by writers living in the royal court. This practice was exercised both for entirely new colonies and for earlier ones that resulted from the activity of other diadochi.

Notably, Kosmin does not restrict himself entirely to showing the ways in which the Seleucids influenced their subjects, but also looks at the attitudes of the latter towards their rulers. The picture of this stance painted by the sources suggests that their interests were frequently rather different, and this explains the basis of the decentralist tendencies in the Seleucid Empire that ultimately led to its collapse. There were many reasons for this dissatisfaction, including the process of interference in the public space from the rulers, manifested by the building of palace and administrative complexes closed to the royal subjects which led to sometimes insurmountable barriers in the mutual relations. The opposition towards the policy of the rulers that came from the inhabitants of the old cities transformed into colonies was opposition to the official founding legends from earlier traditions. The subjects' emancipation from the influence of the ideological contents imposed by the Seleucids was very much aided by the numerous dynastic conflicts, which allowed various cities to secure greater autonomy from the central authorities, as demonstrated by their minting (pp. 221–251).

These issues are meant only to draw the attention of readers of Kosmin's book to selected matters among the many presented in it. In the space of just a few pages, it is no easy task to discuss even the author's main conclusions, not to mention evaluate or critique the interpretations of various detailed questions that he proposes. Yet there is no doubt that Kosmin's work offers a new perspective on many questions essential to the understanding of the history of the Seleucid Empire. For example, his innovative methodology means that he can demonstrate convincingly that the monarchical ideology created by the first Seleucids is a very complex creature, full of various hitherto undetected subtle nuances. One of the book's most important strengths is the fact that it not only includes many interesting interpretations and valuable observations, but that the image of the history of the Seleucid state that it depicts differs so much from the familiar one that numerous scholars are likely to be tempted to follow in its tracks.

Edward Dąbrowa (Jagiellonian University)

1. *Donum Amicitiae. Studies In Ancient History Publisher on Occasion of the 75th Anniversary of Foundation of the Department of Ancient History of the Jagiellonian University*, ed. by E. Dąbrowa, Kraków 1997, pp. 249; ISBN 83-233-1054-8.
2. *Ancient Iran and the Mediterranean World. Proceedings of an International Conference in Honour of Professor Józef Wolski held at the Jagiellonian University, Cracow, in September 1996*, ed. by E. Dąbrowa, Kraków 1998, pp. 236; ISBN 83-233-1140-4.
3. S. Sprawski, *Jason of Pherae. A Study on History of Thessaly In Years 431–370 BC*, Kraków 1999, pp. 193; ISBN 83-233-1242-7.
4. *Grupy społeczne, ich organizacja i funkcja w świecie starożytnym. Materiały konferencji naukowej PTH, Kraków, 4–6 września 1997* [*The Social Groups In the Ancient World, their Organisation and Functions* (In Polish with the English and French summaries)], pod red. E. Dąbrowy, Kraków 2000, pp. 117; ISBN 83-233-1321-0.
5. *Roman Military Studies*, ed. by E. Dąbrowa, Kraków 2001, pp. 191; ISBN 83-233-1422-3.
6. *Tradition and Innovation in the Ancient World*, ed. by E. Dąbrowa, Kraków 2002, pp. 117; ISBN 83-233-1578-7.
7. *The Roman Near East and Armenia*, ed. by E. Dąbrowa, Kraków 2003, pp. 143; ISBN 83-233-1792-5.
8. *Titulus. Studies in Memory Dr. Stanisław Kalita*, ed. by E. Dąbrowa, Kraków 2004, pp. 151; ISBN 83-233-1849-2.
9. *Freedom and its Limits in the Ancient World. Proceedings of a Colloquium held at the Jagiellonian University, Kraków, September 2003*, ed. by D. Brodka, J. Janik & S. Sprawski, Kraków 2003, pp. 262; ISBN 83-233-1819-0.
10. *Ancient Iran and its Neighbours. Studies in Honour of Prof. Józef Wolski on Occasion of His 95th Birthday*, ed. by E. Dąbrowa, Kraków 2005, pp.126; ISBN 83-233-1946-4.
11. *Greek and Hellenistic Studies*, ed. by E. Dąbrowa, Kraków 2006, pp. 201; ISBN 83-233-2109-4.
12. *Studies on the Late Roman History*, ed. by E. Dąbrowa, Kraków 2007, pp. 113; ISBN 978-83-233-2286-3; ISSN 1897-3426.
13. *Continuity and Change. Studies in Late Antique Historiography*, ed. by D. Brodka & M. Stachura, Kraków 2007, pp. 211; ISBN 978-83-233-2374-7; ISSN 1897-3426.
14. *Studies on the Greek and Roman Military History*, ed. by E. Dąbrowa, Kraków 2008, pp. 155; ISBN 978-83-233-2578-9; ISSN 1897-3426.
15. *Orbis Parthicus. Studies in Memory Professor Józef Wolski*, ed. by E. Dąbrowa, Kraków 2009, pp. 272; ISBN 978-83-233-2821-1; ISSN 1897-3426.
16. E. Dąbrowa, *The Hasmoneans and their State. A Study in History, Ideology, and the Institutions*, Kraków 2010, pp. 228; ISBN 978-83-233-2821-1; ISSN 1897-3426.
17. D. Brodka, *Ammianus Marcellinus. Studien zum Geschichtsdenken im vierten Jahrhundert n. Chr.*, Kraków 2009, pp. 164; ISBN 978-83-233-2845-2; ISSN 1897-3426.
18. *New Studies on the Seleucids*, Kraków 2011, pp. 196; ISBN 978-83-233-3053-0; ISSN 1897-3426.
19. *The Greek World in the 4th and 3rd Centuries BC*, Kraków 2012, pp. 178; ISBN 978-83-233-3483-5; ISSN 1897-3426; e-ISSN 2084-3909.

20. *Colonization in the Ancient World*, Kraków 2013, pp. 176; ISBN 978-83-233-3640-2; ISSN 1897-3426; e-ISSN 2084-3909.
21. *Religion and Politics in the Greco-Roman World*, Kraków 2014, pp. 175; ISBN 978-83-233-3857-4; ISSN 1897-3426; e-ISSN 2084-3909.

Technical editor   *Jadwiga Makowiec*
Proofreader   *Elżbieta Krok*
Typesetter   *Wojciech Wojewoda*

Wydawnictwo Uniwersytetu Jagiellońskiego
Redakcja: ul. Michałowskiego 9/2, 31-126 Kraków
tel. 12-663-23-80, 12-663-23-82, fax 12-663-23-83

Druk i oprawa: Drukarnia Alnus Sp. zo.o.

GPSR Authorized Representative: Easy Access System Europe, Mustamäe tee
50, 10621 Tallinn, Estonia, gpsr.requests@easproject.com

www.ingramcontent.com/pod-product-compliance
Lightning Source LLC
Chambersburg PA
CBHW081654120626
46550CB00010B/2903